The
PERCEPTION
of MUSIC

The
PERCEPTION
of MUSIC

ROBERT FRANCÈS
University of Paris

translated by
W. JAY DOWLING

LAWRENCE ERLBAUM ASSOCIATES, PUBLISHERS
1988   Hillsdale, New Jersey   Hove and London

Lawrence Erlbaum Associates, Inc., Publishers
365 Broadway
Hillsdale, New Jersey 07642

Library of Congress Cataloging-in-Publication Data

Francès, Robert.
  The perception of music.

  Translation of: La perception de la musique.
  Bibliography: p.
  Includes indexes.
  1. Music—Psychology.   2. Music—Philosophy and
aesthetics.   I. Title.
ML3830.F7213   1988   781'.15   87-27197
ISBN 0-89859-688-2

Printed in the United States of America
10   9   8   7   6   5   4   3   2   1

CONTENTS

PREFACE

Having lived with *La Perception de la Musique* for 20 years, I have gained great pleasure from translating it into English. Over the years I had mainly focused on one or another aspect of the book as a valuable resource in conducting research. Now, in the process of translating it, I have come to see it more clearly as a whole. Becoming immersed in it has afforded me many pleasant surprises and rediscoveries in illuminating passages I had forgotten.

The reader may be interested in learning something of the author's life. Robert Francès was born in Bursa, Turkey, in 1919. His early schooling was in Beauvais, north of Paris, and his secondary education was at the Lycée Rollin in Paris, where he received the baccalauréat in philosophy in 1938. He enrolled at the Sorbonne and received his Licence de Philosophie in 1941 and the Diplome d'Etudes Supérieures in 1942. While still a graduate student, Francès took part in the Resistance and was arrested by the Nazis and sent to Auschwitz. He was repatriated in 1945 and received the Médaille de la Résistance and the Croix de Guerre. He completed his preliminary studies in 1947 and taught at Marseille until moving to a research post at the Centre National de la Recherche Scientifique (CNRS), where he completed his dissertation, the present book, in 1958.

In 1965 Francès joined the new Nanterre campus of the University of Paris, being named to the post of professor in 1968. He was instrumental in the establishment of research laboratories in the various departments of the new university and served as Associate Dean for Research and as a member of the Scientific Council of the university. Francès remained active in research himself, founding the Laboratoire de Psychologie Expérimentale et Différentielle at Nanterre, which he directs and which functions both as a research institute and as a graduate training facility. He founded the Laboratoire de Psychologie de la Culture associated with CNRS, for which he was responsible until 1984, and he succeeded Etienne Souriau as Director of the Institut d'Esthétique et des Sciences de l'Art. He served as President of the Société Française de Psychologie in 1971–72 and as Founding President of the International Society for Experimental Aesthetics from (1966 to 1971). In addition to his contributors the psychology of music, Francès has made significant contributions in the areas of the psychology of taste, perceptual development, and the psychology of work.

Now, almost 30 years after its initial appearance, *The Perception of Music* is still worthy of the attention of cognitive and social psychologists, particularly those concerned with music perception. Francès brought to this study both a broad training in experimental psychology, evidenced by the wide range of methods and the astute theorizing seen here, and a deep appreciation for and understanding of a wide variety of music. This can be seen in the range of musical works discussed and utilized in the experiments and in the broad historical and cultural sweep of the discussion of individual differences and expression and meaning in music. Francès's experiments have stood the test of time, and some of them are truly classics in this field. The 16 experiments explore both short- and long-term memory for melodic and harmonic patterns. They do that with "real" pieces of music as well as with more tightly controlled, artificial materials. In addition to recognition memory, the experiments explore a variety of cognitive processes using perceptual judgments, polygraph measures, melodic production, semantic judgments, and preference.

One theme that is developed in a series of experiments centers on the importance of the tonal scale framework for determining the musical functions of pitches and the ways in which melodic pitch is perceived and remembered. Experiment 3 (in chapter 3) shows that brief tonal melodies that conform to the culturally defined scale are easier to remember than atonal ones that do not. Experiment 9 (chapter 6) shows that transpositions of tonal melodies are easier to recognize than are transpositions of atonal melodies. Further, the tonal scheme governs production, so that when subjects are given a pitch with which to begin an improvised melody, they almost always interpret that pitch as a member of the tonic triad of a tonal key (Experiment 4 in chapter 3). Experiment 6 (chapter 4) shows that professional musicians familiar with the atonal materials of serial 12-tone music find them no easier to remember than do professionals who work with tonal varieties of music. This finding suggests that the coherence of a 12-tone row is more a conceptual than a perceptual phenomenon.

Acculturation to the tonal scheme appears to involve the extraction of invariant patterns of stimulation from the musical environment, and Francès presents evidence that in a variety of songs ranging from classical to popular in the western European tradition, the requisite regularities lie principally in the harmonic patterns accompanying the songs (Experiment 5 in chapter 4). Increasing acculturation leads to a taste for wider deviations from conformity to invariant patterns. Experiment 16 (chapter 11) shows that whereas musicians and nonmusicians alike noticed the differences between consonant (conforming) and dissonant (nonconforming) chord progressions, nonmusicians preferred the consonant as more coherent; but professional musicians preferred the dissonant as more interesting.

A corollary of the cultural establishment of a tonal scheme is that pitches will be perceived categorically, as instances of stimuli defined by the framework, even when they physically deviate by a considerable amount from the standard frequencies. Francès shows that sustained pitches in songs sung by accomplished singers and judged "in tune" by experts typically show large deviations of frequency (Experiment 1, chapter 1). And in what is perhaps the most striking experiment in the book (Experiment 2, chapter 3), Francès demonstrates that tonal pitch categories are not merely static frequency regions, but have dynamic properties determined by the melodic and harmonic functions of the notes involved. To show this, Francès lowered the vibration frequency of certain notes on the piano so that they would be judged "flat" if heard outside a musical context. He then constructed musical contexts in which those very same notes had dynamic, functional scale tendencies that pulled them upward or downward toward their immediate neighbors in the scale. Listeners noticed the alterations far more often when the mistuning went counter to the dynamic tendencies of the scale tones. That is, the flatting was noticed when it was of a note that functionally tended upward, but was ignored when it went downward with the dynamic tendency. The perceptual categories of pitch are not rigidly fixed, but are responsive to context.

A second theme developed in the experiments is that of individual differences in music cognition arising from differences in acculturation and training. This theme is closely related to the first; acculturation involves the development of cognitive schemes such as the tonal scale framework, and a principal function of advanced training in music is to bring the procedural knowledge of such shared cultural schemes under conscious control and make it accessible as declarative knowledge. The studies just mentioned typically found differences in performance due to musical experience (Experiments 3, 9, and 16), and a noteworthy aspect of Francès's work is the diversity of expertise represented among his groups of subjects, ranging from those with little or no training to professionals, including music-school faculty and composers. Experiment 12 (chapter 7) showed that musicians performed better than nonmusicians in noticing changes in the harmonic chord pattern underlying a melody. Experiment 8 (chapter 6) showed that both trained and untrained listeners were fairly accurate in indicating phrase endings in a Schubert song, though the musicians performed somewhat better. Polygraph responses (especially EEG alpha-rhythm blockage and GSR responses) while subjects listened to music varying in tension tended to be related to formal properties of the music, especially for musicians and when listeners adopted an "analytic" (versus "spontaneous") attitude (Experiment 7, chapter 5). Differences based on experience and "set" also appeared in listeners' ability to notice the occurrence of the themes in a Beethoven Trio (Experiments 10 and 11, chapter 6). The themes were much more accurately identified when listeners were given some knowledge of the structural pattern of the work before listening. The more experienced listeners noticed themes more readily in a Bach fugue (Experiment 13, chapter 7), and moderately experienced music students showed the most improvement identifying theme occurrences on a second listening.

A series of experiments explored the effects of response set and experience on the attribution of expressive qualities to pieces of music (Experiments 14 and 15, chapter 9). Both musicians and nonmusicians found it easy to assign titles consistently to pieces, whereas children were less consistent. Listeners' drawings also consistently reflected musical patterns.

The reader will find in Francès's discussions of the musical and psychological contexts of these experiments many illuminating comments concerning both music and psychology. Those discussions are also filled with thoughts leading to further insights and empirical studies.

I am very grateful for the care with which Robert Francès and his associates, Bruce Lowery and Nell Rivière, have edited the English text, correcting mistakes arising from my limited knowledge of French and in many instances improving the English phrasing with a distinct gain in clarity and grace. (Any remaining infelicities are fully my responsibility.) And I am grateful to the publisher, Lawrence Erlbaum Associates, for the opportunity to translate this work I had long admired, and to Jack Burton and Carol Lachman for facilitating that process.

W. Jay Dowling
University of Texas at Dallas

FOREWORD

Since the publication of the first edition of this book in 1958, interest in the study of music perception has been growing steadily. The field as it now stands is, happily, free of disciplinary boundaries. Psychologists, acousticians, music theorists, computer scientists, neuroscientists, and others are all contributing ideas, discoveries, and new ways of thinking. The field also has a strong international flavor, which has been fostered by symposia, conferences, and workshops held recently in many countries.

Given this widespread interest in the subject, the translation of Francès classic work comes at a most propitious time. English-speaking readers who are familiar with the contemporary literature on musical cognition and who have not yet read the book will be impressed by the influence that it has exerted on the field. To name just a few issues that are addressed, there are detailed examinations of the effects of tonal framework on the perception of melodic patterns, of processes involved in key attribution, and of the abstract representation of notes and their relationships within a key. We also find descriptions of key-distance and other effects in memory for melodies, and of categorical perception of notes and intervals. In addition, there are challenging discussions of figure-ground phenomena and the role of attention in listening to music.

The book contains a wise balance of cultural and biological considerations. While arguing for the strong influence of exposure and of formal training on the way that music is perceived, Francès draws on the literature concerning the amusias to illustrate his points about the types of cognitive abstraction that are performed by the listener.

Altogether, this book is a notable and highly welcome addition to the English-speaking literature. It will no doubt serve as a source of inspiration for many years to come.

Diana Deutsch
University of California, San Diego

INTRODUCTION

Relationships between man and works of art can be studied both from the point of view of creation and the point of view of contemplation. Man develops through contemplation as well as through creation. A work of art is at once a manifestation of a highly organized form of activity indicative of a particular time and place—often conveying a sort of epiphany of a person of genius—and a manifestation of how the person at present hears, sees, and understands, a manifestation of how the work satisfies ageless artistic needs. There is a dialectic of creation and contemplation. The human importance of a work depends on its generative power, power that permeates the form and content of the object, provided that social forces converge to bring it to life. Its ultimate destiny is to enter into the Pantheon from which the souls of diverse peoples draw spiritual sustenance. As Nietzsche said somewhere, "Tell me what you eat; I shall tell you what you are." This nourishment has always had a variety of aspects.

But this discussion of art works involves more than great artists and their masterpieces. The latter exist only in the context of a multitude of anonymous yet effective productions—effective within a society both in creating and in teaching that ever-changing language of sounds, colors, and gestures that constitute the cultural personality of man in a century or several centuries. We are prepared to enjoy and assimilate perfection by these daily acquisitions, these automatic reactions born of constant unreflective exposure to a mass of secondary works embedded in a historical-cultural cycle. Revolutions in harmonic usage and the visual arts are slow, progressive processes, with occasional decisive crises that lead to changes long dammed up. Never before has an acceleration as rapid as that of our own era been experienced. Those caught up in this process tend to focus on it to the exclusion of all else. For many of us, including many well-trained nonprofessionals, music is defined by the continuum running from Bach to Wagner. It has been remarked—and this is profoundly true—that

1

we had to depart from the framework of the tonal system in order to become aware of its temporal and geographic limits. We were in all respects enmeshed in habits it had formed in us. Form and the violation of form referred back to those habits, just as the uncivilized is defined by what they are not.

The psychology of the music ear finds itself in our time at a critical point that we must seize: our study bears on a complex epoch, which many believe to be a transitional one leading to new modes of musical organization. When Helmholtz (1954) and Stumpf (1883) enunciated the laws of beats and fusion, they intended to provide a physical and psychological justification for the major triad, the basis of tonal music. They also believed they had discovered the laws of Music itself. In our day, when the bending of tonality has been followed by its breaking into smithereens, musically educated persons live in two worlds, in two cultures. The non-musician, who is actually a "pre-musician," has unknowingly developed tonal habits of audition. But both musicians and nonmusicians are exposed to the contagion of new works. No one can prophesy the future of musical thought. It is only a matter of seizing the body of psychological laws tied to the tonal system—along with other laws now rounding the cape of history.

One might wonder if "perception" is always the best term to apply to the phenomena studied here. Cultural objects are privileged in being able to release effects disproportionate to their causes: a few colors, a few sounds suffice to completely disrupt the organism of a connoisseur. Those stimuli are the point of departure for integrative processes, extending to mental operations, properly speaking, to judgments of comparison and preference, and to various levels of semantic judgments. Art can provide motivations so powerful that they can hold instincts and everyday interests in check throughout an entire life. It is to this wealth of effects based on aesthetic "stimuli," and to all the related phenomena, that we must direct our study. The peripheral auditory or visual apparatus is only a threshold at which the message does not stop.

But this initial contact is specific: when music is perceived, it is heard as integrated into sonorous forms and brings into play extremely flexible reflex mechanisms, as well as unique activities developed in large measure by education. There is a type of musical perception that has little in common with simple audition; it is to that we devote our efforts here. In all of its complexity, it is identified with a part of the aesthetic experience, insofar as that embraces equally both experience and creation. We can conceptualize it only as a process of development, and never as simply falling under a "stimulus-response" schema. We must distinguish between the effects of acculturation—unreflective, involuntary, and resulting from almost passive familiarity with works—and the effects of education, where perceptual development is supported by the acquisition of concepts and symbols that provide for the definition of forms, their elements and articulations. These remarks apply to music, but considerable research shows that they apply equally well to the visual arts.

In acculturation[1] there is apparent at a certain level of abstraction a development involving the categorization of the most general types of formal properties, as indicated by nonprofessionals' recognition of styles. But observation has shown similar effects even with culturally unpolished subjects, in terms of frames of reference acquired through contacts with works of a certain type. This acculturation explains the relative ease with which they perceive certain formal properties of visual space or musical syntax and explains the determinants of the aesthetic choices they are led to make. In artistic education these aspects of development are raised to a higher power not only in the exercise of judgments of taste, but also in the ease and mastery attained in perceptual activity, abstraction and schematization in picture perception, and fixation and differentiation in musical hearing. Consideration of these stages of perceptual development should lead us to pose questions of comprehension, taste, and aesthetic judgment in the most concrete manner. However, too many experiments have taken insufficient account of them, and too many tests attribute to aptitude effects due to education. Gestalt theory in particular, although it has had some success in psychology, can be applied to aesthetics only with important reservations. The adaptation of gestalt laws should most often consist of expressing them relative to the history of art and of the individual. Form and formlessness, unity and incoherence, can in most cases be defined only in terms of what one might call the "aesthetic age" of the subject.

These concepts presuppose certain methodological precepts. Experimental research operates in a region between the infinite variety of individual modes of thinking and feeling and the abstractions of (in principal) universal aesthetic experience. In that situation research turns more and more toward definitions that limit the diversity to types and stages that can be defined by objective criteria. It is only comparisons among such stages that permit us to grasp the origins of phenomena and to formulate hypotheses that further experiments will test.

Other, more general rules have been observed here. Present developments in the techniques of analysis and measurement in the natural and social sciences legitimately give us great hope for the study of art. It is very much in the aesthetician's interest to base certain steps in his arguments on solid data and to verify his intuitions and their consequences at

---

[1]The meaning given here for this term seems more legitimate than that given it by certain cultural sociologists. One can speak of the "acculturation" of transplanted adults only if one supposes the initial absence of culture. Otherwise one should say "transculturation."

least in part through empirical suggestions. But bringing together a science with techniques it has long ignored can precipitate a crisis of adaptation. We know that such a crisis has been felt in psychology and sociology, especially in the excesses of an exaggerated "operationalism" and the non-sense of certain statistical formalisms.

These sorts of difficulty are not new to aesthetics. They appear where, in the design of an experiment, account has not been taken of the specific character of the artistic activity or the aesthetic experience. They arise every time an experimenter places undue confidence in technique itself. The meaning, the import, and finally the utility of an experiment depend not only on the techniques employed, but also on the viewpoint in terms of which the variables were chosen, presented, and measured.

One of the difficulties of aesthetic research involves inferences from the general to the particular. No doubt the general laws of psychology and sociology partially condition the facts of aesthetic creation and contemplation. Attempts have been made to deduce these facts from intrinsic general properties of the human mind, from fundamental requirements of intelligence that show up with respect to widely varying contents. However, the attentive study of works of art repeatedly reveals the wide variety of needs they express through the styles of various schools and periods. For example, neither the need for simplicity (as in mathematical theories of music) nor the laws of equilibrium and combination of pleasant experiences (as in Fechner's theory) in themselves can account for the essentials of a cycle of musical activity such as the development of classical harmony, nor for the Italian development of perspective in the visual arts, nor for the distinction of those cycles from those that preceded or followed them.

These modes of deductive thinking belong to studies in the 18th and 19th centuries inpired by "faculty" psychology and Pythagorean mathematical realism. Later work, penetrated by empiricism, presents the illusion of submitting the facts of art to scientific treatment, but without taking account of the special character of productive activity and aesthetic contemplation.

In effect, art has always been a discipline (or cluster of disciplines)— an activity structured according to specific norms. Those norms guide both production and apprehension and, in certain cases, interpretation. The various disciplines leave their mark on the objects at different levels of analysis: even in the simple choice of materials, as well as in the establishment of a syntax of sound and of color, and in the composition of groups. The disciplines operate hierarchically and constitute dialectical systems within which they often participate in reciprocal patterns of control. They nourish themselves on traditions, often very ancient, that have been enriched throughout the course of history. In such systems is the freedom of the artist born—freedom enveloped in requirements some of which come to seem natural.

This disciplinary aspect of the arts, which one encounters in the forms great and humble, determines the accessibility of true aesthetic problems that might or might not be subjected to experimental or simply quantitative techniques. Lacking that guidance, such an application will always produce an arbitrary and violent dislocation of the object and experience of art, of which one will not know how to discover the true articulations. This seems true at the levels of analysis both of objects and of their structures.

Physical and mathematical analyses are fruitful only if they are conducted in harmony with the true articulations of the object, because the latter result from particular causes and goals of expression. The subliminal level of microevents is of only indirect concern to the specifically artistic message, insofar as it provides perceptible results that are not accidental but, rather, are intentional aspects of structure.

All the same, to give sense and significance to the application of experimental techniques repeatedly employed since Fechner (such as the methods of choice, variation, reproduction, comparison, identification) one must take the artistic disciplines as a point of departure, but only insofar as they permit a reconstruction of the true aesthetic elements involved or of operations playing an effective role in the aesthetic experience.

Paradoxically, this concern for specificity is what gives research in the psychology of art its scientific and philosophical character. If that research can teach us something new about humanity, it will be when it does not attempt to reduce to general functions what belongs to a concrete activity having its own specific qualities. This is a patient science and philosophy of which the sole prerequisite is to aim at discovering the real, without any extraneous additions. This specificity is the price of the true synthesis.

From these considerations we see why so few artists would be surprised by the nature of this work: in most cases it does nothing but establish, through experiments and calculations, facts they knew already, since those facts were already components of the practice of their art. We have sought rational explanations for these facts while guarding against the myths that tradition has handed down to us. I know very well that certain myths are based on causality, at least psychologically. Belief in the existence of "natural harmony" is sufficient to perpetuate its rules. The art of music has never been a pure technique, isolated from the contagion of prevailing ideas and ideologies. In some cases, those have influenced musical practice; in other cases, they have not. It is a question of weighing the effects. Music has at times been reduced to a game of pure, sonorous forms; at other times, inflated with expression and raised to the level of a sublime language. These ideas have not only influenced composers; they have structured the attitudes of the public, preparing them to listen in a particular manner. In these situations, psychological experimentation cannot be other than circumspect. Its conclusions must be interpreted and placed in their proper sociological and historical contexts.

Since the appearance of the first edition of this work, there have been numerous studies on the same subject by a variety of authors. I have included the most important of these in the Supplementary Bibliography. In particular, recent work utilizing up-to-date methods extends the area covered by the present book to include children's music perception and describes the structure of children's musical capabilities (Zenatti, 1969). The field of musical semantics is also enriched by contributions from psycholinguistics (Imberty, 1978, 1981). And I have extended the psychological implications of this book in my own work, chiefly through the construction of a course of programmed instruction in solfège based on the essential results presented here (Francès, 1983).

Part I
SYNTAX

Chapter 1
SOUND
AND MUSIC

PRESENT THEORIES OF AUDITION

The periphery of the auditory system has received special attention from physiologists since 1870, when Helmholtz (with Hensen) proposed that the transverse fibers along the basilar membrane resonate selectively to different frequencies. There at last, it seemed, was a clear theoretical picture, in keeping with what was already known about the physical properties of resonators. However, this view had to be abandoned for various reasons. For one thing, the fibers are neither freely vibrating nor anatomically separate and because of that cannot mediate distinct perceptions of different frequencies. Second, the fibers vary greatly in length, but not in mass or tension; and although there are many of them (about 2800 over the seven octaves where discrimination is good), there are not enough to explain the subtlety attained by the musical ear.[1] In fact, the idea of specific places of stimulation for different pitches has now been abandoned, without giving up the general idea of a place model of pitch perception altogether. The general notion has theoretical support (Blondel, 1934; Caussé, 1944; Gribensky, 1951) and is approximately correct on a practical level: fibers in a specific region respond to a particular tone, with the region situated toward the basal end of the membrane for high tones and toward the apex for low tones (cf. van Esbroeck & Montfort, 1946; Wever, 1949). All the same, this approximation is not without difficulties, because it increases still more the number of fibers required to explain known discrimination abilities. Moreover, if an increase in intensity enlarges the region of stimulation, it ought to produce a decline in discrimination, but

---

[1]Wever (1949) supposes it possible to distinguish up to 64 different pitches within a semitone around 1000 Hz, which implies the need for about 5300 fibers for the seven octaves under consideration).

that is not the case. And the simultaneous perception of several neighboring tones at high intensity would be impossible because of the interference of the neighboring regions of stimulation.

Such difficulties gave rise to the theories mentioned earlier and shifted the locus of auditory discrimination from peripheral to central processes. These theories held that the message transmitted to the brain via the auditory nerve is not yet identified by means of peripheral resonators, but rather consists of a pattern of excitation—a frequency of nerve firings determined by the frequency of vibration received. The discovery of electrical currents corresponding to auditory activity in the cortex by Beck in 1890, and in the auditory nerve by Beauregard and Dupuy in 1896, was refined by Wever and Bray using more highly developed techniques in 1930. We now distinguish the cochlear response recorded from the basilar membrane from the neural response. The former reproduces the waveform of the stimulus; the latter has its own distinctive pattern. The neural response has a higher intensity threshold than the cochlear response. And, most important, the cochlear response is capable of following a wide range of frequencies, whereas the upper limit of neural synchronization is around 4000 or 5000 Hz. At higher frequencies, the place mechanism comes into play.

But synchrony at such high frequencies is not consistent with a neuron's refractory period. A single fiber could not transmit such rapid excitation. The cooperation of several fibers relieving each other in tandem is required to convey a volley—a cluster of responses for each peak of stimulation; hence the name *volley principle*. Wever supposed that the volley principle would operate in the range of 400 to 5000 Hz, whereas a modified place mechanism would handle frequencies beyond that. "Pitch therefore has a twofold representation, in terms of place on the basilar membrane and hence of particularity of nerve fibers, and in terms of composite input frequency "(Wever, 1949, p. 189) The process of audition is different depending on the frequency range considered: from 15 to 400 Hz, the auditory nerve transmits the frequency just as it receives it; from 400 to 5000 Hz, it encodes it in volleys; and from 5000 to 24000 Hz the response is tied to place of excitation on the basilar membrane. For midrange frequencies, the volley principle operates jointly with a more or less precise place mechanism, which nevertheless plays a minimal role in pitch analysis.

For the origin of the cochlear microphonic potentials, we must look in the organ of Corti supported by the basilar membrane, rather than in the membrane directly. The disturbances it receives are transmitted to the hair cells, which rub intermittently on the tectorial membrane, initiating electrical potentials that are transmitted to the auditory nerve (Wever, 1949; Gribensky, 1951).

Thus, beginning with an explanation of pitch perception based on a single mechanical principle, we progress to an explanation positing several principles according to the frequency range in question, implicating cortical activity to decode each message in accordance with its specific pattern. Certain recent considerations regarding this central processing theory involve difficulties, however. Although certain authors admit the dual-process model of Wever (e.g., Caussé, 1944; Gribensky, 1951; Stevens & Davis, 1948), others proffer two sorts of objections. First, pure tone auditory stimulation evokes an electrical response at the cortex over the entire area of reception, but without point-for-point resolution of frequencies. Cortical projections of single-frequency stimuli only show a tendency toward localization, in which specific *regions* of the cortex respond (cf. Piéron, 1945). Second, the duality of Wever's model creates difficulties for its use as an explanation of a function that exhibits such a manifest continuity across the entire scale of frequencies (cf. Piéron, 1945).

THE GENERALITY OF AUDITION AND THE SPECIFICITY OF MUSICAL PERCEPTION

It seems reasonable to start, therefore, by piecing together a coherent explanation of the auditory mechanism. Yet we are still speaking only of simple tones without harmonics and of isolated tones without rhythmic, harmonic, or melodic relationships with other tones. For even if these simple phenomena were thoroughly explained, the study of the three psychological attributes of sound—pitch, loudness, and timbre—would still not provide us with specific contributions to the psychology of musical perception. Of course, analysis is the time-honored procedure of all the sciences, and it is not clear how one could inaugurate a new one by starting with the complex. Even so, the simple phenomena with which one does start must belong to the domain being researched or at the very least should be linked by successive approximations to the complex phenomena they support.

Concerning the object of our study, the audition of simple and complex tones provides a basic point of departure only if those tones can be related to the combinations into which they are always integrated. The history of music has seen just one genre based on a monotone,[2] and even that

---

[2] See Sachs, 1943. Literate Chinese in playing the ancient zithers Sê and Chhin can execute a succession of tones that differ not in pitch but in mode of attack, timbre, and vibrato, of which there are no fewer than 26 varieties. Thus, they anticipated Schönberg's aim of creating a melody of timbres (Klangfarbenmelodie).

coexisted for the same listeners with genres involving a variety of tones. One wonders what the effect on such a listener's musical ear would be if *Klangfarbenmelodie* had been the only influence on its formation. It seems to us a simple matter, then, for the range of study to be exhausted by the study of the three aforementioned attributes, along with some related additions concerning noise and attack transients. Therefore, the approach to music cannot be made from the direction of the nonmusical; though it is easy to suppose that the nonmusical sets conditions for music, it clearly does not constitute it. There is no doubt that music is embedded in a complex social reality that envelops it. In its aims, as well as in its causes, music is social; and it is no less certain that its material, whatever the sound object, is determined by the laws of physics, is perceived, and is subjected to physiology and psychology. But what *music* consists of, is precisely *relations* among sensory qualia—among sensations of sound. To grasp what that object is, as a specific mode of human activity, is the fundamental task out of which arises the study of reactions evoked in the subject through the action of that object. We shall not seek, therefore, to reduce music to such nonspecific elements as pitch, duration, and loudness; nor aptitude at musical perception to the sense of pitch, of duration, and the like.[3] Such a reduction would seem to destroy or ignore what belongs most closely to the object, which is reducible neither to concept nor experience, but which presupposes a technical approach to the discipline in which it has been fashioned. The psychology of music (like the philosophy of music) has often strayed into bordering regions, which involve certain relevant physical and physiological considerations but are too vast for one to expect to encounter in them a well-defined structure for the object. Often the psychology of music has also oriented itself toward a metapsychology in which one seems to get at the truth and where, in a curious paradox, one connects again with the nonmusical under the guise of religious sentiments or metaphysics. In each of these cases, a human fact that has its own laws and scope is reduced to laws that are otherwise foreign to it, or at least only indirectly linked.

I shall cite only one example of this abstract and general approach— an instructive example in that it is revealed by its own consequences. Starting with the self-evident principle that "all musical expression of emotion is communicated in terms of pitch, intensity, duration, and extensity," Seashore, after making careful measurements on recorded fragments,

---

[3]Seashore (1919) analyzed the musical mind into five factors: sensation, activity, memory and imagination, intelligence, and emotion. The components of the first factor are the sense of pitch, of loudness, of duration, of space, and of their complex derivatives—the sense of rhythm, of consonance, and of volume. Not only did sensitivity result from innate natural aptitudes, but the other factors of the musical mind could be traced back to more general faculties as well.

elevates the principle of "the deviation from the exact" to the status of a universal necessity of beauty in music (Seashore, 1928; Seashore & Metfessel, 1925). Among the deviations reported, those of pitch and duration will occupy our attention. It is certain that those in themselves could not be the actual elements of artistic expression. Accidental deviations in mediocre performances sometimes result from insufficient psychological or physiological mastery and are destructive of melodic and rhythmic form. Intentional deviations, in an artist of bad taste, result in equally serious disorders, producing interpretative caricatures incapable of serving as vehicles of aesthetic emotion. The principle Seashore posits seems, therefore, insufficiently precise with respect to the domain under consideration. Deviations in an interpretation in written values can only be specified when done according to the way the work is articulated in its cultural context or in conformity with more or less rigid norms (performance practices) associated with those articulations. Thus, concerning rhythmic fluctuations, especially those of tempo, Brelet (1953) has aptly emphasized the need for a certain amount of rubato, that is, a certain amount of liberty in the synchronization of a song and its accompaniment at specific moments in specific works, under equally specific conditions. Otherwise, rubato is nothing but a clumsy and exaggerated affectation. Liberties in performance are to some extent necessary, in the sense of deviations from constraints other than natural ones. Without doubt, the internal necessities of artistic production, insofar as it is conventional, achieves its ends by means of natural processes—through a slowing of arm and hand, through contraction of a vocal interval. Such events can only be measured with the aid of recording techniques already in use in sciences such as psychology and physiology (although there is nothing to prevent experimental aesthetics from developing new techniques). But the study of these processes furnishes us with knowledge of art only if we gather them from central instances among art works and aesthetic structures. They are instructive only when illuminated by that internal necessity that we need to describe in order to distinguish between the perception of music and mere audition.

That this is so in no way implies that we must return to mystical conceptions involving art in transcendental principles and nonrational ways of knowing. The *additus naturae* appropriate to art is a human thing and as such falls within the range of scientific investigation. It must be considered as a highly differentiated region of behavior, involving the development of certain natural functions through prolonged interaction with socially defined art works and techniques. It is more interesting to study this development itself, tracing its roots in general human capabilities, than simply to reduce it to functions already understood. This approach arises not from a conception of a hierarchy of facts of humanity (which would be much more in the province of philosophy than of psychology), but rather from a concern for scientific exactitude. Thus it is for the sake of precision that we need to affirm a radical distinction of musical perception versus audition taken as a general physiological process. To be precise, we need to maintain the distinction between a conception of expressive performance as "deviations from the exact" and a cultural conception according to which those deviations differ in their occurrence in keeping with different structural locations in the work. We have seen that this is true of temporal deviations. We shall see later, in reviewing Abraham's experiments, that pitch deviations follow a set of specific laws: some of them concerning melodic movement (the hierarchy of pitches within a melody), and others strictly dependent on tonal functions assumed by each tone and conferring on each of them a more or less stable sense of direction according to the norms of usage of the generative tonal system.

It is important to understand that faithful description of the simple requires knowledge of the complex. We must interject here a basic distinction between logical, and psychological, simplicity. In a conceptual system such as Euclid's geometry, the elements (point, line, surface) are defined in terms of each other and provide the basis for the diagrams and demonstrations. In just such a way the exposition of a system can follow a course of synthesis such as one finds in certain philosophical systems— truly a highly privileged way. In a cultural system such as that of music, seen not as the demonstrated facts of music theory, but rather as a system that is psychologically integrated into experience, with its own pattern of development. In such a system the description of an element involves in some respects certain features of the system as a whole. All attempts at naive understanding are precluded. All phenomenological reductions that "parenthesize" the institutional context of the culture in an attempt to retrieve the living event in its manifestations are without object. One obtains a simple element only by tearing it out of the ensemble of which it is a part and by virtue of which it acquires its specific properties. What we call a perceptual given in reality derives from an objective sphere (that of works and the techniques on which they are based) that must be known before we explore the contents of consciousness.

It is not only because of oversimplification but also because of its misplaced "naturalism" that it seems arbitrary to take the work of art as the result of synthesis beginning in simple auditory phenomena. We have seen in numerous analyses the psychological difficulties arising from the attempt to reduce all the properties of musical events to wholes, forms, and structures such as have been propounded by the Gestalt theorists (cf. Francès, 1951).

In their tendency to construe the developmental character of the physical acoustical forms out of which the subject's experiences arise, the Gestalt psychologists (whose discoveries constitute a real contribution) give their explanations a distinctly nativist turn. For them good form and its opposite often seem to be immediate perceptual givens. They do not take these givens as events in individual psychological development, or as growing out of a social process like that of linguistic change. Language is determined by cultural institutions that make it appear to be "natural," until a new language is substituted—one that generates new "good forms" that a century earlier had seemed "bad forms." How would the contemporaries of Grétry have been able to hear the *patterns* of Debussy's *Preludes*—the whole patterns as well as the details? Debussy's contemporaries, like many of our own, not hearing in the *Preludes* a tonal organization in all its purity, could (then and now) grasp in them only isolated tones and passages whose coherence in the new system escaped them. The immediacy of the sensation of "good form" of a musical passage or work is relative, usually, to a system of connections already established in the listener from contact with other works. Beyond that, in the central works of a particular period or school, symmetry, regularity, and continuity are not necessarily the only criteria for coherence (not to mention aesthetic value).

SPECIFICITY IS NOT FOUND SOLELY IN THE PARTICULAR AIMS OF MUSICAL PERCEPTION

In a sense, one could reject the very use of the phrases "musical perception" or "the perception of musical sound." If one adopts a biological definition of perception phrased in terms of its adaptive value, one ends by conferring on object perception a pragmatic and utilitarian stability, which, in contrast, relegates the contents of the perception of art to a disembodied state. The usual function of the perceptual act is to be a means and not an end— a feature of the process linking need and action (Piéron, 1945). Nothing in this process is directed toward sounds or sound patterns that are signs of either potential satisfactions or of dangers. But there is in the case of music a sort of "pure perception" carrying with it its own aims and accompanied by a pleasure arising *sui generis*[4]—literally a case of "rapture" (Pradines, 1947).

There are several ways to attenuate the rigor of these dichotomies. The psychological life of humans in all its manifestations is far from being

---

[4]See Ehrenstein, 1954: "Ordinary perceptions are related to objects; they are not pure but linked to their objective causes. In contrast, listening to a piece of music is a case of pure perception. Here the fact of listening (Gehörerlebnis) is an end in itself" (p. 7).

devoted, either more or less directly, to the necessities of needs and actions. In the entire cultural sphere, and in almost all highly socialized behavior, perceptual acts occur under conditions of very limited or strongly mediated biological stimulation. If it were otherwise, the field of perception could not include reading a book, hearing a conference, or such multisensory activities as sorting documents and typing. In any case, to make the perception of art a disembodied act lacking contact with biological and human motivations in no way follows the scientific evidence. Rather, it opts for just one ideological conception of art among many against which one can invoke numerous facts, if only the mundane social interest aroused in hearing a new piece or a new interpretation, or the desire to expand one's cultural horizons in order to cope with social competition. It does more justice to our conception to seek the specificity of such perceptions in the cultural structure itself.

NOTE ABSTRACTION

The perception of musical tones arises from a certain power of abstraction and generalization. A musical tone is a "note," that is, a concept subsuming approximate physical values, having a variability whose extent and form we are far from assessing. Investigators with some knowledge of the nature of musical facts have described the approximate character of the tone very well and have noted the unimportance of the speculations of physicists concerning mere intonation and the power of the ear to discriminate minimal intervals (Lloyd, 1940). The musical ear, although very sensitive to tuning deviations affecting components of standard chords or essential in the composition of the tonal structure of a pattern, tolerates large irregularities as long as they leave intact the framework of the structure. Curiously, these are the very physicists who helped establish the lack of physical exactitude in the events of real music, thanks to phonophotography and frequency analysis. Already in 1923, Abraham had made tonometric observations on the singing of moderately trained and well-trained subjects and showed that the mean deviations between frequencies of notes emitted and perceived as in tune and the frequencies of the corresponding notes of the tempered scale were 39 cents (0.39 semitones) for ascending intervals, and 52 cents for descending.[5] These deviations fall well within the range of those detectable by the musically untrained ear (Abraham, 1923). Seashore, who obtained even more precise measurements by means

---

[5]Ellis' *cent* is a logarithmic unit in common use in German- and English-speaking countries, and equals 1/100 of a tempered semitone. The *savart* is sometimes used for ease of calculation and equals 4 cents.

of phonophotographic recording, showed the various components of this variability of the parameters characterizing a note:

1. Pitch vibrato consists of frequency modulation around an imaginary center, with a mean extent of a semitone and with a frequency of about 6.3 to 6.8 Hz (Seashore, 1936). Vibrato is not a voluntary process, but rather a constant and spontaneous physiological response of the vocal organs; it can be found in string playing under analogous conditions and with the same generality (Small, 1936). The recordings analyzed were by artists of the first rank, and the "correctness" of the interpretations is beyond doubt. Undoubtedly the group of sound sources that generate vibrato excludes instruments of fixed tones. It probably includes woodwinds and brass in addition to strings and the voice, although physical analysis of those instruments has not yet been done. Furthermore, the characteristics of frequency modulation in these instruments tend to rule out stability in the given frequency. Vibrato is a continual periodic fluctuation whose limits and rate are known.

2. What, then, is the "pitch" of a musical tone emitted by these sources? The authors I cite represent it as a line at the mean pitch level, cutting through the middle of the sinusoid traced by the vibrato (see Fig. 1.4, (p. 23). This line "denotes the general tendency" of a pitch level as if the cycles of the vibrato were absent (Seashore, 1936, p. 48). The line does not really exist—it only arises out of the temporal distribution of "pitches" of which the maximum deviation covers a semitone. Here is a basic example of a sound *quality* arising from a periodically varying population of *quantities*. "Sound quality" in music, to use Piéron's (1945) expression, is often abstracted from a large population of neighboring but not identical frequencies sinusoidally distributed in time. Is it only that? We cannot decide that question without admitting the legitimacy of the mean pitch line as a representation of perceived pitch. And that line appears only exceptionally at pitch levels predictable by objective criteria and only occasionally during the duration of the note. For instance, only 20% of the notes were at their prescribed pitch for their entire duration; 25% never were; and 55% were at times.

The mean extent of fluctuation was about 1.0 semitone for singing (Seashore, 1936) and about .2 semitone for the violin (Small, 1936).[6] Most of the deviations were never perceived as such, even in the analytic conditions of a laboratory experiment. To speak of errors here would be a contradiction in terms, for it is a question of deviations with respect to a higher order standard of correctness, whether in the mathematical or

---

[6]For 62% of the notes, the deviation was between .1 and .2 semitones; for 34% of the notes, it was greater than .2 semitones.

physical aspect. Such deviations, which the ear would not tolerate on the piano or organ (Seashore, 1936), demonstrate the abstracting character of tone perception: good singers and listeners have a difference threshold of 1 or 2 Hz, but they do not "perceive" much more striking deviations that occur in performance, so long as those deviations do not occur in melodic structure (the nature of which we explore later).

3. Finally, apart from fluctuations of intonation, there is in the acoustic signal of most tones a lack of pitch unity during the attack and transition. All observers noted that the incidence of "sliding" attacks was greater than expected from considerations of the aesthetic procedures voluntarily employed by the artists at specific moments. Miller reports that 58% of attacks take the following form: the tone begins below the pitch, which is reached by a sliding glissando with a mean extent of 0.45 semitones for artists (0.3 semitones for amateurs), and with a mean duration of 0.18 and 0.17 sec respectively (Miller, 1936). The glissando sometimes overshoots the target pitch, and then the attack is prolonged with a gradual decline in pitch. Transitions from note to note show the same pattern—notes are reached via ascending or descending portamenti. Small (1936) has described 32 transitions of this type out of 42 notes analyzed from the playing of great violinists. The size of the interval covered was 2.5 semitones, and the transition was either tied to the note that had just been played, or to the following note, or it linked both of them in a smooth curve. In any case, sliding attacks and transitions are perceived as such only when they become artificial and are longer than average: "There is an adaptation or anticipation of tonality that tends to mask the gliding attack and make it seem as if it were an even attack" (Miller, 1936, p. 169).

In summary, at least in the case of singing and stringed instruments, the ear extracts *notes* from the periodic fluctuation of pitch around a mean. This mean is seldom stable, and seldom at the desired pitch throughout its duration. During a good portion of that duration—in attacks and transitions—frequency varies abruptly before establishing the tone. One can see the complexity of these processes and the difficulty of reducing music perception, even the perception of an "element," to a schema of audition such as has been established for sinusoidal phenomena. Yet up to now we have been examining only the aspect of pitch, which seems to be the most important because, with duration (more than timbre and loudness), it brings into play the most differentiated mental processes of music perception. There is, however, an intensity vibrato equal in rate to the pitch vibrato (6.3 Hz), with a mean amplitude of 4.4 dB and affecting 76 notes out of 100 (Small, 1936). Intensity deviations within notes had a mean range of 12.8 dB, but this mean hardly tells us which intensity variations were perceived, and which remained subliminal.

EXPERIMENT 1

In the study I am now going to describe, I proposed to evaluate as exactly as possible the objective frequency fluctuations of stimuli that corresponded to perceived *notes of music*. My aim in this research was not only to show that a note is never just a single "sound," but also to disclose, if possible, regularities in the distribution of frequencies that make up the stimulus.

(1) In the work we have just analyzed, the authors were engaged in the study of particular phenomena, such as vibrato and inexact intonation, but did not aim at a global representation of the objective structure of musical stimuli. It is this representation that we seek.

(2) In those works, the temporal course of the sound frequencies was the fundamental object of the investigation, as was only natural given the goal of discovering how a performer "does" his notes, to use the expression of some artists. Our perspective is different: we attempt to grasp the physical substructure of the phenomenal unities that the listener actually perceives as unities, whatever their duration or whatever the temporal distribution of frequencies, such as might produce a rising or descending effect during a part or all of the duration of a note. It is certain, for example, that for the listener a B is a B in spite of vibrato or any movement of intonation and that this identity rests on the specific distribution of instantaneous frequencies that makes up the stimulus.

Note abstraction refers to the sensory process in which tonal qualities[7] arise for the musical ear—qualities corresponding to diverse stimuli, diverse not only in the form of the sound wave, but also in the degree of stability of frequency. Of these stimuli, those involved in singing are certainly the most complex and the least stable in terms of frequency. The following study gives an idea of the limits of this complexity, that exists without doubt in bells and percussion instruments that have frequency spectra closer to that of noise. In such sounds, however, the ear still perceives notes, but does not find the unitary impression belonging to sung notes. Sung notes are subjectively assimilated to the notes of variable-pitch instruments (for which pitch fluctuations are less important) and of fixed-pitch instruments having very stable pitch.

In this study, I aimed at an analysis of sung notes not produced in isolation, but integrated into a melody. Three experienced female singers were asked to perform a simple vocalise (see Figure 1.1). As it was necessary to provide as much technical support for good intonation as possible,

---

[7]The adjective *tonal* is used here without reference to any musical system of tonality, but rather in the sense used by physiologists distinguishing between noise and tones having definite pitch.

Figure 1.1 Score of the vocalise recorded by the singers, with the accompaniment they heard over earphones.

the singers read the score and heard the accompaniment during the performance.

General Method

The vocalise was performed on the vowel "ah" in order to avoid interruption of the sound by other phonemes. Performance was supported by a piano accompaniment made up of chords indicating metrical beat, tonal functions, cadences, but not containing the notes of the song. Difficulties of intonation were thus avoided, while the voice retained its freedom to form notes without being restricted by the presence of an identical model. This accompaniment was recorded on disc and played on a fixed-speed turntable in a listening booth in the recording studio. The singers heard the recording over headphones. Only the sung part was audible in the studio, and only it was recorded. The studio[8] was well isolated and specially outfitted for this use. The sung part was also communicated to the booth, where it was recorded simultaneously during the playing of the accompaniment.

The three female singers were upper level voice students of the Ecole Normale de Musique de Paris, and all held Concert Performance Certification. The singers, of course, were sure to possess the required technical ability, especially in intonation. They had previously learned the vocalise and had performed it twice while hearing the accompaniment. Thus, conditions were highly favorable for good intonation in their singing. The

---

[8]Recording Studio of the Phonetics Institute of the University of Paris.

recordings were also submitted to competent judges, whose task it was to assess that aspect, first globally and then with analytically. In the latter case, the judges followed the score, underlining notes of doubtful intonation as they went along. The 10 judges as a group agreed that the vocal interpretations were of excellent quality, especially in intonation, and the incidence of notes judged "unstable" or "approximate" was only 5.7% of the possible elements. (The judges did not always agree on questionable elements.) Based on these assessments, the recordings could be considered globally as "musically cogent," and so we proceeded with the photographic analysis of the fundamental frequencies of the longer notes as described below. The relative error of this visual analysis was 0.8 savarts, or about 0.03 semitones.

Technical Methods of Film Recording and Analysis

Apparatus.   The speed of the turntable was controlled to a first approximation by a stroboscopic disc illuminated by a neon lamp at 50 Hz. The disc was played by means of a low-impedance, high-fidelity pickup cartridge, whose output was fed to the oscilloscope amplifier (bandwidth: 0.1 to 10,000 Hz). The divagations of the spot on the oscilloscope were filmed by a camera whose speed provided temporal callibration. A connection for the listener provided for auditory control of the phenomena filmed.

The camera, placed at a suitable distance, had a film speed of about 90 cm/sec. In order to track variations in film speed, a simultaneous time-signal was registered by a Siemens-type mechanical-loop oscillator fitted with an electrically coupled vibrator, producing a 1000-Hz signal with a precision of about 0.000001 Hz.

The connection for listening consisted of a power amplifier and loud-speaker. The amplifier input was taken off the lead from the pickup cartridge (see Figure 1.2). To verify the constancy of turntable speed, a small magnet was attached to the bottom of the turntable. On every revolution, this magnet passed a magnetic sensor whose variation in resistance produced a time-signal that was recorded along with the 50 Hz trace. Thus, the time markers indicated the number of rotations per second, as well as providing for the measurement of rhythm.

Measurement and calculation.   The film recordings were coded in the following manner. Since the vocal performance was supported by an accompaniment regulated by a metronome, we could, given the film speed, retrieve the position of each note on the film. Also, once we had analyzed the first note of the vocalise as played on the piano in the accompaniment recording, we knew precisely the reference frequency the singers were

Figure 1.2 The apparatus. On the table: the cathode-ray oscilloscope on the left and the camera on the right. On the shelf: the turntable on the right.

using. Thus, we could identify onset and offset phases of the sung notes, including sliding attacks. Since we sought to eliminate transient phenomena in isolating pitches of *notes*, we excerpted only the steady state phases, that is, that sustained portion where the note had already been reached. The portions of film thus defined were analyzed by using the time markers as a standard and by dividing the notes throughout their duration into ten-period sections (see Figure 1.3). These sections provided mean instantaneous frequencies, established on time intervals of between 0.02 and 0.032 sec (since the frequencies measured were between about 500 and 310 Hz). For certain notes, the number of measurements obtained was not sufficient for statistical reliability, so we retained only those long enough to furnish at least 30 component measurements, after the elimination of onset and transition phases.

Results and Discussion

With this method we collected mean frequencies for 46 notes (strictly defined). The distribution of these frequencies could be studied as a function of time, or as a simple statistical distribution across time.

Temporal Distribution. The four curves shown in Figure 1.4 are good illustrations of the irregularity of the succession of mean frequencies. Given

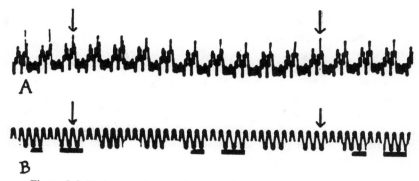

Figure 1.3 Technique of measuring mean frequencies on the photographic recording of sung notes: (A) cycles of the fundamental frequency; (B) 1000 Hz calibration trace. The distance between the two arrows on (A) equals ten cycles, and the elapsed time can be read on (B).

that these are measurements on the phases of notes that followed the onsets and preceded the transitions, they do not illustrate a continuous evolution of the note, but rather a series of oscillations around a mean frequency, the mean frequency itself being systematically flatted or sharpened to a greater or lesser degree.

Statistical Distribution. The statistical distribution can be taken as a representation of fundamental characteristics of the frequency, although lacking the fine detail of its quantitative and temporal variations. One might suppose that although hearing a *note* produces an incontestable

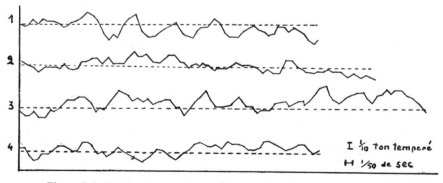

Figure 1.4 Distribution over time of fluctuations of pitch of four notes sung subjectively "in tune." Graphic representation of logarithmic values of instantaneous intervals forming the notes. The dashed line indicates the equal tempered pitch. Instantaneous intervals were calculated from mean frequencies over 10-cycle periods. (1) and (2) were notes with descending tendencies; (3) and (4) were notes with ascending tendencies.

impression of musical unity and simplicity, the cochlea is beset by vibratory phenomena with a distribution of frequencies having certain specifiable properties.

The three curves of Figure 1.5 show clearly that this distribution varies across notes, always, however, with a marked central tendency and a greater or lesser degree of asymmetry. Calculation of arithmetic means and standard deviations was therefore not always appropriate.[9] We made quartile cuts and present ranges, interquartile ranges, and deviations of central frequencies for the 46 notes in logarithmic units (savarts) in Table 1.1, together with means across notes.

Column A. Range of Deviations: Instantaneous mean frequencies oscillated between maxima and minima between which the mean range (in logarithmic units) was 26.245 savarts. The variance of these deviations was calculated across the 46 notes, and was a relatively small 2.561. There is an important fact: the instantaneous frequencies that make up the pitch of a note have generally a range of deviations somewhat greater than a semitone (25 savarts).

Columns B, C, D, E. Ranges Within Quartiles: Between the minimum frequency and the limit of the lower quartile of frequencies lies the first within-quartile range (column B) with a mean of 7.791 savarts. This represents the musical interval separating the minimum frequency from the frequency below which 25% of the frequencies fell. Columns C, D, and E show logarithmic values for the remaining within-quartile ranges, that is, the size of intervals separating the limits of 50, 75, and 100% of the frequencies comprising each note. The means of these intervals were 4.832, 4.809, and 8.607 savarts, respectively.

Column F. Interquartile Range: Between the first and third quartile lie 50% of the measurements. This range corresponds to the central cluster of frequencies displayed by most of the curves. These ranges are more or less grouped according to the notes under consideration but in the aggregate have a mean of 9.641 savarts (more than a third of a tempered semitone).

The pitch of a sung note, perceived as *simple* and *in tune*, and assimilated by the musical ear to notes of instruments, is thus determined by a complex pattern of stimulation—by a population of frequencies having a range greater than a semitone and a central cluster of frequencies (indicated by the interquartile range) covering an interval of more than a third of a tempered semitone.

---

[9]The entries in Table 1.1 indicate mean values. Variability *among notes of the same name* is quite apparent. For example, C4 has a range of mean frequencies of 502.8 to 514.4 Hz.

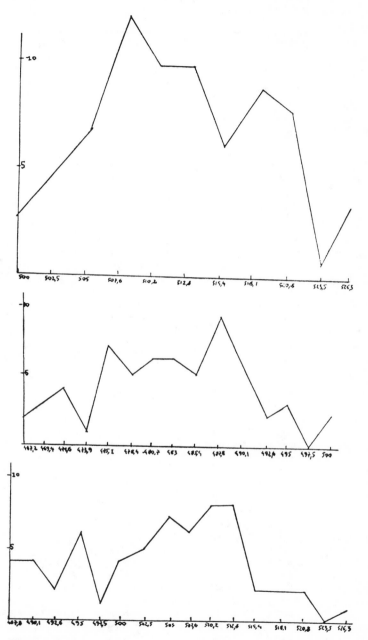

Figure 1.5 Distribution of mean instantaneous frequencies (calculated on 10-cycle periods) for three sung notes (numbers 16, 20, and 25 in Table 1.1). Frequency is on the abscissa, and number of instances in each frequency region is on the ordinate.

TABLE 1.1

Distribution of Mean Instantaneous Frequencies Calculated on
10-cycle Periods for the 46 Song Notes.

					Interquatile Range (Savarts)			
				A	B	C	D	E	F
Note Number	Number of Time Periods	Mean Frequency[1]	Range of Deviations (Savarts)	1	2	3	4	Deviation of Central Frequency (Savarts)
1 G3	29	379,6	26,13	7,27	1,61	8,32	8,93	9,93
2 G3	54	381,1	33,5	4,9	9,79	1,79	16,55	11,55
3 C4	85	514,4	22,26	10,97	0,00	4,57	6,82	4,57
4 B3	42	483,9	21,28	4,17	2,07	4,30	10,75	6,37
5 A3	67	432,5	26,54	7,42	1,91	1,80	15,41	3,71
6 E3	42	316,9	22,02	6,87	6,75	6,92	1,48	13,67
7 C4	43	513,2	33,82	2,16	8,81	8,97	13,88	17,78
8 C4	52	512,3	19,94	7,66	3,31	5,14	3,83	8,45
9 C4	30	513,4	22,26	8,77	2,20	2,20	9,09	4,40
10 B3	61	482,6	29,47	8,19	6,25	4,30	10,73	10,55
11 C4	82	507,1	32,99	10,73	6,55	4,42	11,29	10,97
12 A3	49	430,2	20,49	7,78	3,74	3,71	5,66	7,05
13 G3	30	382,6	29,79	12,92	6,71	1,69	8,47	8,40
14 F3	61	339,9	26,47	11,64	5,76	4,56	4,51	10,32
15 E3	34	321,1	27,88	8,12	3,53	2,02	14,31	5,55
16 C4	75	512,3	17,70	6,55	4,42	4,47	2,26	8,89
17 A3	52	432,8	24,52	5,44	3,23	6,50	8,75	9,73
18 B3	55	485,5	18,92	6,19	4,22	4,19	4,32	8,41
19 A3	48	431,1	28,15	3,69	3,66	5,63	17,17	9,29
20 F3	54	338,8	27,99	90,2	3,99	4,40	10,52	8,39
21 F#3	58	354,8	29,46	10,58	6,85	5,53	6,40	12,48
22 C4	65	502,8	24,13	6,51	4,34	4,39	8,89	8,73
23 A3	49	428,1	27,78	9,04	7,35	5,63	5,76	12,98
24 B3	40	482,1	23,06	7,16	3,17	5,30	7,43	8,47
25 C4	62	504,5	28,43	8,55	6,50	4,45	9,00	10,95
26 A3	60	429,1	31,78	9,11	3,72	7,45	11,54	11,17
27 B3	47	479,1	25,10	4,07	6,22	6,30	8,51	12,52
28 A3	31	428,4	26,10	5,49	5,53	7,45	7,63	12,98
29 F3	65	359,2	26,45	10,63	4,74	4,68	6,46	9,42
30 C4	58	503,7	30,67	8,55	6,50	4,45	11,17	10,95
31 A3	46	430,1	20,37	7,30	5,58	3,71	3,78	9,29
32 B3	49	475,6	18,74	2,04	4,14	8,26	4,30	12,40
33 A3	36	432,3	24,42	6,56	6,57	3,70	7,69	10,27
34 A3	46	430,1	21,55	10,66	3,05	3,16	4,68	6,21
35 C4	48	502,7	26,17	6,36	8,69	2,23	8,89	10,92
36 A3	57	424,1	20,24	5,41	5,54	1,84	7,45	7,38
37 B3	45	467,4	30,35	11,8	94,02	8,19	6,25	12,21
38 A3	40	421,7	29,02	10,55	5,49	3,69	9,29	9,18
39 F#3	70	358,4	23,26	9,04	4,65	4,70	4,77	9,35
40 A3	40	421,7	34,50	11,39	5,52	7,60	9,99	13,12
41 E3	43	318,4	30,67	8,20	4,11	5,55	12,87	9,66

(Continued)

TABLE 1.1
(Continued)

				Interquatile Range (Savarts)				
				A	B	C	D	E	F
Note Number	Number of Time Periods	Mean Frequency[1]	Range of Deviations (Savarts)	1	2	3	4	Deviation of Central Frequency (Savarts)
42 F#3	58	359,2	32,63	13,64	4,74	4,32	9,93	9,06
43 G3	66	378,5	19,72	4,90	4,84	3,31	6,67	8,15
44 C4	43	503,3	34,80	14,42	4,54	6,61	8,93	11,15
45 A3	71	430,1	24,22	9,14	1,82	3,83	9,43	5,65
46 G3	67	380,2	31,55	7,01	5,98	4,99	13,57	10,97
		Mean	26,245	7,971	4,832	4,980	8,607	9,641

[1]The A3 of the accompanying piano by which the singers were guided was tuned to 425.4 Hz.

THE PHYSICAL DIVERSITY OF AUDITORY STIMULI AND THE ABSTRACT UNITY OF THE MUSICAL NOTE

This rigorous inductive acoustic study provides a demonstration of one of the most complex physical events that underlie the psychological construct of the musical note. Sensory reception is, to be sure, the seat of a different order of molecular fluctuations, which we have not considered here: dynamic fluctuations, fluctuations in the harmonic spectrum, variations resulting from the musicians' performance, and the like. But across these microevents (occurring in time, and in certain cases when taken singly perfectly perceptible to the ear), the listener arrives at those simple phenomenal unities familiar to us as graphic symbols in our music books— a process we call *note abstraction*. Upon this infinitesimal level of sensory synthesis there is superimposed a broader level at which the listener hears the same music, whether played in different halls and on different instruments[10] or sung, transcribed, transposed, or recorded with a variety

---

[10]In comparison with the frequencies of an equal tempered instrument such as the piano, the *same note* on stringed instrument or brass (French horn) shows the following deviations (respectively): for E, 0.36 and −0.64 commas; for A, 0.27 and −0.73 commas; for B, 0.45 and −0.55 commas. (The minus sign indicates that the tempered note is sharper.) The D, F, and G were not identical, but differed only slightly from the tempered frequencies, in the neighborhood of 0.18 and −0.09 commas. Since the difference threshold for pitch is around 0.28 commas, these differences would not be negligible to the practiced ear. Except in the criticism of theoreticians, no one has ever heard that the coexistence of the three types of instruments in concerts had provoked reactions among musicians, nor that composers had foresworn writing for ensembles in which they played together. That is one of the principal indications that favors the notion of an abstraction of notes arising from disparate acoustic phenomena.

of apparatus with any number of distortions. If, despite modifications of the physical "message" that carries it, the listener claims to recognize the same piece of music, it is because the fundamental reality on which its identity rests has been conserved, across fluctuations on physical ranges of a different order. This split between levels has long been recognized by physicists and philosophers. I seek here, however, to give it a correct and heuristically valid interpretation.

First, one possible interpretation consists of "canonizing" (so to speak) the divorce between physical values corresponding to the notes and the conceptual reality, thus turning the study of music in a transcendental direction.[11] That way lies a Platonic temptation we should avoid (though the notion of reminiscence applied in this instance would, as we shall see, correspond exactly to the known psychological facts). Although notes—the basic material of music and perceived as phenomenal unities—do not correspond to the same unity in terms of physical causes, it does not follow that their origin must be extraphysical, that it should reside in the realm of ideas. The disparity that appears here between a psychological unity and a physical multiplicity is not limited to the world of music—we must be cautious about making a general ontological distinction. All sensory reception involves a synthesis achieved by the neural centers operating on a multitude of physical events presenting a notable dispersion of quantitative features. This disparity has a structure and peculiarities that we must study in order to understand better the nature of note abstraction. It does not seem heuristically useful to move from facts to values, but rather to go from a summary of facts to a finer description and from there to research directed at an explanation. Let me therefore say, without anticipating the demonstration that follows, that the basis of musical perception is in syntactic *relations* among tones and that those tones can be recognized by the educated listener, even when the acoustical values of their components are altered or fluctuating. The ear seeks, across inexactitudes produced in these relations by notational approximations, musical entities (having a particular psychological status) to which it has become accustomed by frequent repetition. It is the successive and simultaneous combinations of these entities (intervals and chords) that serve as the focus of attention. Up to a point, all musical perception involves recognition of these entities deposited in the mind, not during some preterrestrial experience, but in the course of psychological development going back to infancy. One learns to "hear" the intervals across note values, just as one learns to classify

---

[11]According to Vial (1952), "Everything happens as if there were a Being or an Idea of middle-C" (p. 88). Such an interpretation is somewhat equivocal—it is accurate only in so far as this being and this idea are conceived in terms of events in psychological experience—as potential products of learning and not as a transcendant categories.

colors, by setting boundaries in the sensory continuum, according to the norms corresponding to the divisions most frequently encountered or to those sanctioned by social usage. There is, however, a difference between these two processes. Children isolate the primary colors at the same time as they learn their names. Language categories provide decisive support in that learning (Gelb & Goldstein, 1925; Gelb, 1933; Goldstein, 1933). In contrast, experience of intervals takes place before any naming. Children can sing in tune between 3 and 4 years, but it is rare at that age that they know what a fifth is. Experience is clarified and differentiated during acquisition of verbal and graphic symbols of the tones. But, on the other hand, musical experience enjoys the privilege of an almost absolute standardization of the stimuli on which it is based. Intervals, chords, and scales—including the approximations we are about to describe—are governed by divisions unknown in the scale of colors presented to the young child. Moreover, social sanctions, which are more rigorous concerning errors in tones, contribute to the fixation of more or less strict models. Children who sing out of tune will be corrected, yet they are allowed to call "red" any of a diversity of nuances in the spectrum.

A second interpretation consists, inversely, of placing the musical fact in the domain of physical diversity. Here the unity of the note becomes an "abstraction" in the sometimes pejorative sense of that term. Physical music becomes the only true music. Those distinctions we provide "exist only on paper, or are written with an highly restricted number of artificial symbols—'notations'—themselves subjected to a large number of rules . . ." (Moles, 1953, p. 281). Moles, though providing an interesting study of physical constraints on the "musical signal," appears to suppose, in accordance with the principles of information theory, that the listener hears something other than notes, namely, phenomenal unities designated by the symbols in the score. The process of musical perception actually consists of a refinement and a gradual differentiation of capacities to discriminate *musical* elements written in the score and to ignore subliminal physical elements and miniscule variations in the acoustical message. The level of reality appropriate to music is defined as the cultural message conveyed by perceived signs at *a certain grain of analysis*—itself the result of systematization and peculiar to each culture—of divisions established in the sound continuum. The musical note is not a degraded and approximate physical reality, a product of infirmities of our senses, but rather a reality situated on a different level of analysis with its own intrinsic properties. As we shall see, the laws of musical syntax (tonality, orientation, polarity) are not merely conventions by which composers put together the sounds that are the vehicles of musical meaning. Rather the connections the laws establish are an integral part of that meaning, and, to a point, contribute to the constitution of the "sound message." The stability of sounds in perception and memory, their hierarchical differentiation, and even their more physical properties (such as pitch) are subordinated to a certain degree to the functions conferred on them in the totality of sound by the syntactic laws, with the result that they can be produced by artists and perceived by listeners.

Chapter 2

THE MATERIAL

THE IMPORTANCE OF INSTITUTIONALIZED RELATIONSHIPS OF PITCH

We have seen how the ear of the musician adapts itself to very approximate sound elements—aggregates of all sorts of impurities and of fluctuations of pitch, timbre, and loudness. Surely, compared with noise, musical sounds present a simple structure, but compared with the constant and pure sinusoids of tone generators, they are enormously complex. What is really essential in musical objects—and essential as well for aesthetic consciousness even at the most rudimentary levels—is not just their frequencies, but *relationships* of a certain type, not molecular but molar, not isolated but integrated into a system, not provided by nature but contrived by technology out of natural materials. The musical ear, constructed by the action of these relationships and constructing them in turn, is more a mental than a physical apparatus, governed by habits that guide the apprehension and production of sound materials.[1] The timbre of a musical sound is generated by the cluster of relationships of the frequencies and intensities of its harmonic components. This complex system presents itself to the ear as a simple perceptual quality with emotional power and intrinsic beauty. Yet everyone knows the conventional character of timbre judgments, expressed in spatial, dynamic, or temperature terms (for example, flat, soft, hot, and their analogs and opposites). Our western ears accustom

---

[1]This is even more remarkable than the fact that the differential acuity for pitch is perfectible to a considerable degree by practice. The relative difference threshold ($\Delta f/f$) can vary among individuals by a factor of 20. A number of researchers have demonstrated this perfectibility, notably Wolner and Pyle (1933), Wyatt (1936), and Lundin (1953). Seashore (1938), on the contrary, claimed that acuity stabilized in childhood and remained constant in spite of practice. This claim was based on a study of 25 children exposed to passive training, without feedback. R. Seashore (1935) showed with adults that after a week of active training the mean score of subjects on the Seashore test rose from 6.6 to 45.0.

themselves only with difficulty to the singing of the best Japanese artists, to their instruments, and to the patterns of sound in their orchestras and accompaniments. And even within a particular culture, vocal and instrumental timbres are differently appreciated in different periods and schools.[2] Finally, there are typical timbres that are colored by association with their source, their mythology, and their historical and social context; for example, the sound of the accordion seems "vulgar" to many, the sound of the organ mysterious to some; to others, the flute is bucolic, the horn evokes the forest.

The difficulty is in conceptualizing the nature of *pitch* relationships. The musical ear is formed to distinguish relationships along a dimension fixed by history, which guides it according to more or less stable norms. We refer to the constituent pitch intervals within an octave as the *musical material*. Starting with the pitch C, there are 12 different intervals, going from the minor second (C-Db) to the octave (C-C'). Among melodic intervals larger than the octave, those larger than an eleventh (an octave plus a fourth) hardly ever occurred before the beginning of this century. Today instrumental music employs larger intervals, sometimes larger than two octaves.

Harmonic intervals are those that the ear perceives among simultaneous sounds from the same scale in its repetitions through the series of successive octaves. The order of intervals is not the same here as for melodic intervals. It happens, of course, that a melody contains groups of notes forming broken chords, giving a succession of the same notes as those of a chord. But, at least as often, the notes of a melody present a sequence of intervals not used in harmony, for example, a diatonic or chromatic scale or scale fragment. Classical harmony does not permit the simultaneous occurrence of more than two adjacent intervals. The harmonic equivalence of intervals is enlarged by one or several octaves, of an interval and its inversion—an equivalence that we will need to explicate later but that we mention here only because it does not occur melodically. Neither octave substitutions nor inversions retain the most basic aspects of a given melodic fragment that embodies gesture and movement—a contour of pitches.

The ear is thus formed to evaluate—or, more simply, to perceive— distances among sounds defined by fixed, institutionalized standards for the intervals generated by the scalar division of the octave and homologous processes. This division, different for different cultures, poses bothersome problems for the philosopher of music, problems such as the "true" source

---

[2]Physiologists, such as Husson (1953), recognize the *ethos* of timbre: "The same voice can be said to be too 'white' or too 'dark,' too 'small' or too 'large,' by this or that voice teacher." The beauty of a timbre is a function of the subject's prior auditory experience and the way it is presented.

"correct" intonation in scales of all the possibilities that have been chosen in other times and other places. We will examine these possibilities for their psychological aspects.

To be sure, the term "distance" is rigorously applicable only to melodic successions in which qualitative and quantitative impressions are mingled in the perception of an interval. The qualitative impressions arise from frequency relationships, and the quantitative impressions of interval size stem from prior associations to spatial images of distance in which vertical or oblique lines cut the horizontal.[3] The impression of the relative sizes of melodic intervals grows gradually from the comparison of different intervals, and then only insofar as the subject receives an education of a specific sort, that is, training in the analytic dissociation of elements from the groups into which they are usually integrated. It is certain that interval qualities become individually and clearly differentiated only after such training, including naming. For the subject, a 3/2 frequency relationship (and its close approximations in equal temperament) becomes a *fifth*, with all the relevant cultural meanings and including the ensemble of its structural components, such as the tonality it defines, the major and minor thirds from which it is formed, which either determine mode or leave mode undetermined, and so forth. These properties of intervals do not reside in a conceptual plan, but rather are implicit in thought and action; that is, they are associated with the hearing of an interval just as much as are any other virtual properties of the physical sound stimulus. Insofar as their acquisition may have been experienced through simple exposure to musical works, those properties might even appear in themselves before being isolated in a network of abstract and general relationships. It is there that we are struck by the sense of Combarieu's (1907) remarks concerning intelligence and musical ideas. Understanding music, even insofar as it involves only simple relationships such as intervals, can occur without "theoretical" concepts: "Excluding concepts definitely does not imply excluding thought, and may on the contrary favor the freest and least superficial sort of intellectual activity" (p. 264). "To be intelligent is to *understand*. Understand what? The thought that *is* the melody. It is to be able to see a meaning there, where there are no concepts, no words; a 'logic' there, where all the processes of the verbal dialectic are excluded, replaced by a sort of direct intuition" (p. 251). Of course, this process will reflect back on those thoughts, that logic, that ontological ground,

---

[3]This spatial imagery based on flow and apparent movement is tied to the temporal distribution of sound stimuli. Physiopathologists consider it to be an indispensible condition of normal perception. In a pathological state the movements lose their continuity, causing intermittences—false summations that produce unpredictable, gapped sound structures (cf. Ombredane, 1944). However, Riemann (1906) supposes an "immanence of spatial representations" in the perception of both successive and simultaneous (chordal) intervals.

and on the necessity of musical relations and systems. Nevertheless, Combarieu's remarks capture an essential psychological fact: the lower bounds of musical comprehension are set by this intuitive grasp of hierarchical relationships which operates in the subject through the effects of implicit abstraction (sometimes made explicit by training), arising from entirely passive experience of music.

That boundary thus falls outside simple auditory perception, and so at this point I will introduce direct and indirect evidence from other areas.

EVIDENCE FROM PSYCHOPATHOLOGY: AMUSIAS

Out of the great variety of clinical observations on amusical patients there is a good part that, because it concerns subjects without technical education in music, permits the definition of a mental deficit appearing in those afflicted as an incapacity to grasp musical relationships in the perception of sounds. The peripheral auditory apparatus remains intact, and sensory reception is undamaged, yet the subject has lost the possibility of *identifying* intervals, of *comparing* them, of attending to a succession of them *as a melodic form*, or even simply of grasping in that succession any *hierarchy* or *ordering*. Music becomes for such persons a succession of discrete *sounds*; they are unable to identify those often experienced relationships that form the familiar framework of musical discourse.

The most extensive, and the least analytical, classification of amusical subjects of which I know is that of Brazier (1892), who distinguishes tone-deafness, note-blindness, and motor amusia. In most cases of tone-deafness there is a link between amusia and aphasia, and the amusia is observed only as a (nonobligatory) correlate of aphasia. Wallaschek (1891) clearly distinguishes between *Tontaubheit* and *Worttaubheit*. And Brazier himself observed a case of restoration of language in conjunction with persistent tone-deafness.[4]

It is in this category of subjects incapable of hearing, but still (or newly) able to express themselves verbally, that we find the basic differentiation of general deafness and tone-deafness (taking the term in the broad sense, without direct reference to the system of tonality). Brazier observed a subject afflicted with aphasia and sensory amusia to whom a year later

---

[4]This often observed concomitance between the two disorders is instructive in itself. It places musical activity and perception far from sensory functions and closer to symbolic functions than is usually believed. Probst (1899), reporting ten clinical-anatomical observations of amusical subjects, noted this concomitance in all cases. Oppenheim (1888) gave 17 observations from which one can draw analogous conclusions, Dupré and Nathan (1911) came to the same conclusions.

speech gradually returned. Hearing seemed unaffected. The subject, a musician of modest attainments, was able to recall many songs and melodies. When *La Marseillaise* was played, he reported hearing "only a meaningless series of noises, with no aesthetic connection . . . a confused noise, in which he could discern nothing musical" (Brazier, 1892). For all that, the term *noise* as used by this patient is vague and lends itself to two interpretations. Either the subject heard musical sounds, but without connections between one another; or else, in the cluster presented to his ear, he was not able to separate out of the sound fluctuations and impurities that we have described those abstract unities called notes. In the latter case, he would have been hearing only noise—successions of sound elements without the possibility of synthesis. In a case of congenital failure of musical development, Dupré and Nathan (1911) also speak of noise in connection with the sound impressions experienced by their subject, a 30-year-old physician:

> Nothing to note in hereditary and personal antecedents. Psychological and somatic development normal through childhood. But a complete absence of the sense of music was observed early. He does not recognize songs that were repeatedly sung to him; he cannot repeat notes played for him on the piano; he is absolutely incapable of making a synthesis of sounds. (p. 15)[5]

Of course, as these authors observe, such a deficit could be appreciated only by comparison with the previous state of the patient. To get some idea of that, one needs careful interviews with witnesses and recourse to compositions (if there are any), to try to discover any rare or exceptional circumstances bearing on the case. But in the simple observation of the present state of the subject there is at least this typical fact: The *dissociation of peripheral reception from synthetic perception of the simplest musical groupings*—a dissociation that, as we have seen, can either be congenital or acquired later.

In the observations that follow, we see that tone-deafness itself breaks down into three distinct incapacities, which seem to give good evidence of the complexity of the corresponding function: incapacities involving the sense of interval direction, of interval size, and of interval quality.

Some patients lose the ability to recognize *qualities* of intervals without, as a result, losing the ability to distinguish their relative *size*. Such was the case of the music hall violinist and song writer (described by Dieulafoy in Dupré & Nathan, 1911) who commited gross errors in this sense and the case of an excellent musician (observed by Révész, cited in Ogden, 1924) who, while retaining the sense of pitch level, took the interval of

---

[5]Dupré & Nathan (1911) discuss failures of musical development. See also Ireland, 1894.

a fifth for an octave and vice versa. The case of Heinrich R., described by
Käufer (1931) over a period running from 1918 (when he was wounded
in the temporal bone) to 1930—one of the most rigorous sets of observations we possess—leads to the same conclusions. He could identify even
very faint noises of objects. Differential pitch sensitivity was intact—the
patient, a professional tuner, adjusted slight tuning errors in a piano on
which several notes had been mistuned, but he could not specify the
direction of the differences. It was all the same to him when a phonograph
was played at different speeds. As a correlate, interval qualities were
obscured: a fourth was confused with a fifth and vice versa, major and
minor thirds were confused with each other. As for sixths and sevenths,
they could not obtain verbal identification. In order to identify a fifth the
subject made use of an interpolated third between the outside pitches,
whistling all three notes. (That indicates the preservation of the perception
of relative interval size and shows at the same time the relational character
of qualities of intervals in a musically trained subject.) Finally, the patient
described by Dupré and Nathan (1911) (a former musician—a tubaist)
was just as prone to errors in the identification of intervals (he confused
fourths and fifths) but preserved the ability to recognize an already familiar
melody by its simple melodic movement, that is, the succession of ups
and downs, the rhythm, and relative interval sizes. His case was complicated by problems in sight reading both text and music. The patient was
incapable of synthesizing groups of notes—the groups remained for him
successions of discrete elements without global properties.

Concerning deficiencies in rhythm perception, the observations of various authors diverge, and it seems that none of the following disturbances
is the rule. In general, when rhythm is not disturbed, subjects remain
capable of recognizing fairly long melodic fragments. That, however, seems
to be a matter of recognizing not pitch relationships, but rather temporal
and dynamic relationships and, sometimes, pitch hierarchies. The last, as
we shall see, also affect musical rhythm. What the patient cannot accomplish is recognition of these fragments as being constituted of intervals
and of interval groups with their own properties. The case of Madame R.,
professor of piano, observed by Brazier (1892), is typical. As she recovered
from total musical dislexia (without tone-deafness), she developed, first,
the ability to recognize the durations of notes, and then their pitch. Such
persistances of symptoms can delude observers. For example, Kleist distinguishes sensory amusia (*Tontaubheit*) from melodic amusia (*Melodien-
taubheit*), suggesting that in the former case melodies are well perceived,
"as if the false perceptions of the sounds themselves did not cause the
deficit". It is clear that he is relying on examples in which nonmusical
rhythm and "up and down" pitch relationships permit subjects to identify
melodies from which, for them, specific properties of intervals have been
abolished. It is reasonable to suppose that such subjects would identify

melodies in which the intervals had been enlarged or contracted in some idiosyncratic way, other factors remaining constant.

Finally, although Delacroix's (1927) classification of amusical subjects is based not on direct observations, but on knowledge of work on aphasics in general (especially the work of Head), one can find, besides apraxia and syntactic aphasia, a sort of musical asymbolism analgous to Head's nominal aphasia. That type of disorder, which affects vocabulary, deprives sound elements of their tonal values—their virtual relationships with other sounds—and produces an inability to comprehend musical discourse: "Melody and harmony become confused in the absence of their component elements" (pp. 319–320). However, it is difficult to isolate this form of asymbolism from an "inability to integrate the elements of discourse, to comprehend phrases." In a sense, syntax is not lacking, even in the qualities of intervals and chords—qualities that imply relationships to other tones and chords—dynamic tendencies arising out of acquired familiarity with syntactic relationships. It is difficult to see in the concept of "asymbolism" an exact equivalent to "perceptual amusia." The term is not applicable to subjects lacking specific musical education, for whom intervals, notes, and their combinations have not been brought into a symbolic formulation and thus retain their definition in terms of a purely perceptual reality. To achieve a terminology that casts more light on these matters, we must recall the "primary signal system," which has never been linked to verbal or graphic signs. Might we legitimately consider asymbolism in those subjects who, though musically illiterate, nevertheless have been definitely acculturated through familiarity with certain materials and syntax? Musical signs and their combinations no doubt provide the basis of perception and musical thought, but they can be identified with neither the one nor the other. Lamy (1907) has made an instructive observation in this regard. In the case of Deb. . ., a former music professor afflicted with sensory aphasia and who exhibited all the symptoms of sensory amusia, but with important differences one might attribute to automatic processes acquired in the course of professional development. Here the contribution of the symbolic system was obvious: the patient could not recognize a theme that he had just composed when it was payed to him immediately after; and he could not recognize the *Marseillaise* and other familiar tunes. However, if they were written down, he found them easy. We have here, as in other cases of amusia in professional musicians, a pseudorecognition and a pseudoperception of intervals, consisting of the persistence of their symbolic note to note relationships (visual or verbal). But one should not suppose that these subjects hear the relationships. Everything suggests the opposite.

Along the same lines is another trait noted by Käufer (1931) in his observation of Hermann R. His report is especially valuable because it concerns the perception of chords (concerning which such observations are rare). Major and minor chords were struck and the patient was asked to reproduce them on the piano. Käufer observed that the chords were reproduced in transposition or in inversion, but with the following noteworthy mistakes:

Bb - D - F - Bb	became	G - C - E - G
Gb - Bb - Db - Gb	became	F - A - C - F
G - B - D - G	became	G - C - E - G
D - F - A - D	became	E - G - B - E

The same chords were not identified when arpeggiated; but when they were struck together, a minor chord was clearly distinguished from a major. It seems that lacking here was the precise representation of the quality or distance involved in an interval. The melodic presentation of a chord distributes it into a succession of qualities that, as we have seen, are not perceived. In contrast, simultaneous presentation eliminates difficulties of intervallic distance. What is perceived is a familiar *sound quality* (*timbre*) of general significance—general in the sense of being major or minor—that the subject from prior knowledge translates into notes without actually hearing them. Inversions and transpositions demonstrate that only the conceptual schemas evoked by the sound qualities are preserved, not sound content capable of further analysis.

NATURALIZATION OF INTERVALS IMPOSED ON OTHER DIVISIONS OF THE OCTAVE

Let us now leave observations on the psychopathology of amusia and reconsider the relational perception of sounds in terms of another set of facts. Most people know the "out-of-tune" impression made by African music or the music of Oceania, in which the octave is divided differently from the way to which we are accustomed. This impression shows the power of custom. It disappears only incompletely in the forwarned listener capable of analysis and not trying to interpret unfamiliar systems of intervals in terms of his native language of sounds.

In missionaries' and folklorists' notation of popular melodies, where the non-European material differed from the tempered diatonic pattern, naive assimilation of perceived to known intervals occurs. The European ear, accustomed to tempered tuning and inclined to its own culture—but also as a result of spontaneous perceptual tendencies—interprets melodies in terms of interval qualities arising from acquired automatic dispositions. Here one cannot really speak of "errors of perception"; the disparity between the two kinds of intervals does not remain unperceived. The fact of notation indicates only that such disparity is not an obstacle to the reduction of the perceived forms to a diatonic schema. Departures too important to escape notice are heard, voluntarily or not, as approximations, which do not prevent hearing the melodic line in terms of that schema. The techniques of phonophotography are required to reveal the extent and variety of differences, unless they are always heard as such, in order to arrive at a conception of the specifics of songs using different material.[6] Metfessel (1928), who seems to have been the first to apply these techniques to the study of songs of Black Americans, indicates how ignorance of African music led them to adopt the European system, as seen in copies of native American melodies and African songs in the European style. In contrast, the discovery and recording of Black African music has led authors such as Krehbiel, Work, and Ballenta to associate it with the Black American music that has derived from it.

Metfessel's measurements have provided a basis for more precise analysis of elements belonging to the Negro style. The variety of these elements clearly demonstrates the the extent of the process of abstraction through which living contours become reduced to notes and intervals that often involve departures of intonation become written on a stave (and are thus referable to our diatonic scale). One source of variation, which can be called *stylistic*, involves ascending notes that are entirely unstable, without a steady phase ("intonation tones"), warbling notes, descending ties that take a held note below its pitch level, and various forms of vibrato involving frequency and amplitude variation. Among the most clearly noticed features, as perceptible as those, are falsetto attacks, which give the impression of a brief, plaintive cry at the start of the note; abrupt changes of register and timbre; erratic wavers; slow trills; and ornament sounds encompassing up to five semitones above and below the target note. Among alterations of intervals, neutral thirds (between major and minor) sometimes occur in the melodic division of the fifth, as well as quarter steps and augmented minor sevenths.[7]

Thus, setting aside elements of stylistic variation, when European listeners perceive an exotic song, their spontaneous perceptual attitude is, on the one hand, to assimilate the group of sounds (as measured by other norms) to a sound group fashioned according to familiar articulations and

---

[6]Cf. Sachs (1943): "Western man is never free from adapting foreign melodies to his own musical language; he perforce hears the equal-sized six-fifth tones of Javanese orchestras as alternating seconds and thirds. . . . In the same spirit, painters of the eighteenth and early nineteenth centuries delineated Indians and Negroes with the classical Greek bodies and gestures that academic training had forced upon them" (p. 26).

[7]Metfessel (1928) correctly notes that here the concept of "interval" must be considered as a zone or region or mean distance, due to the statistical nature of the measurements.

to interpret the new interval as a known one. (Here "interpret" is a some-what misleading term in that these judgments are without apparent media-tion.) On the other hand, when the deviation is too important, European listeners feel the unfamiliar interval as a faulty approximation of the familiar—as a technical error. Yet there is considerable evidence of the precision with which exotic scales are measured and of the tuning of the instruments that produce them (Seashore, 1938). Here is, in sum, a pro-jection of our own schema of distances onto material relevant to different norms. This projection is equally apparent in such innovations as the system of quarter-tones introduced at the beginning of this century, in which certain arrangements of melody and harmony were mixed in with equal-tempered patterns: either such differences pass unnoticed (as some trustworthy observers have claimed (e.g., Dukas, 1948), or they appear as intentional fluctuations of intonation aimed at expressive effects, or they are attributed to the ineptitude of the performers, which is the equivalent of a previously observed reaction.

INTERVAL CONSTANCIES

These reactions could be compared with those evoked in vision experi-ments involving color and size perception. Under certains experimental conditions, the identification of a color is affected by *contamination by the familiar object*. The perceived color is what one would expect to find in the object or shape presented, even when the actual stimulus does not correspond to it. In a minimal situation with monocular vision, the rela-tionship between size and distance is perceived in conformity with the requirements of the real object (Bruner & Postman, 1949).

Moreover, the facts involving assimilation of intervals can be compared to certain perceptual constancies.[8] It is necessary to distinguish perceptual constancies from purely qualitative constancies (such as color constancy), in which phenomenal permanence of quality is observed across variations attributable to objective causes (as when different colored light is projected on a surface). In contrast, we have in the case of interval constancy a *permanence of the quality of a relationship, observed in spite of quantitative variations exerted on its components in an already differentiated context*. Size constancy is an equally distinct phenomenon; size relationships are pre-served between the perceived object and the objects in its environment. Here the alteration occurs only in the retinal projection of that relationship, which varies as a function of distance.

---

[8]On constancies, see Koffka (1935), Ittelson (1951), and Piaget and Lambercier (1943).

In shape constancy and object constancy, on the other hand, phenomenal permanence is observed despite objective alteration of the internal relationships in a familiar geometric shape or in the typical shape of a thing—as when a disc tilted progressively in the fronto-parallel plane is seen as a disc and not as an ellipse, even though the distance relationships between the periphery and center are not all equal. If the lateral parts of the disc are masked before the tilt and remain masked during tilting, this phenomenal permanence of form is difficult to obtain. Likewise, a scale or a brief melody in which some intervals have been altered will be heard as in tune (assimilated to a familiar sequence of relationships), whereas the isolated presentation of one or two such intervals will disclose the deviations introduced (cf. Koffka, 1935). Concluding a study of artistic singing involving the phonophotographic measurement of pitch deviations of diverse origin occurring in the most highly qualified interpretations, Seashore (1938) suggested that "though the deviations are often well above the thresholds of discrimination for steady, discrete, and simple tones, they frequently are unperceived by singer and listener," since "by habit we force tonal experiences into our conventional scale" (p. 56). With the analytic and critical attitudes the laboratory, such deviations are perceived.

Object constancy is related to shape constancy in that the phenomenal permanence of a dimension, of a quality, of a relationship holding across variations produced in an experiment, connects with only a minimum of meaning derived from the pattern. Just as shape constancy studied with the usual geometric figures shows the resistance of familiar perceptual unities to deformation, in object constancy form interferes with color (or, in certain experiments, taste with color and consistency) while maintaining a previously integrated pattern, stored in a nonexplicit form of memory. Duncker (1939) showed this influence of knowledge on perceptual judgment. If under red light observers are presented alternately with the silhouettes of a donkey and of a leaf cut from the same bright green paper, they will select as "equivalent" to the leaf sample colors that contain twice as much green or orange as those they select for the donkey. The experimental conditions were such that the apparent color of the silhouettes was actually close to gray.[9]

A question that arises concerning the acquisition of interval constancy is that of the necessity of *attitudes*. A number of psychologists, especially gestaltists, have cast doubt on the possibility of "automatic" influences of past experience on present perception. This controversy is sufficiently well known that we need not dwell on it. In fact, Köhler's (1929) reluctance

---

[9]See also Fraisse (1949) and Francès (1953). A similar result was established by Bruner, Postman, and Rodrigues (1951).

in this regard was determined by a particular type of problem and does not seem related to the problem occupying us here. For Köhler it was a matter of showing that reproduction depended on the form of a whole figure distinct from the ground. The eventual effect of past experience depends on the integration of stimuli into wholes—into groups of relationships. Nothing there militates against the acquisition of interval constancies through hearing complex forms in which they occur. Gottschaldt's (1926) experiments with patterns containing previously presented elements showed that when viewers had a passive set (versus a set for active search) initial exposure produced little benefit, no matter how numerous the prior presentations. But this result arises, as Braly (1933) noted, from the fact that the shapes to be recognized were literally swamped with attached lines in the complex figures, and as a consequence an analytic attitude was prerequisite to any initial fixation. Braly's own experiments clearly established the effects of past experience on present perception. Braly's research using material made up of groups of points plainly showed that such an analytic attitude is not necessary. The influence of past experience is negligible as long as the target groups are simple enough to be remembered after one trial; or, inversely, when after having been presented alone they are submerged in too complex a parasite form. However, in all other cases the effects of experience are considerable. Comparison of results from the experimental group (who viewed 500 tachistoscopic presentations of patterns containing elements to be reproduced later) with those of a control group (not given those presentations) showed that "automatic" learning can modify figural perception. Subjects in the two groups were asked to draw analogous figures. Subjects in the experimental group tended to change the shapes of the figures in the direction of those previously seen or to add elements borrowed from them.

There seems to be a process of perceptual learning approaching that of nonmusicians' acquisition of sound relationships.[10] Note that the subjects in Braly's experimental group were not entirely passive. Their task during stimulus presentation was to draw whatever they saw, and they were kept uninformed only of the subsequent controlled test. Similarly, those whom we call musically illiterate are not entirely deprived of active participation in interval learning. From childhood on, hearing is coupled with vocal reproduction of simple models—reproduction controlled and monitored to some extent by adults. The nonmusical child lacks, on one hand, *analysis* of the interval patterns that make up a melody (where correlation consists of repetition of the entire pattern), and, on the other hand, the *naming*

---

[10]"Nonmusical" refers to subjects deprived of any contact with technical analysis of musical works, and thus ignorant of the graphical system of notation on which it is based. See below, Experiment 3.

of intervals that provides for their explicit differentiation and makes of them definite entities. But it is in these latter processes that we find conditions that contribute to the growth of the *stability* of the melodic stimulus. They are not strictly necessary for refinement of discrimination nor for accuracy of immediate reproduction. By stability we mean the property of persistence of a sound pattern that permits recognition of difference as well as perception of change in later presentations. This is why musical illiterates would be able to judge correctly that someone sang or played "out of tune." In fact, they make such judgments of the playing of Javanese gamelan instrumentalists and the like, without being able to indicate the intervals of whose intonation startled them (much less to indicate the direction of the error), even when the notes were presented separately.

What appears to be acquired—even by nonmusicians and moreso by others—is the absence of naiveté in judgments of intonation. We shall see later that it is impossible to account for this developmental outcome without invoking the effects of certain scale steps with their functional differences, etc. We also find in this connection a definitive solution to certain pseudoproblems that have puzzled the psychology of music for centuries— problems of what the "true" scale might be and what might constitute "perfect intonation," and so on.

THE TRADITIONAL PROBLEM OF SIMPLE RELATIONSHIPS

Insofar as musicology rests on mathematical considerations, on the excellence of simple relationships and the superiority of intervals constructed on that basis,[11] or on the necessity of deducing their dimensions from observation of physical phenomena (as with the spatial dimensions of resonant bodies),[12] the controversy surrounding the *true* division of the octave makes some sense, whether in terms of the aesthetic implications of the results deduced or in terms of the rigor of the scientific methodology brought into play. However, when one seeks to base a musicological theory

---

[11]This is the basis of the "geometrician's scale" of Aristoxenus, Zarlino, Leibniz and Euler. But an analogous spirit informs the construction of the "musician's scale," whose origin is attributed to Pythagoras. It is based on the excellence of the numbers 2 and 3, with intervals ascending from the origin in the following relationships: 1; 9/8; 81/64; 4/3; 3/2; 27/16; 243/128; 2. The only differences in the intervals of Zarlino's scale are: the third, 5/4 instead of 81/64; the sixth, 5/3 instead of 27/16; and the seventh, 15/8 instead of 243/128.

[12]This is the basis of the "physicist's scale" (Helmholtz, 1877/1954) in which the intervals of the major second, major third, fifth, and seventh are equal to those in Zarlino's scale, resulting from a selection from among the first 15 harmonics. Neither the fourth nor the sixth arise that early in a harmonic series based on a common fundamental.

on the *testimony of the ear*, without inquiring into the psychological conditions bearing on that evidence, one eliminates all rigor from the debate and encounters inextricable paradoxes. Lalo (1908/1939) has emphasized the distance separating artistic practice—artistic facts and their conceptual elaboration—from attempts to define an absolute and "exact" music, as if the norms of certain sciences ought necessarily apply to activities relevant to entirely different norms, which must first of all be researched and understood. On the contrary, what is perfectly useful and legitimate is the application of certain *techniques* of the applicable sciences to artistic *facts*, observed and collected in such a way as to appear in all their complexity.

The psychological paradox I wish to outline arises from the following studies. From 1869 (when Cornu and Mercadier published their initial report, to 1946 [the date of the latest experimental report written on this question as of the original writing of this book], various authors, all up-to-date in the techniques of practical acoustic measurement (the earlier used recordings on smoked cylinders, the later phonophotography), asked whether the "true ear" was governed by the Pythagorean or the natural system of intervals. Abraham (1923) close to the truth, had posed the alternative as between tempered and natural intervals. Greene (1936, 1937) and Small (1936) and, later, van Esbroeck and Montfort (1946), extended their investigations into all three possible tunings: Pythagorean, natural, and tempered.

The experiments put forward on the basis of various theories were of three sorts:

1. One type involved the measurement of solo performances on stringed instruments. One might suppose that that the intervals thus produced would provide evidence concerning the musicians' ear, developed through regular practice. (We shall see that, in effect, the values so obtained are closely tied to this technique.)

2. A second type of experiment involved the comparison of melodic or harmonic stimuli presented to perceiving subjects of widely varying musical background (van Esbroeck and Montfort, 1946). There we have an interesting and essentially universal source of data that permits the evaluation of discrimination and judgment of intervals via simple audition.

3. Finally, there were experiments involving performance by singers and violinists having more or less musical experience. Those studies indicate intonation tendencies arising from complex causes (Abraham, 1923; Small, 1936), notably involving the integration of series of intervals in terms of cultural patterns (tonality, mode, accidentals)

or acoustic patterns (melodic motion, similarity of tone height). Those effects are such that it is no longer possible to speak of constant interval sizes without considering an interval's situation in a succession of pitches or the tonal *function* of its constituent notes among the degrees of the scale.

Across this variety of studies, the present review aims, not at finding intervals that are "true in themselves," holding across evidence from diverse groups of subjects, but rather at finding the differences that exist among the various evidences and that can be revealed by a critical review. It is difficult to see the sense of such propositions as the following: "The ear demands in the *succession* of sounds forming what musicians call melody, intervals belonging to a series of fifths making up the Pythagorean scale" (Cornu & Mercadier, 1869/72, p. 425). "The scale of our harmonic music is not that of the physics treatises; it is that of Pythagoras" (van Esbroeck & Montfort, 1946, p. 19). Or "They [artists] unconsciously employ Pythagorean intervals" (Greene, 1937). What would seem to conform more closely with the facts would be a more modest claim formulated as follows: Violinists (and other musicians playing instruments with variable intonation and tuned in fifths) have intonation tendencies which arise out of their tuning and performance practices, that could be labeled Pythagorean. But such intonation is not the only true intonation among musicians. It does not differ appreciably from tempered intonation, the almost universal source for formation of the ear. The ear departs more from "natural" intonation, at least with regard to melodic intervals, because of the relative rarity of instruments capable of producing such intonation.

Further, to determine exactly the sizes of intervals performed on variable-intonation instruments is always a delicate task, producing results subject to caution, given the nature of the variations of frequency grouped under the concept of a "note." Intonation is the result of a variety of factors—setting aside inadvertent deviations arising from physiological lapses of the performer—and certain of those factors militate against the performer's tendency to measure each interval independently of its momentary context. Notes (as we shall see in connection with the laws of scalarity, orientation, and polarity) are subject to complex integrations (of mode, function, and region) that introduce "deformations" that are noticeably greater than the differences between tempered intonation and intonation derived from the cycle of fifths. Those deformations are grafted onto tempered values by singers. And they illustrate aspects of the performers' acculturation in a system that developed through history; namely, the tonal system, that today is beginning to fade due to the production of works on different principles.

Finally, experiments on perceptual comparisons uniformly indicate that virtually only musicians can discriminate among groups of intervals constructed using different dimensions; most others are incapable of such discriminations. Those who are capable tend to select tempered intervals (because of the common influence on the education of their ears), occasionally, Pythagorean intervals, and only rarely, "natural" intervals.

It is difficult, then, to generalize the results obtained from studies of performance and to claim that they alone disclose the demands of the "true ear." Yet those results are interesting because they demonstrate the adaptation of pitch judgments to those integrative schemes that constitute the foundations of articulation within musical forms. Of course, without even revealing itself through acoustic alterations, such adaptation plays an important role in the organization of musical perception, as shown in a variety of studies.

Let us review, as briefly as possible, the research on which these conclusions are based.

Experiments on Performance of Instruments Having Freely Varying Sound

Beginning with the work published by Cornu and Mercadier between 1871 and 1873, we can construct a summary table. Table 2.1 shows (in hundredths of a tempered tone) mean intonation deviations of intervals

TABLE 2.1
Experiments on Stringed Instrument Performance

Mean tuning differences in cents measured with respect to natural, Pythagorean, and even-tempered tuning, according to the studies of (1) Greene (1936), (2) Cornu & Mercadier (1871), and (3) Cornu & Mercadier (1872), with values for 3, 7, and 9 semitones from Cornu & Mercadier (1873).

Tuning	Study	Interval (in semitones)								
		1	*2*	*3*	*4*	*5*	*6*	*7*	*9*	*11*
Natural	(1)	−12	1	−10	0					
	(2)		−1.52	−20.4	18.36	2.5	3.48	−21.64	20.76	24.84
	(3)		3.08		20.72	−5.24	0			23.92
Pythagorean	(1)	−1	1	1	−1	0				
	(2)		−1.52	1.44	−2.72	2.5	1.74	2.2	−1.04	1.82
	(3)		3.08		−1.36	−5.24	0			2.72
Tempered	(1)	−6	3	−2.	+3	−1				
	(2)		1.66	−4.4	5.52	0	5.4	−3.28	4.12	12.96
	(3)		6.16		6.88	−6.84	2.32			11.92

played by violinists, with respect to the values of those intervals in the natural, Pythagorean, and tempered systems. The conclusions that emerge from this are as follows: The sum of mean deviations in each column varies from one study to another, sometimes even doubling in magnitude. There thus seems to be little reliability in these measures. Except for the major seventh (whose increase over the tempered value could be due to attractive tendencies), one cannot firmly conclude that Pythagorean intonation is exclusively preferred to tempered intonation. In the two studies of Cornu and Mercadier, the sums of deviations are clearly more important with respect to natural intonation, notably in major thirds and major sevenths. This fact is the most certain, and it is confirmed by Greene's (1936, 1937) results. Excepting natural intonation, the range of deviation sizes is never larger than the margin of tolerance in the practices of great artists. It is even consistently smaller than the maximum recorded by Greene, which was greater than 30 cents (0.15 tone), from various samples of "in tune" intervals. Mean deviations of less than 1 savart seem absolutely negligible from the point of view of the listener.

Figure 2.1 is drawn from the patient and exhaustive work of Greene. It shows (in hundredths of a tone) means of five intervals measured by ear from recordings of great string virtuosos, in comparison with natural, Pythagorean, and tempered values. In Table 2.1 these results are juxtaposed to those of Cornu, and Mercadier (1871, 1872, 1873). For natural intervals as well, a comparison with intervals in performance leads to clear conclusions. For major and minor thirds, major and minor sixths, and major sevenths (the only seventh measured), the mean deviation is 0.21 tone (41 cents), which falls beyond the margin of tolerance of the ear under similar conditions. Concerning Pythagorean and tempered values, the choice is more delicate, inasmuch as the measurements do not always agree and the recorded deviations are small. The largest deviations are with the major seventh, which clearly differs from the tempered value.

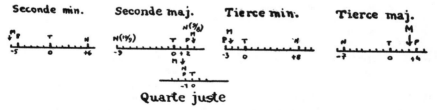

Figure 2.1 Comparison of intervals as performed by the artists, and intervals of even-tempered, Pythagorean, and "natural" tuning in cents (after Greene, 1936): (M) mean of recorded intervals; (T) tempered intonation, taken as zero on the scale; (P) Pythagorean intonation; (N) natural intonation.

But that might be the result of the attractive tendencies discussed later.[13] The means across all these mean differences are 1.63 centitones with respect to Pythagorean intervals, and 4.24 centitones with respect to tempered intervals. One might suppose that there is among string virtuosos a marked tendency to control intonation with reference to a system of ascending fifths, that being the principle according to which they tune their instruments. But it would be an illusion to see in that the effects of a musical "instinct" or to objectify these judgments in order to derive from them a set of values recognized by every "true ear."

Perceptual Comparisons of Three Types of Intervals

Van Esbroeck and Montfort (1946), starting from the work we have just analyzed and seeking to verify the hypothesis of the superiority of Pythagorean values, constructed an orthoclavier[14] having 53 intervals to the octave and on which melodies and harmonies could be played in the three scales in question (as well as in a fourth scale we will not examine here). They presented 1000 listeners (of whom only some were musicians[15]) pairs of melodies and chords played sometimes in one scale and sometimes in another. Among the results, one notes first of all the many judgments indicating insensitivity, indifference, and absence of opinion. For example, in the comparison between the Pythagorean and the natural scales, 57% of the listeners made no judgment (58% and 55% for the melodic and harmonic series, respectively). Among the comparisons involving tempered intervals, a greater number of judgments were made—66% in the comparison with the Pythagorean scale and 72% with the Zarlinian. But those judgments were all in favor of tempered intervals—preferred over Pythagorean by 55% to 45% and over Zarlinian by 60% to 40%.

---

[13]Helmholtz (1877/1954), a partisan of the natural scale, holds, on the basis of a series of experiments, that the sharpening of the seventh (with respect to natural intonation) is quite tolerable, especially in dissonant chords, due to the tendency of this scale degree to an ascending resolution.

[14]That is, the flute stop of a pipe organ with constant intensity. Helmholtz (1877/1954) carried out experiments on himself using a harmonium specially constructed to produce natural and Pythagorean intonation. Those experiments dealt only with harmony. The results showed the importance of adaptation to a system of intonation initially considered "in tune" (in this case natural intonation), and the contrast effect produced by interpolating a chord generated in another system: "When isolated minor chords are struck the difference is, indeed, not much observed. But when long series of justly-intoned chords have been employed, and the ear has grown accustomed to their effect, it becomes so sensitive to any intermixture of chords in imperfect intonation, that the disturbance is very appreciable" (p. 318).

[15]It is unfortunate that the authors do not give a numerical breakdown according to the different categories.

This preference is most clear in the melodic series but much less apparent in the harmonic series. Given, however, that the response set had only two alternatives (yes or no), it is probable that those differences were hardly significant, except for those concerning the comparison of tempered and Zarlinian chords (39% vs. 61%). Even so, there is nothing in this tally that permits certainty, inasmuch as tempered, Pythagorean, and Zarlinian intervals were judged equivalent when compared pairwise (50% vs. 50%, 42% vs. 58%, and 49% vs. 51%, respectively).

Certain emphatic conclusions emerge (van Esbroeck & Montfort, 1946): "The tempered scale received the most votes from the public we had selected. . . . The effects of the preponderance of tempered-scale education in our public shows also that the human ear does not possess the capacity to judge simple relationships [pp. 111–112][16]. . . . The musical scale is in the first place strictly a matter of education; that is, of acquired habits, just as language" (p. 12). The tallies of preferences for the Pythagorean scale over the Zarlinian scale were significant only for the melodic series, which confirms the research of Cornu and Mercadier analyzed earlier.

From these results (in which we have seen the complexity and, to some extent, the confusion) it appears that the formation of the ear regarding intervals owes nothing to natural phenomena of resonance on which the Zarlinian scale is constructed. But it owes a lot to perceptual experience of global acoustic interval sizes provided by the most common fixed-pitch instruments and that determined practice permits one to obtain on the variable-pitch instruments.[17] How might it have been otherwise? Helmholtz himself (1877/1954), who did so much to ground the generation of intervals in the harmonic series produced by a vibrating body, discerned the principle difficulties that militate against the psychogenesis of intervals on the basis of harmonics. Harmonics are never perceptible under ordinary circumstances. It is timbres we perceive, that is, synthetic qualities belonging to one or another vibrating matter. For a trained ear, under specific conditions, such perception requires first hearing the complex tone and the individual partial separately, after which the ear accustoms itself to recognizing that the one is a component of the other. If you first play the melody formed from the first three harmonics of a fundamental and then

---

[16]Note also the work of Meyer (1903) in which he shows that the major third, the fifth, and the octave preferred by subjects are all larger than their "natural" values. That is also the case for the contracted minor third. Small (1936), in a strobophotographic study, likewise established that intonation on the violin tended toward the sharp with respect to both the natural and even-tempered scales. This orientation coincides with with a preference for tempered or Pythagorean intonation over natural.

[17]Cuvelier (1949): "The tempered scale, which has altered our listening habits, appeared in practice at a point when harmony performed with the old, natural intervals was becoming intolerable, and counter to the new logic of sensations and associated sentiments" (p. 52).

vibrate a string at the same fundamental frequency, the ear will recognize the presence of the harmonics in the sound of the string. Still, it is necessary to add, following Helmholtz, that only the first five harmonics are audible; for four of the seven intervals of the diatonic scale we would need hearing capable of discerning fifteen!

One might object that even if the perception of harmonics is difficult, it nevertheless exists *implicitly* in the synthetic perception of timbres and thus contributes to the feeling of the suitability of the intervals of the diatonic scale in conjunction with timbre-producing components. In reality, this argument cannot stand up to the following criticism: Implicit audition, in any causal sense, can concern only the first five harmonics and as a result can furnish only three of the seven intervals of the major diatonic scale. Remaining to be explained is the genesis of the other four—the three minor intervals and the chromatic semitone. We must reach the ninth partial (neglecting, no one knows why, the seventh, which belongs to no scale) to find a tone capable of determining the fourth interval in use. Besides, on fixed-pitch instruments, whose educational importance we have seen, actual interval values militate powerfully against the effects of the implicity heard "natural" intervals—all the actual values differ from the values furnished by the harmonics.[18] The objection bears equally on stringed instruments, except concerning the fifth. It is not conceivable that the principle of the musical formation of the ear resides elsewhere than in hearing and practicing the fundamentals of the arts. It does not reside in physical phenomena that are imperceptible as such, and that among other phenomena underlie heard sounds.

---

[18]Note, however, that I have avoided raising the question of the historical origin of the diatonic scale, because that is outside our range of inquiry. If we place the origin of our heptatonic scale in Greek antiquity (as seems reasonable), two possible modes of generation appear: one by the cyclical repetition of fifths, and the other by the subdivision of the fifth. Intervals other than the fifth and fourth receive different values in the cyclic and subdivision systems. The possible influence of partials obtained by blowing very hard on flutes should be separated out as well—that produces false octaves whose value depends on the size of the bore. Partials involved in timbre, on the other hand, are difficult to hear, and were not known (according to Sachs, 1943) until the later middle ages. It does not seem likely that the origin of the principal intervals of the fourth, fifth, and octave should have arisen from plucked harp strings or the strings of the lyre. The tuning of ancient intervals with respect to certain harmonics arises only from the fact that the numerical relationships of the one and the other coincide. They are two parallel sets of relationships without causal interaction.

Chapter 3
SYNTAX

INTERVALLIC AND SYNTACTIC RELATIONSHIPS

The review of experiments disclosing various forms of integration takes us away from the level of musical material to that of syntax. It forms an introduction to the study of musical syntax, demonstrating its psychological reality, as well as its principal laws and their influence on the formation of perceived musical structures.

In effect, the idea of *material*, as we have just defined it, implies only that subjects accustomed to the stimuli fixate (in the sense of constancies) a certain number of typical qualities tied to relationships of vibration frequencies. However, the unique aspect of the acculturation of the ear is not to be found in that notion. Interval qualities form the elementary level of differentiations and fixations that operate in both naive and educated perception, through the effects of audition or the repeated practice of certain melodic and harmonic articulations of musical "stimuli," as classically defined. Intervals in themselves already constitute a kind of sound syntax, in the sense that tones are linked to one another in pairs. But, in fact, such simplicity in the links is found only in artistic systems far removed from ours. Wallaschek (1891), Sachs (1943), and others, occupied with the innumerable forms of primitive music, have provided examples of tirelessly repeated melodies involving a single tone (as in the West Carolines and Celebes) or a single interval—the "two-tones" style—that may use a "second" or smaller (the Botocudos of Brazil), or a "fourth" (Papua, New Guinea).[1] Syntactic facts of this order are difficult for the Western listener to comprehend. Hearing for the Westerner always involves tonal interpretation. The first or last note is heard as the tonic, depending on duration and accent, a differentiation that does not clearly exist for the native listener.

---

[1] See p. 160, this volume, Figure 6.1 for examples of these songs.

The syntax I propose is that out of which arise the majority of works underlying the acculturation of our subjects, musicians and nonmusicians alike. It is a widespread social fact, of obscure historical origin but ancient enough to invoke the naturalist illusion (whose effects were most strongly felt until the last century, before notions of sociocultural relativism began to trouble the dogmatic sleep of the musicologists).[2]

Certain among the verifiable effects of this syntax could be described as follows: The acoustic values of intervals vary so that, depending on its position in two different melodies (or in two places in the same melody), a third, for example, might be expanded or contracted without thereby being considered an "error" (that is, an accident of performance). In what sense are such effects concerned with the perception of musical forms? They are important when considered as projections of tendencies shared by qualified musicians (string players and singers) toward the accentuation of certain formal features, of certain momentary properties of a note in a melodic grouping and its implicit harmony.[3] Those tendencies clearly indicate that the *facts of syntax* are not merely precepts aimed at the construction of works, but through frequent use and all sorts of emphasis that they give rise to, they have been transformed into states of "requiredness" and perceptual tendencies (according to whether they remain implicit or not). On the other hand, more generally, these facts are not only rules for the generation of forms, but requirements of the ear (by which I mean not the peripheral auditory apparatus, but the mechanisms for reception and interpretation of specifically musical messages—the particular perceptual mechanisms comprising the cortical projections in the sensory and association areas).

CULTURAL AND STRUCTURAL INTEGRATION

Let us distinguish between cultural integration and structural integration. Later I describe several aspects of structural integration. It arises out of psychophysiological effects produced by a group of stimuli on the elements

---

[2]This naturalism extends as well to facts of expression as to facts of syntax. In his study of descriptive music, Goblot (1901), having deplored the fact that a treatise on harmony lacked an explication of the "impression produced" by a particular chord or interval, asked, "How could it be that there is one and only one note of the scale, the tonic, and one and only chord, the tonic chord, that gives the impression of a completed thought, so well that it is impossible to stop definitively on another note or another chord?" (p. 7).

[3]According to Abraham (1923), whose work I cite further on, these tendencies may be far more widespread and may be found in vocal performances of "uneducated" subjects lacking technical training. We have seen, in effect, to what degree musical illiterates are actually potential musicians. See note 4 below.

of which it is composed, without the relationship of the part to the whole being determined by sociocultural norms. Thus, the acoustic phenomena of masking are linked to the effects of one sound source on another. Likewise, the concept of melodic motion described by Abraham (1923) implies an effect of the succession of higher and lower tones of a melody on the perception of intervals, without those effects depending on the learning of a code and without the intervention of social conventions. In contrast, cultural integration consists of an influence of the whole on the parts, inasmuch as the whole is a generator of a sociocultural type. For example, to the extent that a succession of tones is a "tonal" melody—to the extent that the reciprocal relationships among the tones obey certain norms—that melody exerts a specific influence on the sizes of the intervals that make it up.

The sense and import of the distinction is apparent. Features of structural integration are permanent features of musical facts, to the degree that the latter are defined in terms of usage in sound sources and in tonal facts residing within certain limits. Masking effects can be found in all polyphony, melodic motion in all melody—such belong to Balinese polyphony (which is on the whole a heterophony) and to Gregorian and dodecaphonic melody. Features of cultural integration are linked to properties of a musical system fixed in time and space. They interest us as evidences of that complex acculturation of the perceptual apparatus called the "musical ear."

To be sure, the two forms of integration coexist in all musical facts. They continually interact, and in most cases experiments reveal only their combined effects. Thus, the "deformations" of intervals observed in the performance of a melody result to some extent from the effects of melodic movement, and to some extent from the tonal scheme and the attractive hierarchies it contains. Masking effects could be, to a certain extent, counteracted by flexible "hearing out" of certain components in a polyphonic texture—a flexibility that is eminently educable. It is, however, important to distinguish between these types of perceptual integration, because each brings into play different psychological processes and incidentally because, while remaining within the limited sphere of Western music each permits us to explore the present evolutionary stages of art using the conceptual tools of science and to understand certain elements of contemporary aesthetic experience situated (in this view) essentially prior to the disintegration of tonal syntax.

Studies by Abraham (1923; see also Francès, 1948) and Small (1936) provide evidence bearing on the inherent tendencies to cultural integration of singers and violinists. Abraham concluded that intervals executed in a melody, even those with the same label (that is, those one would expect to have identical values), are subject to important deformations in tempered values, varying considerably according to the place the intervals occupied in the melodic succession. Apart from influences due to melodic motion, there was an attractive tendency exerted by certain tones (*Klebtöne*) on others that could be called "transitive" or "conductive" (*Leittöne*). There is thus a hierarchy among the component tones and an *orientation* of one in relation to another, such that the interval they form is diminished by a flatting of the transitive tone. These facts were already partly known by musicians under the name of "leading-tone attraction." The experiment showed, however, that it is necessary to suppose, besides "ascending leading-tone attraction" (already known), a "descending leading-tone attraction," as well as "leading tones" above and below the dominant. According to Abraham, the law of attraction could be extended even to notes that precede the neighboring notes of the principal degrees of the tonality: "The principle tones of a melody attract less important tones nearby, so that intervals are smaller than the sizes indicated by their names." Abraham observed these attractions among subject with highly varied musical training.[4] The performance took place without accompaniment, and the results can be attributed only to the way in which the subjects set their sights on melodic tonality.

It was the same with the violin performances of virtuosos analyzed by Small (1936). He found among the performers tendencies of *attraction* as well as tendencies to accentuate certain *contractions* and *dilations* of characteristic intervals. The former effects are those we have just defined. The leading tone ascending to the tonic was raised in 85% of the cases; the "leading tone" descending to the mediant (the fourth degree descending to the third) was lowered 80% of the time. Small did not mention the attraction exerted by the dominant, nor that exerted by the tonic on the upper "leading tone." His exposition is not exhaustive and contains only examples of tendencies he labeled "diatonic."

The diatonic tendencies observed by Small consisted of accentuations of the characteristics of certain intervals by augmentations and diminutions of their values, going in the direction of their characteristic tendencies. Thus the minor and diminished intervals were contracted in 51% of the cases; the major and augmented intervals were enlarged in 44% of the cases; and chromatic alterations were exaggerated in 50% of the cases. Small (1936) concluded, "In reality an implicit harmony is usually, if not always, present, even in a solo melody without accompaniment.

---

[4]Two musicians having absolute pitch; three singers without absolute pitch; three non-singer musicians; three moderately trained musicians; and an indefinite number of subjects with no musical training.

EXPERIMENT 2

The experiment about to be described aimed at providing evidence concerning inequalities of tuning that would be tolerated or not by the ear, depending on the melodic and harmonic functions of notes in a group. More precisely, I wanted to determine to what extent different forms of *attraction* among notes, and of *contraction* and *dilation* of certain characteristic intervals, are required by the ear. Until now, those phenomena have in effect been presented either as facts, based on the analysis of instrumental playing and vocal interpretation, or as consequences deduced from the precepts of harmonic writing. To draw an example of the latter case, the theory pronounces that "the leading tone submits to the attraction of the tonic," which means only that in a chord progression the leading tone must ascend to the tonic for the progression to be correctly resolved.

It was interesting for a theory of the development of musical perception such as ours for us to see in what measure the precepts of writing have been transformed into perceptual tendencies, resulting in the tonal integration of tones into a whole. Might these influences, linked to harmonic resolutions, be the only ones known to the tonal ear? Or might they also admit of modifications of tempered tuning such as tend to accentuate the characteristic sizes of certain intervals? This raises the question of modal notes. Analysis of stringed instrument interpretations has demonstrated the reality of certain tendencies to contract minor and diminished intervals and to dilate major and augmented ones. Is this a matter of practice being tied to the style of violinists, or does that practice itself arise out of its relationships with more general structural properties already grasped in perception? Does the ear accept imperfections of tuning that emphasize modal differences?

Finally, this experiment aims at a general examination of perceptual tendencies. By presenting subjects the same melodies solo, and then with a harmonic accompaniment, I attempted to learn whether, even without explicit harmonic progressions, the ear would ascribe an implicit harmony to the heard melody.

Underlying Principle of the Experiment

If we take as a base the tempered tuning of a piano, and lower the pitch of two of its notes, we would expect this alteration to be less noticeable to the listener when those notes contribute to a structure where they are subject to descending influences (in keeping with the tendencies defined earlier), than where they are subject to ascending influences. For example, if the same note in the context of a phrase is a descending appoggiatura and in another context is an ascending appoggiatura, the objective flatting of the note should be better tolerated (that is, less noticeable) in the former case than in the latter. In the former case, the flatting conforms to the harmonic influences on the note; in the latter case, it runs contrary to them.

Method

Materials Presented to Subjects.   I composed two short pieces for piano (See Figure 3.1) in which two notes (Eb4 and Ab3) occurred a certain mumber of times in each with influences pulling in opposite directions. Thus in the first piece (in C minor—Fig. 3.1A) the two notes were:

1. mediants (thirds) in perfect minor chords (8 instances: notes numbers 1, 6, 8, 29, 36, 45, 49, 51);
2. sevenths in seventh chords, resolved (5 instances: notes 13, 21, 26, 33, 55;
3. ninths in ninth chords, resolved (2 instances: notes 15, 58);

Figure 3.1. Two pieces for piano recorded with flatting of two notes in the melody: (A) Piece in C minor in which notes numbers 1, 13, 15, 40, and 44 have a descending tendency; (B) Piece in E major in which notes numbers 1, 5, 10, 38, and 41 have ascending tendencies.

Figure 3.1. Continued.

4. upper appoggiaturas, resolved (2 instances, notes 40, 60); and
5. descending melodic note (1 instance: note 44).

In the second piece (in E major—Fig. 3.1B) the critical notes were:

1. leading tones resolving to the tonic (10 instances: notes 1, 5, 13, 16, 23, 26, 51, 55, 63, 66);
2. unresolved leading tones (2 istances: notes 73, 77);
3. roots of perfect chords (2 instances: notes 30, 34);
4. mediants (thirds) in perfect major chords (2 instances: notes 38, 46);
5. lower appoggiaturas, resolved (4 instances: notes 10, 41, 60, 70);
6. fifth in perfect chord (1 instance: note 48); and
7. upper appoggiatura, resolved (1 instance: note 42).

The two pieces were conceived as melodies that could be heard as solos or with a simple harmonic accompaniment that would make their tonal functions explicit. They were recorded on tape with and without accompaniment in three different versions:

First Version: instrument tuned to tempered tuning, A3 = 440 Hz;
Second Version: the critical notes (Eb4 and Ab3) lowered about 13 and 12 cents, respectively;[5]
Third Version: the critical notes lowered by a greater interval, about 20 and 22 cents, respectively.[6]

In order to mistune the critical notes, we employed the technique of beats. The two notes had been previously recorded at their initial pitches. The number of beats heard between the recording and the pitch obtained after mistuning being equal to the frequency difference, it was easy to calculate the degree of flatting obtained and to control it after a few attempts. To find suitable values by which to lower the notes, I relied on the calculations of Cornu and Mercadier (1869/72; 1873) and of Greene (1936). In both cases those values were supraliminal for isolated tones. The corresponding notes, moreover, appeared to the experimenter to be clearly altered in both the second and third versions, as well as to several *forewarned* listeners who heard the pieces with the critical notes indicated.

Nevertheless, among the 22 subjects who subsequently heard the pieces, six judged the first piece to be free of imperfection of tuning, and four judged similarly of the second piece. The other subjects succeeded to a greater or lesser degree in identifying the critical notes.

These subjects all had some technical contact with music. They had had an extended course in theory (4 to 10 years of solfège, and 2 to 4 years of harmony) and had played one or two instruments over a period of at least 10 years. Four were composers who had produced several works. Their ages varied widely: 13 were between 19 and 24 years; 8 were between 24 and 32; and one was 44.

Procedure. Eight subjects who were students in a special music class served in a group session; the others in individual sessions. The test for the two versions containing the critical notes (that is, the second and third) was subdivided into four phases:

1. Global listening to the melodies. The subjects listened to the melody in C minor, having been instructed to attend to any possible imperfections of tuning. That issue was raised prior to listening. After

---

[5]Corresponding to beat frequencies of 5 and 3 per second.
[6]Corresponding to beat frequencies of 7 and 5 per second.

listening, they wrote their judgments of the melody as "in tune," "slightly out of tune," or "clearly out of tune." Then the procedure was repeated with the melody in E major.

2. Analytic listening to the melodies. The subjects who had noticed an imperfection of tuning were asked to find those notes that had appeared imperfect to them. To do this they were given a text of the melody in C minor on which the notes were numbered. They were asked to underline the imperfect notes in pencil while listening to the melody for a second time. This operation was very easy for subjects who had had several years of active instruction in solfège.[7] This phase was then repeated with the melody in E major.

3. Global listening to the accompanied melodies. The subjects were told they would hear an accompanied version of the melodies they had just judged but that "there would be somewhat different tuning." They were asked not to take their initial impressions of the melodies into account and to classify the melodies, as distinct from their accompaniments, as "in tune," "slightly out of tune," or "clearly out of tune."

4. Analytic listening to the accompanied melodies. The subjects were given a new copy of the text of the melody (without the accompaniment) and asked to underline the imperfect notes, as indicated for phase two. The injunction to disregard their prior listening was repeated.

These four phases occupied about 15 minutes. After a rest of 3 minutes, the subjects returned to the task and listened to the third recorded version, in which the critical notes had been flatted by 20–22 cents. Given the rather long duration of this group of operations, it was not possible to impose on the subjects by having them listen to the first version (which was completely in tune). In three cases when the good will of the listeners permitted us to do this, we obtained unanimous assent to the correct intonation of the two melodies, accompanied or not.

Results and Discussion

Results of the global listening phase are shown in Table 3.1. For both the second and third versions, the judgments of "in tune" and "slightly out

---

[7]Nevertheless it is true that in the case of our second melody (where the succession of notes was more rapid), notation did not always keep up with perception, especially in the reprise of the initial theme (measures 16 and following). Some subjects perhaps thought it unnecessary to underline the same notes. All the same, that would place greater weight only on the collection of responses already verified for that melody, motivated by musical factors that were the object of the experiment.

TABLE 3.1

Global Appreciation of Intonation in Two Pieces for Piano

Judgment:	Second Version						Third Version					
	In Tune		Slightly Out		Clearly Out		In Tune		Slightly Out		Clearly Out	
	M	M+A	M	M+A	M	M+A	M	M+A	M	M+A	M	M+A
Piece:												
First	15	13	4	7	1	0	7	9	7	7	8	6
Second	10	8	8	6	2	6	5	4	5	4	12	14

Numbers of subjects making each of three types of judgment (In Tune, Slightly Out of Tune, Clearly Out of Tune) to two pieces played on the piano. In the second version (N = 20) the critical notes were flatted by 12 to 13 cents, and in the third version (N = 22) by 20 to 22 cents. M = melody alone; M + A = melody with accompaniment.

of tune" were applied more often to the first piece (in C minor) than to the second (in E major); the latter received more judgments of "clearly out of tune." These variations in judgment went in the same direction for both the accompanied and unaccompanied melodies, except in one case. We are therefore justified in seeking an overall conclusion for the two pieces by summing for each of them the judgments made of the accompanied and unaccompanied melodies. I was also led to make this summation in order to apply the chi-square test correctly, due to the smallness of the original cell entries.

For these reasons the numbers in the "clearly out of tune" column were added to the "slightly out of tune" column for the second version. This established a simple distinction between judgments of "in tune" on the one side, and the two degrees of "out of tune" on the other. The differences between the frequencies of the two judgmental categories applied to the two pieces were significant (chi-square = 5.112, $p < .01$). For the third version it was possible to apply χ^2 across the three categories of judgments. Here again the differences were significant (chi-square = 6.646, $p < .01$). We can conclude that *the global impression of correct intonation was greater in the first piece (where the flatting of the critical notes conformed to the descending influences they had each time they occurred) than in the second piece (which exerted ascending influences on the same notes).*

The results for analytic listening confirmed and extended those we have just examined. They are given in Table 3.2.

a) The frequency with which the flatted notes were recognized as out of tune was greater for the second piece than for the first, and even greater in the third version. Apparently the greater alteration of the critical notes in the latter version produced an accentuation of the disparities between those frequencies. The deviations were in the same direction for both the solo and accompanied melodies.

b) There was throughout the responses to the two pieces, accompanied or not, an appreciable number of out-of-tune judgments applied to notes *neighboring the flatted notes* (immediately preceding or following them). The intervals formed by the critical notes with their neighbors having been altered by flatting the former, the judgment of "out of tune" was sometimes attributed to the latter and might be considered to be a result of the perception of that alteration. The observed numbers of these judgments confirmed that possibility. They were always proportional to out-of-tune judgments applied to the flatted notes, going from one piece to another and from one version to another.

c) There were always a certain number of erroneous out-of-tune judgments recorded for notes other than the critical notes or their neighbors (columns three and six in Table 3.2). Those indicate some imprecision of judgment. However, their number was greater for the third version, in which the more obvious alteration of the critical notes ought to have prevented such errors.

d) The calculations for chi-square take into account the three types of intonation judgments, the total number of notes contained in each piece, and the number of critical notes presented in each. The result was significant in all cases for the accompanied melody, in both versions. It was less so for the solo melodies. It is therefore certain that *because of a certain implicit harmony, the critical notes were less noticeable in the first melody than in the second. But this difference was more pronounced when the harmony in each piece was made explicit by the accompaniment.*

TABLE 3.2

Frequency of Notes Judged Out of Tune in the Two Pieces, Accompanied (M + A) or Not (M) in Two Versions (as in Table 3.1) for Critical Notes (CN), Notes Neighboring Critical Notes (NN), and Other Notes (ON).

	First Piece			Second Piece			
	CN	NN	ON	CN	NN	ON	Chi-Square
Second Version:							
M	11	21	14	21	26	2	3.301*
M + A	20	16	10	24	29	2	10.622**
Third Version:							
M	85	38	25	113	70	27	5.255*
M + A	69	24	12	108	61	12	10.149**

*p < .05.
**p < .01.

TABLE 3.3

Distribution of Notes Identified as Out of Tune in Three Different Chordal Contexts in Third Version of the First Piece. M = melody alone; M + A = melody with accompaniment; CN = Critical Note; NN = Neighboring Note.

Context: Instances: Note:	Third in minor chord 8		Seventh in seventh chord 5		Ninth in ninth chord 2		Upper appoggiatura 2		Descending melodic note 1	
	CN	NN	CN	NN	CN	NN	CN	NN	CN	NN
M	41	20	24	12	12	3	5	1	3	2
M + A	26	13	22	9	10	2	9	0	2	0

The initial hypothesis was thus verified: influences resulting from the tonal structure of a melody act on its organization, not only in the way it is performed (on an instrument with free intonation), but also when it is perceived. Nevertheless this action, established globally for the two pieces, can be analyzed in detail according to the specific nature of the influences presented by each of them. Tables 3.3 and 3.4 show the frequencies with which the critical notes were identified when they had various functions. Due to the weakness of the partial figures for the second version, I have restricted myself to presenting only those for the third version in the tables. Each column is headed with the name of the harmonic function filled by the critical notes, and the accompanying numbers indicate the number of instances in which those functions occurred in the piece in question. The half columns below that contain, to the left, the number of out-of-tune identifications for the critical notes, and, to the right, the number of such judgments of their immediate neighbors.

Tables 3.3 and 3.4 show that the frequency of identification of critical notes was, for each function, closely parallel for the solo and accompanied

TABLE 3.4

Distribution of Notes Identified as Out of Tune in Three Different Chordal Contexts in Third Version of the Second Piece. M = melody alone; M + A = melody with accompaniment. CN = Critical Note; NN = Neighboring Note.

Context: Instances: Note:	Leading Tone Resolved 10		Leading Tone Unresolved 2		Root in chord 2		Third in major chord 2		Fifth in chord 1		Lower appogia- tura 4		Upper appogia- tura 1	
	CN	NN	CN	NN	CN	NN	CN	NN	CN	NN	CN	NN	CN	NN
M	65	38	9	3	14	5	6	5	6	7	10	8	3	4
M + A	66	36	10	2	9	10	7	3	9	6	3	2	4	2

melodies. To make this comparison statistically, I calculated chi-square for each piece by adding the number of identifications of the critical notes and their neighbors (which can be considered linked to the effect being studied). Moreover I have combined the numbers in the two last columns in order to obtain theoretically sufficient numbers in each cell. Evaluated in this way, the chi-square test *indicates no significant difference between the distribution for the solo melody and the accompanied melody.* This is true of both pieces. Thus, it is confirmed that *the harmony implicit in a melody confers on it the same tendencies as explicit harmony.*[8]

Finally, I wanted to determine whether the influences present in these pieces were all of equal force, that is, whether in sum they provided equivalent numbers of recognitions of critical notes of whatever type. This was a matter of testing the null hypothesis among the different categories of influences designated by the columns of Tables 3.3 and 3.4. The total chi-square (across the solo and accompanied melodies) was 11.754 for the first piece and 52.600 for the second, *values that permit us to affirm the existence of significant differences among the categories.*[9] However, due to the weakness of the entries in certain columns, it was not possible to carry out pair-wise comparisons.

BASIC PROPERTIES OF TONAL SYNTAX

The foregoing facts guide us in isolating some of the basic properties of tonal syntax.

Scalarity

Perceived musical tones are integrated into a scalar system; that is, they are heard as degrees of a scale having a point of origin—the tonic (first degree)—and seven other degrees making up the octave. This integration presupposes the implicit perception of the tonic as the center of reference with respect to which the level of each other degree is evaluated. Each tone is therefore implicitly referred to an acoustic standard, that is, to a fixed note (the memory of which, we shall see, is constantly maintained

---

[8]We ought to introduce here the following reservation: The melody alone had previously been heard by all the subjects with its harmonization (in the second version). It is therefore possible that some subjects were retrieving a memory of that when they heard this melody alone in the third version. But that memory could consist only of a vague impression, as we had asked the subjects to judge the intonation of the melody (accompanied or not), without attending to the harmonization.

[9]$P < .01$ in each case, with $df = 3$ in the first case (where the data were collapsed across the last two columns), and $df = 5$ in the second.

by ceaseless repetitions of that note in musical works). Between the tonic and the other degrees there exist (in the most common diatonic scale over the past three centuries) standard intervals called "intervals starting from the origin." Between any two of the latter there exists and interval of a tone or semitone called a "successive interval," the location of which in the scale (equally standardized) varies according to two main cultural types, the major and minor modes. (Those are the only surviving modes out of the seven church modes in use through the 16th century.)[10] In the major mode, the semitone occurs between the third and fourth, and the seventh and eighth, degrees; in the minor, it is found between the second and third, the fifth and sixth, and seventh and eighth. The scale degrees may be lowered or raised by a semitone by "accidentals," in which case the preceding and following intervals become diminished or enlarged. An accidental implies a feeling of ascending or descending influence, according to whether the degree was altered by a sharp or flat. In practice, however, since tempered instruments have come into general use the pitch of a sharped note is the same as that of the next higher note flatted.[11]

A related idea merits particular attention—the scale degree affected by an accidental can signal passage to another tonality. That is, it may announce the displacement of the origin of the scale in which you are situated. That is the case with *constitutive* accidental alterations. For the ear, the strangeness of the accidental note then becomes the springboard for an hypothesis to be confirmed immediately by context. The altered degree of the scale where you are is a "natural" degree of the scale that it introduces and that the following notes establish. Accidentals characteristic of change of mode fall in the same category, but indicate no shift of the scalar origin. In contrast to the above uses of accidentals there are *passing tones*— modifications of the pitch of a scale degree without the context shifting to some other tonal integration. In that case the ear hears a *foreign* note in the scale, of which the origin remains mentally present. The foreign note is interpreted as an ornament, a transition between "natural" degrees. In all these cases the mechanisms governing the perception of accidentals are to be found in the preexistence of an acoustic model of the scale, laid down during the listener's development. That model is a pattern of interval

---

[10]These very simplified historical facts will be made more precise later. Moreover, we are not taking into account the difference between the melodic and harmonic forms of the minor mode, since that difference did not figure in the measures on which we are relying.

[11]See Chailley and Challan (1947): "Tonality is a natural feeling in the hierarchy of pitches by which each appears to us as ordered with respect to the others, their meaning being determined by the basic note called the tonic" (p. 49). In d'Indy's (1897/98) celebrated definition, of equally naturalist inspiration, tonality is "the ensemble of those musical phenomena that human hearing can appreciate by direct comparison with a constant phenomenon—the Tonic—taken as the invariant term of the comparison" (p. 108).

sizes that have become usual or "natural" and with respect to which judgments of alteration can develop (Chailley & Challan, 1947).

Scalar relationships can provide for differentiations other than simply ordinal. The labels employed by classical music theory to designate the seven tones include qualifications such as *tonic, dominant,* and *leading tone,* which indicate a role or a certain degree of importance—a melodic function (even though the term "function" might properly be reserved for harmony). The other labels are explicable in relation to the tonic and dominant: supertonic, subdominant and superdominant. Psychologically the differentiation of melodic functions is strictly dependent on harmony. Each melodic degree becomes gradually associated with one or with a few of the chords to which it is assigned according to the rules of classical harmony. In that way there develops a coloration peculiar to each, because each almost always occurs in a chord that maintains specific relationships with the tonic. Of course, such a chord is not unique. The seven notes each participate in several chords, as shown in Figure 3.2.

On one hand, however, certain chords are infinitely more frequent in classical harmony than others. Hence the probable tonal quality of a particular scale degree involves, as a practical matter, a choice among two or three possibilities. The chord on the seventh degree is seldom used. The chord on the third degree is almost never used in the major mode, and in the minor it is strictly prohibited.

On the other hand, these tonal qualities are largely determined by the harmonies that precede them, inasmuch as chord progressions are, as we shall see, rigorously regulated by the precepts of part-writing. The usual term "implicit harmony" thus means that each note is implicitly endowed with its probable harmony, that it "suits" it by virtue of involving its most frequently occurring associations. (This is at least true of those notes that have sufficient duration or are initial or final notes, but it excludes ornament tones, grace notes, and the like.) At the same time, a sort of coefficient of movement or repose is added to this differentiation of tonal quality and of tonal relationship, which is a result of the underlying implicit chord. It also seems likely that the fleeting character of the leading tone ascending to the tonic has some connection with the fact that it is supported by the dominant seventh chord (or in general, the dominant)—an essentially unstable chord that calls for a tonal conclusion. When the context requires a tonic perfect chord the instability of the dominant is drawn to the stability

Figure 3.2. Variety of chords including each note of the major diatonic scale.

of the first scale degree by the probable implicit harmony. That stability is made finally to last, to conclude, to settle and define, and to resolve tensions and expectancies.

These associations naturally presuppose an educated perception—not necessarily a knowledge or practice of harmony, but frequent acts of attention bearing on the suitability or unsuitability of a particular harmony or scale note. It often happens when one is listening to inner voices, or even in impromptu vocal harmonizations of three voices made upon a given melody by subjects practiced in choral singing but who do not know harmonic writing. This interest brought to perceived harmony, insofar as it neutralizes the spontaneous tendency to focus only on the melody and suppress the lower voices, belongs at the origin of the harmonic differentiation of melodic scale degrees.

These scalar relationships are transposable, both from one octave to another and from one key to another. That is, they remain unchanged as long as the point of departure, the tonic, is shifted up or down by the same amount, whatever the degree of displacement. In a classical tonal work there may be several displacements of this sort (modulations), but a return to the initial tonal center is obligatory. Modulations are relatively rare in classical works of the 17th and 18th centuries, and are in general limited to a shift of the tonic to the fifth or fourth, or sometimes the sixth, degrees. Even in the course of a modulation the ear retains a memory of the initial tonic through the effects of the persistence of the first tones and chords in sensory memory (a persistence we shall see at work in the experiments on melody). This effect is enhanced by the frequency of occurrence of nonmodulating passages. One might suppose that in a classical work—a song, a symphony, or a piano piece such as those that provide the foundation for the music education of the majority of our subjects—all the tones are perceived as degrees of a tonic with which they maintain specified relationships, standardized according to two principal types. What is new in this scalar integration, beyond the accommodation described earlier under *material*, is that here acoustic distances are evaluated not only *between two successive tones* (under which rubric they were already standardized) but also *between each tone and the tonic*.

The integration I have just defined as one would in a theory text is in reality a widely applicable psychological fact that is likely to affect the perception of musical tones, even a small number of them. It is attested to by Small's (1936) results on the augmentation of major and augmented intervals and the contraction of minor and diminished. In effect, for those four interval types there is an accentuation of the movement suggested by the notation and a translation of that movement to the neuromuscular level. The major intervals appeared, as before, to be augmented, and the reverse was true of the minor. The influences indicated by these alterations were inscribed in the phrasing of the artist, and they guided that phrasing in their transmission through the alteration of intervals, hyperchromatisms, and so forth. Perception here surpasses, in a sense, simple audition. Already present in the listener's interpretation of sense data is an induction of motor mimicry tied to comprehension of the cultural message.

EXPERIMENT 3

In a series of experiments on the fixation of melody, I was able to find evidence concerning the structuring role of tonal scalar integration among subjects at different levels of musical education. To isolate melodic factors as far as possible, I controlled for the length of the melodies (in terms of number of notes) and eliminated metrical and temporal differences that go along with rhythm.

Method

Subjects.   It is useful to note, concerning training, that in the domain of music it is hardly possible to employ pretraining with the stimuli to be used in the experiment and to suppose that the control group would be free of all contact with analogous stimuli. As we shall see, the effects of tonal acculturation are felt among all the subjects and are revealed by the ease with which certain melodies become fixed in memory, in comparison with others of equal length. To this general acculturation are added the very noticeable effects of voluntary learning, namely, musical education in its various aspects.

It would therefore be impossible to institute a training program in the course of the experiment without taking account of these facts, at least to the extent that with different subjects, the various stimuli, being learned more or less well, might easily have different effects. We were thus limited to the qualitative evaluation of the effects of acculturation and training already established by education, since one or the other intervenes as a condition in all previous training. As a result, on the basis of the following questionnaire given to subjects before the experiment, the subjects were distributed into three groups: (A) musically illiterate, (B) performers, and (C) complete musicians.

Questionnaire

1. Have you studied music theory: solfège, harmony, counterpoint, fugue, composition? If so, for how long?

2. Have you practiced music: instrument, voice, chorus, ensemble? If so, for how long?

3. Do you attend concerts: frequently, rarely, never?

4. What are your age and occupation (or your parent's if you are a student)?

Of course, this classification into just three categories was not always done without difficulty, notably in separating the illiterates from the performers. Some subjects had practiced an instrument or voice for only a short time (1 to 6 months), sometimes in childhood. Others had lessons but were not grounded in solfège, not even at an elementary level. This lack put them on the borderline of group B because they did not conform to its cultural norms. We removed those subjects from group B without, however, putting them in group A. The use of the term "illiterate" is justified as a designation of a category of subjects *without active training and without technical knowledge concerning music.* Everything we know about acculturation prohibits us from considering them to be deprived of all perceptual contact with music. Some may have had historical knowledge of composers, works, interpreters—in that sense they were musicians of a sort. But such matters are difficult to control. Most subjects in group A responded affirmatively under the third heading of the questionnaire, often stating that they listened only on the radio. In a study using the Seashore and Kwalwasser tests, d'Annibale Braga (1956) gave subjects a questionnaire asking for the composer, the orchestra conductor, and the opera they preferred. Certainly responses to such questions cannot furnish objective and sure criteria for the classification of subjects—they cannot guarantee actual contact with music. [On the contrary, questions concerning training, or knowledge of a technical matter, posed before a test whose nature they did not know, should incline subjects to prudence, for fear that they might be about to experience an exercise that would involve one or the other.]

The classification into three groups of subjects was justified by its basis more on *qualitative* than on quantitative criteria and its concern with specific types of activity and types of analysis of musical matters. I classiffied as "performers" (group B) only subjects who had played an instrument or studied voice for between 2 and 7 years, with preceding or concurrent study of solfége. Group C consisted only of music students[12] who had achieved the level of final examinations or recital at the end of their studies. These subjects had played for 10 to 16 years, and their work was grounded

---

[12]Of the School of Music Education and the National Conservatory of Music.

in a relatively specialized course of fundamentals (advanced solfége, harmony, analysis of works and styles, and occasionally fugue and counterpoint). We shall see later the formative role of these elements of training.

Materials and Procedure. The auditory stimuli consisted of a series of brief melodies played on the piano and recorded. Each series contained 12 pairs, each made up of a melody and its repetition in which *one note* was changed. All the melodies in a series were of the same length (three, six, or nine notes), making 36 pairs in all. The form of the melodies varied only in terms of melodic motion: ascending, descending, zigzag, V-shaped, and inverted-V (see Figure 3.3). The melodies were composed entirely of unaccented quarter-notes proceeding at a uniform tempo, which enabled the isolation of the melodic factor (in the sense of the "constellation" of pitches) without rhythmic differentiation. The battery of 36 pairs proceeded without interruption, except for a 30-second pause between the series containing melodies of different lengths, during which the experimenter announced "three notes," "six notes," or "nine notes."

As a precaution, the session was preceded by a rudimentary audiometric examination administered to the group. This was intended to discover any characteristic hearing difficulties in our subjects, and consisted of four sets of pure tones of different frequencies[13] recorded on tape and played over loudspeakers at a level the experimenter judged to be around threshold. The subjects were told to count each of these sets and to write the total they found in each of them on the back of their individual questionnaires. As a result I was able to eliminate a few doubtful cases in which one or more frequencies were not perceived.

Figure 3.3. Examples of melodies of different shapes excerpted from the two batteries of Experiment 3: (A & B) Ascending motion, 3 and 9 notes, Tonal; (C & D) Descending motion, 3 and 9 notes, Atonal; (E) V-shaped motion, 3 notes, Atonal; (F) Inverted-V-shaped motion, 6 notes, Atonal; (G & H) Zigzag motion, 6 notes, Atonal and Tonal.

---

[13]Of 512, 1024, 2048, and 4096 Hz, respectively.

After the audiometric exam the taperecorder presented the following instructions:

> You are going to hear brief melodies played on the piano and grouped into series of three-note melodies, then six notes, and finally nine notes.
>
> As soon as it has been played, each melody will be repeated. The repetition will be identical to the first melody, except for a change of one of its notes. The change might be on the first, or last, or one of the middle notes. For examples, . . . [Here the example in Fig. 3.4 was played].
>
> The experiment consists of listening to each of these melodies and its repetition, and trying to recognize which note has been changed in the repetition. Then indicate the position of the changed note by putting an X on the grid you have in front of you. Each trial (that is, each melody and its repetition) is separated from the following trial by a few seconds of silence during which you can make your response.[14]
>
> The sheet before you has three grids—one for each series of trials. In each grid the boxes going across a row correspond to the order of the notes. The twelve rows in each grid correspond to the twelve trials in each series.
>
> If you do not find the changed note on a given trial, it is absolutely necessary to leave the corresponding line blank, and go on to the next line.

The battery of 36 pairs was followed, after a 3-minute rest, by another battery of equal length, differing from the first only in specified musical characteristics.[15] The rules of classical tonality were followed in the construction of the first battery, giving each item "a frankly tonal feeling," as a musician would say. This effect was achieved, first, by beginning and

Figure 3.4. Example played with the instructions, illustrating the change of an intermediate note.

---

[14]The silent periods observed between each melody and its repetition, as between each pair and the pair following, were proportional to the length of the melodies and were respectively 2 and 5, 2 and 6, and 3 and 7 quarter-note values. Metronome speed was 124 quarter-note values per second. Each listener had a sheet of paper printed with grids like those of crossword puzzles. Each of the three grids had twelve rows and three, six, or nine boxes. The rows were numbered in the margin from 1 to 12.

[15]It is important to emphasize that the nontonal melodies had *the same number of different notes* as their tonal homologs. In other words, both presented the same number of stimuli and the same number of pitches. All that were changed were the intervals between the notes (by increases and decreases of a semitone). Owing to these experimental controls, we were not able to accentuate the atonal character of the nontonal melodies. The experiment showed that in spite of this limitation, the difference between the two batteries of melodies was effective.

ending on the tonic; second, by beginning and ending on notes of the tonic triad; third, by using only notes of the diatonic scale, major or minor (harmonic or melodic), without accidentals; fourth, by frequently employing sequences of two or three notes drawn from the principal chords of the tonality (tonic, subdominant, dominant, and dominant seventh).

The changes of notes in the repetitions followed the same principles and did not disturb the tonal character of the melodies. Further, the changes never involved accidentals, but rather substitutions of one scale degree for another.

In the construction of the second battery, the aim was, in contrast, to destroy systematically the tonal feeling of the melodies. Identical in length, in tessitura, and form of melodic movement, the melodies of the two batteries had opposite tonal character, because the principles enumerated earlier were contradicted by numerous alterations: (a) the first and last notes did not belong to the tonality suggested by the intermediate tones; (b) they sometimes did not belong to the same tonality; (c) the intermediate notes taken in threes did not belong to the principle triads of any tonality, or if they did, that tonality was violated by the immediately preceding or following note; (d) in a melody or in its repetition the notes taken together did not belong to any one diatonic scale in any key.

The two batteries were played on a Barthe Supertone record player over a fixed loudspeaker mounted 2 meters above the floor, at levels consistently greater than those of the audiometric test. The listeners were seated in front of the speaker, in essentially the same sound field, and concentrated on filling out their own grids. After hearing the first battery they were asked to hand in the sheet they had just used and to prepare for an experiment similar to the first, but with different melodies. We thus avoided any influence that the first answer sheet might have had on the second experiment. In those infrequent cases (3 out of 150 cases) in which, after the two batteries, subjects were observed to have produced the same pattern of Xs on their two sheets, both protocols were eliminated.[16]

Finally, there was the predictable practice effect that made the second battery easier following the first. It was necessary to reverse the order of presentation in alternate sessions so as to assess the relative difficulty of the two batteries. Let us designate the first, tonal battery T, and the second, atonal battery At. An equal number of protocols from each group of subjects was obtained from sessions in which the order of presentation was T→At as in the reverse condition At→T.

---

[16]These experiments were carried out in the recording studio of the Phonetics Institute of the University of Paris for subjects in groups A and B, and in a room of the School of Music Education for subjects in group C.

TABLE 3.5
Mean Percent Correct Responses to Melodies of Three Lengths in the Two
Batteries for Three Groups of Subjects.

Length:		Tonal			Atonal		
		3	6	9	3	6	9
Group:							
A	(N = 36)	76.16	59.95	41.43	67.59	46.06	23.39
B	(N = 72)	90.75	83.91	59.60	85.99	61.65	46.63
C	(N = 38)	97.60	96.52	75.60	93.28	80.78	62.03

Results and Discussion

Effects of Education: Inter-group Differences.   The results of Experiment 3 are shown in Table 3.5, in which correct locations of changed notes in repetitions are scored as "good responses," and incorrect locations and omissions are scored as errors. It is evident that the percentage of successes improved from one group to the next for each series of trials. However, there are difficulties in the way of a precise evaluation of these intergroup differences. The distribution of successes was not always normal, as can be seen in Fig. 3.5. Certain of the distributions were J-shaped, especially for the results of group C, indicating that the test was easy for the majority of those subjects. The maximum for each curve occurred at higher and higher values as we go from group A to group B to group C. But, given the distribution, tests of significance involving the standard error of the means would be inappropriate. I therefore used the chi-square test to compare the distributions of the groups taken in pairs. As Table 3.6 indicates, only the differences between groups A and C were significant.

Interpretation of these results is not easy. One might dispute the very nature of the experiment described, saying that it did not bring perceptual functions into play in the strict sense. From that point of view, in effect, what was measured was the *fixation* of the first melody of each pair, and consequently elementary musical memory, rather than the simple possibility of realizing a cluster of excitations. To this one might reply that such a fixation itself is the initial condition of any perception, prior to being that of memory. Only the length of the series, and the delay between listening and response required of the subjects, introduce functional differences.[17] It is in the nature of temporal sequences, once they surpass a

---

[17]See Fraisse and Fraisse (1937), who distinguish between memory proper and sensory persistence. The latter is a function of capacity of immediate apprehension of a plurality of elements without any intervention of an associative unity among them. This apprehension is thought to be operating in the reproduction experiments after a very brief period of a succession of sounds being struck. Fraisse and Fraisse also note the difficulty subjects had in not counting them. The idea of the number of elements occurred to them after listening, even if they had avoided counting during listening.

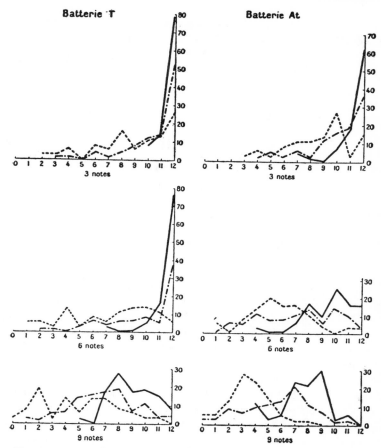

Figure 3.5. Distribution of numbers of subjects achieving different numbers of correct responses (out of 12 possible) for 100 subjects in all conditions of Experiment 3. The three groups were (A) nonmusicians (dotted lines), (B) moderately trained subjects (dots and dashes), and (C) music students (solid line).

certain number of stimuli, to be apprehended in chunks—in a series of partial glimpses that persist to some extent after the disappearance of the stimulus and become integrated into the succeeding moment.

Incidentally, one could also raise objections of another order concerning the analytic character of the acts implied in this experiment. The discovery of the changed note supposes, one might say, something besides the spontaneous conscious apprehension of a form—of a whole sound pattern. This research bears on the *apperception* of a difference, rather than on the naive encountering of a stimulus.

It is true that perceptual activity can be studied at different levels of vigilance, but here we must avoid the illusion that analysis begins only

TABLE 3.6

Comparison of the Distributions of the Three Groups for the Two Batteries
of Experiment 3.

Melodies	Comparison	Tonal			Atonal		
		df	Chi-Square	p	df	Chi-Square	p
3 Notes	A–B	10	9.986	.45	9	13.185	.15
	B–C	9	4.285	.90	8	8.114	.40
	A–C	10	17.697	.06	9	23.638	<.01
6 Notes	A–B	11	16.847	.11	11	11.526	.40
	B–C	10	15.694	.11	11	13.578	.25
	A–C	11	32.983	<.01	11	29.153	<.01
9 Notes	A–B	12	12.997	.45	11	15.284	.18
	B–C	11	13.343	.27	11	15.542	.18
	A–C	12	23.406	<.02	11	31.855	<.01

with a conscious and voluntary "analytic attitude." In reality analysis takes place at nonreflective levels of consciousness. There is no actualization of a structure without decomposition and the emergence of privileged elements. The differentiation of members of a whole, even if it is not explicitly verbalized, is already a latent analysis. McCleary and Lazarus (1949) have shown the existence of such an analysis on a subliminal level using tachistoscopic presentations too brief to produce consciousness of shape. In other words, every apperceived difference is first a perceived difference. The analytic attitude does not introduce a natural opposition between two ways of apprehending sensory contents, so long as it is not a question of explicit formulations. All the exploratory techniques of perceptual consciousness bring analytic processes into play. Not to recognize this is only to identify analysis with one of its especially lucid stages.

Put briefly, we are justified in taking the operations brought into play in these experiments as evidence bearing on the clarity of perceptual contents as they appear in the spontaneous conscious experience of the subjects. It remains for us to consider the psychological nature of the observed differences among the results of the three groups. One would not be able to connect those results with the effects of familiarity of the stimuli without knowing what that term signified in each group. Nothing indicates that the subjects of groups A and B had less auditory experience of musical intervals than those of group C. The more important difference is, rather, the advantage acquired by group B over group A as a result of practical familiarity with intervals and groups of intervals linked to their habitual production, to motor and visual associations with the sound stimuli, and to the grouping of sounds according to symbolic formulas. In group C all these modes of learning were systematically developed, without doubt involving a preponderance of automatic analysis based on their knowledge of note names and especially their melodic functions. For subjects in group C a note of a tonal melody[18] was differentiated by its function, that is, by a sort of hierarchical qualification derived from a conceptual system. Each note was immediately heard "as mediant," another "as dominant," another "as leading tone." The change of the note in the repetition of the melody thus struck these subjects as the substitution of one function for another.

These remarks on the effects of symbolism, however, need to be clarified. At the end of each experiment, we asked the subjects if, in the course of listening, they had thought of the names of the notes or their functions. In reality those operations were only infrequently indicated in group C, and then only with battery T and not with battery At. It is thus not necessary to appeal to introspective evidence from the subjects to conceptualize the actual role of this symbolism: the names of notes, like the names of functions, can affect perception in the absence of an explicit naming of those elements. Everything happened as if in a continuous stream of which the successive moments were not named as they occurred; but those events were more easily fixed in the memory of a listener with an acquired disposition to name and analyze intervals and their functions. Automatic analyses, once established, can operate without being consciously accessible to the subjects themselves. What is given in consciousness is a feeling of familiarity of interval qualities and functions.

Influence of Tonality on Melodic Fixation: Comparison of the Results of the Two Batteries. The preceding results might appear predictable from common sense alone. It is not surprising that trained musicians should be able to remember a melodic line better than musical illiterates and to compare one melody to another. Only the quantitative evaluation of those differences and the hypotheses used to account for them might then hold our attention.

In contrast, the following results introduce a differentiation between the tests that, in spite of its being quite basic, has not been respected by psychologists of music. Seashore's (1919) test of melodic memory (tonal memory), based on operations involving the identification of changed notes, mixed tonal and nontonal melodies without distinguishing between them. As in the experiments of Guilford and Hilton (1933)[19] who used the same stimulus materials, the only factor affecting difficulty among the

---

[18]I showed, through comparison of results of the two batteries and through the privilege shown for the critical notes in the tonal melodies, that this functional differentiation was implicitly operating in all the subjects, and in terms of the "physiognomic" qualification of notes in the melody, and not on a conceptual basis, for subjects in groups A and B (Francès, 1954).

[19]We are indebted to Guilford and Hilton, from whom we borrowed this procedure of comparison with substitution of a note.

melodies was length; that is, the number of notes contained in each of them. Now, as we shall see, the maximum memory span—the melody length that could be taken as the limit of fixation for all the subjects— varied from one battery to another. For two melodies of equal length and of equal tessitura and similar contour, the tonal, but not the atonal, melody would be fixated. The stability of the notes that make up a melody is a function of the relationships that they maintain and the conformity of those relationships to the historical reference system of tonality.

In the presentation of the quantitative analysis of correct responses for the same group on the two batteries, we encounter the following difficulty. The relative facilitation arising from the tonal character of melodies in battery T tends to be obscured by the incidental facilitation of each battery that results from being heard after the other. As described earlier, these effects of practice in the course of the experiment were controlled by the batteries' being heard in counterbalanced order (T before At, and At before T), with an equal number of protocols derived from each order. I therefore calculated the difference between numbers of correct responses for each subject obtained from one battery and the other, to find out their distribution in the group. These differences (T − At) were positive when T was easier than At, and negative in the opposite case. Table 3.7 shows the group means, including the means of the halves of each group that experienced different orders of presentation. The results of Student's t are

TABLE 3.7

Comparison of the Results for the Two Batteries Across Different Testing Orders, Melody Lengths, and Groups in Experiment 3. Mean shown are for Tonal–Atonal number correct. Half the subjects in each group served in each order condition.

Order:		Atonal-Tonal		Tonal-Atonal		Combined	
		mean	t	mean	t	mean	t
Group Length (N)							
A	3	2.28	5.16	−1.61	−2.33	0.33	0.63
(36)	6	2.11	4.95	0.83	1.20	1.47	3.54**
	9	1.94	3.39	0.94	1.86	1.44	3.72**
B	3	1.64	5.14	−0.64	−2.02	0.50	1.92
(72)	6	3.75	8.72	1.72	4.44	2.74	8.81**
	0	2.31	5.57	0.83	2.55	1.57	5.69**
C	3	0.84	1.88	0.11	5.24	0.47	1.88
(38)	6	2.26	5.17	1.42	4.02	1.84	6.42**
	9	2.32	5.35	1.90	0.74	1.53	4.46**

**$p < .01$.

~ The groups being compared did not have normal distributions, either for one of the orders or for both. The formula employed for t was that for matched samples.

shown for the T − At comparison for the subgroups and for the group as a whole.

Table 3.7 shows the following results. When battery At was presented first, the results obtained by subjects in all three groups were clearly superior for the tonal battery. In that case, the effects of order were added to those of tonality. When battery T was presented first, the results of that battery were superior, except for the three-note melodies. In that case, the advantage arising from order of presentation went to battery At. Columns five and six of Table 3.7 give the means and values of t for the two half-groups, providing a global estimate of the effects of tonality. That effect was weak for the three-note melodies—the differences, though always positive, were not significant. The differences were significant beginning with the six-note melodies. These results might mean that three-note melodies do not establish a tonality, do not provide a tonal feeling. But in reality a tonal feeling arises from the perception of just two notes, maybe even one, as several authors have pointed out. Hearing a pitch already involves the structure of a system of relations with a multitude of other implicitly thought pitches. The weakness of the observed differences between the two batteries in this instance comes from an opposite source. With three notes, the stimulus cannot decisively contradict the laws of tonality and of tonal feeling, even by design. There is always a tonal interpretation, despite alterations. For example, the items in Fig. 3.6, drawn from battery At, can be heard in E major, F major, and Bb major, respectively.

The privilege of battery T nevertheless existed with three-note melodies, though to a lesser degree. That should be attributed to the fact that in that battery the key (C) remained unchanged from one section to the next of the experiment, favoring immediate interpretation with respect to a single system of reference.

There was marked effect of tonality with series of six and nine notes for all the groups. The results thus support the idea of a general acculturation, existing prior to technical education, among listeners from the three groups. In a sense, this effect was consistently greater than that of education, at least according to the criteria used to define that for groups B and C. Recall that, overall, the between-group differences, while always measurable, were significant only between the extreme groups A and C.

Thus, to return to our problem of scalar integration, the experiment just described demonstrates the global structural effect of tonality among subjects grouped as musicians and nonmusicians. The analyses and experiments that follow will show what that effect—a synonym of "tonal

Figure 3.6. Examples of three-note melodies excerpted from the Atonal battery.

feeling"—consists of and how it might be explained by developmental psychological processes.

Hierarchy, Functions, Orientation

Already manifest in scalarity is the existence of a certain privilege of the first degree over the others, for which it serves to fix the pitch level of the scale. It remains for us to define three other properties of tonal syntax, inseparable from each other and difficult to separate from the first. The seven scale degrees are differentiated not only by ordinal properties arising from their common origin, but also by functional properties—they differ qualitatively or, better, structurally. Each has a role to play in the musical totality of melody and harmony and even, to some extent, rhythm. These functions can be explained only by the close cooperation of the perception of successive and simultaneous groups of tones, that is, of melody and harmony. Tonal functions are formed in the listener beginning with the reinforcement of certain scale degrees introduced in chords underlying the melody. Temporal factors come equally into play—the privilege of the tonic is explained, in part, because of its *initial* and *final* position in a piece (and often in a phrase), in melody or harmony. A particular focusing of attention affects the initial and final positions. I will limit myself here to defining these three properties, and to establish them by means of experiment as facts of perception. They will be explicated below through quantitative analyses of musical works.

The functions of each scale degree are coefficients attached to each of movement and repose, of instability and stability, of polarity and opposition. They are normatively defined by the theory of classical harmony, but through frequent use they come to determine expectancy reactions—momentary perceptions entirely saturated with knowledge or containing a small degree of uncertainty. Thus, the first degree (the tonic) and the components of the tonic triad (the third and fifth degrees) have a function of resolution when they accompany other elements, heard harmonically. The fifth degree, the dominant, has a function of preparation and calling forth—it draws forth the tonic and the tonic chord. Elaborated as the dominant seventh, it suffices to determine a tonality even when the tonic has not yet been heard. The second and fourth degrees call forth the fifth. They thus lack their own stability; they are nonessential and relative, whereas the fifth, as the pole opposite the tonic, can engender a certain stability if not a definite resolution. *Pedal points* are harmonic procedures that involve only the first and fifth degrees, in which those pitches are held (usually in the bass) while the other parts engage in varied motion on the other scale degrees, altered or not. In cadences (harmonic formulas that end phrases and works) the tendencies of the different degrees are found in a pure state, with their polarities and coefficients of movement and resolution. The second or the fourth precedes the dominant, which in turn leads to the tonic and definitive resolution. In a broken or "suspended" cadence, the dominant is followed not by the tonic, but by the sixth degree, whence arises a deception of the expectation of the tonic—an instability that calls for another, conclusive cadence.

The experiments by Abraham (1923) provide an illustration of these forms of integration. The tonic and its octave, the fifth degree, and then the fourth were subjected to inifinitely less deformation than the other degrees. When a fifth was divided into two thirds, the outer tones (tonic and dominant) were more in tune than the middle one, which was often played as a "neutral" third.

These functions establish a network of relations and temporal connections among the scale degrees, and, as we shall see, the appeals of one to another are all the more powerful for being frequently repeated. But this amounts to recognizing the notion of *hierarchy*—the tonic and dominant have the privilege of stability, of longer duration, of frequency of occurrence, of intensity, and of rhythmic accent. Those are designated as being *tonal functions*.[20] Classical theory turns them into good notes, or good degrees, and recommends their preferential use in harmonization. At the same time upper and lower neighboring notes are subjected to physical attraction (like mental attraction) arising from their subordinate, preparatory, and transitory character. The attraction of the lower leading tone is the most emphatic deformation in vocal and instrumental melodic interpretation. It is implicitly mentioned in the observations of Cornu and Mercadier (1869/72; 1873) and of Greene (1936, 1937) under the label of "augmentation of the major seventh." It is found in Abraham's (1923) and Small's (1936) studies along with the other forms of attraction.

Tonal syntax thus consists of a double network of relationships established among scale degrees: harmonic relationships among chords based on different degrees (or the among the components of those chords), and melodic relationships among notes neighboring the principal degrees. The strength of the former, however, far surpasses that of the latter. Harmonic sequences of functions are much more rigidly controlled by theory and practice than are melodic sequences. Melodically there is only one note whose motion is obligatory: the leading tone ascending to the tonic. Yet even it can be found dissociated from its neighborhood in certain melodic inflections (for example, arpeggios). The upper leading tone to the mediant must descend to the mediant only in the resolution of the dominant seventh. Melody is the synonym of liberty; harmony of rigor. In the historical evolution of music as an art, the flexibility of melody preceded

---

[20]On the concept of melodic tonality and on melodic functions, see Roiha (1956).

that of harmony. The melodic flexibility primed the harmonic through the use of passing tones, appoggiaturas, and foreign tones. Harmony was able to submit to successive enrichments of *coloration* of chords, without changing the fundamental structure of the temporal order of functions.

The importance of these integrating aspects of syntax has been often recognized, at least when psychologists have had more intimate contact with musical reality. In effect, in order to be implicitly efficacious, they are not explicitly recognized by subjects even in the light of reflection. Knowledge is required to reveal the forms that affect perception as a result of its education—forms that typically are heavily layered and that have taken on the status of reflexes that escape consciousness. Among psychologist musicians we might cite Lloyd (1940), who understood the nature of the musical ear in the present sense. According to Lloyd, the question of "interval" sizes is a false problem if it is not subordinated to the question of scale degrees and functions. The pitch scale of any sort of music is a flexible instrument, as much today as in the past. Musical art has never encountered the difficulty of using an acoustically imperfect scale. The musical ear is very sensitive to deviations of pitch when they affect the component notes of a chord or a tonality. Intonation can be flexible as long as the essential intervals are respected. Modulation introduces a flexing of the pitch of a single tone to the extent that it changes its scale degree (when the note is common to two tonalities). Lalo (1939), who presented measures of isolated intervals played on a sonometer and asked subjects to judge their intonation, notes: "When the subject thinks a precise tonic or a scale fragment, the results change, in virtue of the fact of interpretation" (pp. 204–205 note). Later we return to the psychological nature of these integrations and the likely mechanisms of what is commonly called tonal "interpretation." Let us limit ourselves here to showing by means of an experiment that such phenomena exist and have widespread effects.

EXPERIMENT 4

This research was aimed at showing that *hearing a single note* brings about the constitution of a system of hierarchical relationships in subjects in such a way that the tones put in relation by imaginative operations are almost always tones of the diatonic scale (major or minor). These tones maintain relationships with the heard sound, not only of belonging to the same *tonal community*, but also of a functional hierarchy. In other words, the issue was to find out, first, with what frequency musician and nonmusician subjects were capable of *spontaneous tonal interpretation* of single tones heard several times; and second, if such an interpretation were to exist, in what it might consist, that is, what function would be most frequently attributed to a note through the relationships that it induces in the subjects' imaginations.

Method

The subjects, turning their backs to the piano, were alone with the experimenter. The experimenter gave them the following instructions:

> I am going to have you hear, three times in a row, one note on the piano. Starting with that note as a beginning, try to imagine a short melodic phrase that you sing silently to yourself. It doesn't have to be either beautiful or original. When you have finished, sing the melody out loud; or, if you prefer (and can do it) play it yourself. I will tell you the name of the first note.

Whether sung or played, the imagined melody was immediately written down. Then the procedure was repeated with three other notes.

The four notes given were G4, Db4, A1, and Eb1. The two last were taken from the low register so that they could be interpreted as bass notes. To avoid the possible persistence of interpretation from one trial into the next, the four notes were chosen so they each in turn did not belong to a triad in which the preceding note served as either root of fifth.

Table 3.8 shows unequivocally the fact of tonal interpretation of an isolated tone taken as the initial note of a melody. That tone was, in the great majority of cases, heard as one of the three components of the tonic triad (root, fifth, and, more infrequently, third). As for the four other scale degrees, the lower part of Table 3.8 shows that they were rarely chosen (six and eight times out of a total of 75 and 70, respectively). Final notes

TABLE 3.8
Distribution of Beginning (B) and Ending (E) Notes of Different Types in Melodies Composed by Subjects After Hearing One Note.

Scale Degree	Mode	First Melody B	First Melody E	Second Melody B	Second Melody E	Third Melody B	Third Melody E	Fourth Melody B	Fourth Melody E	Total B	Total E
Tonic	Major	7	6	4	7	6	7	6	7	23	27
(first)	Minor	2	4	2	2	2	3	3	3	9	12
Dominant	Major	4	5	6	4	4	2	3	2	17	13
(fifth)	Minor	4	1	1	1	3	1	3	3	11	6
Mediant	Major	2	0	3	1	1	1	2	1	8	3
(third)	Minor	0	0	0	1	1	0	0	0	1	1
Other	Major	0	2	1	2	2	2	1	2	4	8
	Minor	0	0	1	0	0	0	1	0	2	0

were equally in a majority among those three degrees. The mediant was more frequent in the initial position than the final. The major mode was always chosen more often than the minor.

ANALYSIS OF TONAL INTERPRETATION

The three experiments presented in this chapter are mutually complementary but yet do not provide any explanation of the integration of the musical stimulus. The first showed us the *effect* of scalar integration on memory fixation for melodies. The second demonstrated the existence of a *privileged interpretation*, among the possibilities affecting the perception of a single tone. An explanation of this group of results such as the following seems to be applicable, as being valid in the majority of cases and as representing the pattern of the more complex cases:

First, hearing a tone, the first element in a melodic sequence, brings about an interpretation as tonic or dominant (or, less frequently, mediant) in the corresponding tonality. This interpretation is linked to the fact that throughout tonal works the beginning of a melody is one of those three degrees and that the initial chord (the tonic triad) always contains it as a component. This is a simple associative effect maintained by the frequency of occurrence of such associations in experience.

Second, when the tones that follow *come from the diatonic scale having as its tonic or dominant the intial tone*, the interpretation is confirmed. It is anchored (a "centration") on the actual or virtual (underlying) tonic and the *revival of relationships laid down by experience* that exist between the tonic and the seven other degrees. Each note is then interpreted as a scale degree and its fixation in memory facilitated by the association established between it and the tonic.

Third, when the tones that follow come from scales other than the initial one, the interpretation is contradicted, the hypothesis of a possible tonic is rejected, and a new hypothesis can be elaborated concerning the subsequent tones, and so on. To the extent that none of these hypotheses is confirmed by subsequent tones, the melodic grouping does not favor any centration, and the group produces only a diminished fixation because no revival of associations was possible along the way. To the extent that a tonal hypothesis might have been momentarily established (that is, where there was a group of notes belonging to and suggesting the same tonality), this revival occurs and facilitates the fixation of that group more than the other notes.

Fourth, it seems likely that there is a markedly retroactive role of recent notes in confirming or contradicting an interpretation, conceived earlier, that reinforces or inhibits the associations evoked. In effect, when there is a contradiction, a new hypothesis is immediately elaborated, to the detriment of the preceding one. The last note, like the first, has a privileged status of very clear stability. Those notes engender particularly powerful relationships, and it is important that those be compatible with the relationships established in the middle part. The most favorable case is that in which the first and last notes are the tonic.

Two cases remain to be examined that are not covered by the above rules:

In the first case, the first note is neither tonic nor dominant (nor even mediant) with respect to the contextual tones, while belonging to the same tonality as they do but in the category of another, less important degree. There then occurs a delay in hypothesis formation—a multiple interpretation or absence of interpretation—until in the procession of successive tones one of them constrains a definite choice among the possibilities. Beginning with a certain number among them, the configuration engendered by four or five degrees leaves no doubt concerning their respective functions. The tonic is thus placed and the first notes intepreted in retrospect, but not by a present effect on something that has ceased to exist. Rather, present traces of sound elements become integrated into a system currently evoked, to whose evocation those elements had initially contributed, while remaining in memory as not yet integrated traces. There is reciprocal action—feedback—between one another.

In the second case, the tonic itself is understood all the way through the melody. Teplov (1947), citing certain experiments of Ephrussi, presented evidence that children of 8 to 11 years were able to finish an "incomplete" melodic phrase (that is, one that had for its last note some degree other than the tonic or member of the tonic triad), extending it by the addition of several notes so that it ended with one of those notes. Here again there is an effect of the progressive elimination of possible tonics and a choice of one that is compatible with the heard tones. Even when it remains implicit and without acoustic reality, the tonic *is evoked through hearing the other degrees just as powerfully as it evokes them, when it alone is present.* There is a reversibility of effect and cause and, as in the preceding case, the verification and fixation of heard notes through the effect of an understood tonic and the network of relations that it involves.

I have outlined here some of the principles that govern tonal interpretation and that are concerned exclusively with the *pitches* of tones. It is nevertheless certain that rhythmic factors have an extremely important effect wherever the pitches do not clearly determine the choice of an hypothesis, notably when there are just a few notes. Relative duration, intensity accents, and relative pitch height can without any doubt come into play. For example, the four notes in Figure 3.7 can be interpreted as in either C or F major, depending on their relative duration, their accent, their pitch, and so forth.

Figure 3.7. Influence of rhythmic factors on tonal interpretation: (A & B) Influence of relative note durations; (C & D) Influence of intensity of accent. (A) is heard in C major; (B) in F major; (C) in C major; and (D) in F major.

THE PSYCHOLOGICAL PROCESS OF INTERPRETATION

These facts of interpretation have such psychological and aesthetic importance that here it is worthwhile to attempt to clarify the concept with the aid of the best established theoretical principles presently available. Tonal interpretation appears to cross seemingly different psychological processes that nevertheless relate to a common underlying reality:

1. The assimilation of a melodic pattern containing intervals foreign to the tonal material with a "usual" pattern, by means of the subjective correction of intervals, or the judgment of "out of tune" made against those with too obvious deviations. This assimilation presupposes a choice of tonic from among the tones heard and an ordering of the other tones with reference to it.

2. The assimilation in immediate memory of a nontonal melody with a tonal melody having the same contour. This process is analogous to the preceding, except that the "corrected" intervals are borrowed from material deposited in memory. They are only perceived as incompatible, incongruent, with a tonal interpretation—not as "approximately in tune" as in the preceding case.

3. The perception of an isolated tone or of a group of sounds too impoverished to determine a tonality as a function of its most likely center of reference; in sum, the *projection* of an integrating network conforming to the scalar and hierarchical rules of tonality on one or several of the elements.

4. The effects on perception and memory of reinforcement of tonal patterns, relative to nontonal patterns with the same characteristics of length, contour, and so forth.

All these facts—and one might cite others—presuppose tonal interpretation. To a great extent, tonal interpretation has conditioned the evolution of music as an art since the 16th century—a period that saw the codification of the distinctive principles of tonal writing, supplanting the modal system in Europe. All the innovations of composers tended to introduce as much diversity as possible into harmony and rhythm, and flexibility into melody, while at all times respecting the requirements of order and functional polarity inherent in tonal interpretation. In this sense it is correct to see there—more than in the antithesis of consonance and dissonance—the pivot around which events in the history of music since the 19th century have been articulated. The line of cleavage that separates the new music from the old is not placed between a consonant art (that admits common dissonances) and an art that would enlarge the circle of dissonant sounds. Rather the separation lies between an art in which *tonal syntax subsists as a quality of common perceptual experience* (that is, making possible the interpretation of sound materials) and another in which such a syntax is no more than one empty category of experience, or else an art that made place for a new syntax that may or may not have audible effects.

Similarly, for the majority of the public the line of cleavage between music and nonmusic should be drawn with respect to the possibility or impossibility of the tonal interpretation of a group of sounds. Incoherence, arbitrariness, strangeness, and inconsistency—such are the qualities the average listener attributes to the new forms of syntax. And, surely, the listener does not experience this incoherence solely at the level of sections, periods, phrases, and phrase segments. No, the work as a totality will not attain structure in those instances where the parts, themselves unstructured, do not become fixed in memory, where the working out of themes, however real it might be, is not apparent to the listener because of the lack of perceived themes. Music and nonmusic, form and formlessness, the beautiful and the ugly can only be defined for many listeners as aesthetic categories with reference to these tonal integrations, and those in turn grow from the history of musical thought considered together with other social facts.

How, then, should we conceive of the process of interpretation that alone renders this integration possible?[21] Let us first underscore the metaphorical character of the term. Here we have to do not with a discursive or mediated process, but rather with an act immediate and intuitive in appearance. Each note, each group of notes, is "felt as"—"heard as"— a tonic or as requiring a complement in order to have meaning with respect to an implicit tonic. This is not an explicit inference, not a choice made among imagined possibilities. It is the establishment of an equilibration among heard sounds, beginning from the moment when there are enough of them, when they maintain sufficiently determined relationships to exclude

---

[21]In effect, these two notions, bound up with one another and closely related, ought to be distinguished. *Integration* concerns the perception of an element (a note or chord) as a part of an actual group (a tonal phrase). It is integration that produces tonal groupings having functional differentiation. *Interpretation* refers to the conditions of the possibility of perceiving the grouping, but it could very well be demonstrated in the presence of just one element—the interpretation of an isolated note as the tonic would not be regarded as an integration. Let us note again that interpretation is integration in terms of a fictive grouping, that is, in an array of *virtual* relations, sedimentary products of culture.

all tonics save one. That tonic is not necessarily heard, or even thought, but implicitly stressed. It guides the progress of the subject whom one has asked to complete an unfinished phrase; it orients auditory assimilation. The process is thus *implicit and unreflective*. Everything happens as if one were in the presence of one of those unconscious conclusions that the intellectualist philosophers (primarily Helmholtz) described for us in connection with the perception of distance, depth, and size constancy. Nothing, however, permits a parallel supposition here, and the phenomenal appearances are against it. The term "hypothesis" that we made use of earlier is equally metaphorical, and only in rare and well-defined cases could it be taken literally. An educated subject, to whom the concepts of tonality, functions, and the like are familiar, may hear in an initial fragment as yet tonally indeterminate a succession of explicit inferences and hypotheses concerning the tonal center that may or not be expressed. But that is a question of intellectualization and of an *a posteriori* verbal review of a process that occurs automatically in everyone without the intervention of language.

Yet the appearance of immediacy is not enough to satisfy us. One might put forward here such concepts as the establishment of "good form," of a spontaneous equilibrium according to the best articulation possible, and so on. It remains for us to prove why such a tonal articulation is in fact the best; why in all likelihood it is not a requirement of every human ear;[22] why also, in the absence of any constraining configuration, a single perceived tone produces in the imagination a whole procession of tonal relationships.

Yet it is this appearance of immediacy that has misled certain psychologists—albeit eminent connoisseurs of things musical—about the concept of interpretation. The equilibration out of which tonal structuring arises seems to take place at the level of sensory function. As it is a matter of an equilibration putting in play a number of elements, we can appeal to those notions that evoke totalities, notably that of "good form." But this concordance between a differentiation and a spontaneous refinement accomplished in the phylogenesis of the auditory sense, and one geographically and historically limited stage in the evolution of music, is not easily explained. The merit of Gestalt theory at this juncture, according to Pradines (1947), "is to grasp that the work of the mind by which we pass from natural perception to aesthetic perception is not an associative synthesis, and that it begins with sensation itself" (p. 254). One recognizes

---

[22]Among the melodies of the "two-tones style" cited by Sachs (1943) are several in which neither note implies a tonal polarization. Many primitive scales are limited to a third or a fourth, and one would not know how to seek in such music for an equivalent of our tonal integration, which presupposes an ambitus of at least an octave and the predominance of a tonic and a dominant.

here the general theory of this author concerning the phylogenetic mutation leading to the "cognitive" senses, vision, and hearing—a generative
mutation of the fine arts. Tonal interpretation may be dependent on this
mutation; it shows itself in the establishment of spontaneous equilibrations
in the grasping of a sound group. However, we must still explain why the
phylogenesis in question manifests itself with equal spontaneity among all
peoples; why, according to the testimony of their musical productions,
many peoples have no "tonal feeling."

If mutation there is, it is developmental and not specific, ontogenetic
and not phylogenetic, associative, and not innate. It takes place at the level
of *perceptions*, not at the level of *sensory reception*. It is well known that
psychologists today distinguish among cortical projection areas, primary
sensory areas (responsible for the simple reception of centripetal inputs),
knowledge areas (on which depend the identification of messages as objective signs), and finally association areas (thanks to which this perception
takes on a fringe of more or less automatic "significations" according
to their frequency of occurrence)[23]. There are mediated associations,

---

[23]This functional duality has been clearly established for vision. According to Fulton
(1947), clinical observations indicate that area 18 is concerned with intraoccipital associations
governing the organization of the visual image (for example, those that are concerned with
integrating light inputs and proprioceptive inputs coming from the muscles of the eye in
depth perception). Area 19 is thought to be the seat of visual associations with other sensory
and motor areas of the cortex. Lesions in area 18 produce poor spatial orientation and
diplopia. A tumor affecting area 19 produces "highly organized" hallucinations. The impossibility of interpreting written words (alexia) can occur following lesions in that area in the
left cerebral hemisphere. (See also Cossa and Paillas, 1944.)

The facts concerning audition are less well established and the functional and anatomo-
physiological relationships are still controversial. Cossa and Paillas even seem to reject the
idea of the existence of a cortical area involving the recognition, identification, and integration
of tones, on the grounds that the abolition of those functions is never encountered in isolation:
"There is no isolated psychic deafness. It is not even certain that a pure verbal deafness exists"
(p. 334–335). However, because those deficits do occur, associated with others, no doubt,
but specifically attached to auditory functions, they must be explained anatomically, in the
absence of deficiencies of peripheral auditory reception.

Experiments with animals led Fulton (1947) to conclude in favor of the existence of a
secondary acoustic area, with well-defined connections in the medial geniculate. This cytoar-
chitecturally distinct area in the cat responds to more intense stimulation than that which
affects the primary area. In monkeys, the secondary acoustic area "undoubtedly plays a role
in the integration of acoustic reflexes similar to that of areas 18 and 19 for visual reflexes"
(p. 348). It seems necessary to distinguish here between ablation studies and studies involving
the recording of responses from the surface of the cortex. Operating on monkeys previously
trained with auditory stimuli, Jacobsen and Elder (1936) did not confirm the alteration of
conditioned responses after ablation of areas 20, 21, and 22. But Ades (1943) and Felder
established (incontrovertably, it would seem) the existence of a secondary acoustic area in
the cat. After having collected evoked potentials in the primary region and thus determined
its limits, they applied strychnine to enhance the transmission of inputs. Thus they observed
secondary potentials in an area situated on the superior part of the lower process of the
posterior ecto-sylvian gyrus. In no case did they observe a secondary response in any other
region. The area thus delimited is not contiguous to the primary area, and constitutes a
"para-receptive zone" or "acoustic association area."

insufficiently maintained by exercise, that appear only after a longer or shorter latency period and hence present themselves in consciousness as associations. This situation also occurs when the attractive term of the association functions in several systems or can serve as an element in several pairs, having long been integrated in several. But some have a *temporal* immediacy and are nonetheless associations. This character arises from their univocacy, from their great stability, from the fact that they are integrated into only one system; and in fact it is they that join graphic signs to words. In the emergence of the word beginning with the successive addition of a few letters, there is also a spontaneous "equilibration," the appearance of a "good form" that resolves the tension. To a certain extent everything happens as it does in tonal interpretation, where group structuring operates on already present elements from the instant when the unique compatible contic emerges from their reciprocal relationships. No one, however, would dream of making the reading of a selected language the subject of a phylogenetic mutation—*although the general possibility of making similar associations would naturally be tied to a certain degree of evolution of cortical differentiation.*

However, as soon as one rejects explanations from the sensualist point of view, even corrected by an evolutionary perspective, one seems necessarily drawn to the side of intellectualism. There are false dilemmas in psychology, due to the survival of dichotomies and antitheses belonging to the philosophy of faculties, that continue to inform (albeit implicitly) the descriptions of some authors. As long as one retains the idea of "sensation" as something passive, elementary, innate, and fixed, one is tempted to attribute to intelligence everything that does not appear to fit this classic schema. Such was the case with Dauriac (1893/95), whose articles on the psychology of the musician are well known: "If moreover you succeed in demonstrating that the act (musical perception, for which we intend to sketch an analysis) is almost entirely inexplicable if you involve only sensation in it—that in addition to its "material" there is an element of form—then its intellectual character will emerge quite clearly" (p. 37). "Sensation" being what I have just described and intelligence being the faculty of inventing or perceiving relationships, it is evident that tonal interpretation occurs on the intellectual level.

Nevertheless, if there is truly intelligence in musical perception (as I believe), it is not at this stage of automatisms derived from cultural learnings that we should look for it. As we shall see, it should be sought, rather, at the level of acquiring grouping structures (*"structures d'ensemble"*) and transformation groups. Piaget (Piaget & Lambercier, 1943), who was especially eager to find differences between perception and intelligence, has taught us not to confuse the *perception of a relationship* with *perceptual comparison*. Although it was in the analysis of vision that these distinctions were made, they can be valuable in audition. The elements of a single figure can be grasped through the perception of a relationship or, if they are too far from one another in time or space, become the object of a perceptual comparison. In the former case, one has a single "centration" followed by a "decentration," because "a centration is a state linked to a static fixation." A decentration is "a coordination of centrations, characterizing also a state, but here a state linked to a group of elements as opposed to particular centrations" (p. 56). If a "transfer" is, on the contrary, "a displacement proceding from one centration to another, but without fixating on either of the two exclusively," a comparison consists of a coordination of transfers. In other words, the perception of a relationship supposes only movement between terms; a comparison between the coming and going of several movements. Now, the latter "is involved in the direction of intelligent activity, since the essential difference between intelligence and perception is an increase in complexity, if one might put it that way, of the spatio-temporal distances between the objects of these two sorts of conduct" (p. 4). But tonal interpretation seems to attach itself now to one, now to the other, of these two cases. When the constituent elements of a tonality are given at once (as in a tonic triad), there is a single "centration," really a single movement, if it involves a melody accompanied by that chord. In some cases (rare, it is true, in classical music, but achievable experimentally and achieved in modern music), all the elements are not given at once, and as a consequence a certain amount of ambiguity prevails for a short period. Should we say that there the reign of intelligence begins? It is true that there is a give and take among the elements perceived and a search for the still absent attractive center. Nevertheless, the equilibration is of the same kind—it intervenes when the compatibility of the sound elements imposes the revival of a schema imprinted under that form or another by memory. The display of interpretation through time contributes above all to making it move from passivity to activity, from the immediate to the mediate. Incidentally, this appears to me to involve an extended concept of sensory association, flexible enough to cover all the experimental instances.

It is appropriate here to distinguish between intersensory associations (which underlie the knowledge processes involved in certain perceptual behaviors) and unisensory associations (on which tonal interpretation is based). The *stability* of a musical pattern in memory, the differentiation of one part in a polyphonic texture, both involve associative processes acquired in the course of a specific musical education in which sound elements were first associated one to one, and then in groups, to visual (notes on paper and on the keyboard), as well as kinesthetic, stimuli (a note corresponding to a finger movement; a chord to a group of fingers). A style of harmonic or melodic contrapuntal writing is a tactile and muscle schema, transferable from one instrument to another with some adjustments, but quite well defined in itself. The intersensory nature of musical objects produces in musicians an intersensory substrate for the *perception* of sound patterns. There is no paradox in this, and one can see the reality of it in perceptual-verbal associations.[24] But in the tonal interpretation of a tone or group of tones, we have the effect of a system of unisensory associations (in nonmusicians) to which (in musicians) are joined the polysensory effects of which we have just been speaking. The tonal interpretation of a tone or tones, the tonal integration of a well-defined sound pattern, both belong to the family of perceptions; that is, they imply the *reception* of a *sensory message* and its *cognitive elaboration*. This elaboration, comparable to that observed in the cognitive perception of objects, involves a placing in relationship with other real or virtual tones that is immediate in appearance and that follows the systematized relationships laid down in development. This placing in relationship leads to an "equilibration" of compatibility or cultural congruence; the tone or group of tones heard and interpreted leads to a feeling of sufficiency and completion when the tonic required by the tones is implicitly thought or explicitly heard. These are in a way the signals broadcast by a tonality, drawing their evocative power from associations constantly present in experience.

In conclusion, it is certainly necessary to distinguish between, and even place in opposition, musical perception and sensation (sensory reception), but it is also necessary to avoid bringing intelligence back into the picture, at least in all its aspects. As early as 1865, Basevi saw this very well in his definition of perception as the "apprehension of tones in relation to others that strike our ear or that spontaneously appear in our imagination" (p. 5). Since sensation is "an impression that does not go beyond itself," perception, in contrast, "relates to the affinities of auditory sensations among themselves, whether heard or appearing in memory" (p. 12). Perception is a faculty very different from auditory sensitivity or that verbal memory which "mechanically" links words in succession and involves a sort of memory for tones heard initially in a sequence that permits comparison with those following. According to Basevi (who here refers to Aristoxenus), from that memory and that comparison the intelligibility of music is born. Be it understood, the latter is—we are in 1865—based on tonality. But there is a specific mode of comprehension of musical facts that is not

---

[24]See Chapter 11. Incidentally, it is a fact that ablation of the temporal lobes seems to affect functions involving visual interpretation. One type of psychic blindness occurs in conjunction with cortical deafness. Finally, the dominance of the left cortex in man shows that auditory interpretation is linked to handedness. Following ablation of the auditory cortex in the left hemisphere (which in right-handed subjects affects use of the right hand), there is not sensory deafness, but rather a disorganization of audition—a psychic deafness both for noises and speech. Cf. Fulton (1947).

identified with mathematical or conceptual intelligence: "The phenomena of tonality on which our system of harmony is based are not the immediate objects of *intelligence*, but of a faculty intermediary between sense and intellect. It is this faculty that I call *perception*" (p. 9). We can see that the principal traits of interpretation and integration have been well observed by Basevi. He lacks, however, a clear conception of the psychophysiological development of these processes, as well as of the historical relativity of tonality.

Teplov (1947), who analyzed a large number of experiments and who himself did experiments with singers that were discussed above apropos of integration, endeavored to define the psychological nature of "tonal feeling." He included in particular an emotional component that it is interesting to add here. The tonal relationships in a melody, by their very nature, produce various impressions of tension and relaxation—of suspension and completion—according as the listener perceives the degrees of resolution and movement of the tonality suggested. Thus the incompleteness of a melody that ends on some degree other than the first, third, or fifth is felt emotionally as a tension requiring a completion—not on a logical level, but on a *sensory* level. This emotional component rests not on a cognitive representation, but on an accumulation of prior perceptions. This occurs not only with musicians, but among all subjects capable of observing their musical impressions with a certain amount of attention.

Chapter 4

PSYCHOLOGICAL ORIGINS
AND DEVELOPMENT OF
THE SENSE OF TONALITY

PRECOCITY OF TONAL ACCULTURATION

Since, as we have just seen, hearing a single note produces by itself a tonal interpretation, it might seem difficult or even paradoxical to speak of the development of tonal feeling as beginning with complex musical structures. Where could we find a sufficiently unschooled ear for which the perception of a musical grouping would not hit on any already established tendency or any predetermined expectancy? Many psychologists have insisted on the precocity of tonal acculturation, whose effects, according to some experiments, should already be evident between 6 and 8 years. Teplov (1947) studied 76 children, 6 to 14 years old, asking them to reproduce melodies or melodic phrases. He observed that even at those ages the easiest intervals to reproduce were those that constituted the tonal framework of the melody, while notes foreign to the diatonic scale and modulating notes created difficulties. On the contrary, the sizes of intervals posed no problem for intonation. Teplov also indicated, on the basis of a study by Astragus, that in children's singing the most surely intoned pitches are those that form the tonic triad. Ephrussi (cited by Teplov) also showed clearly that the impression of completion of a melody that ends on the tonic is present even in children of 8 to 11 years. Finally, Brehmer (1925) and Reimers (1927) both established that the sense of tonality develops during the school years—between 11 and 12 for the former, and according to the latter completely in place by the age of 15 years. Its presence is indicated notably by the need subjects feel to end a melody on one of the three pitches of the tonic chord.

Experimenters who wish to suppress the acquired privilege of tonal music over atonal have therefore to choose between the two following solutions: either they can resort to subjects who have not reached their sixth year; or they can call on listeners who developed in musical cultures different from our own. In the first case, the risk is one of encountering the psychological limits of an early stage of the child's development—the difficulty of explaining the instructions for the experiment and of carrying it out under favorable conditions. That risk does not apply in the second case. It would therefore be useful to compare the results obtained with listeners from different cultures with those obtained from the experiments with children just described. Still, it would be necessary to have groups of subjects that differ only on the characteristics of musical culture, not on age, or intellectual level, or the like. Those conditions are difficult to contrive, but not impossible.

PROBABLE STAGES OF ACCULTURATION: MELODIC AND HARMONIC INFORMATION

It is difficult to form a clear idea of the stages followed by acculturation. Musicologists often conclude that what holds for themselves as conscious and knowing subjects occurs as well in "virgin" subjects in the course of their first contacts with musical works. Thus, notably, feelings for *sequences*— that is, expectancies that one scale degree or chord will follow another— represent a secondary stage with respect to the simple feeling of familiarity born of the frequency of occurrence of certain degrees or chords. In sum, it seems to me that characteristics pertaining to ordering do not appear before characteristics of *familiarity* of scale-degree relationships. The hierarchy and the polarities themselves depend on the alternation between the two fundamental degrees (tonic and dominant) being frequently perceived, if not explicitly observed.

It is essential to grasp this idea thoroughly: "Tonal feeling" and tonal acculturation develop as a system of interconnected perceptual habits, without the subjects' awareness of the objective terms on which that acquisition was based. The subjects do not know what a perfect triad is—or a tonic, or a dominant, or a cadence—until education reveals it to them. Such learning is currently the theme of psychological research inspired by theories of communication and information. (See especially Faverge, 1953a, 1953b; Bresson, 1953.) Numerous studies have shown that the probability of occurrence of an element in a group of elements influences behavior (Faverge, 1953a), memory (Aborn & Rubenstein, 1952), and rapidity of perception of the element (Solomon & Postman, 1952; McGinnies, Comer, & Lacey, 1952), even if that probability is unknown to the subject. Perceiving sequences of letters presented briefly by tachistoscope can be done more rapidly when the sequences are frequent in the subject's native language. In that case, the probabilities cannot be totally unknown to the subject yet are felt in a confused and unreflective way. According to information theory, the number of each type of element perceived is inversely proportional to the quantity of information received via those elements. Along these lines, Aborn and Rubenstein (1952) found that immediate recall of nonsense syllables was linked to the probability of the subjects' predicting the occurrence of an element in context. If we view "organization" as the link between element and context, then we would say that immediate memory varies directly with such organization. The more an element is "unexpected," the less it is deducible from context and the more information it contains. Organization and information vary inversely with each other.[1]

Some processes of this sort are altogether assimilable to tonal acculturation, if one succeeds in demonstrating an organization sufficiently stable across works to induce the automatic operation of the probabilities. The subject listens to pieces of music, learns and sings popular songs. He is completely occupied with the qualitative relationships they contain— qualities of intervals, timbres, rhythms, intensities, melodic contours, the striking of harmonies. And however large the relative frequency of occurrence of certain scale degrees, the relatively constant alternation of certain chords creates in him habits some of whose effects we have seen. Everything seems different to him at first. Each piece, each melody has its own physiognomy, its own individuality. But the quantitative analysis of their elements discloses regularities in them analogous to those in letter sequences whose incidence in a given language is determined. Those regularities lie at the origin of tonal acculturation.

In calculating information, one usually distinguishes between information emitted by a source, which depends only on the source itself taken as an objective system, and information received by the subject, which depends as well on the familiarity the stimuli have for him and which decreases in proportion to increasing familiarity. Now, in the very basic situation with which we are concerned, these two sources are closely aligned and their correlation is 1.0. It is only little by little that a difference appears between them, with received information diminishing until it reaches a more or less permanent level. At that moment, the perception of a chord (for example, the dominant seventh) announced ineluctably its resolution on the tonic chord, and received information tends to zero. Of course, the link between an element and its context is never as rigorous as in this example, representing as it does an extreme case. No other sequence offers such a degree of determination. It is true, for example, that the chord on the second scale degree usually announces that on the

---

[1]It should be noted, apropos of the experiment of Aborn and Rubenstein (1952), that the *organization* of the material presented to the subjects was first made the object of conscious and prolonged training. The subjects learned schemas for the organization of each sequence of syllables before taking recall tests on the same material.

dominant in a perfect cadence, but this rule admits of exceptions. In harmonic sequences that chord might be followed by a chord other than the dominant, whatever it might be. I therefore decided to calculate the total information (along with its distribution among the degrees of the scale) for well-known popular songs (those that make up the basic repertoire of children) and also for works containing harmony, chosen from diverse styles and periods throughout the history of the tonal system. I wanted to find out whether the hearing—even the repeated hearing—of an unharmonized tonal melody involves some regularities in the *quantity of information emitted* (equal by hypothesis to the information received), especially regularities in the distribution of information across the seven scale degress, such as would assure the formation of the fundamental habits involved in tonal acculturation. That would involve, for example, the predominance of the first and fifth degrees and their alternating polarity, and the subordinate character of the other degrees—which, once that was established, could function only as unifying linkages between the principal degrees.

EXPERIMENT 5

I attempted a comparison between two sources of information: the one melodic and the other harmonic. Signals emitted by a melodic source are tones for which the *useful* information is contained in their *scale-degree qualities*, that is, their distances in relation to the tonic. The tonic is most often the first or second note, on a strong beat in the measure (which by giving it an intensity accent makes it appear as a center of reference for the other notes). For a harmonic source the useful information is given by the scale-degree quality of the root, expressed in one of the notes of the chord. The other notes aid in determining that quality through their relationships to the root. The latter note might enter into various combinations with other notes in other chords, but becomes the root only when it is a third lower or a sixth higher than one of the other notes, and a fourth lower or a fifth higher than the other. In perception, the classification of a chord by the scale degree of its root is immediately apparent. In whatever inversion, it is heard as a specific quality arising from the relationships of its components with the tonic.[2] A chord is a complex of

---

[2]This quality is evidently not identical for chords on the same scale degrees when chords of two, three, or four tones are used—the only ones used in the works analyzed. But there is such a numerical predominance of the perfect triads and the dominant seventh chord that one can ignore here the distinction between the one and the other, except for the quite important distinction between a four-tone chord and the other six three-tone chords.

three or four scale degrees associated in a whole pattern and presenting a scalar aspect analogous to that of melodic scale degrees.

The tonal system consists of seven melodic degrees on which the eight popular songs are based and seven harmonic degrees with which the six pieces analyzed were harmonized. Their frequencies of occurrence are shown in Tables 4.1 and 4.2.

Method of Calculating Information

This calculation was simple for the melodic degrees. Each note was classified and counted with respect to the expressed tonality. (There were no modulations in the melodies.) For the harmonies there were some difficulties. Chords are often expressed in succession as arpeggios. (See Figure 4.1) or in other arpeggiated figures. I counted such groups as single chords, no matter which way they were written.

Repeated harmonies (much more frequent than repeated notes in the songs) were always counted. In effect, repeated striking of the same chords should be considered as a factor impregnating the ear. Scale degree was determined in each case with repect to the initial tonality or to the tonality in force after a modulation (change of key).

The information (in bits) contained in each category of signal (that is, in the different notes and chords) is given by the binary logarithm of the probability (p_i) of occurrence of each event in each work:

$$H_d = - \log_2 p_i.$$

This quantity varied to an important degree across melodies.

Results and Discussion

Table 4.1 shows that for the songs the distribution of notes among the seven degrees *accords no privilege to the tonic or dominant* (the first and fifth). *The third and second degrees had comparable frequencies* to the first and fifth, respectively, which could be explained harmonically since degrees one and three, and five and two, are frequently associated with each other in the principal chords of the tonality. But such harmonic connections could not yet be operating at this basic stage of acculturation, at which associations of this type are not yet formed. Melodies are endowed with implicit harmony only when given those values through repeated hearing of chords simultaneously with each scale degree.[3]

---

[3]I should add that, in certain cases, a melody can be interpreted in several tonalities. Then only harmonic support provides a univocal interpretation (cf. Chailley & Challan, 1947.)

TABLE 4.1

Frequency of Occurrence and Amount of Information for Different Scale Degrees in Eight Popular Songs

Song Title and Total Number of Notes	Distribution of Notes of Different Scales Degrees							Amount of Information for Different Scale Degrees								
	I	V	IV	II	VI	VII	III	I	V	IV	II	VI	VII	III	H	R
Au clair de la lune: 47	19	1	0	17	3	1	6	1,307	8,965	0	1,469	7,380	8,965	2,988	1,512	46
A la claire fontaine: 41	12	4	0	7	0	0	18	1,775	6,795	0	2,556	0	0	1,185	1,534	45,2
Il pleut bergère: 54	5	11	7	9	3	1	18	6,795	2,300	2,954	2,590	7,643	5,795	1,590	2,008	28,3
J'ai du bon tabac: 60	10	8	10	16	0	0	16	2,590	2,910	2,590	1,901	0	0	1,910	2,263	19,1
Mon beau sapin: 49	12	7	9	7	1	2	11	2,035	2,816	2,450	2,816	5,643	4,608	2,158	2,525	9,8
Il était une bergère: 35	10	13	0	6	2	0	4	1,810	1,430	0	2,547	4,132	0	3,132	2,073	24,9
Il est né le divin enfant: 82	27	14	9	16	2	0	14	1,603	2,556	3,197	2,358	2,040	0	2,556	2,697	3,6
Ah mon beau château: 50	14	8	2	4	4	6	12	1,836	2,643	4,643	3,643	3,613	3,508	2,058	2,565	8,3

TABLE 4.2

Frequency of Occurrence and Amount of Information for Chords on Different Scales Degrees in Six Tonal Works.*

The two last columns indicate mean information transmitted for each chord in each piece (H) and percent redundancy (R).

Total number of chords for each work	Distribution of chords on different scale degrees							Amount of information for chords on different scale degrees							H	R
	I	V	IV	II	VI	VII	III	I	V	IV	II	VI	VII	III		
Bach: 441	172	140	52	30	25	22	0	1,358	1,657	3,095	3,868	4,158	4,531	0	2,124	24,1
Mozart: 233	95	84	12	18	9	11	4	1,296	1,473	4,293	3,698	4,717	4,411	5,878	2,044	27,0
Beethoven: 202	90	61	23	22	3	3	0	1,168	1,732	3,145	3,210	6,158	6,158	0	1,913	31,7
Duke Ellington: 74 ...	34	27	16	6	3	0	0	1,340	1,675	2,426	3,857	4,878	0	0	1,936	30,8
Diabelli: 94	49	37	4	4	0	0	0	0,940	1,347	4,573	4,573	0	0	0	1,434	48,7
Chopin: 378	180	174	0	21	3	0	0	1,070	1,120	0	4,184	8,380	0	0	1,276	54,3

*The titles of the works were Bach, Concerto in A minor for Violin and Orchestra, BWV 1041, First Movement; Mozart, Piano Sonata in G Major, Kv. 283, First Movement; Beethoven, Piano Sonata in Ab Major, Opus 110, First Movement; Duke Ellington, "Mississippi Moan" for Piano; Diabelli, Piano Sonatina No. 1 in G Major, First Movement; Chopin, Waltz, opus 64, No. 1, in Db Major, for Piano.

Figure 4.1. Calculation of harmonic information. In this excerpt from a Sonatina by Diabelli each of the triplets in the accompaniment expresses a harmonic unit.

In contrast, in the case of the harmonic analysis, the distribution of chords indicated in Table 4.2 was consistently ordered in the same direction. *The first and fifth degrees were always very frequent in comparison to the others*, comprising between 70.7% and 93.6% of the total. Figure 4.2 provides an even more dramatic view of this distribution, reflecting the relative importance of the tonic and dominant. The other chords had variable frequencies, but almost always fell in the same descending order in the table: IV, II, VI, VII, III. The III chord, always exceptional in strict tonality, occurs only within sequences of chord progressions. The IV and II were equivalent in importance, which was always greater than that of the VI and VII chords.

In reading Tables 4.1 and 4.2, note that in certain instances a zero under quantity of information does not really mean null information. On the contrary, theoretically it could mean infinite information, but we cannot consider infinity in the present psychological context. An absent element carries no effective meaning for the perceiving subject, and its rarity in the pieces should accord it a quantitative privilege when it occurs, only for those subjects who know of its existence through experience. For example, Table 4.2 shows that the III chord occurred in only one work. To interpret the quantity of information that it carries correctly, we should take into account not only its relative rarity in the work under consideration, but also its absence in the others. Acculturation arises from the entire set of works, and if we need to determine the mean quantity of information for each class of chords we should attribute elevated coefficients to the null cases.

The mean information transmitted is given by:

$$H = -\sum_{i=1}^{k} p_i \log_2 p_i$$

H gives the mean information transmitted in bits per event—per note in the songs, per chord in the pieces—weighted for frequency of occurrence. That mean was always less for harmony than for melody, because the seven melodic events were closer to equiprobable than the seven harmonic events.

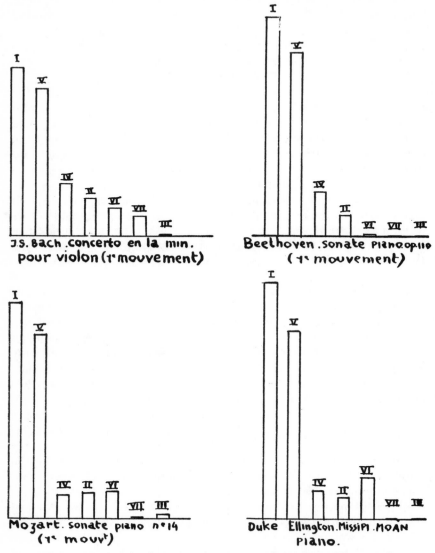

Figure 4.2. Relative frequency of occurrence of chords on different scale degrees in four of the works analyzed. Scale degrees were determined in each instance with respect to the tonality in force at the time, which varied with modulations.

Redundancy (R) is the relationship between mean information transmitted (H) and the maximum possible information in the equiprobable
case (H_m; here, $-\log_2 1/7 = 2.797$ bits):

$$R = 1 - (H/H_m)$$

usually expressed as a percentage. R expresses the degree to which the
information transmitted departs from the maximum possible. It is a notion
complementary to that of information and indicates that, in the set of
events, the selection and arrangement of elements was made with the
novelty and originality afforded by the repertoire in mind. A comparison
of Tables 4.1 and 4.2 shows that redundancy for some of the melodies
was quite low, making mnemonic fixation difficult. However, redundancy
varied considerably, even by an order of magnitude, and that makes fixation
highly variable and hard to predict. Harmonic messages, on the other
hand, were relatively stable in terms of redundancy, varying over a range
involving only about a two-fold increase. Incidentally, the minimum
redundancy for chords was much higher than that for melodies.

In summary, if we wish to compare the developmental resources afforded
by tonal melody and harmony, we should realize that the latter presents
aspects somewhat lacking in the former: relatively stronger and more
constant redundancy to assure assimilation into memory; a quite marked
predominance of the tonic and dominant chords; and a regularly declining
frequency of the other chords. *The harmonic message appears indubitably to
lend itself, under the well-defined conditions described here, to the acculturation
of the ear, and to the creation of perceptual habits born of the relatively high
and consistent frequency of occurrence of certain elements.*

Analysis of Harmonic Durations

Further verfication was necessary, however, to establish this result with
certitude. This involved a treatment of the durations of the different melodic
and harmonic signals. Here I wanted to know whether the privileged
frequency of the two tonal chords observed in Table 4.2 was compensated
by a lower duration relative to the other chords. Likewise, in the case of
melodies, I wanted to see whether the irregular numerical distribution
across the different scale degrees would correspond to a certain amount
of regularity in their durations. Note that the analysis up to this point has
been based only on the *frequency of attack* for notes and chords—a factor
that can legitimately be considered as the fundamental basis for acccultur-
ation, not differing in its effects from the frequencies of letters and syllables
that characterize a language (whose importance in perception and memory
for those sorts of messages was indicated earlier). However, something

that belongs particularly to music is the variety of temporal values of the sound signals involved in a work—a diversity that language permits to a much smaller extent.

To the preceding analysis we need to add an analysis of the *durations* over which events hold. This factor, along with frequency of occurrence, is an integral part of what one might call the statistical structure of discontinuities in the acoustic message. In these discontinuities information derived from frequency of occurrence measures the degree of "originality" or unpredictability of each element in the message, while information derived from durations measures the degree of saturation of the message with one or another of those elements. This is a consideration that cannot be abstracted psychologically: Signals that are rare but prolonged can have an effectiveness in perception and memory comparable to that of signals that are frequent but brief. I therefore calculated, for all the pieces previously examined, the temporal distribution of the melodic and harmonic signals, and those results are shown in Tables 4.3 and 4.4.

It is interesting for purposes of comparison with Tables 4.1 and 4.2 to consider these durations from the point of view of information theory. One might suppose that for the virgin listener whose tonal acculturation is nonexistent, the durational units of a piece would carry sound signals *independently* of each other. The listener does not yet know how to foresee what note or chord has just been announced by the note or chord he now hears. He does not know at all what the following instant will hold, save for those periodicities and repetitions we abstract momentarily. One could thus take each work as a sum of discrete units of duration, with each one carrying a certain amount of information. In this sum, signals that are prolonged, or that have a long duration overall, carry relatively little information. Those are the ones that impregnate the ear more than the others and that form the basis of its perceptual habits. Brief signals pass unnoticed at this stage. It is only later that their shapes emerge, after the elements of the ground have been laid down and assimilated.

Tables 4.3 and 4.4 confirm the results of the analyses of frequency of occurrence. *For the melodies the durations for which the seven scale degrees were held were very differently distributed.* The first and fifth degrees were not on the average more important than the second and third. *For the harmonies, on the other hand, the tonic and dominant took up between 68.9% and 93.6% of the total duration of the works,* which agreed precisely with the results obtained for frequency of occurrence. Figure 4.3 illustrates this similarity.

What the duration measure contributes that is new involves redundancy. A comparison of the last columns of the four tables shows that for six songs out of eight redundancy is lower for duration than for frequency of occurrence; while for four out of six harmonic works it was higher.

TABLE 4.3

Overall Duration of Different Scale Degrees and Amount of Information Contained in Temporal Units in Each of the Eight Popular Songs (as in Table 4.1)

Song Titles and Number of Temporal Units in Each Song	Distribution of Durations on Different Scale Degrees							Amount of Information for Different Scale Degrees								
	I	V	IV	II	VI	VII	III	I	V	IV	II	VI	VII	III	H	R
Au clair de la lune: 64	25	4	0	20	5	1	9	1,358	4,011	0	1,680	3,680	6,058	2,836	2,075	26,9
A la claire fontaine: 50	17	5	0	7	0	0	21	1,556	3,321	0	2,836	0	0	1,251	1,784	36,3
Il pleut bergère: 93	11	21	12	14	5	1	29	3,083	2,152	2,954	2,736	4,237	6,643	1,685	2,457	12,2
J'ai du bon tabac: 95	14	14	18	27	0	0	22	2,766	2,766	2,403	1,810	0	0	2,114	2,269	18,9
Mon beau sapin: 80	18	11	13	11	3	4	20	2,152	2,867	2,625	2,867	4,756	4,321	2,000	2,584	7,7
Il était une bergère: 64	21	21	0	8	6	0	8	1,608	1,608	0	3,000	3,426	0	3,000	2,122	24,2
Il est né le divin enfant: 164	64	29	15	31	3	0	22	1,358	2,506	3,457	2,403	5,795	0	2,899	2,230	20,3
Ah mon beau château: 64	20	10	2	6	4	6	16	1,680	2,580	5,011	3,426	4,011	3,426	2,000	2,481	11,3

TABLE 4.4

Overall Duration of Chords on Different Scale Degrees and Amount of Information Contained in Temporal Units in Each of Six Tonal Works (as in Table 4.2)

Song Titles and Number of Temporal Units in Each Work	Distribution of Durations of Chords on Different Scale Degrees							Amount of Information in Chords on Different Scale Degrees								
	I	V	IV	II	VI	VII	III	I	V	IV	II	VI	VII	III	H	R
Bach: 581	249	222	77	59	47	30	0	1,457	1,625	3,158	3,539	3,878	4,539	0	2,171	22,4
Mozart: 634	292	244	26	33	32	3	4	1,126	1,384	4,643	4,293	4,351	7,965	7,380	1,736	38,0
Beethoven: 655	311	256	55	31	4	8	0	1,098	1,380	3,608	4,442	7,380	6,380	0	1,662	40,6
Duke Ellington: 202 ..	105	52	16	13	16	0	0	0,946	1,960	3,662	3,965	3,662	0	0	1,825	34,8
Diabelli: 105	56	40	4	5	0	0	0	0,907	1,395	4,717	4,411	0	0	0	1,399	50,0
Chopin: 378	180	174	0	21	3	0	0	1,070	1,120	0	4,184	8,380	0	0	1,276	54,3

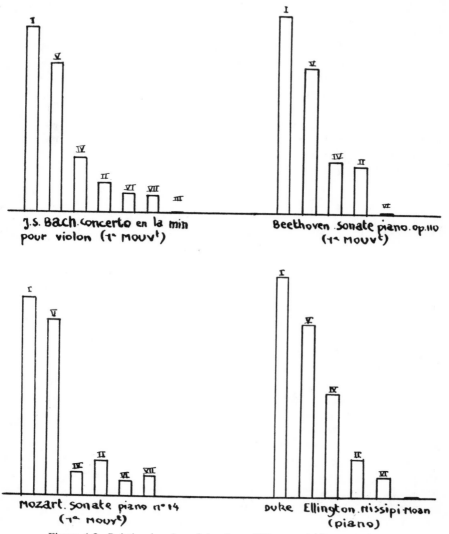

Figure 4.3. Relative duration of chords on different scale degrees in four of the works analyzed. Scale degrees were determined in each instance with respect to the tonality in force at the time, which varied with modulations.

We can conclude that effects on perception and memory are even less important with melodic notes, given the distribution of their respective durations, and even more important for chords. According to their statistical structure, the harmonic patterns were thus eminently apt for shaping tonal habits. The frequency of occurrence and duration of the tonic and dominant chords varied little from one piece to another. The information carried by the tonic had a mean of 1.225 bits; and by the dominant, 1.5 bits. (For each chord the probability of occurrence was not far from .50, for which the information would have been about 1.0 bit.) Likewise, in the temporal progression of a tonal work each durational unit had a probability close to .50 of being occupied by a tonic or dominant chord (averaging 1.267 and 1.477 bits, respectively).

FORMATIVE ELEMENTS APART
FROM DURATION AND FREQUENCY

We should not believe, however, that the factors of duration and frequency are the only ones to play a role in acculturation. Other factors, whether or not shared by melody and harmony, often intervene effectively to reinforce the groundwork laid down by the principal chords.

Experiments have shown that in a melodic phrase, the first and last notes are more stable than the intermediate notes; that is, that they have greater persistence in memory (see Guilford & Hilton, 1933; Francès, 1954). In most phrases the initial and final notes are drawn from the tonic or dominant chords and often are the tonic or the dominant. In harmonized phrases the initial chord is tonic at the beginning of a piece, and the end of the phrase is marked by a cadence, that is, a succession of chords of which the last is tonic (in perfect or plagal cadences) or dominant (in half cadences) or, seldom, the superdominant (in deceptive cadences).[4] To this initial or final pattern we should add the metrical accent affecting the end of the phrase and the relative length of the terminal note or chord. More generally, metrical and durational accents occur on the tonal chords, whereas the other chords serve as transitions—as hinges—more or less briefly.

---

[4]More precisely, as Chailley and Challan (1947) have shown, "The first assumption is given by the first perfect triad encountered; but this assumption requires confirmation" (p. 74), either by other notes or by the alternation of chords based on notes of the scale. But we might add that this assumption (analogous to the hypothesis involved in the tonal interpretation of a melody) is an index of the acculturation of the ear.

HISTORICAL EVOLUTION
OF THE SENSE OF TONALITY

The quantitative analysis just presented represents a simplified schema of acculturation, deriving from works exemplifying tonal structure in all its rigor. But we are well aware that our own epoch has seen the multiplication of musical systems following the progressive dissolution of tonality. That dissolution itself was preceded by a long period of *expansion* (to use the musicologists' term) during which the underlying foundations of tonal organization preserved their effectiveness, in spite of distortions of tonal relationships. One might thus speak of an evolution of the sense of tonality in that such organization became gradually less and less manifest as efforts at harmonic and melodic invention expanded.

Here again, the analyses of the art historian and the psychologist diverge to some extent. Innovation, for the latter, does not often have remarkable perceptual effects in that it is immediately "comprehensible" to the listener; that is, susceptible of being integrated into the tonal framework. On the contrary, starting from a certain moment in evolution, the relationships that the musical text reveals with the aid of concepts are no longer perceivable by the listener. The listener is plunged into a new world that he tries vainly to order in accordance with his perceptual habits. The tonal sense is in this case entirely contradicted by new modes of formal generation which recieve from other sources the guarantee of history, following a series of erudite parallels that utilize a detour through concepts, without emerging, however, at perceptual analogies. I wish to retrace briefly the ups and downs of the tonal sense through the body of work that followed on romanticism, trying to mark the moment when this contradiction became established in a decisive manner.

The earliest studies I have found on the expansion of the sense of tonality are those of Basevi. As early as 1865 Basevi enunciated the idea of a parallel between the history of harmonic traditions and the evolution of modes of perception for which that history provided the evidence. The deeper and deeper foundations laid by the tonal rules provided composers with the possibility of all sorts of transgressions. But those transgressions were basically only ways of exploiting the latent resources of tonality. The temporal nature of perception permitted delays and anticipations and substitutes for acoustic events that, in the strict tonal system, always occur on time. The ear, accustomed to the sound qualities and ordering of the tonal chords, came to distinguish what was "foreign" to them, what was added out of an interest in ornamentation and coloration—melodic license, "little notes" taken on the beat and then strung out into appoggiaturas resting on chords during part of their duration and resolving during the other part. The ear was not jarred by them; it perceived them in their transitory movement and counted on their rapid passage. Pedal points in all registers, and pedal points in several voices—held notes against which the other parts execute varied motion engendering stronger and stronger dissonances—those must be "understood" in the temporal grouping by imagining their eventual resolution, and not by hearing them as simultaneous and fixed tone clusters. Thus in the example drawn from Haydn in Figure 4.4 the resolution of the A to the G (indicated by Xs in the top part) is long awaited and arrives only after four intermediate notes that attenuate its necessity.

Basevi's (1865) theory consisted of legitimizing these foreign aggregations within the tonal system by conceiving them (and perhaps perceiving them) as transitory; or, in more advanced stages of acculturation (when they no longer carry any effective resolution), by conferring on them potential or imaginary resolutions. In effect, the ultimate stage in the education of the ear, which Basevi called the stage of the "predominance of perception over sensation," is one in which distant resolutions are no longer known. "I mean to consider here," wrote Basevi, "material and perceptible resolutions, since resolutions always exist in our imagination in which, through perception, that tone is generated upon which the dissonance would materially resolve" (p. 46). Thus, consecutive dissonances would be perceived as containing an implicit resolution, since the ear knows the connection that unites the one with the other. Substituted notes, finally, are dissonances that progress by leaps, not leading to the note of resolution but occasionally connecting to another dissonance (see the notes indicatedby Xs in Figure 4.5). These unprepared substitutions at first appear to be errors of copying or of intonation, until they can be grasped (as written notes or sounds) as allusions to other notes that the ear requires in their place.

We have followed Basevi's analyses at some length because of their psychological implications. He was one of the first authors to describe the expansion of tonality, doing that not only as a harmonist but as a psychologist careful to include the perceptual mechanisms governing comprehension of the new works of his time. Of course, the movement to

Figure 4.4. Example of a delay of chord resolution in the melodic line, indicated by Xs in the first violin part. Excerpt from Haydn, Quartet, opus 33, no. 6, Second Movement, measures five and six.

Figure 4.5. Example of "substitute" notes (Xs) in a resolution.

expansion continued on through to dissolution and to the emergence of new systems. Two sorts of tendencies were already apparent in the example given by Basevi.

First, some tendencies contributed little by little to making the usual consonant and dissonant chords on each degree less recognizable through a series of additions of foreign notes. Ninths, elevenths, thirteenths, augmented fifths, chromaticisms, and alterations, employed between 1880 and 1900 by Wagner, Franck, Fauré, Debussy, and Chabrier, constantly enriched the repertoire of harmonies in use. The maximum information in force in this repertoire grew, while redundancy in those works was reduced more and more. Observers were correct in saying that these foreign elements were one after the other *naturalized* and integrated into the stock of sonorities admitted as musical.[5] This did not prevent tonal feeling from being modified little by little by these successive contributions.

Second, other tendencies contributed to blunt expectancies connected with the perception of tone clusters. The ordinal aspects[6] gradually disappeared. The stage described by Basevi is one in which expectancies are satisfied either by substitutions or by the idea of a virtual complement.

In practice, resolutions were seldom avoided, and dissonances seldom led to other dissonances. The habits inherent in tonal syntax remained in their essentials supported in most instances. Chords in irregular progressions (successive seventh and ninth chords, augmented fifths leading to other augmented fifths), losing their constraining character, were able up to a certain point to acquire a symbolic aspect. Indefinite expectancy—movement and unrest—was symbolized by Fauré and Wagner by these sorts of transfers from the syntactic level to the semantic. Even in 1912, successions of dominant sevenths in parallel motion, taken up by Fauré,

---

[5]Cf. Koechlin (1923). The influence of these musicians was above all to "habituate the ear to grasping rather dense clusters. . . . There was as a result a culture of the ear, an advance in auditory perception that proved to be useful" (p. 619).

[6]Cf. Emmanuel (1951): The chords formerly characteristic of a key are no longer destined to establish it, "a chord *in itself* ought to be the focus of attention" (p. 557). And then "the accustomed signals lose their effectiveness in such works" (p. 132–133).

Chausson, and Rousseau, could pass for "exceptional resolutions" (Lenormand, 1912). The violation was not, however, of the ear, but to the mind—or rather of the rules. These resolutions were in fact absences to be supplemented by tonal feeling, grasping the missing complement through its indicators.

The emancipation of dissonance came at the moment when, by their accumulated number and rapid succession, these chords lost their power as signals. Resolutions were no longer thought inasmuch as they were only rarely heard. That stage had already been passed in 1923. As Koechlin (1923) wrote:

> What characterizes the new period is not just that we no longer fear dissonances (as we at times even avidly seek them out), but that certain clusters *previously judged dissonant and 'unresolved' satisfy our musical sense without the least resolution being required; and moreover, they seem to us to be 'at rest' with the same character of stability formerly produced by consonant chords.* (p. 688)

Third, other liberties contributed bit by bit to blunting acquired perceptual reinforcements—the multiplication of cadential formulas, prepared by unusual chords such as that on the third scale degree, without characteristic notes or by an unforeseen return from a key far removed to the initial key. At that point, the ends of phrases took on an imprecise sense; or else the conclusion (when such an idea was unambiguously imposed by melodic and rhythmic means) became for the listener a more extensive concept in harmony than the "classical" cadence. In many cases, final chords ceased to be perfect triads. Sevenths and ninths, unresolved appoggiaturas, and foreign tones of every kind began to color the concluding harmonic signal with a thousand nuances, making the perfect triad lose its particular role. In fact, for educated listeners open to the new ways of proceeding there was a coexistence of two attitudes rather than the maintenance of a single mode of perception for all works (Absil, 1937). Traditional satisfactions were no longer sought in modern music; instead one tried to listen without exactly expecting the anticipated harmonic qualities and sequences. One could accept the style, the epoch, as long as the tonal order left itself ever so slightly discernible. The same remarks apply to the use of modulations, which little by little became more frequent, more rapid, occurring between distant keys. A style prepared by Schubert and fully elaborated by Fauré was based on continual modulation between keys whose triads had no common pivot chord, with the result that most or all of the notes in the chromatic scale occurred within a brief period of time. Fluid syntactic relationships with continually shifting poles— "principal tonalities" to which one is constantly unfaithful and whose course is also cut across with intermediate chromatic harmonies—contributed to changing both the point of view and the course of interpretation. Modulations were perhaps not always identified but could be grasped as passages from one key to another.

This evolution has been well studied, and I will not insist further on these events I have attempted to classify. One of those events was the resurrection of the old church modes in modern music, revived harmonically, although originally they had been used only in monody or polyphony. The assimilation of modes from former French colonies, from American Black music, from the renaissance of national folklores, all contributed continuously to the diversification of syntactic relationships experienced by the ear. But in sundry ways a polar structure for music was preserved, that is, by diverse procedures the preponderance of one pitch among the others was maintained, assuring the presence of a common reference. Tonal interpretation was achieved with difficulty and only approximately, but it was achieved all the same.

THE DISSOLUTION OF THE SENSE OF TONALITY IN VARIOUS CONTEMPORARY SYSTEMS

Since around 1910 composers have defined and put into practice procedures for musical organization that are systematically foreign to tonality. Some of those procedures pertained to tonal material: some departed from the principle of dividing the octave into twelve semitones, pushing that division into 24 or 36 microtones or even smaller intervals; others no longer depended on the phenomena of periodic vibration that had traditionally served to define "musical sound" from a physical point of view (for example, the sound materials constructed by Schaeffer under the name of "dense tones"). The syntactic revolutions preserved intact the tempered material—the twelve semitones in the octave—but organized it in different ways that prevented tonal feeling from operating.

It is difficult to describe all these new techniques precisely in psychological terms. For some of them it is without doubt still premature to consider whether they pose problems. Whether it is a matter of intervals beyond the semitone or of *musique concrète*, their contacts with the public have as yet been too infrequent and restricted for us to be able to determine their effects on the listener except through conjecture. In all these cases we can see what mental activity has given them birth and what is common to all of them: it is a spirit of conceptual generalization, a need to go beyond the limits of the system in force. Exploration grows out of questioning and leads to passing beyond the limits—beyond tonality, beyond single tonalities and diatonicism, beyond the division of the octave into twelve pitches, and finally beyond the exclusive use of periodic sounds. With *musique concrète* we reached, it seems, the pinnacle of this generalization; in the words of J.-E. Marie (1953), Schaeffer "gave the whole universe of sound to music." Among these attempts to go beyond the limits there were some about which the psychologist has something definite to say, namely, those that preserve the 12 tones of our tempered scale while instituting new forms of syntax.

True enough, these techniques were not employed without some theoretical justification that aimed at giving a form of new coherence to musical composition and implicitly offered for comprehension works of a unified style. But—and it is here that difficulties appear—that comprehension was no longer on a perceptual level. The organization was conceptual; it was only but very rarely experienced in audition. The conceptual order no longer gave rise to the perceptual order.

Atonalism was the starting point for all this. It consisted of denying tonal feeling at each instant and as much as possible. Melodically or harmonically, pitches no longer permitted a search for a tonal center in their succession. There are several remarks to be made here:

1. The multiple techniques by which classical harmony had been enriching itself had assured ever new colorations to music because of the underlying permanence of tonal functions. Each innovation remaining within the framework of the tonality had a particular figural quality; it was setting itself off, so to speak, against the sedimentary ground of classical syntax. This is why the harmony of Schumann, of Wagner, and of Debussy immediately acquired a striking individuality, even among moderately educated listeners. The impression of complexity and refinement made by certain harmonies existed only in relation to the tonal framework of discourse. In systematically dissolving that framework, atonality lost the benefit of those relative qualifications and resulted in a nondifferentiation. Melodies whose pitches had lost their functional sense as scale degrees appeared to be merely series of ups and downs, of fluid gestures. Harmony no longer knew the alteration of tension and relaxation except through dynamic effects or through the greater or lesser complexity of tone clusters. The very notion of complexity itself lost its sense, for it had perceptual effects only in relation to "simple"—usual—organization.

For all that, atonalism is seen today as a temporary step leading to other techniques of organization. As J.-E. Marie wrote (1953), "Pure atonality—that is, the abolition of any functional role of a note in a given pattern—seems only to have been a passing phase, providing for the discovery of relations defined in other ways" (p. 71). This entirely negative definition denies all polar structure. It does not go into polytonality either, or into

4. SENSE OF TONALITY 113

the serial technique that, as we shall see, leads to the heart of the contradiction between the conceptual and the perceptual orders.[7]

2. It was, in effect, the search for coherence and unity that was the basis of both orders. But it was a matter of finding out whether coherence and unity in conception and composition would necessarily translate into auditory impressions having corresponding characteristics. In polytonality we have a multipolar mode of generation for simultaneous structures; that is, the composer superposes melodic lines or chords, each of which relates to a different polar center. In certain privileged cases, due to conditions of rhythmic differentiation and tonal distance, it is possible to perceive the simultaneous progress of independent partial forms. But in most cases where such an empirical search has not been tried, the educated listener cannot identify the organization the composer aimed at, for the important reason that, in perception, vertical synthesis occurs at the same time as horizontal synthesis. When they are perceived simultaneously, melodic lines belonging to different tonalities tend to lose their own tonal character. An ear that had developed for structuring sound patterns in terms of a single center of reference and a single tonality common to a whole polyphonic texture, continually vacillates between solutions, one or the other of which is imposed by the piece or by a fragment:

a) One solution involves a centration on one of the lines, "interpreted" according to its tonality, with the other lines constituting a harmonic ground filled with "foreign notes," and the whole pattern forming a succession of unresolved dissonances, appoggiaturas, altered chords, added notes, and so on—the establishment of an equilibrium in terms of one of the lines and its particular tonality. Thus, in the well-known fragment by Milhaud (Figure 4.6) the key of F in the bottom line dominates the key of F# introduced into the upper part beginning in the third measure, in which the notes become interpreted as a function of a center of reference not their own. The interest of this example lies in demonstrating the importance of temporal order in establishing the equilibrium. The first two measures having once imposed the tonality of F, there is a certain anchoring of perception in that tonality, so that the upper line that enters later (that would in isolation be heard in F#) is referred to the initial tonality. The same process sometimes operates in the case of superimposed chords belonging to different keys. One is interpreted in terms of the other in a sort of agglutination of forms that appear independent to the reader, but that simultaneous perception blends into a single, more complex entity

---

[7]This conceptual aspect of musical construction has been well defined by Vial (1952). To say that the concept is here a "pure potentiality of judgment" is quite true, so long as judgments are understood as perceptual judgments. We shall see in the following pages that the ambiguity of this term is the source of certain trends in contemporary music.

Figure 4.6. Example of polytonality with a predominance of one tonality over the other. Excerpt from Milhaud, *Saudades do Brasil*, Botofago.

with respect to one of the tonalities present. Thus in the example of Figure 4.7 from *The Rite of Spring*, a reading of the score discloses the superposition of a Bb major chord and an A seventh chord (the dominant seventh of D). The former is referred in listening to the tonality of the latter, so that one hears a dominant seventh chord in D with three appoggiaturas.

Figure 4.7. Example of polytonality with fusion of one chord in the tonality of the other. Excerpt from Stravinsky, *The Rite of Spring*.

b) In a second solution, the agglutination arising from simultaneity cannot result in tonal predominance, so that perceptual unity remains broken all the way through the fragment or the piece. Conceptual coherence, apparent in reading and analysis, no longer operates on the level of audition—or at the very least becomes transformed via an impression of glistering ambiguity, of refined but arbitrary coloration, which would seem to be the negation of the rigorous intentions inherent in construction. In the example cited in Figure 4.8 from Messiaen's *Epouvante*, we find the superposition of two lines of chords, furnishing in audition a series of complex and unanalyzable forms and, to the reader, a scaffolding of triads

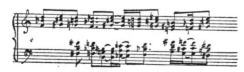

Figure 4.8. Superposition of two chordal lines based on different modes. Excerpt from Messiaen, *Epouvante*.

Figure 4.9. Absorption of middle parts into the tonality suggested by the upper part. Excerpt from Milhaud, Quarter No. 7.

in different tonalities, each of the lines being based on a different "mode with limited transposition." In the example given in Figure 4.9 (from Milhaud's Quartet No. 7) the bass suggests the tonality of Eb, while the first violin is in A and absorbs the middle parts in its tonality.

c) In contrast, in certain much studied conditions, there might be a true polytonality, that is, a perceptible one. Thus, in the example in Figure 4.10 (from Ravel's *Concerto for the Left Hand*) the entry of the brass (in the middle staff) is distinctly heard in G minor over the harmonic and melodic pedal-point on the dominant of D, although the whole pattern could be analyzed as a chord of the minor ninth.

The study of the effects of polytonal constructions is interesting for more than one reason. By varying the characteristics of one of the parts, of one of the chords present, one obtains either the absorption of one tonality in the other, or the abolition of all tonal impression, or the alternate perception of two or more tonalities, or, finally, the simultaneous perception of those tonalities. Among the conditions that determine these phenomena, the most important are without doubt the relative pitch height of the parts or the chords, their degree of rhythmic differentiation, and dynamic and timbral contrasts (cf. Roiha, 1956). It certainly seems, nevertheless, that cases of true polytonality are rare and that we most often encounter constructions of a conceptual order whose structure appeals more to the eye than to the ear. Without doubt we should still admit the

Figure 4.10. Example of perceptible polytonality. Excerpt from Ravel, *Concerto for the Left Hand*.

reality of a dialectic of knowledge and perception, here as in most other domains of music. Each segregation of levels of sound is ameliorated by expectancy—by preparation based on cognition. We distinguish best what we know how to distinguish. Likewise, the mobility of attention and the rapidity of perceptual shifts that come into play here (as in all grasping of structures simultaneously unfolding in time) are functions that develop with age and practice. We were able to show that it is the same with contrapuntal forms (see chapter 7), and it is evident that the same processes come into play in the case of polytonality, with the difference that here the shifts occur between partial structures that must first be placed in some tonality (more difficult than in the case of counterpoint, where they occur between structures belonging to the same tonality). In the first case, it is necessary, through a see-saw motion, to build up sound patterns admitting of distinct centers of reference that must be located, whereas in the second case a unique center is given from the start. With counterpoint, attention shifts among the degrees of a single scale, immediately comprehensible as such. With polytonality, attention shifts among pitches that must be identified as degrees of different scales—that need to be "interpreted" to find their tonal center.

But the contribution of knowledge and practice has limits that can be determined by experiment, and undoubtedly in most cases simultaneous chords or parts belonging to different tonalities produce "field effects" (analogous to those in visual perception) that are practically impervious to the effects of training and reflection.

THE PERCEPTION OF SERIAL MUSIC

Likewise, in the use that serial music makes of the twelve tones, there is a unity and coherence of concept that does not always have a perceptual effect. Of course, one can find examples using 12 tones in works prior to the dodecaphonic school and prior to Wagner, for example in Chopin. But that use, apart from being sporadic, was always integrated into a basically tonal structure, to which it provided an ornament or a chromatic pivot between two tonalities. It was also often reserved for melodic parts, the bass maintaining a functional harmonic line. Even in Wagner, whose chromaticism is often cited to bolster the historical guarantee of dode-caphony, the frequent presence of dominant chords (and dominant sevenths and ninths—even when not accompanied by the resolutions anticipated by classical harmony) assured a sequence of virtual polarities in his harmonic language. The dominant seventh chord, because of its constant association with the tonic that ordinarily follows it, suggests a tonality even by itself, as containing an implicit tonic. In such a case the use of chromaticism is punctuated by familiar sound qualities borrowed from the framework of tonal discourse and that take the place of explicit resolutions. In contrast, the use of 12 tones in dodecaphonic atonalism, by avoiding any combination that could in any way recall a tonality, went to the limit in a way well-designed to disorient listeners accustomed to organizing sound patterns according to the hierarchical polarities previously described. The unity of a work, not being discoverable in syntax, resided solely in its rhetoric—in its rhythmic and thematic patterns.

But one of the most interesting aspects of this evolution is provided by the analysis of serial techniques resulting from the search for a new syntax that grew out of atonalism. The use of a series of 12 tones involves laying out the cycle of tones harmonically or melodically in a fixed order determined by a choice made for each work. This cycle or series of 12 tones can be fragmented, with only a subset of the tones being used, and then another subset or the whole series. It can be used in retrograde (that is, in reverse order beginning with the last note), in inversion (with the direction of intervals reversed), or in retrograde inversion. All these procedures can appear coherent on the level of reflection, and the works that boast their use are the fruit of rigorous elaboration, as analysis shows. A new syntax was born, as conceptually plausible as tonal syntax. But the problem was to find out to what extent this coherence could manifest itself in audition, even after the effort at adaptation required to comprehend any new technique.[8] On this point the theoretical writings of Schoenberg (1949) and his commentators are never very explicit, and one wonders in reading them whether the revolution introduced by serial technique might be more radical than its promoters had ever suspected, in the sense that it took us from a perceptual to a conceptual syntactic unity.[9]

At least this is what the various elements of this syntax lead us to think. Note first of all that the notions of polarity and of hierarchy are replaced here by the notion of order. None of the 12 tones in the series has any more importance than the others. On the contrary, all procedures are avoided that could give them prominence and thereby create an attractive center analogous to a tonic or a dominant. It is the order in which the 12 tones are laid out in the series that forms the basis of syntactic unity in the work. It is intrinsically much more difficult to fix a nonhierarchical series of 12 tones in memory than it is to fix a melody or a chord sequence of 12 elements consisting of functional points of support (that is, a system

---

[8]Roiha (1956) assimilates serial unity to a "form quality" that he thinks difficult to perceive across transformations of the series. "Thus one may conclude that the unifying influence of the serial principle is more theoretical than practical" (p. 61).

[9]Cf. this apt formulation of Schoenberg's (1949): "In music there is no form without logic, and no logic without unity." But the key term, unity, is not defined.

of landmarks common to a whole culture, laid down in the musical experience of the public through a lifetime of learning). Serial works, apart from the division of the octave according to equal temperament, involve no connection at all with the experiences acquired by the listener, since they bring to each work a new ordering of tones. The choice of the series comes first and contains the germ of the style comprising the combinations and sonorities of the work. Its choice is dictated only by considerations peculiar to the work itself and not yet generalized as a form (as, for example, are modes, scales and tonality). The only concern on a general level in the construction of the series is perhaps to avoid anything that might give rise to tonal or modal reminiscences. The choice of a Gregorian mode, of a whole-tone scale, of a tonal system brings into the composition of a work the occurrence of melodic inflections, chords and "standardized" functional periodicities, which in spite of the relaxation and complication of rules brought about by historical evolution, remain typical for the educated listener. One or another of those choices share the stability of social facts—is more or less institutionalized; and the tonal usage that flows from them is free only up to a point. On the contrary, the choice and usage of a series share the unpredictability of individual decisions. They are not limited by any cultural institution, and for artists they manifest that "liberty" in the methods and patterns of thought discussed earlier.[10] That is why, also, those choices are so unlikely to meet the expectations of the public, or at least all those listeners whose experience is tied to structures so socialized as to involve even their syntactic texture.[11]

To grasp the unity of a serial work, the listener needs to acquire a "form" that is new each time—a sort of acculturation, but very different from tonal acculturation. It is not composing with 12 tones rather than 7 (the diatonic scale) that constitutes the originality of the serial procedure. It is creating a system of relationships among the tones, new for each work. When we compare the series from Schoenberg's Opus 25 (Figure 4.11A) with a melody of 12 tones but with tonal polarity (Fig. 4.11B), we can see the degree to which the number of pitches is secondary to the structure of the two patterns, so that the one, unlike the other, makes no appeal to the cultural experience of the subject.

If we now consider the procedures for utilizing the series, is In most cases they do not contribute to the reinforcement of the perceptual unity, in itself fragile, assumed by the series. First of all, harmony in this new

---

[10]Cf. Leibowitz (1949): "The act of composing is involved already in the choice of the initial series. This choice consequently appears linked apriori to the compositional act" (p. 103).

[11]In some very rare exceptions almost tainted (as is the case with the series in Berg's Violin Concerto) with "archaism."

Figure 4.11. Two tone sequences of twelve tones employing all the pitches of the chromatic scale. (A) twelve-tone series from Schoenberg, Suite, opus 25. (B) tonal melody with chromaticism.

technique is entirely dependent on the serial order. Chords and the simultaneous motion of the voices result from the same initial choices as the melody (Leibowitz, 1949). There again, this is a result arising from the "economical" attitude of the founders of the style—a valid attitude on the conceptual level, but one that the facts of experience have not always justified. The harmonic presentation of the series (in simultaneous clusters) is for the ear neither the equivalent nor the analog of its melodic presentation. It is well known that the hearing out of the upper part masks to some extent lower tones given at the same time, so that a given presentation such as in Figure 4.12B is perceptually equivalent to Figure 4.12B', and "recalls" Figure 4.12A only with difficulty. In tonal music, this hearing out (shown to be especially important with less educated subjects) does not fundamentally affect the perception of the underlying harmonies of a given melody, because those are, so to speak, ascertainable as realizations in sound of an already usual functional harmonic line. In certain cases, a detached chord is set off as figure by being unexpected (that is, novel with respect to the usual chords). In contrast, in a series harmonized by itself or by forms derived from it, everything is unexpected; nothing is predictable, nothing can be counted on. Thus the role of hearing out the top part becomes more important, and it is vain to claim to listen for—or to remember from hearing—the nature of such harmony. Whether it consists of a transposition or a retrograde of the series, it is apparent only to the attentive reader.

Figure 4.12. Two presentations of the same twelve-tone series: (A) melodic; (B) harmonic; (B') perceptual equivalent of B. After Schoenberg, Suite, opus 25.

Note among these harmonic difficulties that which results from the fragmented presentation of the inverted series, as in Figure 4.13. There the upper parts give the middle (5–8) and last (9–12) tones of the series; the lower part lays out the first three. This is not an instance of retrograde—we hear tone 4 after having heard tones 5, 6, 7, and 8.

Following this example, one can judge the degree to which the serial order could become a visual order (that is, to participate in the reversibilities proper to space) and to what degree it could be far removed from the requirements of audition. It is the same with procedures such as division (involving presentation of one fragment in the upper part and the other in the bass) and the superposition of several forms of the series (with the straight form and the form in retrograde, for example). Of course, this difficulty becomes practically insoluble in works for large vocal or instrumental ensembles, given the requirement of utilizing only independent parts, that is, of systematically avoiding the doubling of voices in unison or at the octave. In Leibowitz's (1949) masterful analysis of Schoenberg's *Variations for Orchestra*, Opus 31, we seem to reach the limits not only of auditory analysis but those of visual analysis as well.

However, the present aim is not so much to underscore this complexity as to demonstrate the conceptual nature of the new syntax and the intentions that guide the progress of the serial school. Nothing could illustrate this better than the interpretation given in accordance with serial principles of certain tone clusters found in the works of Berg or even of Schoenberg. In Berg's Violin Concerto, already cited, both movements end with chords such as those shown in Figure 4.14A (a minor triad with a major seventh) and in Figure 4.14B (a major triad with a major sixth). Given their long duration, their consecutive repetition, and their arrangement, these chords make themselves understood as tonal conclusions—the addition of a foreign note does not erase the familiar impression they convey. However, on the assumptions of serial analysis, it is necessary to explain them by the logic of serial manipulation. We must understand them as incidental products of the series, ridding our minds of the tonal reminiscences that they almost inevitably invoke. The same idea is illustrated apropos of the superimposed traids found in a passage from Schoenberg's Suite, Opus

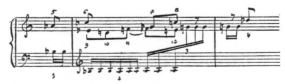

Figure 4.13. Divided presentation of an inverted series, transposed so as to start on Bb. Each part gives a fragment of the series, simultaneously with the others. Excerpt from Schoenberg, Suite, opus 25.

Figure 4.14. Harmonies resulting from the tonal interpretation of a series. Excerpt from Berg, Violin Concerto.

29; but here the case is less clear because of the polytonal architecture by which it is constructed: ". . . The ear grasps these chords, not as super-imposed triads, but as vertical clusters of certain inervals given by the series . . ." (Leibowitz, 1949).[12]

But if conceptual analysis permits us to distinguish what the ear can relate to, it also permits us to relate to what the ear cannot assimilate. This is the case with procedures for utilizing the series, such as transposition, inversion, and retrograde, for which a remote ancestry is claimed—notably that of the polyphonists. Although it is true that these procedures were used within the framework of modal and tonal music, it was in a thematic sense and not a syntactic one. It is themes (that is, formal units indivi-dualized in their melodic or harmonic aspects) that the classical masters subjected to these transformations, taking care that they remained rec-ognizable in some or all of these aspects. The transformation preserved a partial identity of the perceptible thematic unit. We do not find that these masters ever, in harmonizing a melody, used the transposition of its notes presented as chords, in either a direct or retrograde order. Likewise, inver-sion, as used thematically by Bach and Beethoven (with patterns of a small number of notes preserving their rhythmic identity and their situation within the octave), is quite different from serial inversion. One may com-pare, in this regard, an example from Beethoven's Piano Sonata, Opus 110, with another example borrowed from Schoenberg's Suite, Opus 25 (Figure 4.15). Observe to what extent the procedure in the in the former is a vehicle of formal unity and to what extent in the latter that unity remains conceptual and without perceptual effect because of changes in rhythm and modifications of intervals (4–5 being augmented by an octave; 6–7 and 7–8 being diminished by one and two octaves, respectively).

---

[12]The indicative verb "grasps" ought to be, in the present context, replaced by the imperative.

Figure 4.15. Examples of inversion: (A) thematic retrograde (Beethoven, Piano Sonata, opus 110); (B) Serial inversion (Schoenberg, Suite, opus 25).

Therefore, the series is neither a mode, nor a tonality, nor a scale, nor a theme. But serial technique makes use of procedures that have been practiced with one or another of those, due account being taken of complementary requirements and restrictions that assured them of formal effectiveness on a perceptual level. These restrictions are removed in the new technique through a generalization that we have seen to be at the root of many other contemporary elaborations.

EXPERIMENT 6

I decided to submit to experimentation not the possibility of identifying the modes of transformation of a series, but the grasping of its identity across those modes, in connection with the presence of the series itself. It is the latter question and not the former that might be a valid one to raise: If the series is an organizational principle from which flow the formal aspects of the work, it ought to produce a feeling of underlying unity—perhaps just intuitively felt—to the melodies, harmonies, and polyphonic combinations in which it is used. We know that that unity is apparent to the reader, through the inevitable detour of determining the momentary "arrangement" of the series (direct, inverted, retrograde, etc.). It is not legitimate for the listener to take this same detour. Unity may be a global result of the serial order whose partial specifications escape labeling (and perhaps recognition). Since the series is neither a key nor a mode but brings with it a specific unity, there is no way to test that unity with reference to anything else but itself. The only means for an experiment was to ask listeners to distinguish between the unity resulting from one series and the unity resulting from another series.

Method

Materials.   I asked a composer specializing in dodecaphonic serial writing to compose 28 musical examples, of which 24 were on one 12-tone series and four were on a second series (see Figure 4.16). The two series differed only in the order of the last six notes, their initial sections being identical.

Figure 4.16. Series initially presented to subjects: (A) principal series; (B) secondary series.

The aim of the study was not the discrimination between the two series (in which case I would have presented an equal number of examples drawn from each of them), but rather the evaluation of the amount of certitude associated with the more frequently presented series. It was thus *errors of identification of the principal series* (when it was confused with the second) that provided a basis for judging subjective serial unity.

The 28 trials were divided into four categories. The first six trials were pure and simple expositions of the series in its straight version and its inversion and retrograde transformations, transposed and not transposed (Figure 4.17A). The next eight trials introduced rhythmic and melodic differentiation in keeping with the style of serial works, notably the substitution of octave equivalents (Figure 4.17B). In the next seven trials, chords of two or three tones were introduced to verify the persistence of serial unity in harmonic presentation (Figure 4.17C). Finally, the last seven trials were polyphonic, with five written in two linear parts and the other

Figure 4.17. Examples composed on the two series: (A) exposition of series; (B) melodic example; (C) harmonic example; (D) polyphonic example.

two incorporating chords in one of the parts (Fig. 4.17D). Each of these categories included one item composed on the second series. The items in the first three categories each consisted of only the 12 tones of one form of the series; the polyphonic items consisted of one form of the series in each part, with 24 tones in all.

Subjects. The subjects were divided into two groups. The first group consisted of professional musicians having a profound knowledge of serial technique. It included two composers (between 40 and 50 years old), one of them a conservatory professor, who had long finished their studies at the National Conservatory (harmony, counterpoint, fugue) and had been practicing serial technique in some of their works. It also included three young composers (between 22 and 30 years old) who had completed the same course of study and produced several serial works. Finally there were three pianists (between 23 and 35 years old) with a background in composition identical to the others and who had devoted part of their activity to the analysis and interpretation of serial works.

The second group consisted of 27 professional musicians (ages 20 to 24 years) studying to become music teachers in secondary education. All had solid knowledge of solfège (4–10 years) and harmony (2–4 years). But none had had serious technical contact with serial music. This experiment was presented to them by their professor when they completed a course in serial music.

Procedure. After the subjects had filled out individual questionnaires on musical culture, they were told, first, that the experiment had no polemical character; that it was intended only to establish the perceptual facts, and not to promote a critique of the serial system. Second, they were told that the results of each subject would remain secret and that only the group results would be divulged. These two precautions proved useful especially with the first group, with whom an often prolonged discussion of principles was necessary before obtaining their assent.

After explaining in detail the nature of the materials to be presented, the experimenter gave each subject a grid consisting of 28 lines and two columns and asked them to indicate with a cross in the first or second column whether each item seemed to them to belong to the first or second series. Then the subjects listened to each series twice in succession at a slow tempo (one quarter-note per second). After 30 seconds of silence, that operation was repeated, so that the series would be well fixed in memory. Finally, the experimenter presented the 28 trials, announcing each by its trial number. The intertrial intervals were not controlled, and the subjects indicated after each trial when they were ready to hear the next one.

Results and Discussion

Table 4.5 gives the frequencies of *errors of attribution* of the items to the two series for the two groups. The table is divided into four columns dealing with the four types of trial: exposition, melodies, harmonies, and polyphonic examples. Each column is divided in two to show the frequency of errors for items based on the two series.

First let us consider the comparison of frequencies of successes and errors observed for the two groups across the whole experiment. A chi-square test gives a value that does not reach the level of significance that would allow us to consider the two groups as different (chi-square = 3.201, $p < .10$). That is the first important result. The performance of subjects in the first group (who had practiced serial music either as composers or performers) was not clearly superior to that of the musicians in the second group. We can thus consider the results of both groups as indicative of the performance of a single overall population. The last line of Table 4.5 gives the frequencies of errors committed by the 35 subjects along with percentages, which were consistently below 50% only for the first double column (exposition of the series).

In the other columns, the percentages were generally greater than 50%, at least for the examples of the first series. However, in order to evaluate the importance of these errors it was necessary to test the null hypothesis by taking into account the actual numbers of examples of each series within each category. I thus calculated chi-square for each of the four categories, evaluating the apriori proportions of successes and failures using the following formula:

$$(T / 2 \times P) / T$$

where T was the total number of presentations (for example, eight in the

TABLE 4.5
Frequency of Attribution Errors for Examples of the First and the Second Twelve-Tone Series

	Exposition of Series First	Second	Melodic Examples First	Second	Harmonic Examples First	Second	Polyphonic Examples First	Second
Group A (N = 8)	14 (35%)	3 (37,5%)	32 (57,1%)	7 (87,5%)	23 (47,9%)	6 (75%)	30 (62,5%)	5 (62,5%)
Group B (N = 27)	70 (51,8%)	7 (25,9%)	118 (62,4%)	19 (70,3%)	104 (64,1%)	10 (37,3%)	110 (67,9%)	20 (74%)
Combined	84 (48%)	10 (28,6%)	150 (61,2%)	26 (74,3%)	127 (60,5%)	16 (45,7%)	140 (66,7%)	25 (71,4%)

case of the melodic items) and P was the number of presentations belonging to one series or the other (seven and one, respectively, for the melodic items). The results were as follows:

a) **Expositions of the Series.** The frequency of errors was sufficiently lower than that of correct responses to allow us to reject the null hypothesis (chi-square = 6.88, $p < .01$). In other words, the 35 subjects in the total group discriminated between the two series better than would subjects responding randomly. Nevertheless, even in this simple exercise the identification of the first series in its fundamental form produced 48% errors.

b) **Melodic Examples.** Here the frequency of errors was *higher* than that of correct responses to an extent that permitted rejection of the null hypothesis (chi-square = 20.58, $p < .01$). The subjects were thus mistaken more often than subjects responding randomly would have been. The introduction of rhythm and the disjunction of intervals gave the series an aspect that made identification problematic. Notably, the melodies composed on the first series were not attributed to it in 61.2% of the cases.

c) **Harmonic Examples.** The introduction of a few chords perturbed the identification of the series to an equal extent. But here the subjects overall did not commit more errors than did those responding at random (chi-square = 2.98, not significant). This result seems consistent with the remarks made earlier touching on the hearing out of upper parts in a harmonic ensemble.

d) **Polyphonic Examples.** The identification of the series was equally problematic in the case of these examples. The numbers of errors exceeded that of successes in greater proportion than simple random choices would have produced (chi-square = 8.74, $p < .01$). It seems reasonable to suppose that in the present case the interference of two forms of the same series in one example, and the increase in the total number of tones from 12 to 24, introduced special difficulties. Observe, however, that the three preceding categories involved only especially simple "laboratory" constructions and did not include the complex polyphonic texture of serial works (that the examples of this fourth category approached more closely). Incidentally, the pianistic interpretation of these examples was controlled to differentiate the two forms of the series by contrasts of intensity, following a technique in common usage.

The experiment just described without doubt has a reduced impact because of the similarity of the two series and the brevity of the examples. But it sufficiently illuminates the factors outlined in the preceding analysis of serial composition: that serial unity lies more on the conceptual than on the perceptual level; and that when thwarted by melodic motion, rhythm, and the harmonic grouping of tones, it remains very difficult to hear. The modes of transformation (inversion, retrograde) already introduced a diversity that the preceding factors merely increased. An almost infinite possibility of varying a musical idea resulted, and it is that to which contemporary music is dedicated. But the variety attributable to the series itself is not compensated by a sufficient feeling of unity for the connections between one part of the work and another to be always perceptible.

MUSIC NOTATION AS A CONDITION FOR RECENT SYNTACTIC DEVELOPMENTS

We have examined here only some aspects of this movement. True, these are essential aspects, as evidence has shown, but we have examined these only from the angle of syntax. The present generalization had its roots in the purely conceptual manipulation of musical realizations that we have seen at work in polytonalism, as well as in serial atonalism. Formal research into the materials of music (at least up to Debussy and Ravel and not considering its frequent subordination to expressive requirements) aims above all at the elaboration of sound patterns, with the comprehension of a work being based principally on listening—once, or more often in difficult cases—a listening that reading renders more distinct. That research seems to have taken another direction, at least among certain present-day musicians—the arrangement of tones is no longer sought in itself as a perceptible reality. Formal eleaboration is thought of in conceptual terms. And that thought, which carries the whole interest of the work, does not always translate into clear effects in audition. A large part of the treasure dwells "in an absolute domain" where the majority of the public would never dream of looking for it.[13]

How might we, though, conceive of the possibility of so radical a mutation without evoking the behavior that parallel movements in the other arts have gone through? If we examine the case of painting, the dismantling of the representation of space in classical perspective comes to mind as homologous to the dismantling of tonality. This comparison is especially apt in that tonality and perspective each govern specific formal relations in the two arts (cf. Francastel, 1951, and Meyerson, 1953).

Nevertheless, there are exaggerated aspects in the recent evolution of musical syntax that belong peculiarly to it. In substituting a new order for the old one, the activity of painting remained within the limits of a basic

---

[13]According to Leibowitz (1949) it is this thirst for purity, this unshakable resolution to hold composition to an "absolute" domain, cleansed of psychologizing and "aestheticizing" dross, that enables Schoenberg to rediscover the true meaning of all sound construction" (p. 14).

form that is conveyed by the mediation of perceptible phenomenal qualities, without which there would be no artistic product.[14] What, in contrast, permitted music to escape beyond the limits of the perceptual universe is, it seems, the institution of *musical notation*. Originally intended to fix the elements of sound structure on paper, notation played a considerable role in the building up of syntax and rhetoric in the West. Thus was born, little by little, a veritable body of musical thought, whose mobility and combinatory richness were developed for themselves and which became somewhat independent of acoustic reality. Only music could go so far along the road of conceptualization, in a sort of hypertrophy in its use of symbols.

---

[14]Souriau, 1947; 1929, "Form is a perceptual quiddity" (p. 231).

Part II
RHETORIC

Chapter 5

MUSICAL
DISCOURSE

SPECIFICITY OF MUSICAL INTELLIGENCE:
PERCEPTION AND THOUGHT

We have seen, apropos of tonal interpretation, that the integration of tonality into the cultural pattern can be accomplished directly when the notes of a chord or melody explicitly impose the idea of the tonal relationships implanted in the subject (whether or not the tonic is actually expressed). In this case integration is the result of a single focus of attention and arises from a single centration that excites an essentially flexible system of relationships (since many different melodies impose the necessity of a single tonic). It is otherwise when for various reasons this operation cannot be accomplished in one span of attention. The spreading out of tones in time or in different registers, the distortion of diatonic relationships by accidentals, and the like direct the mind to a search that might be pursued through several successive centrations, each of which gives rise to a new hypothesis, until an unequivocal conclusion emerges from the pattern. There is thus a certain number of formal conditions which lead by stages from perception to comprehension.

However, whether mediated or not, tonal integration involves the discovery of a syntactic unity whose essential relationships were defined beforehand. It consists of retrieving an archetype laid down by means of fragmented and variable instances of actual sound. Formal integration, on the contrary, consists in grasping a unity—new within each moment of a work and to some extent unpredictable. Musical invention consists of organizing the parts of a structural pattern according to relationships that reveal themselves in time and that the listener must comprehend in order to remain in control (and not merely to listen passively). Many writers have opposed the active character of composition to the passive character of audition. They were correct insofar as their concept of auditor referred to only one of several categories, namely, those who do not listen or who listen without understanding. We need to make the same distinction if we wish to interpret correctly observations concerning the musical taste of mental defectives and idiots. Dupré and Nathan (1911) described a number of cases in which profound intellectual deficiencies coexisted with a predilection for music, but nothing appeared decisive among their observations. Their subjects were particularly sensitive to rhythmic aspects, which they emphasized by their motor responses, and to timbres, which attracted them with enticing qualities. Their responses were stereotyped. For example, with young Régine F., "the relative preservation of musical faculties contrasted with the profound degree of idiocy. . . . She beat time with her hands all day, and sang continually a song without words. Her voice was in tune and the rhythm fairly exact, but attacks and cadences varied essentially with her momentary moods" (p. 113–116). Another mentally deficient subject "reproduced on the piano melodies she had heard." In none of the cases is there any indication that these mental deficiencies do not prevent the exercise of musical comprehension in its subtle and complex aspects. Observations concerning the effect of mental deficits among musicians are richer in positive conclusions. Legge (1894), who described two cases of composers stricken with general paralysis, indicated that while the patients continued composing, they were incapable of evaluating their own productions or of maintaining unity in them; they left the productions in the same incoherent state in which they had sprung forth. Dupré and Nathan (1911) cite in this regard the cases of two general paralytics, aphasics with serious intellectual deficit. In both, syntactic routines were grossly simplified; accompaniments were invariably reduced to triadic tremolos, for example. The authors note especially the incoherence of pattern, the inability to return to a theme or vary it or to invent a counter-melody. Blondel (1934) reached analogous conclusions drawn from numerous cases of musicians with psychopathological difficulties. Automatic routines functioned in a rudimentary way but were no longer integrated into formal patterns; their productions were banal and incoherent—rhapsodies or structureless jumbles.

In reality, the occurrence of formal integration almost always presupposes some mental activity, depending on the nature of the relationships to be grasped. We encounter here the antithesis between the mediate and the immediate that tonal interpretation demonstrated for us. There are relationships that make themselves felt, as in the repetition or transposition of a musical phrase right after its exposition. And there are relationships that are more difficult to grasp, as in the recurrence of a theme after an interlude or a digression.

Between these two examples we find, raised to a higher power, the antithesis of attention shifts versus perceptual comparisons. Only the latter seems to suppose an act of intelligence, in the sense that it implies that consciousness travels back and forth through the intervening background of sound to achieve an identification. The background is put in parentheses, so to speak, as a result of voluntary inhibition; and if the subject recognizes the theme it is because he has controlled the temporal linkages rather than having been controlled by them. The comprehension of a postponed repetition, characteristic of thematic composition, seems to be an elementary act of musical intelligence that implies reversibility—an imagined return to the earlier instance precipitated by the moment that recalls it. It is the equivalent of a simple identification in arithmetic or geometry arising among elements dispersed in a figure or in the statement of a problem. Here again, it is correct to go beyond the rigid dichotomies of intelligence and perception. The workings of thought, at least in certain of its stages, is always to bring together identical or equivalent signs and forms by running through many mediations. But these signs are also perceptible forms, or else they refer to imaginary forms, to quantitative and qualitative groupings. "Only to the degree that things have form can they serve the workings of intelligence" (Souriau, 1952, p. 77). To discover the partial identity of a theme masked by counterpoint and to find a triangle hidden by other lines in a figure are similar activities.

These aspects of integration reinforce the remarks made by physiologists concerning the quanta or neuronal activity involved in the act of attention and perceptual experience. The number of perceptible elements that can be grasped in one span of attention is extremely small—11 dots in a group, 6 or 8 notes in a melody—as Lashley (1953) has indicated. Undoubtedly there is not an absolute limit here; the spatial arrangement of dots, the tonal and rhythmic arrangement of notes, and the semantic structure of poetry can cause it to vary considerably. Experiments have shown, for example, that counting groups of points in a brief time period becomes clearly more precise with training (Minturn & Reese, 1951). It is not the number of elements that is important here, but the discontinuous manner in which they follow one another (Fraisse, 1956). In mental calculation, in the perception and fixation of a figure or a theme, the organism thus grasps limited groups that follow one another. Yet each element does not correspond to an elementary excitation. Simplicity does not arise from such limitations. Triangles and rosettes can assume this role: "It is not the number of excitations but rather the number of foci of organization that is limited in perception" (Lashley, 1953, p. 430). In the present connection, likewise, one or a few chords, an interval or group of intervals, can be grasped as the result of one centration, can constitute a single quantum of activity. What leads us toward thought is not the number of quanta but the relationships among them. The comprehension of a relationship always presupposes going beyond the given, either by the selection of essential features in a grouping, or by focusing attention on one group among others. This is the place to introduce a notion other than that of the purely additive sum of quanta: namely, that of the dominance of one quantum by another. Thus, Lashley (1953) writes, "While listening to a musical composition the listener can follow the melodic line and abstract it from the instrumental accompaniment" (p. 425–426). This selection can be accomplished only if a certain degree of organization exists objectively in the structures presented to audition; but also, in some complex cases, to the degree that the perceiving subject is led to this mode of selection—if he has experienced analogous types of structure, if his knowledge of the work and of the genre permits the prediction of appearance of themes, and so on. As in other aspects of musical perception, here we encounter components linked to the subject (training, knowledge) and others linked to the sound object, governing the activity of comprehension. We encounter them again in the experiments that follow.

DEFINITION OF MUSICAL RHETORIC

By musical rhetoric I mean those relationships that become established among the parts of a musical work, just as by syntax I meant those that governed the composition of those parts.[1] A theme is composed of tones and a phrase, of words; a work, of themes; a discourse, of phrases. Of course, themes and works present only partial analogies to verbal language. The approximate character of these relationships has often been noted and attributed to a variety of reasons: that thought is external to language; that verbal thought can only designate objects and their relations while musical thought embodies its objects in tones on which it strictly depends; that verbal relationships (at least in nonpoetic discourse), the ordering of propositions, and the succession of phrases are of a logical order, whereas musical "discourse" is of a perceptual order. If there is such a thing as a musical *logic*, it is not to be understood in the same respect as logic pure and simple. Implication and necessity are here on the objective level. They underlie the laws of nature and of society, in this case a formal order, based on convention but produced through artistic freedom (Meyerson, 1948). The relationships of the whole and the parts in a composition depend at once on a generic scheme, on the type of work (sonata, rondo,

---

[1]The former corresponds closely to what Chailley (1951) calls "tonal analysis," and the latter to what he means by "formal analysis." The first "provides and account of the significance of each melodic and harmonic cell in relation to its context (just as logical analysis provides an account of the meaning of words in relation to the phrase) and groups them into tonal phrases." The second "is the equivalent of literary analysis, providing an account of the arrangement of phrases within the pattern of the work; it singles out the themes, and permits us to grasp in them the overall plan and aesthetic intentions . . ." (p. iv).

fantasy), and on the resources of development (new on each occasion) inherent in the themes, in their articulations, and so on. If there is an art of musical discourse, a musical rhetoric, it is not in the same sense that those terms take in connection with the exposition and development of ideas—in verbal discourse. To be sure, in both cases we perceive the organized unfolding in time of wholes in subordinate and coordinate relations: introduction, exposition, development and exploration of inter-relationships, and conclusion. But it is rare that this or that subordination or coordination would be the same in the one domain and in the other. There are easily transferable cases: thus a sonata development may display an affinity to an analysis, but more to an analysis of actual constituents than to a conceptual analysis. The presentation of a theme in terms of its different moments is shown in its articulations, just as a tree-structure analysis might consist of decomposing it into its constituent parts. Likewise the combination of a fugue subject with its countersubject can be taken as a synthesis. But both of those operations can appear in verbal thought in the nonperceptual form of purely conceptual relationships, which are as necessary to thought as the perceptual relationships are to music. A relation such as logical inclusion is foreign to art. It exists only in the order of propositions. Genus and species are sometimes linked by apparent char-acteristics at a certain level in biological classification; but sometimes not, since a hidden link might appear to thought as the result of deeper analysis, without being directly observed. Of course, one might consider all struc-tured mental diversity as form, and say, for example, that each line of reasoning is a form consisting of certain steps—an organization of vectors of thought. From that point, the differences that had been underlined would disappear. We know, for example, that Gestalt psychology sub-sumed under the concept of form, not only the facts of perception but also those of imagination, of memory, in short, every aspect of mental life. It remains true, however, that such representations of mental activities are forms only for the psychologist. They serve as useful schemata, cer-tainly, but schemata construed as abstract concepts standing in for reality. They have nothing in common, it seems, with forms in sound, whose existence can be immediately observed.

One may say that the activities implied in the comprehension of musical rhetoric are connected with those of sensory or sensorimotor intelligence. Twentieth century psychology has contributed to the expansion of the domain of thought in the direction of perceptual organization. Not only is thinking of "events" the source of elaborate activities, but in those activities can be found transposed schemata analogous to the concrete operations of children and animals, yet cleansed of all biological motiva-tion. Mathematics, or better yet, geometry, often involves steps consisting of seeing a group of signs or a figure in terms of an articulation other than that in which it was introduced—of recasting and transforming the given perceptual constellation. It is on this level of thought that we should place what musical comprehension requires in certain cases. But what complexity might not this figural dialectic be capable of attaining with compositions in several parts? For example, how would we evaluate the sum total of operational thought implicated in the comprehension of the *Art of the Fugue*? We can thus speak here of a kind of *geometry in time* to characterize those modes of thought belonging to musical activities.

RHETORIC AND TIME IN MUSIC

Undoubtedly someone will say that such a combining of terms is purely fictive and contradictory. Does it not immobilize what is ceaselessly flowing, and spatialize what exists only in duration? And on the contrary as well, what we know of discontinuous apprehension from attentional focusing and the organization of perceptual groups (or from Lashley's (1953) quanta of activity) prevents us from defining musical time as a continually flowing duration as in the Bergsonian schema. That would be to return to an abstract form of time. There is in perception, and undoubtedly in the reading of music, a succession of acts of apprehension each linked to the next but corresponding to the successive grasping of moments in the structure. Each of them, in making us "comprehend" (in the etymological sense of the term) those moments, lifts us out of the continuous flux. We return to it only to capture the following event in its relation to the preceding, leaping across intervening material when required for the above mentioned comparisons. We shall see later (chapter 10), in connection with the subject of symbolism in music, how we should consider this "pure time," this superstitious vestige of many nostalgic philosophies. It is not pertinent here to enter into discussions of this nature. It is not metaphysical aspects of musical time that I wish to treat here, after work as penetrating as that of Brelet (1947, 1949) that would be to go back over paths already explored. The philosopher can, in effect, reflect on the temporal structure of musical works, on the particular manner in which each of them organizes its different moments into an internal duration. And it is true that then these different manners appear to mirror life experiences having typical characters: one will symbolize a surrender to the flux of Becoming, another the mastery of that Becoming by a constructive will opposed to that surrender. Yet again, there is suppposed to be a struggle between the principle of Becoming and that of Being—"musical time, far from being the pure negation of psychological duration, is the regimen that brings it to its highest power" (Brelet, 1949, vol. 2, p. 425). In brief, the philosophy of musical time leads into an ethic, which, for Brelet, is of a Kantian sort:

certain constructs are conceived as stemming from pure will, from activity, in opposition to others that show us the psychological and pathological side of human nature.

The concept I wish to analyze is necessarily more restricted. Starting with the works and the experience the listener can have had of them, we shall ask what procedures and techniques are applied in their temporal structure and through what psychological processes and activities that structure is recognized in perception. To state the concept, should we say simply: Musical time is that time during which a work is performed? Or should we say alternatively: Musical time, apart from the *event*, is a specific period of time connected to an organization of successive sounds? Clearly, only such a period and such an organization deserve the name of musical time. If music is an art of time, it is not the only one to claim that privilege, which it shares at least with dance and poetry. Our task is thus less to demonstrate the temporal character of music than to describe the specific characteristics of the time intrinsic to it.

This is something to which the experience of the composer seems of little relevance. To the maker of works it does not provide a solution to the problem of continuity between the flow of time he experiences as an individual and that of the object he makes. The latter represents a moment in his life and participates in the particular pulsation inherent in the act of creation. To the extent that (through a sort of projection into the minds of his public) the artist ceases to be actor and producer and participates in the unfolding of his work, the work becomes realized in time according to a specific sequence. At that point, the work passes from a state of conceptual unity, in which virtual time is only implied, to a state of perceptual unity, in which actual time is organized in the present through certain procedures (de Schloezer, 1947) In this projection, the composer thus identifies with a privileged listener who would have full comprehension of the temporal connotations of the smallest morphological details. It is, in effect, through certain given properties of form that the musical work is said to have a temporal *structure*. Of course, everything in it involves succession. But what it is that introduces differences in the succession contributing to the formation of the structure—producing a continuity as well as discontinuities—is of paramount importance for the object of our inquiry. By way of contrast, a break such as the silence intervening between two phrases of a melody is evidently a structural element that can be found in any declamation. We linger there less than on those elements that form the *proprium quid* of musical time, for example, the role played by silence in one of the parts in a polyphonic ensemble.

But do continuity and discontinuity necessarily encounter internal counterparts in the listener, taking into account the listener's psychophysiological constitution? Here we must confront two distinct analyses: on one side there is the temporal structure inherent in the work, implied in its conception; on the other, the temporal structure of activities of the subject brought into the presence of the work. In the meeting of these two structures lies the meat of our problem. We shall see, in the chapters that follow, the purely cognitive aspect in the study of the facts of *recognition* of the *structures d'ensemble*. Before we reach there, we must first see what the present experiment can teach us concerning the global aspect of the relationship, thus defined.

EXPERIMENT 7

The techniques of polygraph recording (despite their present limitations) permitted an objective approach to the conditions of synchronization of the two structures, the effect of musical culture on the organization in time of objective indications of mental and autonomic activity (the latter including respiration, heart rate, and galvanic skin response [GSR], and the effect of voluntary attitudes of the subject on those indications.

1. To grasp the psychological reality of musical rhetoric, it was necessary to abstract it, so to speak, from the cluster of reactions produced by listening to music. In effect, the perceptual contents of music lend themselves with difficulty to being treated as a simple thematic sequence; rather they consist chiefly of successions of quantitatively and qualitatively different events (successive and simultaneous clusters of sound, timbres, rhythms, tempos, intensity changes and contrasts, etc.). I thus sought the physiological concomitants of such successions in the data tracings. In that regard, the synthetic character of polygraph recording was particularly valuable, because we know, especially since the work of Fraisse, Oléron, and Paillard (1953) and Husson et al (1953), that the repercussions of listening to music are to be observed at different levels, involving motor systems and the autonomic nervous system, as well as mental life.

2. From another point of view, we saw the importance of the degree of the subjects' familiarity with the "stimulus," with the various forms, and of their accommodation and conditioning vis-à-vis music. Although of comparable age and intellectual level, the subjects included nonmusicians, music lovers, professional and nonprofessional performers, and music theorists. Though there are, strictly speaking, no individuals deprived of all contact with music, there are yet notable differences between trained musicians and nonmusicians in the ways they apprehend music and its diverse aspects (see

esp. Francès, 1955; Myers, 1927; Ortmann, 1927; Schoen, 1928)—differences that polygraph recording was sensitive enough to reveal.

3. Finally, by means of the experimental situation and the instructions given the listeners, it was possible to introduce among them different perceptual attitudes: passive vs. active, and global vs. analytic, listening. We were thus led to present the same subjects with the same musical works, which they heard once with a "spontaneous" attitude and another time with a discriminating attitude directed at the recognition of certain previously indicated elements.

Method

Recording Techniques

The following experiments, conceived in terms of the foregoing three perspectives, were carried out in 1954–55 at the Electroencephalographic Laboratory of the Clinic for the Mentally Ill and Brain Trauma of the Faculty of Medicine of the University of Paris, using the following recording techniques.

The apparatus used was an Alvar electroencephalograph with eight derived measures. Four channels provided an electroencephalogram (EEG), with the electrodes connected according to a bipolar scheme consisting of the following combinations: (a) frontal median—vertex; (b) vertex—occipital median; (c) occipital—right rolandic; (d) occipital—left rolandic. The fifth channel was used for GSR recording, transcribed by means of an intermittent contact (using the Pessard-Véron method), which avoided distortion of the phenomenon inscribed. Here the GSR appeared as the envelope of the oscillations of the trace corresponding to each contact, the curve reflecting changes in skin resistance with negligible error. The electrodes were placed inside the ankle, below the inside process of the tibia, which left the hands free, as was necessary for the discrimination experiments. The sixth and seventh channels were intended to record, respectively, cardiac rhythm (combining vertex and left leg) and respiration rhythm and amplitude (by means of a thermoelectric system placed at the bottom of a small funnel that collected the subject's expirations. The eighth channel recorded signals emitted by the subject or the experimenter by pressing a button, inscribing them on the moving roll of paper along with the other traces. Thus we could locate not only the beginning and end of each musical fragment, but its larger formal divisions as well—the appearance of those diverse sound elements whose influence on the traces we sought to observe. In the discrimination experiments, which required the indication of those elements to both the experimenter and subject in the course of listening, we connected a second contact to the seventh channel, which did not disturb the general behavior of the electropneumogram, given the brevity of the signal.

A tape recorder was placed in a room next to the laboratory, with its microphone on the laboratory wall near the subject's head. This provided for the recording of all the acoustic messages emitted during the session under conditions closely approximating those of the subject's hearing.

Procedure

The recording sessions took place in a room relatively isolated from exterior noise. The subjects, after being equipped, were seated in a comfortable armchair in the darkened room with their eyes closed (in order to assure optimal conditions for alpha recording). They listened to the music played over a loudspeaker placed 2 meters above the floor. The stimuli were produced by a Barthe record player having a synchronous motor, and whose speed could be frequently controlled by means of a stroboscope, and whose intensity was controlled by means of marks placed on the dial for each piece. The experiment began when the subject, having become accustomed to the experimental situation, declared that he felt no discomfort whatever and was fully attentive. The subject first heard a test recorded by organ, consisting of six isolated tones covering the entire range of pitches used in music (E3, Eb4, G5, A3, Ab2, Gb1), each having a duration of 6 seconds, and separated by silences of an equal duration. Then they heard a series of intervals separated by silences. And finally they heard a third test composed of two harmonic sequences, of which the first contained consonant chords as used in classical writing. The second sequence excluded consonant chords and consisted of very dissonant clusters (five consecutive tones of the chromatic scale, in open distribution) (see chapter 11, Results of the Experiments). This group of tests, lasting 6 minutes in all, was designed to cast light on the types of response of subjects to the different elements of the musical stimuli, in order to facilitate the interpretation of the trace modifications occurring in the course of the following presentations. At the end of each session, the subjects listened again to the recordings made on the tape recorder in the adjacent room, and recollected the memories they retained of their impressions during the preceding listening period.

Musical Material and Subjects

Musical Discourse and Group Differences. To test the hypotheses concerning musical discourse and cultural differences among the listeners, I presented them with a series of six fragments of works belonging to various genres (symbolic music, chamber music, accompanied melodies) in which I had sought a temporal development of different forms of *tension*, clear enough to be perceived by all the subjects, whether musicians or not. This notion of tension, used frequently in the psychology of music, is linked to factors of intensity, pitch level, tempo, rhythm, harmonic texture— alone or combinations of two or several (see chapter 10). In this selection the larger formal divisions were particularly apparent. These considerations justified presenting the pieces to subjects with little or no musical training, on the hypothesis that their grouping structure would be accessible to all. Concerning the necessary motivation for attentive listening, I chose works or fragments that did not exceed 4 minutes in length and of varied nature and characteristics—pieces that could captivate nonmusicians by their free-dom from the arcane, but that had dwelt long in the esteem of musicians. Table 5.1 provides the list of pieces, along with their durations and characteristics.

Forty subjects with a median age of 30 years, 19 women and 21 men, were distributed as follows:

Group A consisted of subjects without any technical training, and having little perceptual experience ($n = 15$).

Group B consisted of amateur performers at a moderate level who had studied an instrument or voice for 5 to 10 years, with a foundation in solfège ($n = 13$).

(*Group C* consisted of professionals in music having more than 10 years training in theory and practice (orchestra directors, composers, virtuosos, etc. ($n = 12$).

Most of the subjects were normal. Fifteen came from Dr. Delay's out-patient clinic at Saint Anne Hospital. Their level of mental functioning and their attentional capacity were assessed by means of an interview that followed the sessions.

Spontaneous vs. Analytic Attitude. To test the hypotheses concerning attitudes, subjects listened to a piano recording of a Fugue by Bach (the Fugue in D Minor from the Chromatic Fantasy and Fugue). This was chosen because of its formal clarity (the principal theme or subject was quite distinct from the accompanying material), and because I had studied it previously in connection with problems related to the segregation of a theme in polyphony (see Francès, 1952, chapter 11). This work was heard the first time in the spontaneous attitude defined earlier and then with instructions to mentally mark the occurrence of the principal theme (sub-ject or response), which the subjects had heard twice initially in isolation so that they could fix it in their memory. When subjects noticed the theme

TABLE 5.1

Musical Works and Their Characteristics Presented in the First Part of
Experiment 7

Composer	Title	Time	Formal Characteristics
1. Franck	"Psyché" from *Psyché & Eros*	3'32	Symphony orchestra. Dynamics of *f* and *ff* for 1'40, then rapid fall of dynamic tension with passage to another theme. Dynamics of *p* and then *pp*.
2. Schubert	Quartet in G (Scherzo)	4'25	String quartet. Agogic and rhythmic contrast: very rapid theme for 1'30; slower melodious interlude (1'32); reprise of first theme (1'20).
3. Ravel	Concerto for the Left Hand (Introduction)	2'59	Symphony orchestra with gradual increase of pitch and intensity going from *pp* to *fff* during 2'13. Brief entry of piano at the end.
4. Bartok	Roumanian Dance No. 4	2'07	String orchestra with solo violin. Slow melody at a *p* level with respise at *mf*.
5. Bartok	Roumanian Dance No. 5	1'28	String orchestra, *f*, emphatic rhythms, agogic cross-rhythms with noticeable acceleration at the end.
6. Schubert	"Der Tod und das Mädchen"	2'32	Female voice with piano accompaniment. Slow introduction, low register, *pp* (34 sec). Then the entrance of the voice: contrast of register and intensity, agogic rhythm (15 sec). Return to first element, with reprise of theme in low vocal register: new contrast.

they were to press the contact connected to the eighth channel of the polygraph. Applying this analytic attitude necessitated our taking diverse precautions. For one thing, we worried that a simple button press might not involve the responses that we wished to treat as evidence for the perceptual activities. We had noted in pilot studies the occurrence of alpha-blocking responses following manipulation of the contact. We therefore asked the listeners to accustom themselves to it for as long as necessary so that it would have no effects on the trace (about 1 to 4 minutes). In those few cases where a doubt persisted concerning the psychological origins of the recorded responses, we verified by asking the subject to mark the occurrence of themes mentally without using the contact. Second, to minimize the examination aspects of these trials, we told subjects that the test did not presuppose technical acculturation in music, that individual results would not be divulged, and that these results were purely of a sensory order and not for the purpose of making qualitative judgments of their personality.

For this research we had in hand the traces of 39 subjects, all normal, with a median age of 34 years (22 men and 17 women). Almost all of them belonged to the categories of amateur performers and professionals defined earlier. Eight were music lovers without musical culture strictly speaking. Since my aim was not to compare the groups, but to assess the effects of the two attitudes, I did not take group differences into account in the statistical analysis. For 21 subjects, the spontaneous attitude preceded the analytic, with the reverse order of conditions for the other 18. These two demigroups were formed with the aim of assessing the effects of the one attitude on the following attitude, especially the effects of the analytic on the spontaneous.

Results and Discussion

Generally speaking, I was less concerned with describing the specifically physiological aspects of the graphs and their probable mechanisms than in finding their psychological significance. In that regard the often noted ambiguity of the elements of EEG and of GSR, or the cardiac and respiratory traces, was effectively cleared up by two means. First, the graphic elements were placed in correspondence with their musical causes by making one or several readings of the trace unrolling at its recording speed (on a table with synchronous drive) along with the music recorded on tape in the course of the experiment. Second, there were the observations in the postexperimental interviews with subjects, in the course of which the subjects' interpretations of the graphic elements could be clarified by their statements concerning the effects produced on them by their musical causes. In connection with each fragment they recalled what they could of the preceding audition, while the experimenter wrote their statements on the tracings.

Analysis of the traces for the first series showed the following results:

1. There was very large individual variability for the different modifications. Concerning EEG rhythms, fluctuations in GSR, cardiac rhythm, and respiratory rhythm and amplitude, one could not statistically predict the occurrence of a response at a given moment in the musical structure, even if one compared traces presenting the same baseline characteristics.

2. Notable was the relatively high number of nonspecific responses, that is, those provoked by nonmusical aspects of the stimulus or of stimulation. Thus, for example (and we shall soon see the elevated

totals), the beginning and end of a piece very often elicited alpha-blocking reactions or GSR responses, a flattening of respiration, or a combination of two or three of them. It was there that manifestations of various discontinuities in the perceptual field could be elicited. Likewise, at certain moments of a development, or even in the midst of a phrase, certain modifications of the trace appeared as consequences of the evocation of an extramusical thought more or less tied to the prior experience of the subject (such as questioning could establish). The same remark could be made concerning moderate respiratory acceleration (16/17 to 17/19 per minute) that very often accompanied the hearing of a piece.

3. Among the specific reactions we can distinguish those that relate to a variety of musical features:

   (a) These effects concerned articulations of form, such as the contrast of a theme and the theme following, a return to a theme after intervening material, or the beginning of a theme after a neutral introduction. In this class were thus musical events associated with thematic construction, that were relatively independent of very apparent sensory changes (such as rhythmic tension and relaxation, dynamic variations, and patterns of timbre).

   (b) Second were effects of formal articulations emphasized by factors on a sensory level that were not specifically musical (whereas those of the preceding class seemed to belong to music *qua* "stimulus"). Here especially were manipulations of vocal timbre, of certain contrasts of intensity, and certain paroxisms of instrumental dynamics.

       Musical events in these two categories were accompanied in certain cases with modifications of alpha rhythms consisting sometimes of suppression and sometimes of a clearly visible depression of that rhythm in which the amplitude diminished by 50% or 75% (blocking reaction, with durations going from 3 to 20 seconds; see Figure 5.1). In other cases the appearance of GSR responses displaying varied shapes and durations (Figures 5.2 and 5.3) can be observed. Quite often EEG and GSR responses appeared conjointly with the theme (Figure 5.3). Brief flattening of the respiratory trace could also be observed coincident with the appearance of a theme (Figure 5.4), a rapid fall in intensity, and the suspension of the melody during a transition. Noteworthy accelerations of respiratory and cardiac rhythms were visible, provoked by agogic rhythms and the

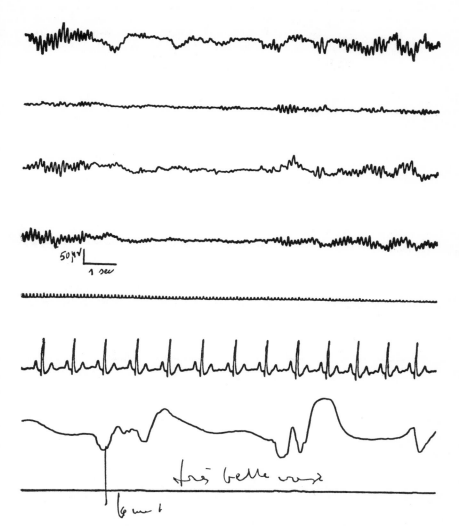

Figure. 5.1. *Alpha blockage following the appearance of a vocal theme* (Piece No. 6). First four lines: EEG derived from the following locations: (1) median frontal—vertex; (2) vertex—median occipital; (3) occipital—right rolandic; (4) occipital—left rolandic. Below: GSR, EKG, respiration, and stimulus marker produced by experimenter.

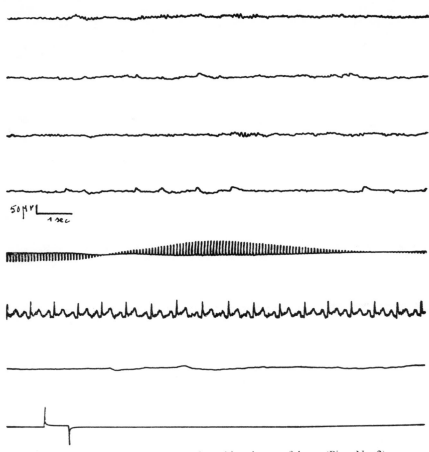

Figure. 5.2. GSR response appearing with a change of theme (Piece No. 2).

rhythm of piece number five (see Table 5.1 and Figure 5.5), along with which alpha blocking and revival, and the appearance of GSR responses, were equally well observed.

(c) Among the specific reactions we can place those due to expression and oveall meaning of the piece, as they were defined in the subjects' statements in either abstract or concrete terms (affective qualities or such general anthropomorphisms as sadness, joy, grandeur; or specific images such as "a forest in September" or "an important event"). There it was not a matter of individual contingent associations, but of judgments of meaning applied directly to the moments of the musical form and found

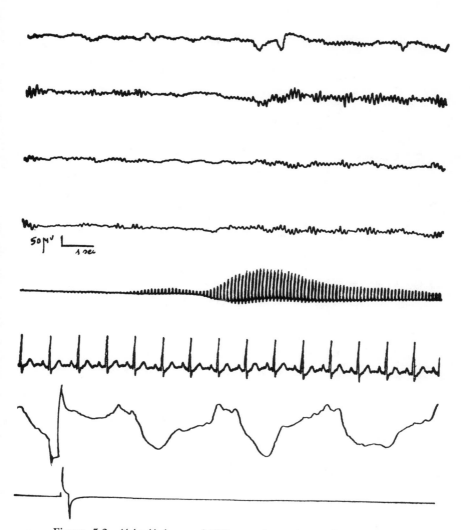

50 μν

1 sec

Figure. 5.3. *Alpha blockage and GSR appearing with recognition of a theme* (Fugue in D Minor, analytic listening). On the last line, recognition response by subject; and superimposed on respiration, the control signal produced by the experimenter.

147

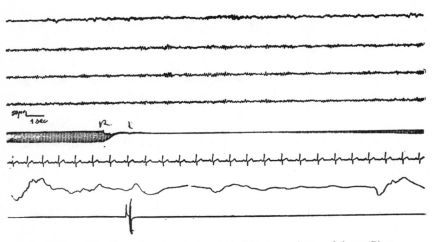

Figure. 5.4. *Flattening of respiratory trace following a change of theme* (Piece No. 1). On the last line, reference signal produced by experimenter.

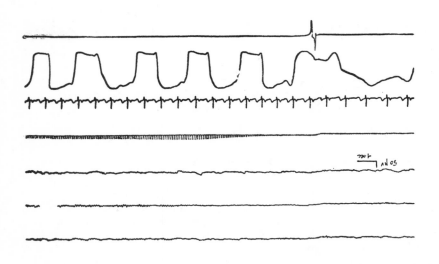

Figure. 5.5. *Acceleration of cardiac and respiratory rhythms at the start of a piece with rapid rhythms* (Piece No. 5). The figure also shows the beginnings of a GSR response and the return of alpha (in the EEG) after some seconds. The alpha blockage before the beginning of the piece (indicated on the last line) was due to the subject's perception of the sound of the stylus on the record.

148

in several subjects (see chapter 8). These were sometimes accompanied by GSR responses of various shapes and by modifications of respiratory rhythms, almost always in the absence of alpha modifications. In a general way these judgments were much more frequent than their autonomic concomitants, at least as far as our techniques permitted us to determine.

These data provide an ensemble of well-established facts that allow us to grasp the perception of music as a global psychophysiological event concerned with mental life as well as with autonomic processes (at times separately and at others together), without it being possible to infer any general rule. That is, *for a well-defined musical structure, there is not a determined physiological behavior, even when (according to the statements of the subjects) the impressions felt were the same among several of them.* For two clearly different sound structures that are well differentiated by the subjects, the responses often remained indistinguishable. The best example in this regard is furnished by the two series of chords presented at the start of the experiment, the one classical and the other ultra-dissonant (see chapter 11).

Differentiation of Cultural Groups

But even if the grouping of facts around structures proves delicate, or in any case arises from individual analyses, it appears much more easily and with greater significance from the perspective of groups of subjects and categories of elements. When we classify the most frequent responses (modifications of alpha rhythm and GSR) according to whether they belong to the *categories* of specific or nonspecific responses previously defined, we obtain a distribution that permits us to differentiate the groups of musicians (amateur performers, group B; and professionals, group C) on the one hand from the nonmusicians (group A) on the other, as well as between the two groups of musicians.

Table 5.2 shows, for groups A, B, and C, the number and mean of the modifications of alpha rhythm and GSR according to whether they were associated with articulations of form, specific moments other than those, or nonspecific moments such as the beginning and ending of the piece. Here we ignore responses occurring at other moments because of the difficulties of interpretation they present, as we have already observed. It is understood, too, that this also ignores the traces of subjects whose alpha was hardly visible, too infrequent, or masked by other rhythms. Table 5.2 suggests the following remarks:

1. The presence of elements of formal articulation and other specifically musical elements is not sufficient to elicit modifications of alpha

TABLE 5.2

Number of Modifications of Alpha Rhythm and of GSR Responses for
Subjects in Groups A, B, and C

*Flat traces from certain subjects and traces masked by other rhythms were eliminated from the
calculations, which has been taken into account in calculating GSRs.*

Groups	Articulations of Form		Other Specific Reactions		Nonspecific Reactions	
	EEG	GSR	EEG	GSR	EEG	GSR
A n = 8 (EEG)	2		9		11	
n = 15 (GSR)		4		10		35
B n = 7 (EEG)	13		22		20	
n = 13 (GSR)		25		25		53
C n = 9 (EEG)	14		22		16	
n = 12 (GSR)		10		17		17

rhythm to the same extent in all groups of subjects. These modifications
were much more frequent with the musicians, for whom alpha blocking
was not simply the sign of a simple discontinuity in the perceptual field,
that discontinuity being almost without effect for the subjects of group
A. In that group the elements in question were undoubtedly perceived,
but not *apperceived* and identified as such. The work of Jasper, Cruikshank,
and Howard (1935) and of Loomis, Harvey and Hobart (1936) concerning visual perception showed that what determined the blocking or
flattening of alpha was the effort—the search—directed at grasping a certain content. Delay (1950; Bertrand, Delay, and Guillain, 1939) has indicated that the effectiveness of the sensory message in modifying EEG is
in large measure subordinate to the mental activities that it brings about.
Finally, Bagchi, (1937) concerning auditory perception, definitely emphasized that the contents—the meanings—of a message lie at the origin of
alpha modifications, more so than do its physical qualities.

Thus, it is necessary to admit the existence of a specific attentional
process in musicians directed spontaneously toward those elements of
formal articulation and other specific features, sensitized to those elements
by analysis and practice of structures of the same type. Such attention can
be detected through the commonplace phenomenon of the alpha-blocking
response, if only one considers it from the perspective of polygraphy.
What is new here, in relation to the works I have just cited, is that here
(at least in the reactions of the first type) the alpha responds not to stimuli
or to interstimulus relationships, but rather to the relationships of relationships (for example, to the contrast between two themes) or to purely
temporal relationships (as in the return of a theme after a long intervening
stretch).

2. The same remarks can be made concerning the occurrence of GSR. For musicians (groups C and especially B) the specifically musical elements were in themselves charged with meaning. The reexposition or the return of a theme appeared to these subjects as emotionally moving events. Here we see a purely playful type of motivation reflected in the GSR.[2] This cultural affectivity does not differ in its manifestations from the affectivity associated with biological motivation. It is distinguished by the causes that trigger it. Thus the flattening of of respiration occurring at the start of a theme or its return was observed only with subjects in groups B and C. That observation leads in the same direction as the preceding one.

3. One can note a decrease between groups B and C in the number of GSRs and to a certain extent also in the number of alpha modifications. This seems to be connected with the predominance in these subjects of a judgmental and critical activity that makes them attentive not only to the slightest imperfections of musical performance, but also to those of recording and playback. Furthermore, in several cases, the composers, or the orchestra directors whom we interviewed appeared to have such sharply defined and exclusive tastes in the matter that it was difficult to satisfy them with a selection of six fragments intended for a broader audience.

Attitudes

Finally, in the second series of experiments I had sought to find evidence for trace modifications resulting from the influence of different psychological attitudes: on one hand, the spontaneous attitude (analogous to that of the preceding experiment) and, on the other, the attitude of searching for a specific sound pattern that had been heard before in isolation, twice in succession, so that the subjects could fix it in memory and recognize it in the course of the piece, where it reappeared on several occasions, either identically repeated or slightly modified.

In the course of experimental work dating from 1950 to 1951, I had explored this domain of the perceptual segregation of themes in polyphony by means of chronometric measures (see chapter 7, Experiment 13). I started out from those results and from the observations made in the experiments of the first series, according to which the recognition of a theme could in certain cases bring about the disappearance of alpha rhythm. The subjects were placed in the testing situation defined earlier. They heard the same fugue twice successively. According to condition, either their task consisted of listening, the only instruction for which was to

---

[2]Lairy-Bounes and Fishgold (1953) showed that those stimuli which produce a blocked reaction more frequently than others are those which have affective content, but they do not specify the nature of that affectivity.

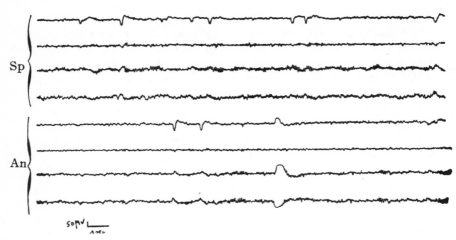

Figure 5.6. In the lower panel (An): *Prolonged flattening of alpha rhythm produced by the recognition of a theme with the analytic attitude* (Fugue in D Minor). The upper panel (Sp) shows the EEG traces for the same listener to the same passage of the Fugue, but with the spontaneous attitude. Note that in general the alpha waves are of lower amplitude and more rare with the analytic attitude than with the spontaneous attitude.

adopt "your habitual attitude" (spontaneous condition); or it consisted of indicating by means of a button press the occurrence of the theme they had heard before (analytic condition).

Here, as in the preceding series, traces were eliminated in which the alpha rhythm was too weak or not clearly enough visible to permit rigorous analysis of its variations in the course of the experiment.[3] Among the individual results, we noted in some a prolonged suppression of alpha with the analytic attitude in comparison with the spontaneous attitude (Figure 5.6). In two cases, this situation lasted for more than 40 seconds with brief episodes of alpha interpolated. In other cases, the analytic attitude brought about GSRs and sometimes a flattening of respiration upon the recognition of the theme, several times in succession. Generally speaking, one could observe through the course of analytic listening a progressive attenuation and even a complete disappearance of alpha modifications, even when the subjects continued to indicate the presentation of themes correctly. There was, without any doubt, a progressive adaptation to the effort of analysis and discrimination. Finally, in several

---

[3]If one refers to the typology established by Davis and Davis (1936) concerning the continuity of alpha waves, one sees that the traces selected correspond to the "alpha dominant" type, that is, presenting that rhythm for more that three-quarters of the total duration during inactivity.

cases the disappearance of alpha preceded the appearance of the theme by 1 or 2 seconds, as if the subject had anticipated that presentation. When this happened there was an episode of strong alpha rhythm that went on decreasing, analogous to the ocular "off effect" (Figure 5.7).

The basis of our statistics[4] was the appearance of blocking responses and flattenings of alpha immediately after the presentation of themes or at some moment during their presentation. Table 5.3 indicates the number of cases of possible recognition, then the number of alpha modifications with the two attitudes, and, for the analytic attitude, the number of actual recognitions. This table suggests the following observations:

1. In the two orders of conditions that we ran, the instructions for the analytic attitude appeared to have greater effects on alpha rhythm (not to mention the effects, more or less sporadic but in some subjects spectacular, that it had on respiratory amplitude and GSR). The number of alpha modifications was clearly superior with analytic listening in comparison with the spontaneous attitude.

2. The differences were significant in the two cases, with, however, a clear decrease of the observed difference in the ratio between the two attitudes according to their succession in time (2.95 when the experiment took place in the order spontaneous-analytic, and 1.36 when it was in the reverse order). We see there the indubitable effect of the persistence of the analytic attitude induced at the start and that the subjects could not abandon during the second part of the experiment when they were asked to.

3. Whatever the order of conditions, with the analytic attitude the total effective recognition of themes was far superior to the concomitant percentage of alpha modifications. *There were thus recognitions that remained without effect on the graphs.*

4. The relationship between the number of alpha modifications and the number of effective recognitions of themes, remarkably constant, was, with the two attitudes, 57.7 and 57.5%. There was no parallelism between the subjective phenomenon of recognition and its EEG manifestations. The clearest differences that we observed in this regard were among the highly trained musicians (notably an eminent organist, the Director of the Conservatory), for whom the study of fugues, and in particular the one that was the object of this

---

[4]It is legitimate to make such a count since in the traces we have been considering the alpha waves occur either in a continuous manner or in zones with their modifications, or blockages coincide in most cases with the presentation of themes, or with erroneous assimilations committed by the subjects and to which they respond as if to effective presentations.

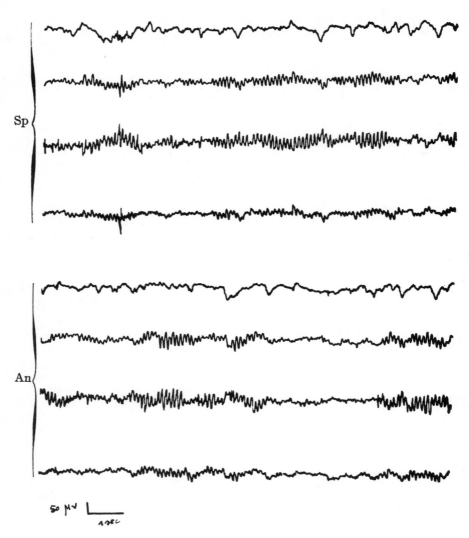

Figure 5.7. In the lower panel (An): *Alpha blockage produced by the recognition of a theme with the analytic attitude* (Fugue in D Minor). The upper panel (Sp) shows the EEG traces for the same listener to the same passage of the Fugue, but with the spontaneous attitude.

TABLE 5.3

Influence of the Analytic Attitude on Modifications of the Alpha Rhythm

The last two columns on the right give the effective number of recognitions and percentage of modifications of alpha relative to that number.

Order of Conditions:	Actual Presenta-tions of theme	Alpha Modifications		Ratio	Chi-Square	Recogni-tions Analytic	Percent Alpha Modifi-cations
		Sponta-neous	Analytic				
Sp-An (18 traces)	182	26 14.2%	78 42.0%	2.95	85.46 p<.001	135	57.7%
An-Sp (21 traces)	169	66 39.6%	92 54.4%	1.37	8.02 p<.01	160	57.5%

experiment, obviated the need for any effort associated with analysis. Facts of this order seemed at first glance incompatible with the preceding remarks concerning the particular sensitization of musicians to the elements of formal articulation. Not so, in my opinion. In the experiments of the first cycle, this sensitivity appeared because of the *unpredictable character* of the formal elements (the structure of the works being less well known, freer, and resting also on a multiplicity of themes). A different level of effort was thus required in the search. In the case of our organist, there was, it seems, a contradiction between the effort demanded by the instructions and the actual ease of the operation (Durup & Fessard, 1935, 1936).

From this group of observations we can draw the following conclusions:

1. Grasped in all its complexity, aesthetic perception appears to us not as a suspension of biological activities, but as a regulating of those activities through the acquisition of cultural attitudes. We have seen that in most cases the perceiving subject is the seat both of mental activity and of autonomic activities concerned with functions such as respiration, cardiac rhythm, and electrical manifestations on the skin. It is incorrect to say that this activity might belong specifically to nonmusicians. More accurately, among nonmusicians these manifestations are disorganized, whereas with musicians, *they tend to accompany the events of musical structure.* Here is a kind of regulation of biological rhythms in terms of the temporal, thematic, and dynamic scheme of the work. Everything happens as if the musician, provided with a focus of attention directed at those elements, had selected them for processing and more or less inhibited the effects of the

rest, Thus, we cannot say that the musician is exempt from non-specific reactions. We can say, though, that the attention of the nonmusician is not spontaneously directed to those elements properly belonging to the nature of the "stimulus"; neither is he incapable of selecting them.

2. We have seen, in the experiment on the fugue, that the effect of instructions can be precisely to induce, to a certain degree, this regulation of biological activity by directing the attention of the subject, thus effectively reducing the disorganized aspect of the autonomic manifestations. But we know that this possibility could be developed fully only after perceptual learning or assiduous practice of music. We shall find here the distinction proposed at the start of this chapter between active listening and passive audition. Surely, what appears along with the application of the analytic attitude in the experiments with fugues is rather the *apperception* of certain formal relationships, that is, their demonstrable actualization in consciousness. But we have already seen how we must understand the relation between this apperception and the simple appearance implicit in a contrast in the perceptual field. All experiments bring into play instructions that disturb to some degree the natural spontaneity of phenomena. But there is continuity between these levels of vigilance. Voluntary attention only brings to light that which exists in a hidden and obscure form in spontaneous attention. And, conversely, the former, with exercise and education, enriches the contents of the latter, as the results in the preceding paragraph indicate.

3. It has been shown that the alpha modifications appear not only when sensory or specifically intellectual activities bring conceptual or mathematical relationships into play, but also when activities intermediate between those two occur, consisting in the discovery of relationships among sensitive patterns—here among series of sound relationships. The apprehension of a similarity or an identity between two melodic shapes, of a periodicity in time, can, especially when a certain threshold of effort is reached, produce alpha blocking. This apprehension is effective even when it does not take place in an empty or neutral field, but in a full, already differentiated field. Then there is inhibition of the effects of the field, and selective action of the element sought after.

4. One can say that the phenomenal contents (that is, the group of subjective events)—insofar as the verbal information or the different signals emitted by the subject give us some idea of them—are much more extensive and richer than their physiological concomitants, at least so far as our present state of technique permits us to detect

them. Alpha modifications in particular lack not only relationship to perceptual qualities, but also numerical relationship to their quantity. This shows us clearly the methodological path that we must pursue in the future. Electrophysiological techniques have taught us that the cognitive aspects of the perception of music ensembles are far from excluding other aspects. The entire organism seems to be engaged in the effects of the sound waves. Even the facts of pure morphology, set, among the professional musicians, autonomic and motor reactions in motion. Furthermore, these facts are not the only ones to give rise to interest and emotion. Timbre, dynamics, the strictly material aspect of the sound field, and induced extramusical associations—all enter into the global resonant structure. Conversely, these techniques give us only a narrow glimpse of the cognitive aspects.

The importance of morphological facts in the total construction, and of the discriminations they imply in the subject, is out of proportion to what the EEG traces indicate, even with the polygraphic correlates. To return to that geometry in time of which we have spoken, it is clear that its different aspects will be revealed to us only with the aid of procedures of another nature.

Chapter 6

PERCEPTION AND LINEAR ORGANIZATION

INFLUENCE OF SYNTACTIC RELATIONSHIPS ON LINEAR ORGANIZATION

The reader may have received from the preceding pages the impression of a trenchant opposition between the relationships of syntax and those of rhetoric. It is true that those two sets of relationships present the psychologist with some essential differences. Syntactic relationships tend to involve automatic processing, at least with regard to a certain phase of music production; rhetoric relationships tend toward free invention. The golden age of tonal music was an age of the development of forms, rather than an age of harmonic revolution. Mozart and Beethoven can be understood in terms of the elementary rules still taught in our textbooks—and Bach to a lesser degree. In the present day, the perspective has been reversed by a surfeit of invention in the syntactic domain.

But we should not underestimate the cohesion that unites the relationships of these two levels: a theme is a series of tonal functions, and a recapitulation takes place in a new tonality that must be grasped as such in order to appreciate the element of novelty introduced. It is the same with modulations that accomplish the transition from one tonal center to another. Certain forms, such as the sonata allegro, require a passage from the initial key to that of the dominant. In polyphony, simultaneous voices continue to form codified harmonic aggregates. In short, perception involves the continual interaction of these two levels, and only the necessities of analysis oblige us to separate them.

Likewise, we cannot speak of *linear* organization without engaging in some abstraction. We have seen that there is no pure melody without understood harmony inasmuch as all melody involves a cycle of scale degrees that imply certain chords. We shall see this in analyzing the various phenomena subjected to experimental control (cadences, melodic transposition, thematic grouping structures). Many musicologists have been right to consider that harmony should be thought of "horizontally," that is, as a simultaneous congeries of melodic lines. Conversely, in the perception of a melody its probable harmonies are implied as a potentiality.

PUNCTUATION OF MUSICAL DISCOURSE: CADENCES

Music appears to us, first of all, as a coherent discourse in which the moments are punctuated by more or less clear suspensions and by conclusions—the former limiting parts of phrases, and the latter whole phrases. This punctuation was codified in classical harmony under the name "cadences," by which is meant "a combination of chords (generally those with roots on the tonic, the dominant, and the subdominant) that indicates that a momentary or final objective has been reached" (Spalding, 1949, p. 63). Among the different types of cadence it is necessary to distinguish the perfect, or final, cadence—a "period" that ends a sentence, based on the opposition of dominant and tonic; the half-cadence, which is thought to be "the equivalent of a semicolon," based on the inverse opposition of tonic to dominant; and the broken cadence, equivalent "to an exclamation point or a question mark," resting on the sequencing of the dominant with a chord other than the tonic, such as that on the sixth degree. This punctuation has not always existed in this rigorous harmonic form. In the monodic music of medieval Europe or in that of other civilizations, it is determined by the simple inflections of the melody. In modern music, at least since Debussy, the underlying harmony no longer conforms to these simple rules.

From the psychological point of view, the nature of cadences appears to be more flexible and extensive than harmonic theory indicates. On one hand, cadences function as *conventional temporal signs* (in the sense that other chord progressions would be capable of providing analogous impressions, as is demonstrated by the evolution of contemporary music). On the other hand, cadences consist of temporal *symbols* insofar as they are affected by melodic and rhythmic characteristics introducing relaxation, suspension, and interruption. (The relative lengthening of a final note is the simplest means to that end.)

The symbolic aspects of cadences, and more generally of "breaths" or "respiration" in musical discourse, appear in the simplest form of what Sachs (1943) called the "two tones style," of which he provided many examples in his works. Thus among the Vedda (pygmoids of the interior region of Ceylon) one can observe a slight relaxation on the final note of the endlessly repeated short phrase (shown in Figure 6.1A), involving an adjustment, it appears, for the necessity of breathing. Further examples confirm the existence of numerous primitive musics without phrases, constructed on a single repeated motive without anything that even remotely resembles a cadence, but with moments of periodic relaxation produced by the relative lengthening of one note among the others (see Fig. 6.1). Note that in the last two examples this repose sometimes occurs on the upper note, sometimes on the lower. It does not seem that in considering melodic respiration we should attribute an exclusive or determining role to descending inflections, contrary to the opinion of Ogden (1924) that "falling inflections" arising from the need for relaxation should lie at the origin of all cadential formulas. We can find in most of the known musics of the world an equal incidence of repose on the upper note of a cadence group, and our own leading-tone-to-tonic relationship is the most typical example of that. Pauses, suspensions, and interruptions can thus be indicated by the relative length of notes in a melody, independently of harmony. The latter, in cadences, constitutes a codification aiming at greater rigor and establishing distinctions of degree between the various kinds of "breath" markings.

It is therefore possible to distinguish two kinds of punctuation in discourse. The first is entirely cultural: in which the temporal signals of harmony, having been learned, are easily interpreted, so that, for example, the suspension inherent in a broken cadence may be discernible from the conclusion of the perfect cadence. The second is more intuitive and deprived of the aid of convention, being based on the varieties of melodic motion in its pauses and interruptions and subject to "misunderstandings" concerning the significance of each of them. Who has not heard these errors of punctuation committed by a nonmusician trying to hum a tune whose notes are remembered, but whose syntax has been distorted because the (actual or implied) harmony has been forgotten or never understood? In this connection, I once happened to hear a phrase of a well-known popular song sung as in Figure 6.2. Pausing for too long on the final note of the first phrase (A) produces an error: because the preceding group of notes virtually consists of a half-cadence, that note indicates a simple suspension,

Figure 6.1. Examples of melodies in the "two-tone" style: (A) chant of the Vedda pygmoids of Ceylon; (B) chant of Toulipang healers, northern Brazil; (C) chant of the Botocudos, eastern Brazil.

Figure 6.2. Erroneous punctuation of a popular French song: (A) end of a phrase constituent; (B) end of the whole phrase.

differing in that sense from the final note (B) marking the end of the phrase.

EXPERIMENT 8

Following this series of experiments utilizing the chronometric method, there will be rigorous discussion of the differences that separate the one and the other syntactic manner of structuring time.

Method

The participants gathered in a room relatively isolated from external noise and were divided into pairs, each consisting of a subject to be tested and a secretary-observer seated face to face across a small table. The observer faced the dial of a chronometer 30 cm in diameter, marking minutes and seconds. The chronometer was synchronous, silent, and visible from all points in the room. The observer noted on a sheet of paper the instant when the subject made a response by pressing the left index finger on the observer's left hand. The subject faced the sound source and did not attend to the chronometer. The subject was to listen to the music with index finger placed on the observer's hand and to react by means of a single or double tactile sign (depending on his judgment of the "suspension" or "conclusion" of a phrase). The chronometer was started at the first note of the piece. The observers, ignoring the music, restricted themselves to writing in two different columns the minutes and seconds at which each signal occurred. The precision attained by this system was of the order of 0.5 sec, which is generally sufficient given the duration of the elements to be recognized.

The subjects responded to the questionnaire already introduced (see chapter 3, Experiment 3) concerning level of musical training and were divided into three homogeneous groups: (A) students of terminal classes at the Lycée who were ignorant of any theory and who had never practiced an instrument or voice; (B) students in the same classes who were amateur performers and who had acquired some idea solfège useful in reading music and sight-reading on an instrument or voice, and who had practiced for between 3 and 10 years; (C) students of an advanced class in Music History at the National Conservatory, all of whom had practiced singing and one or several instruments at an advanced level and who had taken the complete curriculum in solfège, harmony, harmonic analysis, and in some instances counterpoint and fugue. The entire group of subjects was between 18 and 25 years old, with a median of 21 years. The intellectual and cultural level was essentially the same for all three groups, except in music.

Procedure. The choice of musical selection (the first stanza of Schubert's *Ave Maria*, transcribed for violin and piano) was dictated by the following considerations: the melodic shape rests on continuous supporting harmonies whose rhythm and arpeggiated structure excludes the rhythmic differentiations that often stress cadences in classical music. Moreover, the line of the song itself, fairly loud and with long held notes, is devoid of feminine endings, which often give the latter their stereotyped pattern.

The instructions were as follows:

A musical phrase is a group of tones forming a relatively autonomous whole. Like a verbal phrase, it is self-sufficient and has a complete meaning—a beginning and an end, between which various events may unfold. As in the verbal phrase, there can be subordinate groups in the musical phrase—phrase constituents—which require a complement for the meaning to be completed.

Our experiment consists of having you recognize the limits of phrases as well as those of subordinate groups, asking you to indicate them to your observers by a single sign for suspensions (that is, the ends of phrase constituents) and by a double sign for conclusions or ends of phrases.

The work was heard for the first time without chronometry to give the listeners the idea of the whole. Then the experiment proper began.

Results and Discussion

To obtain a global view of the results provided by the three groups, it sufficed to project their chronometric indications on graph paper, with time on the abscissa and the ordinate having a line for each subject. This gave more or less dense clusters of points corresponding to each suspension or conclusion of the phrases, as had been signaled by the subjects. (See Figure 6.3.)

Among the facts that could be established in this way, let us note the existence of "pseudocadences," that is, melodic groups having the weight of cadences although the underlying harmony was not appropriate. (See Figure 6.4.)

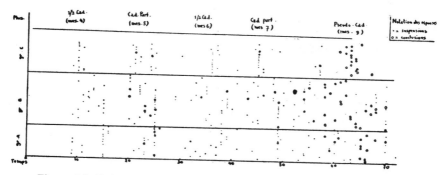

Figure 6.3. Judgments concerning the suspended or conclusive character of cadences and pseudo-cadences by the three groups of subjects. Top line: designation of cadences and pseudo-cadences at specific points in time. Below: judgments of suspension (solid points) or of conclusion (open circles) by the three groups, as they occurred in time. The data points in a given horizontal line correspond to the judgments of a single subject.

Incidentally, in all of the cadences it was clear that the musically educated subjects guided their judgment by the harmonic elements, or sought to do so, without always succeeding so easily. Thus, for example, apropos of the perfect cadences, the frequency of "suspension" judgments (out of 100 judgments) for the different groups of subjects was as shown in Table 6.1.

The great majority of the musically educated subjects (group C) discerned the conclusive sense of these cadences. There was, in contrast, considerable ambiguity in the judgments of subjects with little or no musical training (groups A and B). The other chronometric statistics indicated that the latter subjects waited to evaluate the length of the final note of the phrase before responding, whereas the subjects of group C formulated their judgments at the beginning of that note. Clearly, they were going by the nature of the chord on which it rested.

Nevertheless, whereas the case of perfect cadences provided for the establishment of a marked distinction between musicians and nonmusicians, that of the pseudocadences revealed that the syntactic power of the

Figure 6.4. Example of a pseudocadence from Schubert's *Ave Maria*.

TABLE 6.1

"Suspension" Judgments of Perfect Cadences by the Different
Groups, Expressed as a Percentage of All Judgments

	Group		
Location of Perfect Cadence:	A	B	C
Measures 4–5	28.5	30.4	13.3
Measure 8	33.3	70.0	5.8
Measures 13–14	42.8	28.5	7.1
Mean	34.8	42.9	8.73
Overall Chi-Square:	A–B, p > .05, B–C, p < .01		

Note: Given the weakness of the effects in certain cases for Group C,
the chi-square test was employed on the distribution of the relevant
overall results for the whole piece. Results that might have arisen from
the particular placement of each cadence were thus neglected.

melody had appreciable effects on all the listeners. The sweep of melodic
motion was sometimes sufficient to suggest a suspension and often even
a conclusion to the discourse, without the absence of harmonic signals
being able to prevent it. Table 6.2 indicates in the left-hand part the
percentage of judgments of conclusion or suspension that pseudocadences
gave rise to; and in the right-hand part the frequency of conclusion judgments per 100 judgments.

If the musicians are far from insensitive to the temporal symbols of the
pseudocadences, there is nevertheless among their judgments a relatively
low percentage of judgments of *conclusion*. However, in the whole pattern
the results of group A are closer to those of group C than those of group
B are.

FORMAL SYMBOLS AND CONVENTIONAL
SIGNS IN LINEAR ORGANIZATION

In addition to this metrical learning, there are other, more complex aspects
of cadential symbolism. The analogies between melody and motion—

TABLE 6.2

Occurrence and Syntactic Significance of Pseudo-Cadences According to
Subjects of Different Groups

	Percentage of Judgments for each occurrence			Percentage of "Conclusion" out of total judgments		
Group:						
Location of Pseudo-Cadence:	A	B	C	A	B	C
Measures 7–8	80.0	70.0	30.0	33.3	77.0	20.0
Measure 9	50.0	35.4	55.0	0.0	23.07	0.0
Measure 11	45.0	45.1	75.1	28.5	87.5	15.3

between the movement of pitches and spatial movement—have many times been emphasized (e.g., Helmholtz, 1877/1954; Brelet, 1953). By virtue of a correspondance—not, of course, universal, but constant across various peoples—high and low in space are linked to high and low in pitch; the passage from one to the other is perceived as a lowering and the reverse as a lifting, and both passages taken together as a curve in the state of becoming, with pauses, leaps, attempts, and recurrences (see chapter 10). Whatever their origin might be, high and low sounds are positive psychological givens that play a predominant part in the representation of melody as motion. This representation includes musical rhythm, influenced by the factors of duration, intensity (because intensity accents are different from metric accents), harmony, and pitch. Considered in its unfolding, the form of the motion suggests in its successive moments meanings linked to activities scattered in time. According to the case, the motion is *announced, prepared, accomplished, finished, repeated, resumed, parceled out, amplified, diminished,* etc.

Moreover, once the stage of homophony has been passed, there is a noteworthy action on melodic motion of the polyphonic structures or harmonies that support it. Thus, in an accompanied melody the underlying patterns of the accompaniment emphasize its temporal modalities by symbols of preparation, continuity, and transition. According to their structure, silence in the melodic line is heard as either momentary or final and sketches a temporal articulation defined by the whole pattern. Surely all these symbolic indications are most often based, in classical music, on the temporal signals of the harmony. Thus transitions almost always rest on transitional chords (such as the dominant seventh), or else they contain a note foreign to the tonality we are leaving and that announces the new tonality (a modulating note). But such indicators can also operate by purely symbolic means—through their *structural economy*, as when nonthematic properties contrast with passages that are thematically more dense—simple beats or embellishment, as in Mozart and Schubert, or with repeated notes, as in Chopin. Finally, transitions, as preparations and announcements, can be symbolically determined, as by dynamic factors priming the exposition of a new theme by passing to a different shading; or by rhythmic factors such as the priming of a new rhythm; or by melodic factors as in the sketching of a theme in an introduction where it is given over to the accompanying parts.

By all these remarks on the temporal symbols of syntax we understand the possibility of an organization deprived of the aid of conventional harmonic signals. A nontonal music, without scale functions, modulations, or cadences, can be temporally structured in an effective manner, thanks to cadential *inflections* and to intensive or rhythmic preparations and developments. The abolition of traditional harmonic signals makes a more fully developed elaboration of symbols necessary—a more subtle exploration of

166 FORMAL SYMBOLS AND CONVENTIONAL SIGNS

the domain of the gestural mimicry of melody. And, in fact, it is to these transformations that we must turn in our time when the shattering of tonality has given birth to diverse schools such as atonality, polytonality, dodecaphonism, serial music, and *musique concrète*.

Regarding harmonic *signaling*, of which we have an example in the cadence, in order to define it in all of its extension, it is reasonable to integrate it into functional tonal organization. The tonic plays the role of an attractive pole for all the other tones that depart from it (to one degree or another depending on the interval that they make with it,) to return to, momentarily or permanently, upon the completion of a phrase. The introduction of tonal harmony is the point of departure for significant psychological conditioning. The pole of the tonic and the dominant secondary pole opposed to it are no longer just tones, but chords, whose essential components are the tonic and dominant tones, respectively, but whose other components, as a result of their frequent use with the former in simultaneous combinations, can become substitutes for them. That is why, for example, *mi* and *sol* (the third and fifth degrees), components with *do* (the first degree) in the tonic chord, can be the beginning or the ending notes of a melody and engender the same tonal feeling and the same feeling of completion as the tonic itself. In the listener's experience, consciously or not, *functions* substitute for pitches. Functions, which are in a sense *ordinal concepts*, become capable of being indicated by perceptible global signs—chords or parts of chords, or the notes of a melody. Indeed, in classical harmony, the functions in their mutual relationships are governed by the imperatives of order: the tonic is first, and elsewhere it gives way to the dominant; the latter is prepared by the subdominant or supertonic, and it can in exceptional cases be followed by the superdominant (whence the feeling of surprise inherent in the broken cadence). Psychologically this order of functions constitutes, among subjects educated by analysis and reflection, a primordial acquisition that determines a system of expectancies, of anticipations, of satisfactions and surprises—many temporal intuitions projected on the merest succession of tones. Unquestionably, after certain experimental results this acquisition is also formed in musically uneducated subjects, perhaps with less precision, through their perceptual experience with tonal music.[1]

We have already noted in this connection the research carried out by Teplov (1947) with 7-year-olds who were asked to reproduce vocally and to complete simple melodies. Some of the melodies, ending on the tonic

---

[1]This is illustrated by observations by Lloyd (1954) of a musically illiterate English family whose members performed folksongs in two parts (songs generally heard in homophonic form). The harmonizations essentially preserved tonal functions whose sequencing had been heard in church music.

or on one of the components of the tonic chord, gave the impression of completion; others, ending on other notes, remained suspended, so to speak. The great majority of subjects were able to distinguish the two types of melody and completed those in the second category (see chapter 4). Such tests indicate a feeling for the order of the functions, or at least for the conclusive character of the tonic. Hence the fact that an isolated note, heard as an initial note, is interpreted as tonic. That note immediately suggests, seemingly even to nonmusicians, a system of expectancies for other compatible notes within the suggested tonality. In *modulation* the appearance of foreign notes does not create any incoherence, but does create a determined expectancy, namely that of the new tonality to which those notes belong. Here is the most striking effect of that conventional signaling generated by the experience of tonal functions and of their temporal determinism. The foreign note or chord, not having an assignable function in the present tonality, requires, so to speak, a restructuring that unequivocally calls forth a *foreseeable future*—it is the herald of a new system of reference. In contrast, certain transitory chords, such as the diminished seventh, are ambiguous in that they can lead to several different tonalities.

In classical harmony the interplay of functions creates a system of temporal ordering that underlies all construction.[2] Depending on the style of writing, these signals are arranged in succession under each note of the melody (as in the chorale); or they are more thinly scattered (as in the recitative), leaving the melody greater freedom in the unfolding of its design and intervening to suggest the function momentarily attained or to announce a new tonality. In the procedure of "pedal point," one of the parts (usually the bass) holds the same function over a long period of time while the other parts have a freedom of movement that in no way alters the temporal order, constituting a kind of nonfunctional superstructure supported by a line whose goal is foreseen. The cadenza of a concerto is typical of the significance acquired by the functional order; between the functions of the dominant and the tonic provided by the orchestra is a time lapse, often quite long, during which the soloist performs a series of virtuoso displays that can depart far from the basic tonality without the continuity of the whole being broken, so powerful is the feeling of expectancy for the tonic created by the previous chord in the orchestra.

Thus, the motion of tones and the order of tonal functions are two fundamental temporal aspects of musical punctuation. They coexisted in European music up to the beginning of this century. Since that time, little by little, tonal groups supported by a functional bass have varied in their texture so as to render unrecognizable the chords traditionally used for

---

[2]This part of the exposition is necessarily schematic and notably leaves aside that which concerns passing tones and harmonies.

each function. Moreover, it has become possible to interpose chromatic scale degrees and chords between two functions of the same tonality, and to accelerate the course of modulations and their distance from the original tonality (as in Wagner and Fauré), in such a way that continually deceived expectancies and continually contradicted predictions progressively dull the temporal habits of the listener (as for example by successions of two dominant seventh chords). With Debussy, finally, chords are stripped of their functional values in order to become simple touches of harmonic color without ordinal attributes. Modern music thus proceeds toward a punctuation through motion and symbol, the syntactic forms of the non-tonal systems being unable to assume the role of functions.

MELODIC TRANSPOSITION

The general lesson from this research on cadences has been to demonstrate, in an important aspect of musical discourse, the interference of conventional factors and of such psychologically different factors as motion and respiration. The cadence is at once a signal and a symbol, both elements capable of being dissociated during the history of music. In other words, syntax and rhetoric are linked here. Musical phrases, as forms of completed meaning, would not be perceived as such without some acculturation, at least in the tonal system. The harmonic code, to the degree that it becomes an acquisition unreflectively tied to habituation to tonal structures, is necessarily implicated in the grasping of discourse and its articulations.

This same interference is found in the relationship (conceived as immediate or primitive by the Gestaltists) between sound patterns that is the basis for a supposedly primitive law of perception: melodic transposition (Katz, 1955; Koffka, 1935). The study of this relationship concerns us here because of the role it plays in thematic discourse. After having been exposed at the outset of a piece, the figural unity of tones that constitutes the theme can appear again several times, whether in identical form but transposed into another key or slightly modified in the form of an imitation. In the first case, we have a replica; in the second, a paraphrase.

EXPERIMENT 9

Here I am concerned with demonstrating (a) that the relationship of transposition is not immediately given in perception, notably that to be grasped and differentiated from imitation usually requires the ability to discriminate intervals (and thus a certain degree of implicit analysis) developed by education; (b) that the impression of the identity of two transposed melodic

figures depends on syntax (tonal or not) in terms of which they are construed; (c) that noncultural factors, such as the distance between the registers in which the model and its copy are found, affect the implicit analysis
of interval relationships, rendering assimilation of models and copies easier
and differentiation more difficult; (d) that, in contrast, the simplicity of
the relationships among the notes (whose effects ought to be perceptible
according to the mathematical theories of "simple relationships" (see chapter two)) does not affect transposition to closely related keys, as opposed
to distant keys.

Method

The subjects listened to pairs of melodies consisting of a model followed
by either an exact transposition in another key (or in the same key but in
a higher or lower octave) or an imitation on another degree of the scale—
an imitation that, by the alteration of certain intervals of the model altered
the fine detail of its melodic contour while preserving its rhythm. The
listeners had to decide for each pair whether they heard a transposition
or an imitation.

Procedure. On the basis of the biographical questionnaire on musical
culture described earlier, the subjects were divided into two groups:
(a) musical illiterates and (b) performers. Then the subjects were told of
the conditions of the experiment. They would have to perform 36 operations of discrimination with pairs of stimuli consisting of a melodic model
immediately followed by a transposition or an imitation. The former was
an exact reproduction of the model in a higher or lower register; the latter
was an approximation. The following comparison enabled the nonmusicians to understand these notions better: Suppose a young child wants to
repeat a song that he has just heard from his father's lips. Because of his
physical size, the boy will perform the song in a higher pitch register, but
it will be the *same song*, transposed. There would also be an inverse transposition if the father repeated a melody first sung by the child. In contrast,
it would be an imitation if the model initially heard were altered in the
attempt at reproduction. Even while preserving the respective length of
the notes, the father or child might augment or diminish certain intervals
by mistake so that the new version, though resembling the model, would
not be an exact reproduction.

To familiarize themselves with the sound material, the subjects listened
to four initial pairs whose models were repeated in the same order throughout the experiment. Each subject was supplied with a response sheet having
two columns with rows numbered 1 to 36. The left-hand column bore
the label "transposition," and the right-hand one, "imitation."

Figure 6.5. Models of the four types of melodies presented: (1) and (3), ternary type; (2) and (4), binary type.

Stimuli. The 36 pairs, recorded on the piano, were derived from four types consisting of seven to ten notes, with varied rhythm, and in C major (see Figure 6.5). Two were in binary meters (4/4 and 6/8), and two were in ternary meters (9/8 and 3/4). These four models would each reappear nine times in the same order in the course of the experiment, to be followed either by a transposition or an imitation. The transpositions were presented: (a) two octaves above or below the model; (b) in a closely related key (F major or B major) in the same octave as the model or (c) one octave higher or lower; or (d) in a distant key (F# major or Eb major) in the same octave or (e) one octave removed. The imitations were presented in four homologous conditions: (f) in a closely related key in the same octave or (g) one octave removed; or (h) in a distant key in the same octave or (i) one octave removed. There were thus nine cases to distinguish: five cases of transpositions and four of imitations. The latter were produced on different degrees of the scale, without accidentals, which preserved their tonal character but gave them an altogether different appearance because the tonal function of each note had been modified. It was their final notes especially that had a character distinct from that of the models, since the tonic (expressing completion) was replaced by the supertonic (expression suspension), or vice-versa (see Figure 6.6).

In other cases the dominant of the original major mode was replaced by the tonic of the relative minor (as in Figure 6.7). Briefly, the imitations involved not partial, quantitative transformations of the model melodies (as in the expansion or contraction of one or two intervals), but rather

Figure 6.6. Model and imitation of one of the melodies presented. In the imitation a change of scale degree implies a change of function.

Figure 6.7. Model and imitation involving change of mode.

global transmutations on a cultural level charged with syntactic or affective meaning. They conferred pattern features on the models that allowed them to be distinguished from the exact reproductions—the transpositions.

The 36 trials consisted of four random permutations of the nine transformations, so that two similar cases did not immediately follow one another, except at the boundaries of the permuted series. This order was as follows:

b - g - c - d - f - i - h - e - a-
a - e - h - i - f - d - c - g - b -
b - f - c - h - a - g - d - e - i -
i - e - c - g - a - h - d - f - b

Stimuli were recorded on a vinyl disc and presented at a constant intensity by means of a Barthe Supertone record player with a fixed loudspeaker placed 2 meters above floor level.[3]

Tonality, Atonality and Rhythm. In the course of each session the battery of 36 pairs just described was followed, after a 4-minute pause, by a second battery of equal length constructed on the same principles as the first, with the same melodic types followed with transpositions and imitations presented in the same order. But the second battery was in one condition devoid of rhythmic differentiation (condition TnR) and in another condition devoid of tonal character (AtR). In the TnR condition, the notes of the models and the comparison stimuli were all of equal length, played without accent at a rate such that the total duration of the melody would be perceptibly the same as in the rhythmic version. In the AtR condition, rhythmic differentiation and accent were preserved, but the models and comparisons were altered to exclude as much as possible the tonal character clearly affirmed in the first battery. Of course, given the limited number of notes in each melody, as well as the necessity of preserving the general meldodic contour, this alteration was not always decisive—accidentals could sometimes appear to be chromaticisms or appoggiaturas. In the group of stimuli, however, one can assert (and the

[3]These experiments took place at the Sorbonne (Room S) and in the studio of the Phonetics Institute, under favorable conditions of isolation.

results fully confirmed this assertion) that the tonal structure of the altered battery (AtR) was less clear than that of the tonal battery (TR), which is evident at first glance (see Fig. 6.8).

The sessions of the experiment always consisted of listening to the rhythmic tonal battery (TR), followed or preceded by listening to the nonrhythmic tonal battery (TnR) or the atonal rhythmic battery (AtR). To cancel out the effect of facilitation of any of the batteries arising from being presented in second place, equal numbers of subjects heard the two batteries in reverse order, as follows:

1. TR → TnR, vs. TnR → TR (variation of the rhythmic factor)
2. TR → AtR, vs. AtR → (variation of the tonal factor).

Subjects. This experiment was carried out with subjects aged 23 to 27 years (median = 25), of both sexes, who were students in the year preparatory to the Master's Degree in Psychology. Some were without musical education of any sort (group A); and the others practiced music, having had several years of solfège and having played an instrument for 3 to 8 years (group B).

In the course of each session, once the first battery had been heard the grids on which the results had been marked were removed and replaced with blank grids intended for the second battery, in order to avoid the visual suggestion that the distribution of Xs on the first grid could produce on the second exercise.

Results and Discussion

The results were evaluated by counting as errors every assimilation of a transposition to an imitation, and vice-versa.

Figure 6.8. Alteration of the tonal character of the melodies presented: (A) model and transposition; (B) model and imitation.

Effects of Rhythmic Differentiation. Table 6.3 contains the number of errors committed on batteries TR and TnR; Table 6.4 gives those pertaining to batteries TR and AtR. The distribution of errors was normal for both groups. The comparisons between group means indicated that the differences were invariably significant ($p < .01$) for both batteries TR and TnR. Therefore, *musical education had an influence on the perception of the melodic identity of a model and its transposition.*

The comparison between the means of battery TR and TnR within a given group did not produce a significant difference for the musical illiterates (group A, $t = 0.90$). In contrast, that difference was significant for group B ($t = 3.25$, $p < .01$). However, even in group A the total errors committed with TnR were more than for battery TR. Thus we should posit *a certain effect of rhythm on melodic fixation and, through that, on the discrimination of transpositions and imitations of models,* which is at the basis of the test given to the subjects.

Effects of Tonality. Table 6.4 contains the numerical results bearing on the comparison of the tonal (TR) and atonal (AtR) bateries. The distribution of errors for both groups was normal. The results were as follows:

TABLE 6.3

Number and Distribution of Errors Committed With the Tonal Rhythmic and Nonrhythmic Batteries (TR and TnR)

Series	Order of Presentation	N	Transpositions a	b	c	d	e	Imitations f	g	h	i	Total
GROUP A												
TR	TR–TnR	15	10	22	12	19	16	24	22	15	17	157
	TnR–TR	15	9	19	11	15	12	28	23	18	20	155
	Total	30	19	41	23	34	28	52	45	33	37	312
											mean =	10.4
TnR	TR–Tnr	15	12	25	8	24	10	22	26	18	19	164
	TnR–TR	15	7	22	17	17	16	26	25	18	21	169
	Total	30	19	47	25	41	26	48	51	36	40	333
											mean =	11.1
GROUP B												
TR	TR–TnR	22	4	26	10	17	14	20	16	11	11	129
	TnR–TR	22	6	26	14	17	11	23	26	18	27	168
	Total	44	10	52	24	34	25	43	42	29	38	297
											mean =	6.75
TnR	TR–TnR	22	4	25	8	19	18	31	31	22	13	171
	TnR–TR	22	6	31	14	25	19	22	28	15	21	181
	Total	44	10	56	22	44	37	53	59	37	34	352
											mean =	8.00

TABLE 6.4

Number and Distribution of Errors Committed With The Tonal Rhythmic
and Atonal Rhythmic Batteries (TR and TnR)

Series	Order of Presentation	N	Transpositions					Imitations				Total
			a	b	c	d	e	f	g	h	i	
GROUP A												
TR	TR–AtR	21	9	35	16	38	20	19	37	18	28	220
	AtR–TR	21	10	31	17	33	16	15	27	17	36	202
	Total	42	19	66	33	71	36	34	64	35	64	422
											mean =	10.05
AtR	TR–AtR	21	17	43	16	37	25	27	46	28	42	281
	AtR–TR	21	15	42	18	39	24	17	45	24	35	259
	Total	42	32	85	34	76	49	44	91	52	77	540
											mean =	12.86
GROUP B												
TR	TR–AtR	14	2	14	9	11	9	14	14	12	11	95
	AtR–TR	14	2	12	7	15	13	16	19	9	11	104
	Total	28	4	27	18	26	23	30	34	21	24	199
											mean =	7.11
AtR	TR–AtR	14	9	28	12	18	15	9	21	15	21	148
	AtR–TR	14	7	21	11	19	19	18	17	18	21	147
	Total	28	16	49	23	37	30	27	38	33	42	295
											mean =	10.5

1. Between groups A and B the, differences were significant whatever the nature of the operations. Whether it was a matter of discriminating between tonal or atonal transpositions and imitations (the rhythmic factor being held constant), *musical education always assured a marked advantage to group B*.

2. Within each group, the tonal battery (TR) produced fewer errors than did the atonal battery (AtR). These differences were highly significant for both group A ($t = 4.35$, $p < .01$) and group B ($t = 9.29$, $p < .01$).

To a greater degree perhaps than rhythm, the tonal character of the melodies had an inluence on the fixation of the melodies in memory and on the comparison of the patterns across registers and across keys. But when the tonal structure of a melody was weakened, each of its notes *ceased to be functionally differentiated*, and, as a result, an imitation of that melody ceased to have that qualitatively different character whose presence we had recognized in the imitations of tonal melodies. (For example, the final notes were not clearly perceived as either conclusive or suspensive.)

Imitations in this case were thus difficult to distinguish from transpositions. Transpositions, in their turn, definitely gave a reduced impression of similarity when they were compared to the model because the model itself was not functionally qualified, being merely a series of "ups and downs" signifying neither a modal nor a cadential feeling.

Differentiation and Assimilation. The test given in the four batteries of the experiment called for the assimilation of the transposed melody to the model on one hand, and the differentiation of the model and the various forms of imitation on the other. Tables 6.3 and 6.4 presented the number of errors in the various cases in which the subjects had been performing the two types of operations.

Transpositions to the Octave. We should set aside case *a* (transposition to the double octave), which appears to be especially easy. Indeed, musically speaking, a melody and its transposition to the octave (or double octave) are indistinguishable. The privilege of the octave among the other relationships of tones is well known. Our usual scale is based on the cyclic return of *the same notes* at octave intervals, considered in their frequency relationships as powers of 2 or inverse powers of 2. Partisans of the theory of harmonics explain this privilege by the intensity of the second harmonic, reinforced by harmonics 4 and 8 (and to a lesser degree by harmonic 16). The identity of a melody transposed to the octave is thus supposed to be based on an identity at the physical and physiological level. Listening to a tone or a melody, we hear at once this sound or that melody raised to the octave or to double and triple octaves. Their identity rests on "an unconscious memory" for their previously perceived simultaneity. Although it is true that the subjects recognized the transpositions to the double octave more easily, this difference is decisive only under certain conditions. Table 6.5 shows the percentages of errors committed by the two groups in the case of transpositions to the octave and double octave, and in the other cases of transposition.

From this we can see that:

1. The relationship of the octave was significantly more effective for the subjects in group B than for those of group A. For the two groups I calculated the relationship between the number of errors committed in the other cases of transpositions to the case of transposition to the octave. The comparison of those relationships of frequencies gave a chi-square equal to 3.71 ($p < .05$). It is probable that the threshold of significance would be higher if the comparison had brought into play, in place of subjects of category B (moderate

TABLE 6.5
Distribution of Percentage Errors for the Two Groups on the Four
Batteries

Battery:	Octaves	Group A Transp.	Imit.	Octaves	Group B Transp.	Imit.
TR	15.8	26.2	34.7	5.68	19.17	20.02
TnR	15.8	28.95	36.45	5.68	22.43	25.81
TR	11.3	30.65	29.31	3.57	20.98	24.33
AtR	19.04	36.30	39.28	14.28	31.02	31.35

Note: Battery TR, which out of the necessities of the comparisons were presented to two groups in category A and two groups in category B, provided two different percentages pertaining to errors in the octave condition. This result was undoubtedly due to a difference in sampling between the two groups.

performers), those with a more advanced technical education (category C). In the present case, as shown in Table 6.5 with the tonal series, the superiority of group B was always more marked than for group A. *We can thus assert that the privilege of transposition to the octave, an actual effect for all the subjects, was, however, a function of the musical education of the subjects.*

2. Octave similarity was significantly more effective among the tonal melodies than among the nontonal melodies. In group A the ratio of frequency of errors was 1.91; in group B it was 2.18. Chi-square (calculated on frequencies) attained values off 43.39 and 57.84, respectively ($p < .01$).

The similarity of the transposition to the octave (considered musically to be an identity) was thus doubly relative. It was related to the level of musical culture among the perceptive subjects, and in connection with the melodic patterns it depended on the syntax employed in the construction of the transposed models.

Psychologically this double result should be interpreted thus: The privilege of transposition to the octave, out of all the other cases, arises because the tonic of the model and that of the copy are in a privileged relationship, owing either to the intensity of the second harmonic or to the cyclical character of the diatonic scale.[4] The copy is easily organized around a tonal

---

[4]Révész (1953) proposed that this character is one of the two components of tone perception (the other being tone height). This is what he called "tone quality." While tone height is subject to continuous progression, "tone quality" is subject to a periodic progression in which the size of each cycle is exactly the distance of the octave. These two components are "psychologically blended" in the perception of the tone. But the problem that seems to arise here is that of the origin of this feeling of cyclical periodicity.

center strongly linked to that of the model. Musically, one remains "in the same key." The search for a tonic for the copy is completed as soon as the first intervals are heard. However, that organization is not immediate, because it is to a certain extent due to education. The assimilation of the model to the copy was based, for subjects in group A more often than for those in group B, on a feeling of kinship but not of identity (in that they classified transpositions with imitations).

The dependence of octave similarity on the tonal character of the model and its copy is a new confirmation of the importance of tonality in the perceptual organization of melody. Not only is the model poorly remembered because of difficulties of interpretation and of finding the tonal center, *but the similarity of the components of the copy and those of the model* (all of them in octave relationships) *does not compensate sufficiently for the weakness of the sense of identity of the patterns.* That sense of identity was not easily attained because the immediate memory for the model, itself badly organized, encountered a badly organized perception of the copy.

Influence of Key Distance and of Distances of Register. In the examination of case *a*, the distance of register was considered in its most simple form, because the succession of intervals in the model melody and its copy was identical (transposition) and the beginning note and hence the other notes were situated at a distance of a double octave with respect to those of the model. All the notes in the copy were thus in a 4:1 ratio with those fo the model.

Cases *b* and *c* involved transpositions to tonalities considered to be neighbors by the theory of classical harmony. All the notes of the copy were in a 3:2 or a 4:3 ratio to homologous notes of the model (transpositions to the dominant or subdominant). The same was true of cases *f* and *g*, in which imitations (that is, approximate reproductions) were transposed to the neighboring keys of the dominant and subdominant.

In contrast, cases *d* and *e* (like cases *h* and *i*) involved copies in keys considered to be "distant" from those of the models. If we neglect the approximations introduced by tempered tuning, those frequency ratios were 6:5 for the key of Eb and of 45:32 for that of F#.

If the theory of simple integer ratios is exact, we can expect that transpositions to near keys will be significantly easier to recognize than transpositions to distant keys and that imitations will be easier to differentiate when they are transposed to distant keys than to near keys. For in the first case intrinisic differences due to the partial changing of intervals between the melodies would be added to the complexity of the global relationship between the initial pitch of the model and that of the copy. This formulation is reversible, in that one could maintain that the simplicity of this relationship permits a more distinct the perception of the differences. To test these diverse hypotheses

I combined the data of subjects in the same category for battery TR (whether the other battery had been TnR or AtR), so as to obtain a larger group (group A, n = 72; group B, n = 72).

Certain tendencies were already evident with the groups as initially constituted (as in Tables 6.3 and 6.4). The number of errors committed in the recognition of transpositions did not seem to depend on the near or distant nature of the tonality into which the model had been transposed when care was taken to select cases similar with respect to octave distance. It sufficed to compare the number of errors committed in cases *b* and *d*, and then those in cases *c* and *e*, in order to see that those differed much less than cases *b* and *c* and cases *d* and *e* (in which octave distance varied but not key distance).

Of the two sources of variation just described, we needed to know if either or both was significant and also if their interaction was significant. I therefore estimated the variance of the two factors for the batteries TR and AtR and the two groups A and B, for transpositions and imitations.

Examination of the eight tables of the analyses of variance[5] showed clearly the following results.

1. Whatever the group of subjects and whatever the battery, proximity or distance of tonality did not introduce significant differences in either the assimilation of transpositions or the differentiation of imitations.

2. Whatever the group considered, and for both tonal and nontonal batteries, changing the octave distance was always a significant factor (except in one case, undoubtedly because of the small number of subjects). There were always more errors of assimilation when transpositions were presented in the same register as the models and always fewer errors when they were presented in another register. Concerning differentiation of imitations with respect to models the situation was reversed. There were always more errors when imitations were presented in a register different from that of the model and always fewer errors when the register was the same.

3. The interaction of these two sources of variance was significant in only two out of eight cases.

The first and second observations are complementary and appear to support the same law of perception: *Distance of register facilitates the assimilation of a model with its copy. If that copy is a transposition its similarity to the model is more apparent. If it is an imitation, it is more difficult to distinguish*

---

[5]I have not presented these tables here in order to avoid overburdening the text.

from the model. Indeed, distance of register, in breaking the continuity of melodic synthesis, disrupts the system of reference that the model evoked. When the comparison occurs in the same register, there is a persistence of the tonal reference induced by the model. Because of that—a kind of agglutination of the model and its copy—the notes of the latter were perceived in the tonality that had just been suggested, which did not allow the listener to make an immediate displacement of the tonal center. Hence the impression of dissimilarity of the model and its copy, justified when an imitation was involved. This impression was strengthened in the case of an imitation, thought it did not cease to operate in the case of transpositions. In contrast, this strengthening disappeared with an increase in octave separation, leading to a very great increase in the difficulty of recognizing imitations.

PERVASIVE THEMATIC STRUCTURES

The study of transposition makes it clear that the expression "geometry in time" that was provisionally adopted in the preceding chapter was merely a useful approximation for describing the relationships inherent in music rhetoric. We come to realize, too, that external influences on *present* figural units operate in the perception of an apparently simple identity of appearance, comparable to that of spatial figures when they are not just "similar" but "equivalent" (since the duration of intervallic segments was equal in the models and their copies).

Moreover, to these influences it is undoubtedly necessary to add those of the perceptual field lying between presentations of the two figures. One cannot speak of thematic relationships, of transformations, or of groups of transformations without taking into account the fact that all of them are essentially different in the concept of what they are in time, integrated into a piece, where they must be *perceived* among numerous others. Thus among these relationships Servien (1953) distinguishes *translation* in time (postponed repetition) or along the scale (imitation or transposition), *symmetries* (inversion and retrograde imitation), and *homothetics* (augmentation and diminution in time, or change of tempo). We might add several other types of relationship—the list is not complete—such as the *analytic expansion* found in the development of themes in a sonata allegro movement, or *synthetic superposition* as in the combination of a subject and its countersubject. And what should we say of the amplifying variations to be found, for example, in the organ Chorales of Bach or in Beethoven's *Diabelli Variations*? In these the "invariant"—the musical idea—no longer resides under the heading of figural unity, but after having stripped away all the features of its outward appearance—as a kind of thought revealed through sound, an abstraction resting on a melody of functions—serves as an expanded framework in which the edifice initially planned is recognizable only to the mind. Here the psychologist can only limit the field of inquiry to relatively simple cases, to easily definable types of relationships among themes and their successive elaborations.

A good grasp of the opposition that exists between the concept of a thematic structure and its perceptual reality for the listener is afforded by analyzing the experience of the composer and comparing it to that reality. It is easy to see that if in both cases there is organization, it is not in the same sense in each. For the composer or the analyst, the plan of a work deriving from formal relationships among themes and the various voices, and all the accompanying associations that slip in, participates in the *simultaneity* and *reversibility* of apprehension that characterizes reading. The transparency of the partial structures and of the relationships is much greater, and their identification much easier. The results of analysis—the very intimate knowledge that a composer has of his work—are in a strict sense nontemporal, whether they consist of a schema of organization or of what de Schloezer (1947) calls a "concrete idea." They can be conceived in an instantaneous—or nearly instantaneous—retrospective vision. The experience of the listener, however, is irreversible and successive. The listener engages in an initial perceptual activity consisting of the discovery of a structure in the unfolding of a sound event (that is, in the physiognomical relationships among the successive parts of that ongoing event). The schema—the concrete idea—is in this case a product of the listener's reflection on the temporal field in which the work is perceived. The usual adherence of consciousness to the immediate present must be continually broken by the play of memory and expectation, by synthesis of the past and anticipation of the future, so that the perceptual activity can be summed up and expressed in concepts. Common to the experience of analyst and of composer is movement from a conceptual schema, which is not the work itself, to its realization in time; whereas the experience of the listener is characterized by the reverse process. One finds in both cases the convergence of a certain type of knowledge with a specific perceptual activity. But in the case of the listener, the knowledge, being *generic*, must be recognized in the concrete (and more or less specifically individual) contents of the sound. We shall study in turn the nature and role of perceptual activity and of knowledge in the organization of musical discourse.

Perceptual Activity

Setting aside works with purely dramatic or rhapsodic structure, and those that appear athematic in a particularly contemporary way (too recent for us to be able to predict their future development), we should note that many temporal structures in European music, as well as a good part of those of other continents, involve first of all the segregation of a dominant theme (motive, idea) of a plastic nature. Stated at the beginning of the work or after an introduction, presented all at once or in successive stages, repeated immediately or at longer or shorter intervals, the theme either remains the same or undergoes variations that leave intact certain features that allow for its recognition (Lazarus, 1951). This segregation alone permits the the fixation of the idea in memory and its recognition in the course of repetitions, recapitulations, variations, development, and so on.

The field *intermediate* between the different appearances of the principal idea takes on particular importance. It can be completely absent, as in certain iterative forms of Black music and in our strophic songs. It can be occupied by a fixed secondary theme, as in the chorus of songs with verse and chorus and in responsories. It can be occupied by a variable secondary theme, varied with each repetition, as in the rondo and fugue, or capable of being cut up and worked into a development, as in sonata form. Finally, as in great cyclical works, the principal theme can reappear under very different morphological aspects across separate pieces, as in the movements of a sonata or symphony, the different acts of a music drama making use of the *leitmotiv*, or the melodies in a collection.

Thus there are, in the temporal field taken as a whole, moments of unity and moments of diversity, and it is necessary to take into account the following aspects in terms of perceptual apprehension: (a) the relationships existing between the principal idea and its different appearances; (b) the relationships between that idea and those that are interpolated among its different appearances; (c) the relationships established among the interpolated ideas. Thus one can observe all the levels of difficulty to be found among forms of organization, such as A B A or A B A B A B (song, or verse and chorus), in which A and B remain identical; and A B A′ C A/2 D A″/2 (romantic period rondo), in which A reappears in varied form (A′), truncated form (A/2), or varied and truncated form (A″/2) at various times. The diversity that can exist among the interpolated themes (B, C, D) introduces an element of interest that to some extent militates against the recognition of A. There are intermediate fields involving relaxation, in which the significance of the sound patterns or their cultural interest is weak, as well as others that imply a certain tension. In certain fugues of Bach, the interpolated themes in the episodes borrow elements from the beginning of the principal theme (the start of the *subject*), giving for example the following form, A (a + B) A (a′ + C) A (a′ + E) A . . ., in which the principal theme A is composed of (a + b).

In this case recognition implies the *assimilation* of a pattern morphologically derived from the theme, as well as the *discrimination* of a novel element introduced (variation, amplification, or alteration of harmony or rhythm), and the differentiation of everything that does not belong to the theme but serves as a bridge or hinge, or derives from another theme.

EXPERIMENT 10

In the chronometric experiments carried out with musicians and non-musicians, we saw the important role of these two mental processes and the degree of difficulty with which they occurred, depending on the forms of the themes presented, their mode of presentation, and their reciprocal interactions. Uncertainty arose, especially for nonmusicians, from the interference of the two themes in the course of their alternation in time. The theme, as a plastic figural unity, appears first integrally in the course of the exposition and then in the recapitulation, in contrast with another theme. However, in the course of the development, this unity is divided up and spread out in time (so to speak), so that its constituent elements may be seen in detail. There is the consequent necessity of a synthetic apprehension that is possible only on the basis of a preliminary analysis carried out implicitly during the exposition. To recognize that the elements a, a′, a″ belong to A supposes that one has previously discerned that A is composed of a, a′, a″.

To crystalize the ideas on these different points, let us take the Scherzo of Beethoven's *Trio*, op. 97, as an illustration. The principal theme (A), introduced as a solo at the start of the piece, is shown in Figure 6.9. Rhythmically well structured, and with a frankly tonal outline, its form is stronger than that of the secondary theme (B—Figure 6.10), which has little breadth and a chromatic pattern that does not clearly impose a tonality. The secondary theme extends in one piece over eight measures; the principal theme is divided into two symmetrical wings of four measures each.

To comprehend the temporal structure of the work as a whole, we should:

Figure 6.9. Principal theme from Beethoven's Trio, op. 97, *Scherzo*.

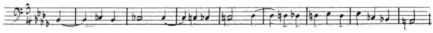

Figure 6.10. Secondary theme from Beethoven's Trio, op. 97, *Scherzo*.

Figure 6.11. Incidental episode from Beethoven's Trio, op. 97, *Scherzo*.

- *First,* isolate the themes as fundamental figural units, as poles of the structure;

- *Second,* recognize when they reappear in identical form or simply transposed;

- *Third,* differentiate them from one another across their alternations in the work, and differentiate the accessory episodes that serve as bridges, transitions, etc., as in Figure 6.11.

- *Fourth,* assimilate to them the different variations and mutations that occur in the course of their development (Fig. 6.12a and b), in spite of changes in instrumental timbre, the combination of A with a countersubject (Fig. 6.12c), the inversion of B (Fig. 6.12d), or its contraction involving a rhythmic change (Fig. 6.12e)—assimilations that involve distinguishing novelty amidst similarity:

- *Fifth,* synthesize the stages of a development; that is, subsume in the same morphological unity a diffused diversity, in such a way as to comprehend that it constitutes one of the major divisions of the work.

To grasp the temporal structure as a whole is to grasp the relationships among the musical events that make it up. If those relationships are of a morphological nature, it is necessary to discern them as such in order to

Figure 6.12. Development of the two themes from Beethoven's Trio, op. 97, *Scherzo*: (a) and (b), mutations of the principal theme; (c) polyphonic additions to that theme; (d) and (e), mutations of the secondary theme.

comprehend the structure. Such are the difficulties that uneducated perception encounters that they can produce the impression of *incoherence*
(through lack of assimilation), of *dispersion* (through lack of analysis and
synthesis), and of excessive *uniformity* (through lack of discrimination and
differentiation).

Method

Procedure.   The experiment took place under the same technical conditions described above for the chronometric research on cadences
(Experiment B). The subjects tested had to follow the following instructions:

> A piece of music is composed according to a certain plan, just as a speech
> is. Ideas are presented (sometimes after an introduction), developed, repeated,
> and they are sometimes separated by transitions, etc. But in contrast to
> verbal discourse, in which the relationships among introduction, exposition,
> and development are logical relationships, in musical discourse the relation-
> ships are purely ones of physiognomy; that is, they reside in the properties
> of the sound patterns observable in perception.
>
> The piece you are going to hear is based on two principal ideas (A and
> B) that are easy to distinguish because of their contrasting shapes. A is
> initially presented and developed by the three instruments, which play it
> sometimes identically, sometimes with variations and transformations that
> are often considerable. Then B is presented and subjected to analogous
> treatment, with intervention of several transitions. Then they return to A.
> Finally, the piece ends with brief allusions to A and B.
>
> There are thus two principal ideas in the work you are about to hear,
> each of which forms a family as a result of the numerous thematic elements
> that resemble them. Please observe, in the course of the first hearing, the
> existence of the two thematic families, as well as to distinguish their phy-
> siognomy and to discern everything that derives closely or distantly from A
> or B. Then in the course of a second hearing, please indicate to your observers
> the occurrence of A and B, and the thematic elements that seem to you to
> relate to one or the other of those ideas. To do that, plese employ the
> following code: For A and its dependents, a single touch signal; For B and
> its dependents, a double touch signal.

Those were the instructions for the "guided method." The subjects,
alerted to the exclusive presence of the two ideas and of their disposition
in time, did not have to bring any *knowledge* to the situation. Under these
conditions there should have been no advantage for the musicians pos-
sessing that knowledge. Perceptual activity was organized in an identical
manner for the subjects in the three groups, by the schema indicated in
the instructions. We shall see the importance of the schema from a parallel

TABLE 6.6
Recognition of Themes by the Three Groups (Proportionate
Recognitions for 100 Subjects)

Groups: Location of Theme or Element:	A N = 18	B N = 23	C N = 20
Principal Theme			
Measures 9–125	489	410	770
— 287–411	520	420	715
— 435–438 (coda)	40	56	80
Total:	1049	886	1565
Secondary Theme			
Measures 126–159	111	153	310
— 182–194	56	49	138
— 218–256	105	114	250
— 412–434	35	75	172
Total:	307	391	870

experiment conducted according to the "nonguided method," apparent in the difficulty encountered by the nonmusicians in separating the two principal ideas from the pattern of the work (Experiment 11).

Results and Discussion

The quantitative results showed the influence of musical education on the *assimilation* of the thematic elements to the principal idea and on the *differentiation* of the two ideas and their dependents, as well as the influence of the formal structure of the respective ideas on those processes, the one theme being a stronger pattern than the other.

Table 6.6 demonstrates that the number of thematic elements indicated as deriving from idea A and from idea B was always superior for group C (conservatory students of age 17 to 20) compared with groups A (nonmusician *lycée* students of the same age) and B (*lycée* students of the same age who had practiced music for between 3 and 8 years).

Table 6.7 shows the relative difficulty with which the secondary theme (B) was recognized by nonmusicians and subjects with moderate training. The first column indicates the number of errors normalized for groups of N = 100. By error is meant that certain subjects signaled the presence of a theme at moments when neither it nor any elements derived from it appeared. The next two columns indicate the mean of the differences between the incidence of errors for the two themes for each subject,[6]

---

[6]These differences were obtained for each subject by subtracting the number of errors committed from the number of recognitions of theme A and of theme B.

186   EXPERIMENT 10

TABLE 6.7
Relative Difficulty of the Two Themes for Subjects in the Three Groups

Group:	Theme: A	B	Mean of the Differences	t
A	194	183	2.249	6.92 ($p < .01$)
B	155	260	1.638	3.50 ($p < .01$)
C	50	0	0.581	0.31 (n.s.)

Total Errors per 100 Subjects (spanning columns A and B)

normally distributed in all three groups, and the corresponding value of
t. The strength of the secondary theme was much lower than that of the
principal theme for subjects of groups A and B, but not for the group of
musicians.

Knowledge

The preceding analyses one may appear to make explicit knowledge an
indispensible condition for grasping the temporal organization of music.
Indeed, in order to explicate the processes of perceptual activity, it was
necessary to have recourse to the concepts in use in the technical analysis
of works. However, as Combarieu (1907) has noted, it is one thing to
know what an imitation is in general terms, but quite another to comprehend one in a particular instance, as in partial melodic identity. The
operative musical concepts desginate the types of transformation of structures having perceptible effects—transformations based on the types of
relationships defined: transposition, modulation, variation, imitation.
Combarieu's critique consists of pointing out that musical comprehension
supposes only the perception of particular effects of those transformations,
independently of all abstract conceptual translation, without explicit reference to the general procedure from which they derive.

But one may wonder whether perception in a particular case might not
be aided by general knowledge; whether the perception of musical forms,
seemingly immediate, might not receive the support of technical know-
how; whether, among the different modes of perceptual activity under
discussion, the significant advantage of subjects in group C (parallel to
that observed in many other experiments) might not have been attributable
to the intervention of that knowledge. On the whole, the problem is to
grasp, in each of its modes, how and to what extent this combination of
knowledge and perceptual organization comes about.

Already, in the simple fixation of a melody in immediate memory, we
were able to see in operation the effects of a certain acculturation or seeding

of tonality and tonal functions, acquired prior to any conscious education and simply through repeated hearing of tonal forms, as well as the effects of conscious education added to them. In that same case, it was remarkable that the automatic processes created by conceptual analysis could operate while yet remaining entirely implicit. Knowledge of labels of tonal functions, intervals, and notes, which the musician subjects acquired through the practice of solfège, does not entail that they should be associated in the course of these experiments with the corresponding tonal elements. But everything happened as if the practice of those associations had facilitated the fixation of melodies in memory. It cannot be doubted, *a fortiori*, that the memory fixation of a theme—a melodic-harmonic unit in which tonal functions are specified by the harmony—benefits under the same conditions from the support of technical education. In a genre such as Theme and Variations, in most instances of which thematic unity (in melodic or rhythmic form) is hardly maintained, it is the succession of harmonic functions remaining constant through the course of the variations that permits the listener to uncover that unity underlying an apparent diversity and to structure the work in its totality. That succession, to be clearly discerned and fixed in memory, must be based at least on the *qualities of relationships* rendered familiar by repeated hearing of functional sequences of the same type. In that case, the harmonic support for the theme, subsisting underneath the melodic and rhythmic changes brought about by the variations, is actually a *melody of functions* to which all that we have said above concerning melodies applies.

In the detail of perceptual activity, assimilation is naturally guided by the concept of the group of transformations in which the particular given cases are arrayed. The growth of the feeling of similarity depends on the prior subsumption of that case under the concept (of variation, imitation, etc.). The untrained subjects generally perceived only close similarities, those preserving rhythm and direction of melodic contour. When the theme was augmented or inverted, assimilation did not operate, especially when the accompanying polyphony took on a certain degree of importance. *Certain forms of thematic elaboration were not immediately comprehensible in perception if the analogous transformations had not been experienced and organized into the same category.* It is possible, in Combarieu's opinion, that this subsumption does not necessarily require knowledge of the technical term applicable to such a particular occurrence. Nevertheless, it presupposes a certain form of abstraction, the constitution of the conceptual substitutions designating the group of transformations in question.

Likewise, knowledge of *generic* concepts has important effects on the structure of the whole group. The idea of a musical genre implies a certain ordering of the themes and components of discourse. It is a formula for organization. To be sure, we must be careful not to overestimate the adequacy of the work to the formula. In most cases the art of the composer consists of playing with the formula, complicating it and making it more supple. Beethoven's last piano sonatas are a beautiful example. Equally important is all that which in each work is interposed among the themes— announcing them, setting them off, attenuating their importance— functioning like connective tissue surrounding the organs, the themes (cf. Schaeffner, 1939). Nevertheless, for the comprehension of musical time there is the guiding principle of the generic concept. The knowledge of that creates in the listener a system of determined expectancies, an already structured attitude that governs apprehension of the pattern and facilitates momentary perceptual activities. The segregation of the principal thematic unit, its opposition to the secondary theme, its return in the recapitulation, and the synthesis of the development are all elements of temporal structure that take on original characteristics in each work. But knowledge of the order in which they should be linked in a flowing sequence assures better structuring of those elements.

Well-determined expectancies and the foreseeing of future contents increase the rate of that structuring and, in a general way, improve it. Expectancies can arise from repeated hearing of the same work, which is also a type of knowledge.

EXPERIMENT 11

In a chronometric study employing the same work of Beethoven, but with different subjects fitting the same criteria, it was possible to cast light on that guiding principle of knowledge by using the *nonguided method*.

Method

The instructions given to the listeners were as follows:

> A piece of music is composed according to a certain plan, like a speech . . . [as in Experiment 10].
> In the piece you are going to hear, there are a certain number of principal ideas that are easy to distinguish because of their contrasting physiognomy. They are repeated by the three instruments, sometimes identically, sometimes with variations and transformations that are often important but that leave recognizable the link binding each idea to its dependents. There are thus several thematic elements attached to each idea. In the course of the first hearing, your task is to find the number of principal ideas contained in the piece. Then, in the second hearing, you should indicate to your observers the occurrence of each idea or thematic element that seems to you to relate

to it. For that you should employ the following code: first idea: single touch signal; second idea: double touch signal; third idea: triple touch signal; and so on.

The subjects included 15 young persons of category A and 15 others in category B, all students in terminal year *lycée* classes.

Results and Discussion

The results showed, first, the large number of subjects who were incapable of bringing together the diversity of the piece into a unity constructed of two themes. Eleven subjects in group A and 10 in group B perceived three themes, and three and two in each group (respectively) perceived four (through lack of assimilation). Along the same lines, the localization of themes A and B was considerably less precise, and the responses less tightly grouped, than with the guided method (Experiment 10). Second, the third and fourth themes were situated indifferently at moments when A or B appeared. A and B were themselves badly discriminated (through lack of differentiation).

The same pair of methods as in Experiments 10 and 11 was applied with the two groups of subjects to a very simple work of Schubert, the Rondo in D Major. The guided method consisted of requesting the recognition of the principal theme across numerous variations and ornamentations. The subjects, even those in categories A and B, succeeded at that easily, given the "good form" of the theme. But with the nonguided method, not only was there a multiplication of themes perceived (going from three to five), but also the eclipse of the principal theme, which was much less often discerned in its elaborations and more often confused with others. It passed almost unnoticed in six out of ten of its appearances. The graphic presentation of the results shows these differences clearly. Fig. 6.13 discloses, by the same procedures used with cadences (Experiment 8), clusters of points corresponding to the same fragment of the Rondo heard by subjects in categories A and B. The top panel shows results from the guided method; the lower panel, from the nonguided method. The lower panel illustrates the rarefaction obtained with the nonguided method of the cluster corresponding to the appearance of the principal theme (X) and the confusion of that theme with a part further on in the work (Y). In the upper panel the points are more numerous and more tightly grouped. They correspond to moments when the theme or one of its variants actually occurred (indicated by +).

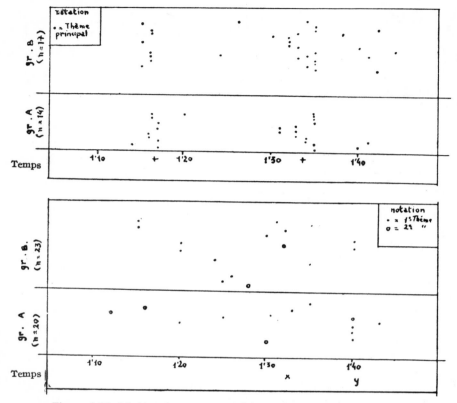

Figure 6.13. Marking the occurrence of themes in Schubert's *Rondo in D Major* by the two groups of subjects. The two panels of the graph represent the responses of subjects of different groups tested with the guided method (upper panel) and the unguided method (lower panel). The two panels correspond to the same section of the work the subjects heard.

Chapter 7
PERCEPTION AND SIMULTANEOUS ORGANIZATION

SOCIAL AND HISTORICAL RELATIVITY

We saw in the preceding chapter the considerable distance that separates perceptual processes from linear organization—in other words, the structure of musical time—in the simple forms of primitive art and in the thematic forms of Western art. This distance is not a question of value judgment. The recordings that brought us into contact with musical sources from the peoples of Asia and Africa have shown us the subtle refinement in timbre discrimination presupposed by certain monophonic Chinese pieces based on 26 ways of playing the same lute string. We have also seen the development—of equal refinement but in another direction—implied by the comprehension of polyrhythmic patterns in certain musics of Black Africa. The same diversity can be observed with regard to simultaneous organization. Our present state of knowledge no longer permits us to restrict the invention of harmony and polyphony exclusively to modern Europe. Texts of Plato (1961) and others attributed to Aristotle (1984; Stumpf, 1896) indicate that in ancient Greece voices were accompanied according to certain rules. Likewise, polyphony (in the sense of the simultaneous progression of independent voices) is not unknown to certain primitive peoples, as has been shown in numerous examples, notably those presented by Sachs (1943). (See Figure 7.1.) In the whole study of forms, it is in this area of simultaneous patterns that we find an infinitely rich scale of steps leading from rigorous homophony (as practiced in

Figure 7.1. Example of primitive dissonant polyphony from the Western Carolines.

191

Europe until the High Middle Ages) to the more exuberant polyphony of Lassus, Palestrina, and Bach—from successions of parallel fourths and fifths to the subtle harmonies of a Fauré or a Roussel.

Among forms of simultaneous organization musicologists generally distinguish harmony and polyphony. Chords would be considered "vertically," and simultaneous melodic figures "horizontally." Of course there is an important difference between structures, such as the accompanied melody and others such as the madrigal and the fugue. But we should avoid defining this difference in terms that apply to composition but that introduce a sharper dichotomy than is appropriate to perceptual reality.

MELODY AND HARMONY: FIGURE AND GROUND

To perceive an accompanied melody is to follow the linear unfolding of the melodic phrase and to undergo at the same time a certain number of "decentrations" in order to grasp the phrases underlying harmonic organization. The focus of attention is unequivocally fixed on the line of the song. But, unless the harmony is only an explicit support for the tonal functions that it implies, this focal attraction must be suspended here and there each time that the accompaniment presents an element of diversity with respect to what is expected—inventions in the chords, melodic figures, and rhythms. The automatic shifts between the song and the accompaniment seem to happen according to the law of Good Form[1] of the one or the other. There are moments of rigorous simultaneity when the harmony expresses itself in a chord-quality that envelopes the melodic passage; and moments of fluctuating simultaneity, of more or less rapid see-saw motion, when the harmony presents some differentiation, such as in pulsating with the beat and in arpeggios. This "good form" is thus to some extent an objective property of the forms being presented. When in one of Mozart's sonatas for violin and piano each instrument speaks in turn, the other is not silent. Rather it carries out motions hardly differentiated from those of the singing part—pulsations, repeated notes, and the like. Attention is focused on the leading instrument, as if drawn to the richer form. In a succession of chords such as those of Figure 7.2a, the ear hears an interior melody in the "contralto" insofar as it is the only voice presenting an

---

[1]This is a matter of purely figural "good form," independent of that which salience of pitch or loudness can confer on a part in a polyphonic texture. It can be defined as the advantage conferred on a more differentiated and unified melodic pattern, compared with another to which it is simultaneously juxtaposed and from which it stands out because of its features, when the whole pattern is apprehended in a nonanalytic way.

Figure 7.2. Interior melody in a chord progression: (a) motion of one middle part; (b) motion of both middle parts.

element of variety relative to the others. This melody is heard less clearly if another part produces motions of equal interest (Figure 7.2b).

Thus, it is not necessary to introduce relative differences of pitch or intensity among the voices for a simultaneously presented pattern to organize itself into figure and ground, though such factors could, of course, enhance the salience of the figure. It is appropriate to call attention to a "hearing out" of the upper part in a simultaneous sound pattern (cf. Spalding, 1949). However, in artistic practice, this privilege can surely be isolated from other factors that might reinforce or attenuate it. Thus, a melody given to one voice or instrument will receive the benefit of salience if it dominates its accompaniment in pitch range. If the opposite is the case, the voice will have to dominate its accompaniment in intensity or in continuity in order to be separated as figure. One of the fundamental problems of orchestration is measuring out the factors of intensity, of pitch, and of diversity of timbre so as not to thwart the appropriate salience of the figures that the composer wished to make appear out of the ambient harmony.

However, these objective factors on the acoustic or formal level cannot be perceptually conceived independently of the education of the perceiving subject. Figure-ground relationships are not unalterable givens of organisms or of conscious experience. When we connect them, as we have been doing, to the play of centrations and attentional shifts, we should understand that they can be modified in the following manner. In an accompanied melody, while the melody remains "figure," the frequency of attentional shifts assures the underlying harmony a presence in perception[2] that is greater to the extent that the subjects, being more educated, are able to produce more rapid shifts.[3] Thus, the general question is one of demonstrating the relationships between education and the more or less marked phenomenal presence of the harmonic ground. The following

---

[2] We cannot speak here of "Prägnanz" because that term is reserved for figure in the the figure-ground dichotomy. Perceptual *presence* in the sense intended here is the simple *phenomenal actuality* of the ground insofar as it is just that (varying with different cases) and of which the degrees are measured by stability in immediate memory.

[3] The effects of this rapidity of attentional shift, described by Piaget in several of his works, have been successfully verified in the visual domain by one of his students (Gantenbein, 1952).

experiment, carried out with 148 subjects, permitted us to establish just that.

EXPERIMENT 12

Method

Materials. Subjects were presented with 12 harmonized melodic formulas recorded with piano. All items were of the same length (five notes) and the same rhythm and duration (four eighth notes and then a quarter note, making three quarter-note beats at a rate of 63 beats/min). The pitch range was restricted to a musical fourth.

Each melodic formula was repeated after a silence that lasted two beats (to provide for fixation in memory). The comparison stimulus was melodically identical, but in nine of the twelve trials contained a change of one chord in the harmonization. The harmony was realized in three parts with one chord on each beat, thus giving three chords for each melodic formula. Changes in the chords were produced by the substitution of one or two notes, while the third note—that of the melody—remained identical. The changes always involved harmonic function and were never simply changes of inversion of the same chord. A tonic chord might be substituted for a dominant, for example.

Subjects. There were three groups of subjects. Group A consisted of 40 *lycée* students in Paris, young men and women aged 18 to 21 years, who were candidates for the second part of the baccalaureate and who stated that they had had no musical training of either a practical or theoretical sort. Group B consisted of 63 students of the same age and cultural background as those of group A, but who had had a certain amount of musical training, including solfège for between 1 and 3 years and the study of an instrument or voice for between 3 and 8 years. Group C consisted of 45 students of similar age and education, but who were involved in the study of music as professionals. These were students of the Ecole Normale de Musique who were members of an advanced class in singing in a private school in preparation for the curriculum in music teaching.

Procedure. Following a rudimentary audiometric examination for each subject as described in Experiment 3, subjects were given the following instructions to read:

> You are about to hear some brief melodic phrases, harmonized and played on the piano. Each of these phrases will be repeated identically, except that

sometimes there will be a change in the harmonization, that is, in the accompaniment. The melody line will remain unchanged. For example, . . . [Here the stimuli shown in Figure 7.3 were presented.]

The first experiment consists of listening to each of 12 such phrases with its repetition and finding whether, in that repetition, you perceive a change in the harmony of the accompaniment, in comparison with the initial version. Your responses should be noted on the sheet you have in front of you. The printed grid has twelve horizontal rows of boxes corresponding to the twelve comparisons that you will make. Each trial will be separated from the following one by several seconds of silence to permit you to carry out that operation. In cases where you find that there has been a change in the repetition, indicate that by the initial "O" (for "*oui*") written to the right of the row corresponding to the trial. If you find that there was no change, indicate that by the initial "N" (for "*non*"). Finally, if a particular case leaves you in doubt, do not write anything and go on to the following line—do not write anything inside the grid.

When this phase was completed, the subjects were given a 3-minute rest, after which they were given the following instructions:

In the second series of trials you will have to specify, for each comparison, the beat on which the change in harmony occurred between one version and the other. Each phrase, as well as its repetition, always consists of three beats. The harmony could be changed on the first, the second, or the third beat. For example, . . . [Here the stimuli in Figure 7.3 were presented.] Here the harmony changed on the third beat.

You will thus have to indicate, for each comparison, the beat on which the change occurred by marking an X in the grid you have in front of you. Each square going across the row corresponds to one of the three beats in the phrase.

Care was taken to have nonmusician subjects listen to the preceding example three times in a row while indicating to them the progress of the voice and its motion, so as to make the verbal explanation perfectly clear. After these instructions the subjects listened again to the twelve examples, marking the locations of the harmonic changes on the grid.

Figure 7.3. Example played during the instructions: harmonized melodic formula with a change in the final chord in the repetition.

Results and Discussion

These two operations—the perception of harmonic changes and of their localization—gave the following results for the three groups:

Perception of Changes. Affirmative and negative responses, corresponding respectively to pairs in which a chord had been changed and to those in which there was no change, were counted as correct. Recall that these responses had been formulated in the course of the first hearing. However, in the course of the second hearing (which had as its goal the localization of the changes) in a few cases it happened that changes unnoticed in the first hearing were noted by the localization (either correct or incorrect) of a changed chord. I therefore added these responses from the second hearing to those previously defined, inasmuch as localization was evaluated by means of the data from the second presentation.

Localization of Changes. Every correct localization of a changed chord was counted as correct, even when it pertained to a trial for which no change had been noted in the first hearing.

Table 7.1 (a and b) shows the percentages of correct responses for the two operations by the three groups. The distributions of these responses were evaluated and found to be approximately normal. Differences between means could thus be evaluated with respect to their standard error. Table 7.2 gives the means and values of Student's t corresponding to the comparisons between the groups taken two by two. The differences were all significant ($p < .01$) for perception as well as for localization, though they were greater for the latter operation (see Figures 7.4 and 7.5).

Comparison of the Two Operations. It appeared at first that localization was distinctly less easy than perception. The former involved the analysis of the pattern, whereas the latter involved a global grasp of change. But, from another point of view, localization implies a simultaneous grouping of melodic and harmonic stimuli, a "vertical" perception in musicians' terms. The perception/localization ratio was calculated within each group for the nine trials in which a harmonic change occurred. That ratio was always greater than one.[4] On the other hand, going from group A to group B, these ratios diminished in six cases out of nine, and going from group B to group C they diminished in all nine cases (see the curves in Figure 7.6 and Table 7.3).

To be sure, the processes implied by localization presuppose memory,

---

[4]The chances of error are not the same for these two operations: they are 0.5 in the first case, and 0.33 in the second. If the subjects were choosing at random, the ratio was would be greater than 1.0.

TABLE 7.1
Percentages of Correct Perceptions and Localizations of Changed Chords in the Repetition of a Harmonized Melodic Formula

	Correct Perceptions (a)				Correct Localizations (b)		
Item No.	%	Item No.	%	Item No.	%	Item No.	%
Group A (N = 40)							
1	70	7	70	1	50	8	55
2	50	8	75	2	15	9	32.5
3	40	9	57.5	4	17.5	10	15
4	52.5	10	55	5	22.5	11	17.5
5	50	11	22.5	7	40		
6	57.5	12	70				
Group B (N = 63)							
1	95.2	7	76.1	1	87.3	8	66.6
2	63.4	8	88.8	2	44.4	9	53.9
3	65.07	9	73.01	4	42.8	10	14.2
4	68.2	10	34.9	5	19.1	11	36.5
5	50.7	11	55.5	7	39.6		
6	61.9	12	84.1				
Group C (N = 45)							
1	100	7	75.5	1	97.7	8	91.1
2	82.2	8	97.7	2	62.2	9	66.6
3	66.6	9	80	4	48.8	10	31.1
4	53.3	10	62.2	5	53.3	11	64.4
5	66.6	11	71.1	7	48.8		
6	66.6	12	82.2				

TABLE 7.2
Comparison of the Results of the Three Groups in the Perception and Localization of Changs in Harmony

	Mean Correct Responses	
Groups	Perception	Localization
A	6.725	2.600
B	8.143	4.095
C	9.067	5.844
Comparison (values of t):		
A–B	3.850	4.424
B–C	3.250	5.754
C–A	5.520	9.216

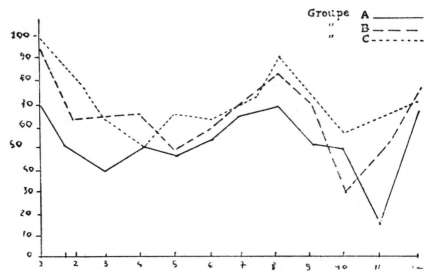

Figure 7.4. Perception of a change in harmony for three groups of subjects: Percentage correct plotted against items, in order of presentation. Items 3, 6, and 12 contained no change.

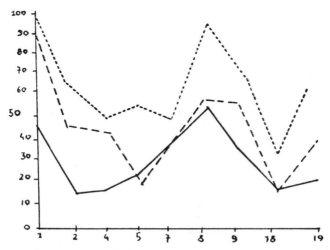

Figure 7.5. Localization of a change in harmony for three groups of subjects: percentage correct plotted against items, in order of presentation.

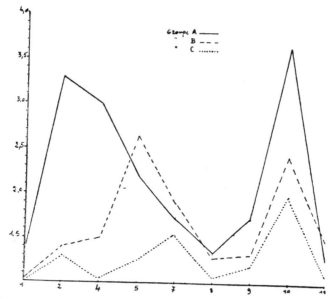

Figure 7.6. Ratio of correct responses for perception vs. localization (P/L) for the three groups of subjects, plotted against items in order of presentation.

since it is a matter of referring a present perception—that of the repetition—being referred to an already completed perception—that of the model. But this retrospection succeeds better as the model becomes better established in memory in its melodic and harmonic aspects at once. Since the melody did not change, and the subjects had been informed of that in the instructions, it follows that the efforts of the subjects in the three groups were

TABLE 7.3

Value of the Ration Between Perception and Localization
Performance (P/L) for the Three Groups

	A	B	C
Item Number:			
1	1.400	1.090	1.022
2	3.333	1.428	1.321
4	3.000	1.592	1.090
5	2.222	2.666	1.250
7	1.750	1.920	1.545
8	1.363	1.333	1.073
9	1.769	1.352	1.200
10	3.666	2.444	2.000
11	1.286	1.521	1.103

directed at reducing the importance of the melody and at attending more to the underlying harmony. We saw in chapter 5 how one could conceive physiologically of inhibition exerted voluntarily in a perceptual field on one group of stimuli, to the advantage of others. This form of explanation is partially applicable here, inasmuch as the subject's attention is oriented by the instructions. But we should not forget that figure-ground relationships persist in spite of instructional efforts to reverse them. Relative pitch level and the intrinsic meaningfulness of figures are factors that are impossible to diminish fully. Such a diminution is in any case contrary to the subjectively intuited impression.

It is well known, for example, that when one looks at one of Rubin's (1915) ambiguous figures, the organization of the grouping makes what was initially ground surge forth in an instant as figure, and vice versa. But nothing of that applies here, where the primitive figure remains on the most basic level. To that extent the melody remains a unit; but, to the degree that it unfolds, the subject retains (or not, as the case may be) the freedom to make a decentration to the benefit of the harmonic ground. The two explications, far from being opposed, seem complementary: It is the possibility of somewhat diminishing melodic centrations that brings about the possibility of multiplying attentional shifts. Further, the necessity for mobility appears greater still in the typical case in which the melody is unfamiliar and accordingly needs to be organized simultaneously with the harmony. The experimental artifice we had to use reduced the role of mobility in favor of inhibition. Ordinary cases should certainly increase it.

VARIOUS TYPES OF FIGURE-GROUND RELATIONSHIP IN MUSICAL WORKS

Clearly, the existence of syntactic relationships is not the only reason that renders the strictly linear comprehension of musical forms impossible. Although there are two ways to structure musical time, one to support the functional signals of harmony and the other to support gestural symbolism, both assume simultaneous perceptions of that which is given "vertically." Gestural symbolism is very rarely limited to the melodic line; it is emphasized by accompanying underlying patterns that can prepare the following gesture or complete the present one. Different harmonization of the same theme at two separated moments in a work, the use of a new accompaniment figure to vary a recapitulation, the superimposition of themes presented successively in an earlier part—all indicate the extent to which linear organization depends on the perception of momentary simultaneities. In a genre such as the classical theme and variations, the diversity of the variations resides most often in the invention of a procedure that changes the ground on which the thematic figure rests. It has become commonplace, since the researches of the gestalt psychologists, to say that the texture of the ground influences the figure. This idea, well established in the visual domain, also holds true of music. The procedures utilized in the variation produce a recasting of the overall organization such that the thematic figure becomes perceptibly modified in character and appearance. In certain instances, a theme introduced with a simple support of chords later rests on more and more rapid figurations (as in Handel's *Harmonious Blacksmith*). In other cases, this procedure is combined with the reversal of pitch relationships, and a figure introduced in the upper register is transferred to the bass, itself supporting figurations in the treble (as in Fauré's *Theme and Variations*).

In the former example both perceiving the figure and establishing its relationship with the ground are immediate, whereas in the latter the formal interest and relative salience of the accompaniment pattern militates against the necessary anchoring of attention in the lower register. There the accompaniment is not a ground but rather a simultaneous figure, perceived along with the other due to a pattern of attentional shifts (see Figure 7.7). It is reasonable to suppose that the distribution of these shifts should follow the rhythm of the slower figure. Between each pair of centrations on the long notes of the slower pattern (quarter notes and dotted eighths) lies a shift to the upper line, during which a whole group of interpolated notes is globally perceived. The continuity of the two patterns perceived simultaneously thus occurs on the basis of a double discontinuity affecting the perception of each of them. We may also have to grant that the centrations on the bass line actually involve very rapid shifts back and forth between the two simultaneous notes (as illustrated in Fig. 7.7). We are thus led to analyze the processes involved in the perception of polyphony.

POLYPHONY

In addition to these considerations, as was noted earlier in connection with the discussion of problems of linear organization), the task of the

Figure 7.7. Probable locations of attentional shifts in the perception of two simultaneous melodic lines (from Fauré, *Theme and Variations*. The direction of the arrows indicates the direction of successive centrations.

psychologist confronted with the diversity of musical facts is to select those which amount to prototypical standards, between which lie innumberable intermediate cases complicated by other factors of various sorts. Musical works are individuals; it is probably impossible to find in one everything relevant to another. This is equally true for simultaneous organization. Between the melody accompanied with chords and polyphony lie an indefinite number of possible structures. These endlessly create new problems, but it seems to me that they involve only a small number of psychological processes. There are differences only in the proportional part taken by each of these processes—its frequency of occurrence, its temporal distribution, and so forth. Between the simple harmonic accompaniment of the previous experiment and the duality of melodic patterns we have just analyzed, there are differences in the temporal distribution of attentional shifts imposed by simultaneities, as well as in the greater effort required for decentration by the second example. But these quantitative aspects of elementary perceptual acts prevent simultaneous perception when they reach a certain threshhold.

The following experiments show that a melodic pattern that the experimenter indicates at the start—known by the subject and listened for in the polyphony—can be recognized by some and not by others. Even though the sensory message is the same for all,[5] recognition of internal organization is determined according to a fixed hierarchy that brings out the figure, while due to their pregnance or other causes the accompaniment patterns are not immediately perceived as ground. This shift from quantitative to qualitative effects seems to me the hypothesis that naturally arises, since it corresponds to the subjects' perceptual learning. How else should we explain the emergence of organization in the pattern of stimuli presented to all, which is realized only for some, namely, those accustomed to musical "behavior" of the same type, be it digital, visual, or perceptual?

The Gestalt psychologists have never denied the development of forms following training and their progressive restructuring. They simply claim that there is a minimal organization that serves as a point of departure for further development. We will grant that without difficulty: no percept is pure chaos. The first glance reveals more or less clear patterns. But the difficulty is to explain the nature of the processes that bring about its development. We know that a number of motor learnings consist in the acquisition of a general facility of movement as well as a rapidity of elementary movements. This is especially true of musical behavior: reading, sight-reading, and memorization. It is probable that beyond a certain point

---

[5]Cf. Stumpf (1883–1890), vol. 1: "The elements of a relationship can be perceived without the relationship itself being perceived" (p. 4).

our observation involves global apprehension, in larger and larger chunks of the succession of stimuli. But this is assured only by long practice carried out with elementary movements, with simple shifts bringing into play a small number of elements. This is typified by the pianist's training in simultaneously playing with both hands. The basic act is the "vertical" shift—note against note, with one or two notes interpolated in one of the two parts. One might say that there is already the apprehension of a "form" because there is a plurality of elements. The interaction is discontinuous, neither of the two parts being perceived globally or "sung." What is gradually learned is the *rapidity* of the shifts and their *richness*. For each shift, the subject can handle more notes vertically. The *amplitude* of the shifts also increases with equal speed—the keyboard is traversed without hesitation over greater and greater distances. These observations are directly related to the object of these experiments. What belongs particularly to polyphony is the independence of figural function in terms of the registers specified, as well as the discontinuity of their relationships and other reversibility. With harmonized melodies the figure is placed constantly in one register and the ground in another. Their functional polarity is indicated by this acoustic arrangement as well as by their differing amounts of inherent pregnance. Attention therefore focuses on the melodic register, and its shifts occur in a constant direction going from this level to the level of the accompaniment. In contrast, with polyphony there is no ground, properly speaking. Melodic motion and variety is not restricted to just one part developing in a constant register. All registers partake of motion and variety to varying degrees. In fact, an equilibrium is always established among these figures, one of them taking on importance relative to the others. Thus one register is momentarily privileged, then another. In the imitative style the listener makes successive sweeps through different registers, each drawing attention to the initial exposition of a motive in one of the parts, imitated in another, while the first continues with a pattern that serves an accompaniment function no matter which register it falls in. Thus polyphony is never an indifferent simultaneity, but, rather, is a hierarchy of levels of sound from which each in turn detaches itself momentarily without the others' being reduced to the function of ground. In fact, figure-ground relationships do not rigorously apply here, because there is not a sufficiently clear opposition here between those two terms. The ground is neither sufficiently neutral nor sufficiently stable to recede entirely. Instead, what we hear is a constant play of the exploration of different registers and of shifts from one figure to another, with more or less stable centrations on those which for one reason or another are capable of provoking them (for example, relative pitch height, internal organization, and, above all, reciprocal temporal and rhythmic linkages among the figures). Depending on the case, there will be simultaneous perception, or more or less pronounced suppression. With practice or education we should expect two sorts of development:

1. Mobility, rapidity, and amplitude of attentional shifts; increasing richness of the partial syntheses of each shift; in sum, a series of factors concerning the scanning of the acoustic field.
2. Inhibition of the phenomenal presence of upper sound levels in favor of the lower, of the pregnance of a figure being followed, which brings about an enhanced presence of other figures and as a result enhances the ease and rapidity of decentrations. There would thus seem to be, in the perception of a second level, degrees of clarity that do not arise from the multiplicity of attentional shifts (though that would be an equally important source of them) brought about by selective activity directed by the subject at the acoustic message.

In the following experiments, the enhancements of elementary perceptual acts result in what we have called the *condensation* of the melodic figure sought in the polyphony. We should not underestimate the temporal character of all the elements involved in the concepts we have been outlining. The contagion of the spatial makes us lose sight of what belongs particularly to them. A geometrical figure is depicted at the moment when it is presented to us; a melodic figure requires successive presentation that imposes a fixed course on our activities. The perception of the former may be successive in a certain sense, notably when beyond a certain complexity it calls forth multiple shifts of attention. But it can be grasped in a single glance if we are not drawn into the details. Any rapid tachistoscopic presentation, for example, is excluded in the latter case. We must wait for its unfolding to be completed in order to be able to contemplate it in itself. If the figure is known and expected, the unfolding must attain a certain completeness in order for it to be recognized with certainty. We shall call the instant of unfolding when recognition occurs the *point of condensation*, with regard to the summation of preceding elements.

EXPERIMENT 13

It is clear that the chronometric method could not be applied to the study of simultaneous perceptions without special instructions. Since the results obtained with musicians and nonmusicians were compared on the important points, it was necessary to provide nonmusicians with a simple means of communicating the structure of their perceptions. We could not, in particular, pose them a task involving musical notation. We decided to present the three groups of subjects compositions in which the same melodic figure recurred several times in various registers, whereas in the other registers were more or less varied accompaniment patterns.

Method

Procedure. The instructions, read and reread after the distribution of the questionnaires, provide an outline of the different steps in the experimental procedure:

> You are going to participate in a series of experiments on the Fugue. A fugue is a work with several voices in different registers, oe of which presents first of all, alone, a melodic figure called the "subject." The subject is then repeated in different registers by each of the voices, sometimes identical to itself and sometimes with slight changes that always leave it recognizable in each of its appearances. The subject, presented solo at the start of the piece, is then accompanied by the other voices, which make various melodic patterns heard simultaneously and which can make it difficult to recognize the subject.

A fragment of a fugue recorded with the piano was presented to back up this definition, and then the instructions continued:

> Our experiment will consist of having you listen to another fugue of which the subject will be first presented to you twice, and of asking you to indicate by means of a hand sign to your observer the exact moment when you recognize it in the course of listening.

The subject or theme[6] was then presented *only twice*, just as it had been presented at the start of the work, and finally the work was presented without interruption, the listeners and observers taking their respective roles.

This same technique was employed with four Bach fugues. For each of them, the experiment was done twice consecutively with the same listeners and observers. That procedure allowed us to form some idea of the consistency of the results and eventually of modifications brought about by the second hearing.

---

[6]The term "theme" is employed here to designate the figural unity corresponding musically to the subject, to the response, and to their multiple transpositions and imitations. This way of proceeding is justified by the fact that, by means of slight intervallic or rhythmic modifications or by changes of key or register, the least educated listeners spontaneously identified or assimilated to the subject proper those patterns derived from it.

Results and Discussion

The results were calculated as follows. To calculate "correct responses," that is, recognitions corresponding to complete appearances of the theme, I counted a response from the listener when there occurred *at least one response during the entire duration of the theme.* Indeed, some subjects confirmed their reaction with a second response before the end of the theme. To obtain the distribution of responses in time, I counted only the first response, that is, the moment when the theme was recognized, and not the second moment, when that recognition was confirmed. But this procedure was not appropriate for the calculation of assimilations and errors, that is, responses that did not correspond to the presentation of the theme. I therefore counted all those responses which occurred between the end of one appearance of the theme and the beginning of another.

To avoid dragging out the presentation of results, I shall give here only those for two of the experiments with fugues. In spite of their incompleteness, the reader will be able to see in them the extent to which factors involved in the formal properties of each work influence the perceptual acts brought into play—this despite the quantitative analogies and constancies they incidentally exhibited.

Fugue in F-sharp Major from Book I of *The Well-Tempered Clavier* by J. S. Bach.

Here we studied the following results in turn, comparing the pattern for the three groups A (inexperienced), B (moderately experienced), and C (graduate students in music) for the two presentations of the piece:

1. The frequency of "correct responses" (that is, those which occurred during the entire duration of the theme);

2. The distribution of correct responses in time (that is, their distribution through the 7-sec duration of the theme);

3. The frequency of "assimilations" and errors (that is, those responses which occurred outside the duration of the theme).

Percentages of Correct Responses. Table 7.4 provides the results for the two presentations bearing on correct recognitions by the three groups, given in order for the seven appearances of the theme along with mean percentages, to provide a general idea of the behavior of listeners in the different categories. The differences in mean percentages between group A and group C were 21.05% and 24.65% for the first and second presentation. Passing from the first to the second presentation, there was a clear increase in the means for group B (8.3%), a smaller increase for

TABLE 7.4

Percentages of Correct Responses to Appearances of the Theme for Three
Groups Listening to the *Fugue in F# Major.*

	First Presentation				Second Presentation		
Groups (N):	A (15)	B (33)	C (26)		A (16)	B (35)	C (27)
Appearance				Appearance			
1	33.3	48.4	80.8	1	44.1	68.5	83.1
2	60.0	72.7	100.0	2	68.7	82.1	96.2
3	93.3	72.7	96.1	3	81.2	74.2	85.1
4	53.3	63.6	61.5	4	56.2	82.1	81.4
5	26.6	48.4	84.6	5	25.0	54.2	74.1
6	80.0	84.8	84.6	6	75.0	85.7	88.8
7	66.6	57.5	73.1	7	56.2	60.0	77.7
Mean:	59.0	64.0	82.9		59.4	72.3	84.0

group C (4.01%), and almost none for group A (0.39%). There was thus considerable consistency in the overall results.

The chi-square test was applied to the raw data for each of the partial results, first with adjacent groups taken pairwise, and then (in all the cases in which those differences were not significant) between the two extreme groups A and C. Yates's correction was employed when the expected values were less than 10. The differences were significant in only seven cases out of fourteen between A and C. But the numbers increased in nine out of fourteen cases going from A to B and from B to C. And they increased in fourteen out of fourteen cases going from A to C. There was thus a general tendency to improved performance with the increasing level of musical training of the groups.

However, in the results for *each group* there were very different numbers pertaining to different appearances of the theme. One could try to determine a hierarchy of difficulty of detection of the theme depending on the moments when it appeared in the course of the piece, insofar as those differences held from one presentation to the other. If such a hierarchy held across groups, that would confirm the constancy of the phenomena on which it was based and invite a formal interpretation. I was thus led to examine the momentary polyphonic structures in detail, following their linkages throughout the whole work.

The theme appeared sometimes with just the accompaniment of the countersubject (Figure 7.8a), sometimes with a less melodic and less meaningful sixteenth-note accompaniment pattern that served mostly to sustain the harmony and that little by little replaced the countersubject after the third appearance (Figure 7.8b), and sometimes with a combination of those two patterns (Figure 7.8c). When the countersubject occurred in the upper part and in the same octave as the theme, it tended to militate

Figure 7.8. Modes of presentation of the thematic subject at different places in the work (Bach, *Fugue in F# Major*): (a) subject in the lower part combined with the counter-subject in the upper part; (b) secondary figure serving to sustain the harmony; (c) subject in the upper part combined with the countersubject in the middle part, and with the secondary figure in the lower part.

against the clear separation of the latter, because of its pregnance and proximity. At least that happened with the first appearance (measures 3 and 4) for listeners in groups A and B, for both presentations.

Where this effect occurred, the percentages of correct responses were among the weakest for groups A and B: 38.6% and 58.4% respectively, both figures below the grand mean. The countersubject did not have this interfering effect when it occurred in a position farther removed from the theme (appearance 2) or when the theme occurred in the upper part (appearance 3). In the latter case, the combination of the countersubject with the secondary pattern just described (Figure 7.8c) did not have a contrary effect. The means for appearance 3 for the two presentations were 87.2% for group A and 73.4% for group B. The interfering role of a contrapuntal pattern in the upper part is thus effective only when there is an extreme coalescence of voices, producing a kind of acoustic interference. We find here an effect of the law established in the preceding chapter following the experiment on transpositions. The case of appearance 5 (subject in the relative minor, measures 17–18) seems to depart from this rule. There we find the smallest percentages for the two presentations (group A = 25.8%, group B = 51.3%), although the separation of the theme and the countersubject (especially with the latter involved only in part) was sufficient to assure the autonomy of the principal part. We may suppose that here the role of imitation was a determining factor. The passage to the minor mode introduced a global transmutation in the character of the grouping formed by the theme and its accompaniment that made its assimilation to the model difficult. The secondary pattern (Figure 7.8c), by its somewhat mechanical unity, constitutes a neutral ground on which the theme stands out in a privileged manner. That is why recognitions were numerous even for subjects with little or no training (appearance 6: group A = 77.0%, group B = 85.2%). However, none of the factors presented to account for the most divergent percentages of groups A and B had any effect on group C.

Distribution of Correct Responses in Time. It seems that here we have to deal with a quite distinct theme resting on a contrapuntal ground that does not hurt its salience, judging from the means of correct responses, which were not higher than those from other experiments with fugues. But we can conclude that, even for groups A and B, responses were clustered in the first 4 sec of the duration of the theme (which averaged 7 sec in length). These means are thus notable for the density of recognitions they display during the first part of the theme. It is certain that the ornament on the fourth beat provided for rapid segregation after the first hearing, even for groups A and B, and this is shown in the curves for the distribution of correct responses over time. (See Figure 7.9, in which the abscissa is divided into the 7 sec of the duration of the theme and the ordinate gives the mean percentage of correct responses across its seven appearances in the course of the piece.) The parallelism of the curves for the three groups is clear. There was noteworthy progress by each group going from the first to the second presentation, marked by a sharpening of the peaks and less spread in the curves. Put concretely, these graphic representations show that melody recognition is both a discontinuous and a cumulative process. Identification of the theme occurs abruptly, at the point of condensation. That is the instant when the physiognomy of the tones already perceived takes on meaning, constituting itself as a theme

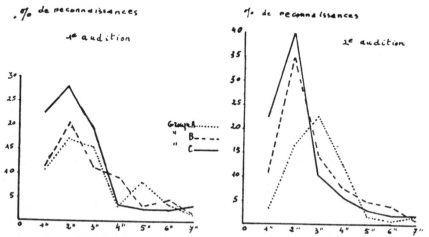

Figure 7.9. Distribution of correct responses in time: mean percentage of recognitions across all presentations for the three groups, plotted against the duration in time of the subject.

arising out of the open and anonymous collection being continuously disclosed. The point of condensation coincides with the anticipated closure of the collection in its development. The numerical data show that its formation is delayed, the extent of the delay depending on the appearances of the theme in the course of the piece and on the category of listeners involved. We can designate the instant when recognition occurs for the majority of listeners in a group the *mean point of condensation*, around which the responses of the group are distributed. This point occurs at different moments in the theme in its different appearances. However, plotting the means of correct responses for each 1-second interval provides us with a global schema of recognition processes for each group. The curves for the distribution of those means (Fig. 7.9) indicate the speed of that process for each group and its recasting from one presentation to the next. The results for group A show a clustering of responses around the 3rd second, and around the 2nd second for groups B and C. The change in the curves follows a parallel pattern going from the first presentation to the second: a change from a normal distribution to a J-shaped one. This change suggests a hypothetical mean point of condensation toward which each group tends, changing with successive transformations in perceptual organization—a point that becomes less and less a statistical abstraction and more and more a concrete reality.

Errors and Assimilations. Substantial percentages of assimilations and errors were obtained not only from groups A and B but also from group C. Moreover, far from decreasing from the first presentation to the second, these numbers generally increased greatly, especially for group C. Between two appearances of the theme, we picked out clusters of responses, often closely grouped, that did not necessarily occupy the same instant when the first and second presentation were compared.

Let us seek the motives giving rise to those responses by lining up the response clusters with the musical score, using the temporal clustering indicated in Table 7.5 as a basis. Cluster number 1 occurred in time intervals 1 and 2 in the second presentation and corresponded (with interval 2 in the first presentation and interval 3 in the second) to quarter-and-eighth-note motives that recall the entrance of the subject, along with the secondary figure in the accompaniment that supplanted the countersubject in the lower register (or else a figure that recalled this last; see Figure 7.10).

The same explanation holds for the cluster in interval 4 (5 in the second presentation), corresponding to an analogous motive in quarters and eighths (measure 18). The other assimilations all corresponded to longer or shorter episodes based in the entrance of the subject. For example, the brief episode in measure 13 reproduced the start of the subject in the relative minor. It corresponded to respose cluster 3 (4 in the second presentation). At measures 23 and 24, there is an episode based on the imitation of the

TABLE 7.5

Percentages of Errors and Assimilations During Different Time Intervals (Indicated in Minutes and Seconds) for Three Groups Listening to the *Fugue in F# Major*.

Groups:	First Presentation				Second Presentation		
	A	B	C		A	B	C
Interval				Interval			
1 0:20–0:27	86.6	66.6	11.5	1 0:20–0:22	62.5	54.2	44.4
2 0:29–0.32	53.3	63.6	38.4	2 0:23–0:27	50.0	37.1	7.4
3 0:40–0:43	33.3	33.3	23.1	3 0:28–0:32	31.2	68.5	58.4
4 0:51–0:57	60.0	54.5	26.8	4 0:40–0:43	50.0	48.5	51.8
5 1:07–1:10	73.3	48.4	34.6	5 0:51–0:57	75.0	51.4	51.8
6 1:17–1:22	6.6	45.4	46.1	6 1:06–1:12	81.2	60.0	81.4
7 1:30–1:32	46.6	45.4	34.6	7 1:20–1:22	0.0	14.2	48.1
				8 1:30–1:33	75.0	60.0	48.1
Mean:	51.3	51.05	30.8		60.7	56.2	55.9

start of the subject in the soprano, with an answer in the alto, with the whole resting on the secondary accompaniment described above (see Figure 7.11). This episode gave rise to response cluster 5 (6 in the second presentation).

Finally, at measures 26 and 27, the theme develops a stepwise descending motion on a motive again imitating the entrance of the subject, with the secondary accompaniment repeated in contrary motion. The end of this episode was, in fact, equivalent to an entrance of the subject in the original key and gave rise to cluster 6 (7 in the second presentation), whereas the imitations in measure 30 corresponded to clusters 7 and 8.

Figure 7.10. Motifs recalling the entrance of the subject (in the upper part).

Figure 7.11. Episode based on an imitation of the entrance of the subject (in the upper parts). In the lower part, the secondary figure already mentioned.

Hence, with the three groups of listeners we are dealing only with assimilations motivated by the presence of thematic elements. Note also that their number grows from one presentation to the other, especially for group C (whose mean goes from 30.8% to 55.9%). This augmentation can be interpreted as evidence of the progressive assimilation in the course of the second presentation of partial structures associated with the fugue subject to the subject itself.

Fugue in D Minor from the *Chromatic Fantasy and Fugue* by J. S. Bach.

This experiment provides us with a basis for understanding what remains constant in the reactions of listeners in the three groups and what varies owing to formal properties of the work presented to them. Those differ here from the preceding work principally because the theme was longer in duration and contained more notes. There were thus more opportunities for it to be recognized in one moment or another of its development. The following divisions can be distinguished, as shown in Figure 7.12: an initial segment *a* formed from an ascending chromatic line of quarter notes ending with a lower-note embellishment—an ascent that is immediately transposed down a fourth; an intermediate segment *b* of two measures destined to lead to the key of D Minor, poorly established in *a* and finally imposed by the cadence in *c*. Rhythmically one could arrive at another division: the last measure of *a* and the first of *b* constitute a motion that is repeated immediately by what follows.

This theme is, from the melodic point of view, easily identifiable, in spite of certain modifications of detail: the mutation in the answer (Figure 7.13a), the ornament in the fifth and sixth measures (Figure 7.13b), the chromatic ornament on the first beat of the first and third measures of Figure 7.13b.

Nevertheless, the harmonic structure of the first two measures (important for recognition) varied from appearance to appearance. The first notes on the strong beats of each appearance called for varying harmonic interpretations involving chords having different functions in the current key. Often the key changed from the first measure to the second, but sometimes

Figure 7.12. Subject and countersubject of Bach, *Fugue in D Minor*: (a), (b), and (c): internal sections of the subject; (d) countersubject.

Figure 7.13. Modifications of the subject in different presentations: (a) change of rhythm at the start (a mutation in the answer); (b) ornamentation of the middle section; (c) chromatic mutation at the start.

not. In the first appearance, those notes were (respectively) the fifth of a dominant seventh chord and the root of a tonic chord in the same key; in the fifth appearance, the third of a subdominant and the root of a tonic in the same key; in the ninth appearance, the root of a tonic chord and the root of another tonic but in a different key, and so on. This factor of syntactic order interfered noticeably with identification of the pattern, in which the notes had a variable role in each group of tones.

Lastly, the theme was organized with a countersubject (Figure 7.12d) composed of long notes interspersed with ascending (measure 2) or descending (measures 4 and 6) motions generated from a rhythmic cell. This countersubject went through varied metamorphoses in the course of the work. At times it overflowed into episodes that borrowed and developed its fertile rhythmic cell; at other times it underwent significant changes and modifications in its role as accompaniment to the theme (whether subject or answer), such that it remained similar to itself only in its first two first appearances (measures 9–15 and 19–25). That is, no similarity existed among the ways the theme was combined with the countersubject. Thus, in the first two appearances an organic pair was formed, whose solidarity was then broken in the remainder of the work. The rhythmic formulas borrowed from the countersubject in the episodes tended to evoke the theme at places where it did not occur.[7] Conversely, the continual distancing of the form of the accompanying parts from that of the theme was an element of interference for the segregation of the theme when it actually appeared. In general, the *divertissements* did not contain imitations of the theme and were formally quite distinct from it.

Percentages of Correct Responses. The amputation and extension of the last part of the theme (its ending cadence) at times made difficult the definition of its duration for the purpose of comparing results from its different appearances. The only solution was to limit it to its first six

---

[7]This is confirmed by the observations of several listeners of Group A, noted in their protocols, who had judged that "The theme is everywhere," or else, "It is repeated indefinitely."

measures, leaving out the cadence. This did not alter its physiognomy in the least and preserved the essential parts of its 10 appearances. Reduced in this way to 6 measures, its duration was 9 sec.

Table 7.6 presents the percentages of recognitions and their means for the three groups. Progress from one presentation to the other was negligible for groups A, B, and C (1%, 3.2%, and 5.0%, respectively). In contrast, the differences between groups A and C were considerable: 23.9% and 31.25% for the two presentations, compared with 10.1% and 12.3% for groups A and B. Those were the most significant intergroup differences we had observed to that point. Chi-square calculated on the frequencies of correct responses for groups A and C was significant at the .01 level for seven out of the ten appearances for the first presentation, and in eight for the second.

Group A seemed to behave with a certain amount of autonomy, and the most interesting partial percentages came from them. For example, the figures for appearance 7 departed from the group mean by 18.15% and 19.5%. For the other groups, those differences were 3.4% and 9.4% (group B), and 10.4% and 3.7% (group C). These results appear related to the relinquishing of the countersubject and the introduction of contrapuntal parts, in favor of a more continuous and denser structure cast in an interfering role many times during appearances 5, 6, 7, 8, 9, and 10.[8]

TABLE 7.6
Percentages of Correct Responses to Appearances of the Theme for Three
Groups Listening to the *Fugue in D Minor*

	First Presentation				Second Presentation		
Groups (N):	A (18)	B (28)	C (24)		A (16)	B (31)	C (24)
Appearance				Appearance			
1	72.2	82.1	83.3	1	83.3	74.1	100.0
2	61.1	67.8	95.8	2	83.3	93.5	91.6
3	50.0	71.4	91.6	3	50.0	67.7	83.3
4	61.1	60.7	91.6	4	44.4	64.5	87.5
5	50.0	64.2	62.5	5	44.4	51.6	83.3
6	50.0	53.5	66.6	6	61.1	61.2	83.3
7	38.8	64.2	70.8	7	38.8	61.2	83.3
8	61.1	78.5	87.5	8	50.0	87.1	87.5
9	77.7	57.1	83.3	9	72.2	87.1	79.1
10	50.0	67.8	79.1	10	55.5	58.6	91.6
Mean:	57.9	67.1	81.2		58.3	70.6	87.05

---

[8]Moreover, concerning appearance number 5, it is necessary to take into account the rhythmic change occurring on the first beat of measures 1 and 3.

However, these indications could be taken into consideration only after examination of the distribution of correct responses in time, since the contrapuntal structure we have been discussing operates only in the first four measures of the theme—the two last measures bringing about a clear conclusion by means of chords or other procedures (see Figure 7.14). It was thus of some concern whether the listeners of group A found it difficult to discern the theme within those four measures, and the global percentages of correct responses could not tell us that.

Distribution of Correct Responses in Time. As in the preceding analysis, I examined the way in which correct responses were distributed among the 9 sec of the duration of the theme (truncated to six measures). It happened that there were relatively few correct responses during the first 5 sec (the first four measures) of appearances 5, 6, and 7, giving 16.6%, 11.0%, and 16.5% respectively (compared with a mean of 29.8% for the first 5 sec). Thus there was in these three instances a noticeable delay in condensation, due to the contrapuntal combination noted earlier. But this delay hardly occurred further on, with appearances 8 and 10, even though the same combination was present. This effect did not occur very much for listeners in group B, and especially not for group C. Finally, this delay did not recur for group A with the second presentation. There was, then, already in the first presentation a certain amount of accommodation to discerning the theme as *figure*. Here there was a process of progressive structuring of the tonal pattern resulting in the functional distribution of its elements—some assuming little by little the function of ground, others organizing themselves with the help of previous repetitions as figure on the primary level and focus of attention. In some of the earlier appearances, the organizational weakness of the patterns presented in the other parts favored its emergence as figure. If we take appearance 4, for example, inspection of the tables of the temporal distribution shows that listeners in group A produced 44.3% and 44.2% correct responses during the first 5 sec of presentations one and two, compared with means of 29.8% and 38.1%. We must attribute these elevated figures to formal conditions in the polyphony, in which the theme was presented in the middle part and the upper and lower parts moved as shown in Figure 7.15.

Figure 7.14. Fragmented presentation of the subject: In the first four measures the subject is presented in the lower part, then after that in the upper part.

Figure 7.15. Apparent presentation of the subject in the middle part.

In measures 1 and 3 of this example the upper part is limited to developing the harmony by means of arpeggiated chords in syncopation, leaving the theme easy to detect, while the bass furnishes an almost immobile support. In measures 2 and 4 the upper part takes on the rhythm of the theme, emphasizing it, while the bass takes on a motion borrowed from the countersubject. Several conditions converge here that center attention on the theme and make the rest of the pattern appear as a neutral ground. The conditions doubtless hold for a single appearance. The pregnance and neutrality of figure and ground are relative to each other and constitute a functional equilibrium that enjoys a certain flexibility. The addition of a detail would not necessarily compromise it (as in the polyphony of appearance 1, measures 9–16, which is in some respects simpler than that of appearance 4).

The processes generating the distribution of the functions thus rest, as with all learning, on the passage from behavior *derived from* the forms to behavior *applied to* the forms. The behavior of concern here consisted of staying with the line of the theme under the various conditions created by the neutral or interfering forms presented with it.

If for each appearance of the theme the conditions of its identification were new, what meaning can a graphic representation such as that of Figure 7.16 have? We cannot claim that it represents a typical distribution of responses for a group, because that distribution varied noticeably from one appearance to another, at least for groups A and B. However, we can see here a clear indication of a difference between those groups, on one hand, and group C, on the other. It shows not only the existence of a more rapid mean condensation in group C (especially in the second presentation), but also a greater uniformity in their reactions across appearances of the theme. The curve representing group C, especially for the second presentation, can be considered typical of their collective behavior. The curves for the other groups appear bimodal and irregular. Comparing this figure with that representing the results for the *Fugue in F-sharp*, we can see the degree to which groups A and B were surpassed here by group C in the formation of the point of condensation.

Errors and Assimilations. As shown in Table 7.7, there were significant differences among the responses of the groups. Setting aside the cases of clusters 3 and 7 (3 and 6 in the second presentation), the percentages for

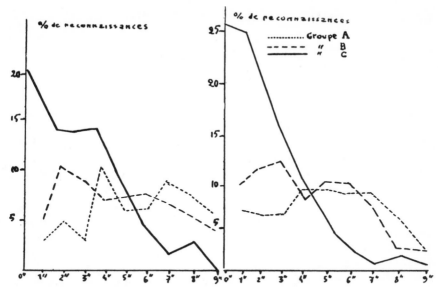

Figure 7.16. Distribution of correct responses in time: mean percentage of recognitions across all presentations for the three groups, plotted against the duration in time of the subject.

TABLE 7.7
Percentages of Errors and Assimilations During Different Time Intervals
(Indicated in Minutes and Seconds) for Three Groups Listening to the
Fugue in D Minor.

	First Presentation				Second Presentation		
Groups:	A	B	C		A	B	C
Interval				Interval			
1 0:39–0:43	22.2	14.2	0.0	1 0:38–0:44	33.3	29.0	8.3
2 0:44–0:55	22.2	35.7	16.6	2 0:45–0:50	22.2	25.8	4.1
3: 0:57–1:02	38.8	42.8	50.0	3 0:57–1:03	55.5	67.7	37.5
4 1:17–1:23	38.8	42.8	4.1	4 1:19–1:25	54.4	32.2	12.5
5 1:25–1:29	66.6	53.5	8.3	5 1:26–1:28	27.7	32.2	8.3
6 1:42–1:45	16.6	25.0	8.3	6 1:49–1:53	88.8	77.4	37.5
7 1:47–1:52	55.5	57.1	33.3	7 2:07–2:13	38.8	32.2	4.1
8 2:30–2:35	27.7	39.2	4.1	8 2:34–2:38	44.4	35.4	8.3
9 3:09–3:13	22.2	42.8	4.1	9 2:59–3:05	33.3	25.8	8.5
				10 3:06–3:13	44.4	41.9	4.1
Mean:	34.5	39.2	14.3		44.3	36.7	13.3

217

Figure 7.17. Motifs recalling the start of the subject (a) and the answer (b).

group C were invariably quite a bit lower than those for the other two groups. As it turned out, the two cases just noted corresponded to moments in the work when assimilation could be based on formal elements that made sense musically; namely, in measures 39–40 a progression in the bass clearly recalled the start of the theme, and in measures 72–73 there was a free imitation of the start of the answer (Figure 7.17a & b).

Other clusters coincided well in temporal localization from one presentation to the other; for example, clusters 1, 2, 4, 5, 6, and 9 (10 in the second presentation). Certain clusters referred to episodes that borrowed elements from the countersubject (measures 26–28 and 30–34—see Figure 7.18a). In these cases the solidarity of the theme and the rhythmic cell of the countersubject came into play, linked by an indissoluble bond to other episodes that recalled neither the theme nor the countersubject at all. These clusters were thus evidence of collective but aberrant assimilations (measures 51–54, 56–58, and 127–130).

Cluster 6 belonged to the first category because of the presence of the rhythmic cell imitated from the countersubject (measures 69–70), whereas cluster 8 in the first presentation belonged to the category of aberrant assimilations (measures 100–102, Fig. 7.18b).

The clusters that formed in the second presentation were of these two types as well. Cluster 7 corresponded to measures 84–86, in which the already familiar rhythmic cell appeared in the two upper parts. Clusters 8 and 9 were aberrant assimilations (measures 103–104 and 122–125). The former had its equivalent in cluster 4, whose musical motive corresponded to a transposition of measures 103–104. This motive could in a way evoke the start of the subject, only with a modification of its chromatic progression (see Figure 7.19). The first note of each beat, emphasized in the performance, gave the pattern this tendency to evoke the theme.

In general, setting aside the first two assimilations, which were based on clear formal principles, the mean percentages for the other types of

Figure 7.18. Rhythmic cell borrowed from the countersubject involved in aberrant assimilations of the subject.

Figure 7.19. Motif recalling the start of the subject, but with a modification of its chromatic progression.

assimilations for the two presentations were as follows: group A: 24.03% and 28.8%; group B: 28.1% and 25.4%; and group C: 5.05% and 5.8%.

In the case of the aberrant assimilations, rhythmic suggestions and motives too obscure to comprehend had only relatively weak influence on the listeners of group C. The means for the other groups, although important in their overall behavior, were nevertheless well below the level of the means for correct responses for the same subjects.

Conclusions. In conclusion, the perceptual activities of the three groups were more clearly distinguished with this fugue than with the preceding one. Although it is true that the means of percentages of correct responses were more or less the same, their distribution in time was very different and contrasted group C with groups A and B in forming the point of condensation. Moreover, the figures for errors and assimilations showed more clearly than for the preceding fugue the importance of musical education in the development of thematic *differentiation* in polyphonic situations. We saw earlier with linear organization that pattern organization was assured to a great extent when an equilibrium was reached between the capacity to assimilate what was actually presented to the theme and the capacity to differentiate from it what was foreign. Here, likewise, in all cases where there was nothing objective to justify it, insufficient differentiation was the rule, especially among group A and B listeners. Consistent with that result, assimilation was insufficient in passages where the theme appeared. However, these two forms of perceptual activity were here not identical to those described in the preceding chapter. With linear organization, they consisted principally of shifts accompanied by suppression of the intermediate field and partial or total identification of present perceptions with a previously perceived figure.

The role of activities pertaining to simultaneous organization is relatively weak in works in which the style of writing is of the "melody-with-accompaniment" type. But with polyphonic writing, assimilation and differentiation combine those activities with attentional shifts and decentrations required for the inspection of simultaneous registers in which the theme should be sought. Active listening for the theme involves a continual sweeping across superimposed melodic lines. The formation of a point of condensation is actually a cumulative process based on the disclosure of the notes of the theme as well as on the frequency of shifts that the listener is capable of producing in searching the polyphony.

THE IDEA OF INTEGRAL PERCEPTION

We now come to the idea of *integral perception*, synthesizing the activities (defined separately earlier) that coexist in varying proportions in the perception of any nonmonodic form. This can mean two distinctly different things:

First, it means the result of all the tonal and temporal relationships inherent in a work—relationships of pitch, of duration, of intensity, of timbre. Here we have the perception of its concrete *rhythm*. The reader may have been surprised to see that rhythm has not to this point been the object of any special analysis because it can be clarified in music only on the basis of all the aspects that we have distinguished through abstraction. De Schloezer (1947) showed the inadequacy of definitions of rhythm based only on duration, or metrical accents of intensity, or pitch. All of those factors occur in the total rhythm along with, in the case of polyphony, the reciprocal action of simultaneous "horizontal" structures and the effect of the harmonies they engender. It is true that for de Schloezer the rhythm of a work is what it makes of itself, conceived as becoming, that is, *in statu nascendi*, developed in time, or finally perceived. As we have seen, insofar as rhythm is a formal concept it can even be apprehended outside of its time by the analyst or composer. There will thus be an integral perception beginning at the moment the information conveyed by the tones is clearly perceived in each unit of time. It will be defined in a purely quantitative manner as an output fluctuating more or less, abundant or rare, rich at one moment in diverse elements of one order or another— an output that a machine or group of machines could record.

Second, in contrast, by integral perception we can mean a process of actualization that is not just quantitative but also qualitative and in which, besides these analyzed relationships, others are actively discerned. It goes without saying that both of these concepts are at once connected and contradictory—connected, because the more information there is, the greater the likelihood that the listener will detect subtle or remote relationships. We have seen in particular (apropos of the perception of changes in chords in the harmonization of a melodic formula) that the greater or lesser "presence" of the underlying harmony allowed musician listeners (more than the others) to localize alterations with certitude. As we have seen, the speed and mobility of the elementary acts improve the chances of recognizing a theme in a polyphonic texture. Conversely, to perceive a qualitative relationship in the linear or simultaneous structure is to abolish all that is foreign to its terms, to select them in order to reconnect them. There is in the hearing of a thematic work a certain discontinuity of psychological tension. Certain key moments completely occupy us because of their importance to the comprehension of the whole: exposition, recapitulation, passage to another idea, cyclic return; and certain others because of the formal invention they display, such as the thousand and one ways to vary a theme, superpositions, and shape-preserving transformations. The polygraphic experiments provided evidence of this. So it is that, in the series of tonal and temporal relationships analyzed, there arises that relation that allows us to organize them—a relation that doubtless does not require verbalization, but that itself assists us in retaining them long enough to comprehend at last the idea of the structure. Other moments bring relative relaxation that prepares us to detect further patterns. We now give ourselves over to the flow of information provided, whereas earlier we were looking for hidden information.

The necessity for retrospection also contributes to the discontinuity of integral perception. Establishing linear relations always implies reversibility, possible instantaneous, of apprehension. To grasp the relationship of the present with what has passed is to lose contact with what immediately follows, in order to establish a mental connection. What follows breaks the hold on the present, which is no longer perceived except peripherally.

Thus conceived, integral perception should not be confused with the automatic recording of the flow of information. *It is doubtless conditioned by the quantity of sensory elements that the listener can grasp at each instant, and by their amount of presence or of pregnance (depending on whether they pertain to ground or figure). But the listener who seeks to comprehend the unity of the pattern, its variety, its characteristics of invention must abandon a part of this wealth of elements. The perceptual integration of form cannot be merely a redintegration, but must in some sense be an active and abstracting dialectic.* To grasp the rule structure of the pattern and its appropriate time is to break the continuity of sensory adherence to the irreversible. Likewise, to grasp the organization of a simultaneous structure is to establish there a hierarchy, leaving obscure certain sensory givens (even while perceiving them) in favor of others one seeks to recognize. In other words, integral perception—which in this sense is intelligence—is made of temporary breaks in what is perceived, breaks which eventually bring out relations the character of whose terms do not permit them to be immediately perceived.

Part III

EXPRESSION
AND MEANING

Chapter 8
THE PROBLEM
OF MEANING

THE AESTHETIC CONTROVERSY

For the psychologist there is perhaps no problem more difficult to pose and to resolve than that of expression and meaning in music. As long as we were concerned only with classifying and describing partial or global tonal structures, or with researching their development in the course of experience as the result of acculturation and training, we remained on a strictly empirical level of establishing facts and finding explanations in other facts.

However, as soon as we try to submit to the same treatment aspects that are not inherent in the sound, we encounter innumerable possibilities for negation and affirmation. Even the notion that we have here matter for serious research can be disputed from the outset.[1] A proposition such as "In a melody the tonic is the final and most conclusive note" is essentially different, it seems from another such as "Compared to the major triad, the minor triad appears sad and sombre." Why is that so? It is not that only one of the two propositions can be subjected to rigorous experimental treatment so that its accuracy might be established or rejected. Rather, it is with the former proposition, and not with the latter, that we can find in the work (or in habits that similar works have stimulated) distinct reasons for the effect. For the latter proposition, certainly, explanations are legion. But as is often the case with arguments that attempt to account for conventions of ancient origin, they reach only a certain degree of validity.

---

[1]See Souriau (1929): ". . . Of all the speculations belonging to the philosophy of art, only those (interesting as the rest may be) have scientific value that contain a strict empirical study of form" (p. 36). Likewise Lalo (1908/1939) thought that we could "separate the expression from the essence of the music" (p. 14) and that we do not need to refer to it to know the work itself.

225

That this problem is not, in itself, strictly empirical is evident in the interminable controversy to which it has led since the advent of the scientific approach to these matters. At a time when *ethos* governed the expressive power of the Greek modes and when, in other civilizations, the elements of music (scales, notes) were associated in the codes of scholars and priests with the elements of the cosmos—with the points of the compass, the planets, the seasons (in China), the hours of the day, or the ages of human life (Java) (Sachs, 1943)—at that time the institutional character of the attributes of sound precluded the possibility of doubting them or of raising questions concerning them in any but theological terms, according to the norms of the "universe of discourse." Rules for tonality, numerous in western Europe until the 19th century, essentially raised the issue of analogous mental processes. To learn music then was not simply to learn the arrangement of notes compatible with the tonal system, but also to penetrate the intricacies of a system of significations that was not always either explicit or coherent. Nowadays, in contrast, apart from the imprecision of psychological data concerning musical expression, a number of aestheticians emphasize the hierarchically lower position of such systems in the comprehension of musical works.[2] The significant form—the musical ideas—becomes an end in itself. The true connoisseur is satisfied with the enjoyment that it brings. Expression comes in addition to that enjoyment (Hanslick (1854/1957). Among the varieties of aesthetic experience, only those that put form first are adequate to the "essential nature" of art. Others are inadequate and thus unworthy of interest (Schoen, 1928). Finally, this hierarchical argument sometimes results in a simple denial of the expressive power of music, its power to describe or to signify in general. The approbation of the public, their reactions and ways of understanding music, is of concern to neither art nor aesthetics. Only the freedom of the artist matters. Artists engage in the development of pure forms, and their freedom requires us to set aside the myth of expression.[3]

"Formalism" thus has diverse nuances of meaning, and its usage is difficult because it can characterize doctrines and opinions that, for a variety of reasons, give the study or contemplation of forms a predominant or exclusive place in both aesthetics and cognition. In addition, there arise from this formalism antitheses in two directions. Many musicians, as well as many aestheticians, have chosen expression as an indispensible factor

---

[2]See de Schloezer (1947): "The aesthetic attitude thus consists in attention being directed exclusively to form" (p. 259).

[3]"Do we not, in truth, ask the impossible of music when we expect it to express feelings, to translate dramatic situations, even to imitate nature? . . . And it is quite illicit, to my way of thinking, to set the public up as a jury by entrusting it with the task of rendering a verdict on the value of a work" (Stravinsky, 1947, pp. 79 & 138).

in comprehension and as the reigning feature of artistic studies. Many put respect for artistic creation first, which in the case of masters cannot be characterized without belittlement as gratuitous playing with notes. Dukas (1948), for example, asserts that "expression is an indispensible element in music. An ignorant but sensitive person is more valuable than an adroit arranger of notes."[4] Would anyone say that he was not enough of a musician to have an "adequate aesthetic attitude" toward his art? Others have indicated that the expression of emotions is inherent in the works themselves and can be heard in them (e.g., d'Ollone, 1952) such that "every musical form is in itself a representation of emotion. It seems to us that it symbolizes emotions. There is probably no inexpressive music" (Delacroix, 1927, p. 303). Still others support the thesis of the priority of expression. For them expression is not merely an addition to primary perceptual experiences, but, on the contrary, an immediate effect of the global apprehension of the object—the ground of awareness; whereas the details of its construction and its diverse formal elements, although they serve as underlying implicit motives for expression, will be only marginally present in consciousness (Arnheim, 1949).

From the many possibilities, these two contradictory approaches have been selected by the literature of the last 50 years. This seems to indicate an odd division in contemporary opinion regarding the problem that concerns us, a division that was shown to be dichotomous in a 1918 study by Vernon Lee (1932). Lee sent questionnaires (translated into each language) to numerous musicians in England, Germany, and France. The responses of half of the subjects disclosed the existence of a coherent extramusical message that in its variety sustained their interest in listening to music; the responses of the other half maintained that music was just music.

IMPORTANCE OF SOCIOCULTURAL ATTITUDES

But what does all this mean for the psychologist who is concerned not with endorsing one theory or the other, but rather with determining the facts that these theories capture? In a sense, the methodological prudence

---

[4]See also d'Udine (1910): "A fugue of Bach, a sonata of Mozart, are, like a page from Berlioz or Wagner, works of transposition, and to claim that these old masters were seeking only pure combinations of sound would be to recast their admirable creations on the same level as student exercises or academic products. It would be to refuse them that human component that in fact made them immortal."

of those who eschew these contradictions seems to be justified by the contradictions themselves; we should restrict all empirical studies of music to morphological facts. However, in my view, these opinions and evidence, apart from stimulating the curiosity of the researcher, indicate what is the psychological nature of the facts of musical expression and semantics. The facts are not of the "stimulus-response" type; they invoke (whether or not they appear in the listener) a relationship to cultural stereotypes concerning the nature of art, particularly the art of music. Our epoch lies at the confluence of cultural streams and opposing ideologies. If the question posed by these facts is not, as we have said, strictly empirical, it is not because these facts do not exist. It is rather that they exist only to the degree that the subject experiencing them accepts general norms of expression and signification. Without, for the moment, trying to find out which of these significations are "natural" and which are "conventional," we can nevertheless admit that the mere presentation of the "stimulus" is not always sufficient to trigger the appearance of extramusical psychological contents linked to it by semiotic relationships; or, more precisely, that nothing in the individual's idiosyncrasies must contradict the general idea of a possible correspondence between the musical structure and contents of that sort. As we shall see in analyzing the results of the studies, the majority of subjects who refuse to admit such a correspondence with regard to a given fragment invoke general principles that involve the essence and specificity of art or some theory of the self-sufficiency of form, or the like. They do not claim to be incapable of performing that operation (and at times even indulge in it in spite of a theoretical denial), but they find it lacking sense, prejudicial, and a sacrilege, vis-à-vis what *ought to be* a veritable contemplation of the music.

Therefore, we should sketch the outline of a more empirical conception of perception as a basis for the problem to be treated experimentally.

Musical expression and signification are adventitious occurrences whose appearance is tied either to ideological contexts or to actual (possibly ceremonial) contexts, both of which are associated with institutions and not dependent on individual contingencies. The normative character of aesthetic contemplation has often been emphasized. Texts concerned with initiation to a musical work indicate not only *what* must be seen or heard, but also *how* one should approach a given work or class of works (Fallot, 1951). The presentation of a painters or musicians as yet unknown to the public requires not only that they be situated in the historical genealogy of their time, but also that the nature of their language, the problems that they set themselves, and their expressive or formal intentions be specified. There is something *ritualistic* in the perception of art that prevents us from considering it according to the schema of perception in general—an aspect which, in certain civilizations, is still evident in the institutions governing the construction and upkeep of instruments and the creation and performance of works.[5] The way to listen is thus implicitly suggested by all this context, independently of whatever significance is attached to the particular social function of the ceremony: sacred and secular festivals, births, and funeral rites. The autonomy acquired by music in our civilization and its promotion to the rank of an activity with no other goal than to assure its own performance lead to the appearance of a new way of listening that nevertheless coexists with more ancient ritual features. The attitude of "rapture" (Pradines's (1954) term), certainly frequent in our civilization, cannot be considered to be directly released by sound. Rather, it appears as a tradition, common to a whole historical-cultural cycle marked out by myths known to everyone—the music of the spheres, the orphic lyre, Platonic reminiscence—coming down to us across intervening centuries of Christianity.

The "abolition of the will to live"—detachment—according to Schopenhauer (1844/1966) is only one of the attitudes traditionally constituted interdependently with belief in the transcendent origin of music. According to other traditions, the revelation of its mystery might bring about exaltation; trance states; motor, respiratory, or vocal excitation, carried to paraxysm, exhaustion, or death. The singer becomes possessed, racked by supernatural forces evoked by the sounds, by the repetition of stereotyped rhythmic forms, and by the increase of loudness and tempo. This communicative possession, imitated by the audience and striving for a shared ecstasy in a sort of collective frenzy, has been noted by many observers (e.g., Sachs, 1943; David, 1951). The secularization of norms and myths in contemporary art criticism and aesthetics should not make us lose sight of their historical character. Their public diffusion gives rise to attitudes as little "spontaneous" as the rapture and frenzy just described, attitudes that condition the perception of sound patterns as either deprived of or endowed with significance.

Apart from that, it is easy to see that once constituted in the listener, the attitude will be generalized and will operate effectively with all music, producing with regard to one or another school or period judged not to conform to the aesthetic ideal one has formed, either dislike or a projection into the music of features inherent in the attitude. "Expressionist" or "formalist" norms in the broader sense have doubtless ruled musical production just as they have influenced the public. To be sure, composers

---

[5]See David (1951). For many primitive peoples, musical sound has a magical origin and power. It is not man who produces it—he is just the occasional cause. Instruments must be used in accordance with strict norms. In matriarchal societies only the women can make use of them. Their use by the opposite sex brings death. In East Africa, the royal drums rest on a bed in a closed-up hut, guarded by two women who maintain a continuous hearthfire. The sorcerer's flute has the power to alienate or attract affection.

almost always avoid elaborating theories, but none can escape his time. As Lalo (1908/1939) noted, two doctrines served to determine absolutely only two periods in the historical evolution of art. The former held for romanticism, and the latter for classicism. It is not for us to settle here questions related to the history of music or to classical or romantic conceptions of art. But it is undeniable that, even if the limits in time of these conceptions are imprecise, the creators of music have not always striven in the same direction.[6] Not only have sound structures' forms of adaptation to expressive, descriptive, or symbolic content been different through the course of history, but the search for a particular adaptation cannot be considered to be a permanent preoccupation of composers. The evolution of musical language is not limited to innovations in the realm of syntax and rhetoric. Dukas (1948) and many others even thought all innovation of that sort to be dictated by imperatives inherent in the expression of a content, varying from one case to the next, at times bordering on the imitation or description of natural processes and at times turning to the translation or expression of character, passions, and emotions, even of ideas. Dupré and Nathan (1941), as well as Delacroix (1927) insisted that beginning with Beethoven, evolution went in the direction of hypersubjectivity: "With the evolution of artistic taste and the progress of orchestration, music became more and more subjective. The composer no longer described just to describe. When he had recourse to description it was for purely subjective ends. He expressed internal emotions and states of mind through the symbolic imitation of external things" (Dupré & Nathan, 1941, p. 47–48).[7] This attitude is necessarily constituted as a single attitude within the individual, and it is applied impartially to works of the recent past as well as to those of the present. All music offers at once a formal arrangement and the possibility of semantic judgments and expression. That is why general opinions of this art, taken as a whole, can have a unilateral character. Our judgment, based on historical knowledge and analysis, occasionally succeeds in distinguishing features that arise prior to formal research or expressive intention. But most of the time in perception we do not achieve this discrimination. Rather, we look in the

---

[6]See Dukas, 1948: "It is only since Beethoven that music has taken on, in general, this aspect of *translation* from the psychological order to the musical order. We may even state that the greater part of the pleasure that today's listener takes in music is provided him by the impression of *struggle* that the composer had to engage in, in order to arrive at the musical expression of more and more complicated interior phenomena" (p. 142). In this regard Dukas distinguishes the objective *description* and the direct *translation*, more recent than the indirect *expression* of feelings." (p. 195). He also adds a form of *symbolic description* (affect-laden allusion to natural scenes or effects) introduced by Debussy. See also Francès, 1951.

[7]Snyders (1955) showed that in France, in the 17th and 18th centuries, in spite of fluctuations in musical taste, one principle developed by composers and justified by philosophers remained stable: *Music is an imitation of feelings*.

works of the masters for that which some of them have shown us to be excellent. In the time of Dukas (1948) there was not only a retrospective reevaluation of the work of Mozart, but a certain transmutation of his general meaning. Listeners were not satisfied with the beautiful organization of forms but found in him a subtle translation of subjectivity and even a metaphysical content that seemed inseparable from genius. In the 18th century, noted Delacroix (1927), "the general public, infatuated with the cult of the meaningful dramatic melody," (p. 2) heard the symphonies with an inattentive ear. Stratagems of development gave the impression of a multiplicity of themes, and listeners had false perceptions of form. Further from our time, in an epoch that we shall have occasion to discuss in detail, when there arose in Germany the conception of romanticism in music—according to which music left off being an arrangement of tones in order to disclose the secret and the profound in man and the universe— Haydn, Mozart, and even Bach were heard from that perspective. They were made romantics before there was a Romanticism.[8]

In our time, when a formalist tendency has developed among many musicians, emphasis has been placed retrospectively on hints of polytonality and dodecaphony in Beethoven (Scherchen, 1946). According to Scherchen, the introduction of the human voice in the soloists and choir in the Ninth Symphony evidences only Beethoven's a need to resort to a group of timbres different from those of the orchestra, without any expressive intention. Between Mozart and Beethoven there would be differences only in "language"—writing, style—language being defined primarily by "the persistence of certain melodic formulas, of harmonic and rhythmic phrases, of constructive schemas, etc.—the sound patterns being as expressive as they are in virtue of the structures themselves" (de Schloezer, 1951, p..

Thus, besides acknowledging the historical diversity of works, it is necessary to recognize a parallel diversity of modes of apprehension— forms of satisfaction pursued that constitute one aspect of the cultural personality of the individual and that spontaneously spring into action for every production. Our age, heir to so many traditions ceaselessly resurrected by books and reviews, in which aesthetic theories attach themselves to philosophical, ethical, and political concepts,[9] does not offer the psychologist a simple field of investigation. All that is said and written concerning music enters as an integrative factor in the attitude of the listener. In the listener's ideology, there might be either inhibition or facilitation

---

[8]This trend of ideas was developed in various German reviews between 1798 and 1805. From that time, the expressionist conception triumphed and brought about a romantic interpretation of the art of the past. See especially texts published beginning in 1799 by C. F. Michalis in the *Allgemeine musikalische Zeitung*, cited by Boyer (1938).

[9]De Schloezer (1951) notes correctly that all theory and opinion concerning art brings to bear philosophical consequences and a whole Weltanschauung.

of any spontaneous extramusical thoughts. What, therefore, can serve as method for an experiment consistent with the foregoing remarks? What might be the import of such a study? It is tempting to limit the questioning of subjects to their general conception of art.

RESULTS OF PSYCHOLOGICAL INVESTIGATIONS

Since the birth of empirical psychology there have been a great many studies and experiments that are useful to examine at the outset. All of them depart from the conception of music taken as a *stimulus*; that is, they conform to a schema that we have just discussed.

To start this examination, brief as it is, we must keep in mind a nomenclature that provides us orientation amid the varying terminology utilized by the authors. These studies are based on the analysis of one or more of the following types:

1. *Objective judgments or objective tendencies* concerning: (a) abstract properties of the stimulus, timbre, tempo, vibrato, etc.; (b) characteristics of musical form, its identification as to genre, its historical genealogy, or merely different moments in its development; (c) the technical structure of the form: the type of writing, the details of construction, etc.

2. *Normative judgments*, formulated as either personal appreciations or appreciations referring to to cultural norms and as a result having a certain objective intention. The subject will say, according to the case, "I found the theme banal," or else, "The theme is banal."

3. *Statements of an introspective (intrasubjective) order* related to the psychological effects felt by the subject: activation or inhibition of ideation, depression or enhancement of affective or motor tone, etc.

4. *Judgments of signification* consisting in the attribution of extramusical content to a certain local or global form, at once different from the physical and aesthetic qualities of the sound pattern and from the effects that the subject is aware of in himself. These judgments establish a relationship between sign and thing signified permit us to consider music as a language in a sense close to that of verbal language.[10] The modalities of this relationship are of three sorts:

---

[10]This juxtaposition constitutes an entirely provisional way to consider the relationship between sign and referent appropriate to music. I do not believe that it consists, as it does in language, in a *designation* (as Meyer, 1957, thought). However, we can join them by means of the fact that in the two cases the referent is not an internal property of the sign. This brings us back to extra-musical realities.

(a) It can be individual. The signification can relate to some personal exprience *without there being a simple association by contiguity*. It can be accompanied by imagery or not.

(b) The signification may be concrete or semiconcrete. It can relate to some aspect of nature or some general dramatic situation without direct relationship to the subject.

(c) Finally, the signification may be abstract. It can express itself in terms of psychological traits or emotions apart from any immediate causation: cheerfulness, playfulness, serenity, universal representations of nature such as order, disorder, hierarchy, etc.

As we shall see, these categories are well supported by clinical observations and common experience. But they are equally consistent with the research methods that have been employed. A common feature, however, of the majority of studies is the misunderstanding of this consistency and a lack of reflection on the methods used. The methods have been of two types:

1. *Noninductive methods* consist of asking subjects about the effects that they experience in listening, without first specifying them—for example, "Describe what happened within yourself."

2. *Inductive methods* are those in which the experimenter specifies in the question the type of response expected from the subject: an image, a concrete or an abstract signification, an experienced emotion, an internal change. Induction can be more or less precise depending on the extent to which the subject is led by the terms of the question. Thus there are *guided* methods of induction ("Choose among the several adjectives presented those that describe the emotion"), *semiguided* methods ("Use an adjective to describe the emotion"), and *free* methods ("Give a description of the emotion in words").

The method and the formulation of the instructions are important to the nature of the results obtained. Depending on whether the questions bear on general effects experienced, on agreement or disagreement, on the general signification of an image, we obtain a scale of responses that differ *qualitatively*. The results show that *there is a possibility of inducing different psychological states using the same musical content*. The music can lend itself to varying effects: it can be felt and lived through by way of direct effects on the motor or affective level, or it can be interpreted and translated into memories and associations. What should be emphasized is the influence of verbal induction on the attitude of the listener and the importance of that attitude in determining the psychological state linked to a musical element. This effect of verbal commands is found in the typological classifications to be discussed later. Several authors have observed that musically educated subjects, perceiving music according to the norms of a formalist aesthetics, hardly ever give any introspective responses. Others, appreciate music affectively when interest in form relaxes. Likewise, these subjects have a certain amount of resistance to interpreting music with the aid of images. In short, aesthetic norms, as another aspect of verbal commands, can induce various types of psychological states.

Some social conditioning is established by education in the effects of music. Concerning likes and dislikes, Ortmann (cited in Schoen, 1927) observed that children preferred pitches in the neighborhood of a low C (75% of choices) and rejected pitches around middle C (10% of choices). However, a similar discrimination could not be obtained with adults because of their habituation to the higher frequencies. With regard to dissonance, Ortmann showed that after 2 months' conditioning, the disagreeable experience of hearing a major-seventh chord was neutralized for 7 year olds. Husson and his colleagues (1953) also noted that the threshold of what is musically disagreeable fluctuates because of inhibition exerted by the cortex and adaptation phenomena. We know that slowly but surely the concert-going public is growing accustomed to rhythmic and harmonic innovations of nonclassical composers. A sociological study would show that it took more than 25 years for the augmented fifths and whole-tone scale of Debussy's school to cease offending the ears of concert lovers yet still retain their peculiar psychological resonances. Sokolov (1952), resuming researches in the Pavlovian tradition, found that language can inhibit strong excitations, including dissonance.

Thus by means of all these reservations, and by emphasizing the relative and historical character of psycho-musical correspondences, we can attack the problem. By analyzing a number of classifications, we observe that they cluster into two principal groups: typological classifications and semantic classifications. The former were obtained with free induction, generally by eliciting from subjects associations between the music (the inductive element) and a verbal response (the induced element). The contents of the induced element provide the principle of classification. For semantic classifications, obtained with the semiguided method, the inductor is always a fragment or piece of music, but the induced element is limited to a designated region that excludes other responses: in general the area of emotions, anthropomorphic characters, or dramatic situations. With the guided method, that region is restricted still further to nuances of emotion.

Semantic classifications, then, can occur as a particular case of typological classifications, because the latter almost always allow a semantic type of response. However, the method of free induction seems, on reflection, to be essentially different from the others in that it does not uniquely orient the listeners toward perception of the stimulus.[11] The focus of attention could as well be the subjects themselves—the modifications that they observe in themselves and the images that appear in their minds. The response provided is not necessarily tied to the musical effect; it might be the continuation of an antecedent thought. In contrast, procedures resulting in semantic responses incline the subjects to perceive significations *in* the musical pattern, which remains the center of attention and which must be characterized. Here there is an objective process of pairing words and music, different from the vaguely introspective, even equivocal, attitude that consists in asking oneself "what one felt."[12] Of course, this pairing could in itself give rise to reservations. It implies as a postulate the non-specificity of the systems of both expression and objectivization. It is not evident a priori that the significations of music, as it is perceived, invariably have verbal correspondences, such that there would always be a possibility of translation. In fact, the word condenses an infinite variety of affective nuances, of individual differences in the *experience* of the same stimuli, of stages of development of the same socialized expression. These verbalizations thus play the role of substitutes, summarizing groups of impressions whose detail is impossible to express except through the musical structure itself.[13] We cannot deny this approximate aspect of the studies, which is clear from the experimental results. Listening to music determines regions of possible meaning concerning which verbal language is at once too precise and too lax. On one hand, subjects cannot decide if the nuances that the words introduce are fitting. On the other hand, the word chosen is a makeshift—it captures only the overall appearance, the physiognomy, the affective tone of the signification. But within those limits it is felt to be appropriate. Moreover, if the word socializes the expression and confines it to the use of preestablished categories, it also contributes to some extent to the socialization of subjective experience according to the same

---

[11]This is a case, in effect, of a noninductive procedure, according to which music does not necessarily generate associations, but can become the occasional cause of some state or another.

[12]In that case the procedure conforms to certain preoccupations of aestheticians: "In truth, it is the music itself that appears tender and of such poignant and melancholy aimiability. . . . What have you just told me of Schubert? What have you just told me of myself? It is the same—the work—that just now wept, that just now developed and stopped in such poses—itself completely alive with its own life" (Souriau, 1929, p. 117).

[13]As de Schloezer (1951) showed, the opposition here is that of the general designation (in the verbal system) and the individual concrete expression (in the musical system). But the abstract always grasps something of the concrete, and conversely, the musical concrete is abstract and general in certain of its aspects.

norms. In one sense, what one experiences becomes sharpened when one collects it into a familiar form classified by language.

Typological Classifications

As early as 1897, Downey showed, in a study of 21 musically untrained subjects, that three types of responses could coexist in the same listener: the concrete response (definite imagery), the subjective response (concerning the affective tone attributed to the stimulus), and the sensori-motor response (perception of finger movements, thrills, etc. in response to the music). The quantitative distribution of results disclosed a clear advantage of first two types over the last.

Delacroix (1927), relying on a number of literary documents and on individual observations, distinguished four types of responses, of which some could coexist in the same listener:

1. *Egocentric imaginative type*, with a hedonistic base. Musical stimulation awakens in these subjects sensory excitations and a reverie centered on personal themes. This is the case with Stendhal, Sully Prudhomme, and several of the subjects that Delacroix examined. This type included developmental sequences of two sorts, tending either to the formalist type (when musical culture was developed) or to the paroxystic type (characterized by the states of musical extasy described by Diderot and several of the subjects. In these cases conscious awareness of form is weak or nonexistent.

2. *Imaginative allocentric type*. Images here have little apparent relationship to the subject's life. Though at times dependent on it, they are not integrated into comprehension of the musical form (for example, perception of color schemes, color hearing, and photisms). These phenomena are observed as often among musicians as among subjects deprived of musical culture. This type can even lean toward a type of formalism in which the perceived schemas adhere to melodic contours and rhythmic patterns—visual images of gestures and moving contours.

3. *Formalist type*. This type is focused on the development of the sound patterns, with apprehension of the vertical and horizontal textures of the groupings, an apprehension that is facilitated when the subject commands a technical vocabulary but that can occur to some extent even among untrained subjects.

4. *Associative type*. Here adequate images are evoked and intelligible images arise, flowing ultimately from the literary theme that serves

as a basis for the work, with an occasional symbolic spectacle or dramatic development adapted to the events that it contains.

In Ortmann (cited in Schoen, 1927), we find a three-way classification:

1. *Sensory type*, characterized by the subject's adherence to the stimulus as such.
2. *Perceptual type*, in which local stimuli are integrated into a global synthesis in which they become organized into motifs, phrases, contours, progressions, and contrasts.
3. *Anticipatory (imaginal) type*, in which substitution of harmonic elements in the melodic phrase occurs, as well as imaginative anticipations of movement and articulation in the work.

Myers (cited in Schoen, 1927), seeking to assemble evidence concerning individual differences that could exist among 15 listeners of the same general culture but with varying musical education, started off with pure tones and then progressed to musical works. Although there was not a clear correlation between the results of the two types of experiment, there was a certain tendency for subjects to respond in one manner rather than in another, whether by "intrasubjective" remarks on the physiological effects experienced and memory images evoked; by objective remarks concerning physical or cultural characteristics and the formal structure of the music, or by judgments of signification (affective or personalizing) and the attribution of anthropomorphic characteristics to themes and rhythms. Myers made an astutely observed the frequent disparity in the same subject between the signification perceived as inherent in the music and the affective state experienced at the same time. There was not always an accommodation of the one to the other. The signification could be antecedent or even contrary to the feeling that was experienced.

Thus we observe that even the noninductive method employed in these studies gives rise to many judgments of signification, bearing not on what the music *is* or *appears to be*, but rather on what it *says* relating to the listener or to what it expresses in general.

However, with the semiguided method of induction we see a considerable increase in the proportion of semantic responses. At this poiint new problems arise, namely, problems of consistency of the significations (indicated by the frequency with which they are attributed by a subject population to a particular musical pattern), problems of their coherence and the limits of that coherence, problems concerning their historical origins and of their psychophysiological basis, and so on. These problems, whose solutions are of consequence for the science of art as well as for applications of music to the theatre and broadcasting, cannot be entirely resolved by psychological inquiries, though the latter facilitate the work of historians and physiologists. For example, the affective signification of the major and minor modes has long been a puzzle to physicians and physiologists insofar as those modes had been attributed to mysterious properties of the stimulus. Psychological research has shed light on the weakness of those explanations by revealing the considerable cultural and historical relativity of these significations. Gilman (1891/92) showed, on the basis of a study of 22 amateurs of music, that the major and minor modes do not determine affective tone in a decisive manner. Heinlein (1928) showed that *ethos* could not be attributed in a fixed way to major and minor *chords*. Hevner (1935, 1936) seems to have established that *ethos* is tied to melodies and to melodic-harmonic complexes. The adjectives that expressed *ethos* best were "happy," "light," and "lively," applied to the major, and their opposites applied to the minor. The adjectives that expressed *ethos* least well were "calming," "exciting," and "secular." However, there was no automatic and universal attribution of *ethos*. Thus, the adjective "light" was attributed to the major 374 times, as opposed to 171 times to the minor, in connection with the same stimuli.

Semantic Classifications

Gilman (1891/92) used the method of semiguided induction with some variation in instructions. Sometimes he asked his subjects to describe an opposition of themes in the same piece; at other times, he asked them to provide a dramatic interpretation; and in still other cases, he asked them to define the general feeling of a work, the atmosphere that it created, and the like. The results obtained corresponded closely to the type of question he posed, and there was a clear convergence of affective tone in the responses in spite of the variety of verbal expression, notably: indications of movement, of activity, and of conflict applied to themes and relationships among themes, to agogic rhythms, and to polyphony. Emotions and impressions of the patterns were coherent, but closely related nuances were not distinguished. For example, "melancholy," "discouragement," and "dispair" were applied to the same piece.

Guided induction has been employed most frequently, doubtless because of the ease of calculating the results. Gatewood (in Schoen, 1927) showed that the frequency and coherence of words and expressions used to characterize music were variable. Next to coherent areas, including *greatness, lines, movement*, and *dramatic genre*, there were incoherent areas that included *color* and *season*, for example. This study could be criticized for its supposition that unity of signification should hold across a whole work, which is doubtful. Furthermore, it is obviously arbitrary to apply the same classes of significations to different works. Some works simply could not lend themselves to questions concerning color or temperature, whereas those questions were justified in other cases.

This sort of difficulty was mitigated in a study by Hevner (1936) in which the listener was asked to make a new choice from an adjective list at selected moments indicated by the experimenter during the piece. The list consisted of 66 adjectives expressin psychological states and qualities, clustered into groups having similar meaning. The results showed that although the same adjectives were not chosen to correspond to a given passage, others were chosen from the same group. In other words, there was some commonality of affective tone in the choices of the listeners. To refine these results in a causal direction, Hevner later presented original and altered versions of the same pieces to different groups of subjects. The altered versions involved changes of mode, chordal complexity, rhythm, or direction of melodic movement. Variations in adjective choices from one version to another demonstrated that the modification of one element while the other elements remained constant introduced new significations. The most noteworthy changes in meaning were associated with mode and chordal complexity and, to a lesser extent, with rhythm. Changes in melodic direction had almost no influence on signification. Watson (1942) made the same use of adjectives in a study of abstract significations. Watson's conclusions agreed with Hevner's regarding degree of precision and consistency with which the choices were made. And the same notions were expressed by Campbell (1942) in a study of basic affective patterns applied to music. The limitations of his tentative results in expressing nuances of listeners' responses led Campbell to conclude that "music expresses overall emotional patterns much more clearly than it expresses internal aspects of those patterns." If, for a given work, 90% of the choices were of "cheerful," it is impossible to determine in the course of a second hearing whether this cheerfulness was carefree, joyful, or lively.

REFLECTIVE OBSERVATIONS OF MUSICOLOGISTS

Finally, we should not disregard the interest of semantic classifications obtained without experimentation, but simply by reflective description. Musicians and musicologists have gone out of their way to systematize the observations they make of themselves concerning musical language. In truth, it is often difficult to untangle in their works what reflects ancient myths or traditions already dead in contemporary thought from what remains alive and psychologically relevant—that is, perceptually real.

Later we take into account certain observations relative to cultural significations. There is no doubt that writings of this genre, when their contents converge on observations common to several authors, consist of facts that are just as valuable as those from experiments (which would in certain cases be difficult to carry out).

Certain musicologists of an empirical bent have become involved with *explaining* the expressive means of descriptive music and with analyzing the underlying associations on which a number of objective significations are based. Combarieu (1893), in developing the consequences of a theory that puts song at the origin of all music, sought to show that the association of pitch height and physical height was primitive, arising from kinesthetic sensations situated in the head and thorax. As a consequence, successions of pitches were immediately placed in an imagined space in the form of movements, directions, and so forth. Music could thus translate form, duration, rhythm, direction of movement, and the numerosity of objects, including the relationships of their motions in space (via polyphony) and their distances (via tonal distance). To these were added less well-defined associations, such as those of the serious and the somber, as well as more explicable notions that conferred affective qualities and evocative power on instrumental timbres and that related melody and declamation by way of the laws of "instinctive language," the borrowings by composers of rhythms, themes, and modes having a well-defined imprint of time and place.

The views of Goblot (1901) were not very different; he saw in the suggestion of imagined movement one of the principal resources of musical description. In contrast to Combarieu, he denied music the power to give perceptible form to an idea except through motoric induction. Moreover, there is in Goblot an echo of the research of his time connecting hypnotism and suggestion with the musical stimulus.[14] The motion represented in consciousness would arise from muscular resonance set off by the direct action of the stimulus on the neuromuscular system: "A melodic pattern produces the idea of movement since it induces us to move ourselves"

---

[14]Despine (1880) presented evidence for the appearance of an "emotional pantomime" in hysterical subjects that was set off by music and regulated by the expressive features of the musical form. The experiments done by Rochas, Dauriac, and Poiré (1900) with a normal hypnotized subject demonstrated a considerable diffusion of the reflex motor accompaniment that besets the listener and was most clearly seen in the way it affected the larynx. As described by those authors, this accompaniment involved the entire muscular system, with, however, a localization corresponding at times to the degrees of the scale, and at times to different components of the sound structure. For example, the accompaniment of a waltz was mimicked by the legs, while the arms sketched the melodic contour of the song. We may wonder up to what point this experiment (which has never been repeated) can be taken literally in all its aspects. The audiomotor parallelism is almost too perfect.

(Closely following the experiments of de Rochas, Dauriac, and Poiré (1900), Goblot proposed that the degrees of the scale correspond to definite places in the body, going from the feet (*do*) to the head and lips (*si*). This description is thus intimately tied up with the direct action of the body, although it is not clear how to get from *sensation* to *cognition*— from motor accompaniments to the representation of movement. The order and size of melodic intervals, and the relations of high and low, become translated into spatial relationships. These translations need to be distinguished from those that use musical imitation without recourse to represented motion—the songs of birds, the noise of thunder. Both mechanisms are nevertheless more intelligible than the affective impact of a simple melody, chord, or mode. There we find sources of signification that cannot be traced to mimetic description nor to sonic imitation, and for which we cannot find an explication in Goblot's terms that would be wholly satisfactory.

What gives value to these reflective classifications, apart from their contributions in analysis and explication, is that they include so much evidence that is not just individual but representative of a category of especially well-educated subjects, reflecting traditions and aesthetic canons that in some instances have been widely diffused throughout the public. The public *learns to listen* in a particular manner as a result of their influence. Conversely, it is likely that a certain formalist attitude developed among music lovers through the influence of the ideas and productions of composers and aestheticians defending the thesis of the superiority of such an attitude over others. In several of the studies discussed here we can see that where subjects refused to give a meaning to a musical fragment that they heard, they added to their response a normative or theoretical justification. Music, according to them, *must not be interpreted*, just as one or another master had established. Quite as much as associations between sign and thing signified, the inhibition of such associations could become established as the result of transitory norms developed by authorities in the matter of art and its understanding.

What meaning and what import can we confer on this body of empirical work (whose treatment here is far from exhaustive) from the perspective that we believe correct? This typological research clearly indicates the polysemy of a given musical content, and the semantic research provides evidence of the multiplicity of significations potentially present in a given structure or class of structures. From a psychological point of view, we can conclude that music, in many of its forms, can be the point of departure for a variety of semantic inductions, as well as for objective, normative, or introspective judgments. The decisive effect of verbal instructions on those inductions leads to the thought that different psychological states can occur in relation to the same musical structure, depending on the work and its formal properties, the various attitudes governed by different rituals, and (which is the same thing) contrasting ideological conceptualizations. Every inductive method is closely related to an aesthetic ritual, before which the possible resistance of the subject seems easily overcome. The varieties of expressionism or of theoretical formalism, as we know them, consist of accentuating one of the four types of state previously described, while conferring on others a lesser importance and lower value, or passing over them in silence. Hanslick (1854/1957) eulogized object judgment, with which he connected the apprehension of beauty.[15] He disparaged the importance of "intrasubjective" judgments[16] and contested the possibility of a consistency of semantic judgments, relegating to them the role of merely vague and indeterminate schemata that chiefly express the evolution and dynamics of feelings. In contrast, Hoffman (1949) glorified judgments of signification, which he placed at the origin not only of the beautiful, but of individual emotion.[17] All purely formal inquiry was for him an "enemy of music".[18] D'Udine (1910) making of the comprehension of a work a process that follows back through the progress of creation, had comprehension start with an immediate impression, the product of affective empathy and aesthetic surrender, leading to a judgment of signification concurrently with the "generative sensation." De Schloezer (1951), in contrast, took knowledge of the work as the point of departuture for comprehension, which consisted essentially of grasping the spiritual meaning, of which the psychological meaning was merely the unfolding in time. To the extent that there was expression, it was to be found only in the "expressive power of the form. . . . The work reveals only its own being, which is a system of forms in the process of becoming. . . . However, that which is there—that presence—suffices to give me fulfillment. It speaks, but only speaks of itself" (p. 231). Everything was subsumed in some way under the objective judgment, of which the signification was only the effulgence.

It would be easy to undertake other analyses of this tyoe. They would only confirm our certainty of the primacy of attitude, constituted on the basis of sociocultural norms concerning the "effects" of music. Here, then, would be a good place to work out a reciprocal interrelation of cultural

---

[15] 1957 "Musical beauty is musically beautiful" (p. 64).

[16] "The less the resistance imposed by education, the more music has power in the pathological sense" (p. 94).

[17] "Isn't music a mysterious language from the far away realm of the spirit—a language whose marvellous accents find their echo in our soul, where they awaken a higher, more intense life?" (p. 205)

[18] In *Kreisleriana, the enemy of music* (Kreisler himself) is described with the traits of a young man whose hostility to music is directed at contrapuntal forms, concertos, Italian operas—at all that is not simple, mystical, and directly expressive.

analysis and structural analysis. We have already seen the importance of the former; now we must develop the latter, to determine in what the mechanism of expression and signification consists, when it occurs. Is it purely arbitrary, or does it rest on some latent isomorphism that experiments can reveal? Is it, in its manifestations, linked to individual contingencies? Is it necessary to speak of evocation, signification, meaning, symbolism, or expression in relation to these "psychological states" triggered by audition?

EXPRESSION, EVOCATION, AND SIGNIFICATION

As we have seen, the most general terms that are appropriate are *judgment* and *assertion*. *Objective* and *normative* judgments are judgments of attribution or identification that pose no particular problem: "That is a ninth chord"; "The woodwinds are not used well"; "That theme reminds me of Fauré." Introspective statements are essentially judgments reflexive on the self: "That leaves me indifferent"; "It gives me an image of movement." It is best to avoid here the use of this term to designate semantic judgments, whose formulation might be closely related but are in essence no less distinct. In fact, judgments of signification (or semantic judgments) differ from the others in two principal ways. First, they attach to the perceived sound pattern attributes that would not belong to it, such as spatial qualities ("grandiose") or anthropomorphisms ("graceful," "noble"), or that spring from unclear identifications ("a wait that drags on," "a passionate argument"). Second, these judgments do not implicate the perceiving subject but are stated with an unequivocal implication of inherence in the work. When the subject states "That is a wait" or "I have an impression of grandeur," it is clear that it is not he who waits and that the grandeur, even if it is only an impression he feels, is a grandeur observed in the sound pattern as one of its attributes.

But are these judgments simple *evocations*? That would mean that they would be simply mechanical associations whose links with the properties of the form would be nonexistent and would activate only the traces of circumstances in which that work (or a similar work) had been heard. Note here that the opposition between *evocation* and *signification* is not precisely the individuality of the one and the generality of the other. Music is a social product, and the circumstances of its performance can activate related memories in several subjects, as when those memories are connected with stable institutions. For example, a prelude for organ will evoke sacred places with which that instrument is associated. What distinguishes the two terms is rather that signification remains anonymous and impersonal concerning the circumstances that can initiate it and the associations that link it to the present structure. Evocation, on the other hand, is always somewhat introspective. It appears to the subject as personal and contingent, not as a property of the musical structure but as an occurrence in the subject. It lacks the appearance of objectivity that signification has in seeming to result from observations on the work itself.

Do significations have something in common with expression? We sometimes use this term to emphasize differences of psychological level: signification partakes of critical distancing; expression seems protopathic, less polished, at a lower level than signification. The sign itself is consciously accessible and lucid, whereas expression is subconscious and mysterious. Ruyer (1955)[19] has provided examples of expressivity that are closely related in their diversity to the semantic judgments that experimentation with music provides us. "You are a beautiful sky of autumn— clear and rosy," wrote Baudelaire ("Causerie," 1961, p. 123). This is an example of a proposition that, in its present form, has neither operational nor predictive value. It cannot be verified, but it is not simply a noise. It discloses an expressivity. This example is of one of the identifications that Ruyer wished at all costs to distinguish from signification. In my view, the two are indissolubly linked together. Judgments of signification condense expressive properties read in the musical stimulus into verbal form. *And at times they are connected with verbal statements blended with perceptions.*

Expressivity appears as a raw given inherent in the structure; signification as an elaboration of that given tends to become reduced to a concept, a rationalization, even to an explication. This elaboration is not concerned in any way with the spontaneity of the signified, but only with the sign, whose properties it gleans in order to match them to the signified. One could say that semantic judgments disclose the musical expressions perceived by the subjects. They are *semantic* only for the psychologist who seeks to account for them and to dissipate the mystery by analyzing the relationships between sign and signified belonging to each.

It is the analysis of these relationships that will permit us to distinguish among judgments of signification what is a pure sign and what is a symbol— the one arbitrary and related to the signal ["index," in C. S. Peirce's (1931– 35) terminology; *trans.*]; the other closer to an indicator ["icon" or "symbol," for Peirce; *trans.*], resting on analogies of form, on relationships, on stylized transpositions. Finally, this analysis permits us to explore the hybrid nature of what becomes symbolically grafted onto the sign when it has secured its signifying power.

---

[19]According to Ruyer, expressivity is to expression as signification is to meaning. This last is always marked with finality (for example, the meaning of a behavior is its particular goal), so that the term has a signification that is, in fact, that behavior.

Chapter 9

CONSISTENCY AND COHERENCE OF SEMANTIC JUDGMENTS

THE VIRTUAL CHARACTER OF SIGNIFICATION

A review of the group of studies included under the label frequently used by their authors—"the effects of music"—has led us to the observation that the paradigms of the experiments and the kinds of questions they pose influence the results obtained. That review did not show that the subjects in those experiments, left to their own spontaneity, would have formulated judgements of signification in their minds, although the typological classifications they made would lead us to think so. What came out of our review was that the great majority of subjects lent themselves to such a formulation, and that, incidentally, the judgements were consistent. "Abstract" significations were, from all the evidence, associated with processes in which the musical form was the source of the thing signified; those judgments did not appear, in the way they were stated, to depend on individual personalities. They were not, however, just "responses to stimuli" in the sense of deriving from automatic perceptual reactions. The signifying musical pattern could have been the point of departure for normative or empirical judgments if the *semantic attitude* had been for some reason excluded by the subject. Musical signification is thus not identical to signification with words or images, which derives directly from the *univocacy of attitude that those engender*. We can doubtless take some interest in the typographic presentation of a text, or in the composition of an image, and thereby become distracted from their significations. But signification is still immediately given, before all other considerations. We might similarly suppose that semantic judgments apply to music only as the last links in a process that, in order to remain in some cases nonverbal, is nevertheless no less real and effective at the prereflexive level. To the extent that the musical signification is potential, that potentiality necessarily resides in a psychological reality that remains latent, in the form of a vague impression, as long as the subject's attitude does not require an explicit verbal response of it.

This is a plausible hypothesis that still lacks direct experimental tests. Everything we know concerning musical significations is based on the analysis of verbal responses and the sound structures that engender them.

EXPERIMENT 14

The following experiment was aimed at clarification of the following points:

1. Is there a marked effect of musical education on the establishment of relationships of signification?

2. What degree of consistency is obtained with the same musical fragments using the three methods of induction of responses: guided, semiguided, and free?

3. The method of free induction, in which the choice of response is left entirely to the initiative of the listeners, has never before been applied. It is this method, nevertheless, that can provide decisive evidence concerning signification, since the limitations imposed by other methods orient listeners' choices to some extent. If free induction leads to the appearance of some consistency in responses, then we shall have to investigate their nature. A common element, if it exists, will furnish the semantic kernel out of which responses become elaborated when guided induction is used.

4. Can we isolate the bases of signification through analysis of the fragments, and what hypotheses can we legitimately formulate concerning the mechanisms by which "factors" inherent in the musical form give way to semantic interpretations? In other words, what is the nature and the development of the relationship of signification?

Method

The methods employed consisted of asking the subjects to attribute a *title* to each musical fragment that that were to hear. They were to choose the titles from a list or could make them up themselves. The titles were to be related not to musical genre or to details of musical structure or performance, but rather to the semantic content of the fragment. The instructions differed depending on whether the method of induction was guided, semiguided, or free.

Guided Method of Induction. Before hearing a musical fragment, the subjects were given a slip on which were listed six titles, from which they were asked to choose the one that appeared to them to be most appropriate to the fragment. These titles were worded without any literary pretensions, to avoid influencing the choice through the relative attractiveness of one over the others. All had some fairly obvious sense in which some particular aspect constituted the adequate signification of a musical fragment. The musical fragments are listed in Table 9.1 by the titles given the works by the composers themselves. The fragments were selected to illustrate best the subjects with which those works are concerned. That choice, as well as the draft of the six titles, was submitted to judges who were musically very competent. For example, fragment C of Series II (concerned with effects of light) was from Respighi's Fountains of Rome: *La fontana di Trevi al meriggio* (from rehearsal number 15, measure 9, to number 16, measure 11). The titles provided for the choice of listeners were:

1. Midday in full sunlight
2. Threatening sky
3. Gray day
4. Deep night
5. Summer sunlight
6. Joyful breaking forth of morning

Of the titles proposed, three were concerned in varying degrees with the "subject" of the fragment (numbers 1, 5 and 6), and the other three were not concerned with it at all (numbers 2, 3, and 4). The six titles all concerned aspects of the time of day or the season or degrees of luminosity—they differed only relatively.

In addition to these six titles, the subjects were given the possibility of making up different titles themselves if none of the ones proposed were satisfactory, and also of indicating that the musical fragment they heard did not, in their view, signify anything. These latter possibilities were explicitly mentioned on each slip following the titles.

Semiguided Method of Induction. Before listening to the music, the subjects were told they were going to hear six brief fragments of musical works for which they had to find titles that were as well adapted as possible to their expressive contents. These titles could vary in length and might, if appropriate, consist of a single word. Given the nature of the different fragments in each series, each title should concern, as much as possible, a psychological state or feeling or dramatic situation. The titles need have

TABLE 9.1

Musical Fragments Presented in Experiment 14

Composer	Work	Excerpt	Duration (sec)
Series I: Water and Aspects of Water			
A Debussy	Images	*Reflets dans l'eau* (first 17 measures)	58
B Ravel	Jeux d'eau	first 24 measures	67
C Respighi	Fountains of Rome	*La fontana del Tritone al mattino* (beginning to No. 8)	85
D Smetana	Ma Vlast	*The Moldau* (E meas. 9 to F meas. 5)	70
E Debussy	La Mer	*Jeux de vagues* (edit. Durand, No. 33–38)	92
E Debussy	La Mer	*Jeux de vagues* (edit. Durand, No. 19–23)	50
Series II: Seasons, Times of Day, Lighting			
A Debussy	La Mer	*De l'aube à midi* (first 30 measures)	73
B Ravel	Daphnis et Chloé	*Levée du jour* (edit. Durand, p. 184, No. 155–157 (meas. 3))	68
C Respighi	Fountains of Rome	*La fontana di Trevi al meriggio* (No. 15(9–24) to No. 16(1–11))	66
D Respighi	Fountains of Rome	*La Fontana di Villa Medici al tramonto* (No. 22–23, last 20 meausres)	69
E Ravel	Daphnis et Chloé	*Nocturne* (edit. Durand, p. 84, No. 70–63(meas. 3))	64
F Respighi	Pines of Rome	*Pini presso una catacomba* (measures 1–9)	67
Series III: Feelings, Psychological States, Dramatic Situations			
A Franck	Psyché	*Le sommeil de Psyché* (measures 1–15)	70
B Franck	Psyché	*Psyché et Eros* (R to S, measure 24)	75
C Mozart	Quartet in C, K 465	Rondo, allegro molto (measures 1–54)	42
D Stravinsky	Elegie for violin solo	first fifteen measures	60
E Bartok	Out of Doors Suite	*La poursuite*, measure 5–42	54
F Berlioz	Roméo et Juliette	*Roméo seul*, measures 1–20	88

no relationship to the titles of the works from which the excerpts had been drawn. The listeners were asked, however, to indicate the names of the composers and the titles of the works if they knew them. The semiguided method was employed with the six fragments of Series III (Feelings) and with the six fragments from Series II (Light). In the latter case, the instructions indicated that the titles ought to be related as much as possible "to the season, to the degree of luminosity, or to the different times of the day."

Free Method of Induction. Before listening to the fragments, the subjects were instructed without further specification to find for each fragment a title that was as well adapted as possible to its semantic content. The titles could be brief, if appropriate, and could even reduce the whole contents into a single word. They could be without relationship to the titles of the works from which the fragments had been excerpted. The listeners were asked, though, to indicate those titles, as well as the names of the composers, if they knew them. The free method of induction was used with the six fragments of Series II (Light) and with the six fragments of Series III (Feelings).

Why this diversity of method? Several reasons. Until now, the guided method of induction had been the most frequently used because of its apparent rigor. In the analysis of the results, experimenters found themselves confronted with well-defined choices, generally an adjective chosen from a list. The results were calculated by counting the frequency of choice of a given adjective for a given musical fragment. Listeners found themselves confronted with a limited field of verbal elements, and experimenters were not exposed arbitrarily to a subjective clustering of responses. This rigor in computation was balanced against the artificial character if induction of the responses. In fact, the objectivity gained in the clustering had already been lost as a result of the manner in which the responses were obtained. For example, in many studies of this sort published in the United States, subjects were presented with adjective lists relating to affective states (sad, lively, melancholy) or to personality traits (stately, amusing). The artificial character of this method appears in the course of even these experiments, when the same musical fragment is *always seen to furnish* verbal responses of an extreme grammatical variety: adjectives, common nouns, adverbs, proper nouns, and long or short clauses of varying complexity. Even in the present use of the guided method, the grammatical presentation of the verbal formulas proposed has been left flexible. They are not always adjectives but sometimes nouns accompanied by adjectives ("light gaiety"), or longer formulas describing a global aspect or the dynamic development of a fragment ("the setting sun and the falling of night"). It seems questionable to try to characterize a whole piece with a single adjective: it is difficult enough to use several words to characterize a fragment only a few seconds long.

Furthermore, this objection to the guided method is connected with two other objections. First, abstract significations appear to be artificial products of an elaboration of semantic contents that the subjects formulate spontaneously. If, as was shown in chapter 8, semantic responses condense living expressions for which the subject could be led to find a verbal *analog,* we can say that in most cases the verbal response garbles the expression, makes it lose its specificity, and schematizes it in the extreme. That is the case for abstract significations imposed on the choices of subjects in the experiments described. In comparing the results obtained with different methods for the same musical fragment, we have an additional observation: The subjects feel that the choice of one proposed verbal formula, although preferable to the others, is still only makeshift.

In addition, the guided methods constitute an excessive intervention by the experimenter in the research. Either the expression could be suggested by the word that appeared least arbitrary—a sort of accommodation of the one to the other—or else it would undergo in the listener the transmutation that the experimenter must carry out on the basis of the responses that manifested it. When the listener is asked to attribute an abstract adjective to a musical phrase, a chain of identifications is set up, based on the subject's analysis of the original expression. The expression no longer figures in the response provided and remains unknown to the experimenter. However, it is in the first link of this chain that the expression itself can be found, not in the successive equivalents that the listener must elaborate in order to choose an element in the questionnaire. The effort of abstraction that enables the grasp of the essence of a musical signification should not be required of the subjects. It would distract them from the effort of trying to translate individual living expressions into words. Abstraction can legitimately intervene only as a reflection on spontaneous judgments, in *analogies* conceived by the subjects themselves. At the same time, only those judgments—only that reflection—can reveal to us the structure and development of musical signification.

Nonetheless, the guided and semiguided methods have, psychologically, a certain amount of justification. *They do correspond to the usual forms of musical usage.* Every time music is preceded by a concrete title, or accompanied with words, or mingled with action or discourse, it introduces psychological situations analogous to those which these two methods produce. There is, in all these cases, a polarization of the representative effects of the music by the verbal elements given before or while listening to the music.

In contrast, the method of free induction corresponds to uses of music in which the music itself precedes the apprehension of the verbal element.

The overture of an opera, or the music during the opening credits of a film, creates a climate—an objective or affective atmosphere—before the unfolding of the action. It can also, to some extent, inform us concerning the situation produced by hearing works that have no titles other than formal ones (symphony, quartet, concerto, etc.). Although, in that case, the attitude of the listener does not consist in an orientation toward finding representational elements, *they still impose themselves in the margins of consciousness* because they are inherent in musical form. A melody is a physical movement; a rhythm is a form of behavior; a dynamic change is a prototypical process that we feel implicitly, even when we do not seek to formulate them verbally. These infrarepresentational elements are no less real. They are at the root of the global impression that arises from the music, even among listeners whose attention has been constantly occupied with analyzing the composition or performance from a technical point of view.

Procedure. The subjects gathered in groups of 10 to 20 in a relatively well-isolated room.[1] They first completed a questionnaiare on cultural level (see Experiment 3). Then the instructions, differing according to method, were read slowly and summarized. To make sure the instructions were well understood, the experimenter asked the subjects if they had any questions. Then the fragments were played, each twice in a row, on a Barthe-Supertone record player of excellent quality and amplified over a fixed loudspeaker hung on the wall about 2m above the floor. Between each fragment and the one following, the subjects were given a pause of 40 sec to choose and enter their responses on the slips. They were instructed to indicate, if they believed they recognized the work, knew the title of the work from which the fragment had been excerpted, and the composer's name. Even if they knew the original work, they were to select or make up a title closely related to the particular fragment. During data analysis, it bacame apparent that most of the responses concerning the actual titles and composers of works were erroneous. When they were erroneous, the corresponding responses were eliminated from the calculation of the results.

Stimuli. The stimuli consisted of three series of six fragments each[2], listed in Table 9.1 with the exactly corresponding place in the score and the duration of the performance selected. Each series had a general title that

---

[1]This was either in the Center for Radio-Television Studies of the R.T.F., in the studio of the Phonetics Institute, in the S room of the Sorbonne, or in a classroom of a major music school (the National Conservatory or the Music Normal School).

[2]Fragments of pieces from commercially recorded discs were dubbed onto flexible discs or magnetic tape.

served as a theme for the selection of pieces. The first two series were presented using the guided method as an initial test. Then Series II and III were the objects of research with the semiguided and free induction methods. Most of the works included had a concrete title that indicated the descriptive or expressive intention of the composer. But it is certain that representative contents could be placed in evidence using excerpts of "pure music" (as we shall see later concerning fragment C of Series III). Technical analysis of these fragments shows that that intention is realized, definitively, by the placement in the works of a small number of means that can be found separately or be together in works intended as formal.

Thus, it is not of works employing exceptional means that we have been thinking, but of works in the ordinary concert repertoire, having, however, a *defined* character. The fragments excerpted here are those in which that character was particularly apparent. That is why they did not last longer than 100 sec. That condition was very important for the rigor of the experiment. We have often seen other experiments of this sort in which the subjects were presented with entire compositions and then asked to describe the general feeling that the compositions expressed. It is certain, however, that such a feeling is rarely maintained constantly throughout the course of a piece of 5 or 10 minutes' duration. The impressions summarized by the listeners in their responses thus represented either a compromise among related nuances of feeling or else a brief impression evoked by one moment in the piece that it was no longer possible to identify on the basis of the responses. Hevner (1936), aware of this difficulty, thought of asking her subjects to indicate, in response to her signals, new choices at different moments during the course of their listening. But that is a rather artificial procedure in terms of the experimental conditions that it involves and the attitudes that it engenders in the subjects. I therefore adopted the following solution, namely, to take from the works excerpts whose musical characteristics would be *as well defined and homogeneous as possible* throughout the duration of the fragment. The first of these conditions imposed a minimum duration; and the second, overriding limits that varied for the different works.

Furthermore, in order to test a current thesis according to which imitative elements take a preponderant role in the induction of expression. I was careful to include among these sound montages two fragments in which such elements were integrated: the imitation of birdsongs (Series II, fragment B) and of bells (Series II, fragment D). The problem was to find out if the presence of these realistic elements would assure that those fragments should have better consistency of significations, relative to the others.

Subjects. There were 628 subjects: 316 tested with the guided method (including 44 children), 161 with the semiguided method (including 45

TABLE 9.2

Number of Subjects in the Four Groups and Three Conditions of
Experiment 14

Method	Groups			
	A	B	C	Children
Guided	136	110	26	44
Semiguided	60	39	17	45
Free	72	73	0	0

children), and 145 with the method of free induction. Table 9.2 shows the distribution of these subjects into groups based on their questionnaire responses concerning musical culture. Group A included those who had had no musical education, either in theory or in practice. Their development was entirely perceptual, involving listening to music without analyzing the stimulus and without conceptual support. They were recruited from varied social milieux—they were employees of the French National Railroad, firemen, office workers, students.[3] The subjects in Group B had had vocal, choral, or instrumental training for at least 3 years, involving the study of elementary solfège, as well as the perceptual background shared by Group A. Group C consisted of professional musicians and music students from the major conservatories. They had practiced an instrument or voice for at least 10 years and had advanced theoretical training: advanced solfège, harmony, harmonic analysis, formal analysis, music history, and sometimes counterpoint and fugue. Most of the subjects of Groups B and C belonged to different social milieux from those of Group A. They were generally students at the lycées (high school seniors or university students), office workers, and (in Group C) musicians.[4]

The children tested were distributed as follows. The 44 children tested with the guided method consisted of 16 in the range of 8 to 9 years, and 28 in the 10–12 year range, students in the Maison d'Enfants de Sèvres. All had had a certain amount of musical training conceived according to the ongoing methods employed by that school: choral singing, comparative listening with commentary, group dancing; but only the older children had received the rudiments of solfège. The 45 children tested with the semiguided method were between 4½ and 5½ years old and were students at a nursery school. They had had no contact with music other than the elementary choral singing in use in such establishments.

---

[3]The results of these groups had first been examined separately, in connection with the guided method. Then all the results that showed no significant differences among them were treated together.

[4]Here also the results showed the relative independence of the appearance of consistent semantic judgments in relation to cultural level in general and musical background in particular.

Results and Discussion

First we should note that the semantic judgments were seldom accompanied by images. People speak too frequently of music imagination, which tends to confer on the semantic relationship an individual and contingent character that it does not have or at least not to speak of. Musical imagery supposes the awakening in the subject of a flux of infinitely varied evocations, without any real basis in the properties of the musical form, and released by a play of accidental and unforseen associations in the subject's psychological structure and momentary state, in antecedent thoughts, and so on. In fact, what is observed most frequently is the appearance of a conceptual form that seems adequate to the musical form but that the subject gives as a representative *analog* to what he has heard. Even when the image is clearly signaled, it takes on an objective character, the character of an external "sign," foreign to the momentary or permanent peculiarities of the individual subject. In very rare cases, subjects have indicated that the image contained in their response was associated more with a specific memory than with the properties of the sound pattern.

Frequency of Semantic Responses.   The frequency of semantic responses for the entire set of conditions requires thorough discussion. These responses do not represent all the effects that can be obtained from the presentation of these fragments, but they do consist of precisely those determined by instructional conditions. These effects are partial, but they correspond to the principal goals of the research.

Tables 9.3, 9.4, and 9.5 show the results for the different groups. Table 9.3 contains the percentages of nonsemantic responses observed with the guided method for stimulus Series I, for Groups A and B and the children. Table 9.4 shows the same percentages for Series II, for Groups A, B, and C, and the children, tested with the three methods. Table 9.5 provides for the comparison of percentages from Group A and B tested with Series III with all three methods. There are, unfortunately, gaps in these tables. Table 9.3 offers no comparison of methods and, like Table 9.5, includes only subjects from Groups A and B among the adults. Table 9.5 lacks

TABLE 9.3
Frequency of Nonsemantic and Negative Responses in Series I of
Experiment 14

| | Groups | | | | | |
| | A | | B | | Children | |
	n	F%	n	F%	n	F%
Guided method	48	4.8	67	3.4	19	1.7

TABLE 9.4
Frequency of Nonsemantic and Negative Responses in Series II of
Experiment 14

| Method | Groups | | | | | | | |
| | A | | B | | C | | Children | |
	n	F%	n	F%	n	F%	n	F%
Guided	52	5.3	43	3.1	26	1.2	25	0.6
Semiguided	24	9.7			17	5.8		
Free	37	5.4	31	9.6				

scores for Group B on the guided method. And Table 9.4 contains four gaps in the last three columns. Nevertheless, some indisputable results appear in the examination of the diverse sets of data.

1. Whatever the method, and whatever the series of fragments, the tally of negative and nonsemantic responses was apparently the same for subjects in Groups A, B, and C. No important differences could be established within a given series among the group percentages taken in pairs. This is a result that appears to contradict other observations and hypotheses according to which the semantic attitude, being frequent only among uncultivated listeners, should have been foreign to the musicians' perceptions. Quite the contrary. In certain cases, we can observe a slight tendency toward an increase of semantic responses among subjects of Groups B and C compared with the untrained group. This is apparent in the first two lines of Table 9.4, the third line of Table 9.5, and in Table 9.3. Semantic induction is thus a general possibility. It can be found as well with the children, beginning at age 8, as shown in Tables 9.3 and 9.4 for the responses of the 44 children in the Sèvres School. That group evinced no surprise or difficulty at the idea of "interpreting" music in extramusical terms. We shall see later that, in addition, they performed this operation with as much discernment as the adults. These children's choice of titles

TABLE 9.5
Frequency of Nonsemantic and Negative Responses in Series III of
Experiment 14

| Method | Groups | | | | | |
| | A | | B | | Children | |
	n	F%	n	F%	n	F%
Guided	36	1.2				
Semiguided	36	13.8	39	15.3	45	20.7
Free	35	15.8	42	13.4		

was never arbitrary. On the contrary, we find there a tally of meaningful choices as useful as those of their elders.

2. In addition to the foregoing analysis, we might raise the possibility of achieving at least a cursory understanding of musical significations going back to early childhood. The experiment tried with 45 children between the ages of 4 and 6, students at a nursery school in Vincennes, produced the results contained in Table 9.5 (columns 5 and 6).

Because of the ages of the subjects, the experiment was run as follows. Only fragments A, C, and D of Series III were presented, so that the duration of the session did not exceed 15 min. We had first explained to the children:

> Pieces of music are not all the same. Some are happy and others sad. Some pieces make you think of one thing, other pieces of something else; for example, of sleeping, of dancing, of playing, or crying, or being happy or bored.
>
> You are going to hear, each one twice in a row, three little pieces of music. Listen closely, and then tell the woman or man with you what the music makes you think of.

The sessions were run with groups of 10 children in a schoolroom well isolated from external noise. Adult recorder-observers were assigned to pairs of children seated one behind the other at separate tables; the children could not communicate with one another. The observers questioned the subjects after the second presentation of each fragment and wrote down their responses. If necessary, they repeated the instructions in a quiet voice and solicited a response.

Adults of Groups A and B gave the three fragments in question a mean of 16.8% negative and nonsemantic responses, whereas the children produced 20.7%. We might be tempted to suppose that since the difference was not significant between the two results, age was no more important for this stage of analysis than for the others. However, this would be a risky conclusion. These figures do not take into account the conditions under which the responses had been obtained. All the observers charged with collecting the responses emphasized at the end of the experiment the reticence shown by the children regarding the problem they had been given. Most children's spontaneous response was, "I don't know." The observers insistence on overcoming this resistance succeeded in obtaining responses that took the form of echos, such as: "Is the music happy?" "Yes, it is happy." "Or sad?" "Yes, sad." Taken together, many of the responses seem to have been the result of chance. We see the confirmation of this fact in the analysis of the *contents* of these responses, whose consistency is relatively weak.

3. If we now examine the nonsemantic and negative responses, we can observe a difference attributable to method. There was a constant tendency among the subjects in the three groups to provide more semantic responses in experiments involving the use of the guided method. This trend is particularly clear in the results for Series III (Table 9.5). For the same fragments, with the untrained subjects, the guided method of induction provided only 1.2% of nonsemantic and negative responses. The use of the other two methods led to significantly higher percentages: 13.8% (semiguided method) and 15.2% (free method). The other tables indicate similar but less pronounced tendencies.

We might suppose that here is a tendency that is not entirely explained by the nature of the experimental procedures, but that touches on something more substantive concerning the way in which the signifying aspect of music is understood in its relationship with verbal language. Certainly one could interpret these differences by maintaining only that it was easier for subjects to choose a title from among the six presented than to make one up themselves, taking account of the characteristics of the musical structure. The risk of an inadequate result was perhaps greater of the latter operation than for the former, and that would be sufficient to deter some of the subjects.

In fact, though, this finding must be placed in the context of what was said earlier concerning the reciprocal accommodation of expression and the verbal formulas proposed to the choice of the listeners. The presentation of a title or of an adequate abstract signification, among a set of others, elicits an orientation and limits the number of interpretations possible to the subject. Clearly inadequate titles were immediately excluded upon confrontation with the characteristics of the musical pattern (which indicates that the title was not chosen arbitrarily). To the extent that the experimenter and his colleagues have caught in the title an actual lively expression, it can be retrieved by others on the basis of the signification. As I shall attempt to demonstrate, musical significations are always based on properties of the musical form, which, in the multiplicity of its aspects, can give rise to different interpretations. Reading a title that implicitly emphasizes certain of those aspects has the effect of placing the listener in a selective attitude and of grasping that form from a certain perspective. The grasp of the subject is thus neither forced nor left to chance—it is oriented.

Everything happens, up to a point, as in listening to program music, or more generally to music that bears nongeneric titles. The words not only elicit a semantic attitude, but lead to the implicit emphasis of certain aspects of the sound pattern, which could have been apprehended in another way. We shall see the truth of this statement in the excerpts of "descriptive" music that (spontaneously in the case of free induction and under the constraint of instructions in the semiguided method) could have been meaningfully interpreted from a subjective point of view.

4. Let us now look at the varieties of nonsematic and negative responses. They appeared to be either admissions or claims of inability to do the task, or refusals to do it. The former case was a matter of *partial* negative responses involving one or more fragments, but not stated as a refusal or inability to respond in principle. These responses were indicated by question marks, blank lines, or more explicit phrases (especially in the case of methods requiring the subjects to make up their own responses: "don't know," "none," etc.). Out of a total of 547 adult subjects in the three groups, producing a total of 3282 responses, there were 196 (5.9%) partial negative responses. *Global* negative responses, though fewer in number, were more instructive. They better clarified the attitudes of the subjects toward the task required of them. The page was blank or erased all the way across—sets of six partially thwarted responses never occurred. The subject seemed to have refused, immediately and categorically, to try to find a response. Most often that refusal was accompanied by remarks expressed in general terms—sometimes polemically—that interpreted certain aspects of the subject's own aesthetic. There were 11 such cases among the 547 subjects (2%).

For example, one listener wrote that "being touched directly" by a particular melody or harmonic combination, she refused to introduce "an anecdotal and false" (in her terms) meaning in trying to find a title. Another listener wrote, "I protest the explication of musical impressions by words, infinitely too precise to be true." (This listener provided, however, six perfectly adapted titles, that is, titles conforming to the themes of induction defined by the group of subjects.)

Another listener, a highly cultivated man of letters, indicated: "Classical music hardly inspires me with anecdotal titles." Then, later, apropos of a fragment of Bartók: "For modern music, it is impossible to give any other title than just 'music'." Yet this same listener provided three titles out of six that fitted the character of the fragments quite well.

Other responses expressed the same normative trend: "It disfigures music to give it a title," or, "Symphonies evoke no other title," or "To give a title to an excerpt is to empty it of meaning. The only names that should be given are fugue, concerto, largo, andante, etc." And here are some more cutting assertions: "Music does not signify anything outside of itself. It is a pure expression of individual feelings that each person experiences while listening." "A piece of music does not have to be translated so as to signify something in another domain." "No, no, no. Music is music. I do not see how it can be the source of emotional or literary divagations."

The detail of these responses shows in a sense the roots of a nonsemantic attitude linked to certain "formalist" or "formalizing" cultural tendencies. In fact, the subjects of whom we speak opposed in principle the application of extramusical signification to *all music*. Their responses do not indicate that after trying they found it impossible to achieve a result (as would be the case with parial negative responses). Rather, such an attempt appeared to them in general absurd and contrary to the nature of music. Sometimes, as we have noted, this refusal in principle was accompanied by a performance of the task in fact, which appears to confirm the "cultural" nature of the negative attitude. Nevertheless, this attitude was not encountered among the subjects of Group C, but rather among those of Groups A and B, who belonged to milieux of a generally average cultural level.

These global negative responses all the same constituted only a small part of the nonsemantic responses. There was a series of response types that were in fact only disguised refusals, which can be classified as follows:

1. *Generic Responses.* "Excerpt from a symphony," "Etude," "Aria," "Improvisation;" to which we might add the those that sought a historical placement of the work: "School of admirers of Wagner, d'Indy, or Dukas," "Influenced by Ravel, if it is not by him," etc.

2. *Functional Responses.* "Movie music," "Information bulletin," "For a cartoon;" or responses in which the fragment was placed in a social context, according to a series of stereotypical associations. Note that these responses already contain a rudiment of signification, in that they can be explicated in extramusical terms. But they only condense an abstract and anonymous aspect, in some sense traditional. Thus "For a cartoon" is the equivalent of a group of significations themselves attached to a series of agogic and rhythmic schemes, forms of writing, etc.

3. *"Formalist" Responses.* Here certain elements of structure, of instrumentation, or of performance were provided: "Dissonances," "On two strings," "Rapid at the start, slowing down as it went along," "Duo," "Concerto for violin and orchestra."

Normative and introspective responses were hardly ever encountered, with the exception of a few introspective responses such as "Heard before," or, "I would like to hear what followed;" or normative responses like "Arid discords," "Very beautiful chamber music," "Monotonous," "A very singing type of music."

Were negative and nonsemantic responses more frequent with "pure" music? This was the question addressed by including the excerpt from a

Quartet of Mozart in Series III. This fragment was presented with the semiguided method (with the directive theme: "feelings and psychological states"), and then with the method of free induction. The percentages of negative and nonsemantic responses were slightly higher for the semiguided method (16%) and clearly higher for the free method (28.5%), compared with the other fragments (12.86% and 10.04%, respectively—see Table 9.6). Although the values for the Quartet were not high on an absolute scale, they still cast some doubt on its capacity to signify. However, if we refer to the way in which many of these responses were actually filled out, we find that conclusion to be the result of an abstract deduction rather than of an immediate impression. In the responses, the identification of a genre or an epoch prevented any semantic interpretation. This fragment was easily attached to a category of works—to a composer known to avoid concrete titles. So we also found responses like: "Chamber music," "Mozart," "Sonata," and "Minuet." Furthermore, in most responses connected with 18th Century dances (responses that were erroneous: "minuet," "rigaudon," "gavotte"), there was a bit of semantic interpretation: those dances were imagined less from a generic angle than as conventional stereotypes covering feelings, a festive atmosphere, graceful gestures, and youthful vivacity. Several responses showed this: "a soirée of Louis XV," "Versailles," "Intoxication of a ball of yesteryear," "Ballet theme: Spring." These examples do not support a conclusion of the qualifiable nature of a fragment of pure music. We are tempted, rather, to recall the words of Schumann, for whom each fugue of Bach was a piece of characterization having its own physiognomy, despite the formal rigor imposed by the rules of that genre (d'Ollone, 1952).

Content of Semantic Responses. The most interesting aspect of this study was the contents of the semantic responses, which, as we have seen, constituted the majority of responses obtained.

TABLE 9.6
Tally of Negative and Nonsemantic Responses for
Series III

Fragment	Method	
	Semiguided (n = 75)	Free (n = 77)
A	12	10.3
B	14.16	11.6
C	16	28.5
D	12	11.6
E	14.16	5.1
F	12	11.6

The Consistency of Semantic Responses and the Existence of Themes of Signification. Were the significations produced by the group of listeners, as one might think, indefinitely variable from subject to subject, or did they display common characteristics suggesting that they had an objective basis in the properties of the form? To what extent did this commonality exist, and of what did it consist? The great variety of the responses has been noted above. It involved adjectives, common nouns, proper nouns, and combinations of several words ("Retrospective, elderly, the calm of old age") or phrases ("Lively battle of a few persons in a twisted and sombre landscape," "Dance with pursuit").

The use of the guided method provided for a convenient solution at the outset: it was sufficient to evaluate the number of choices of titles considered adequate in order to find out the degree of consistency of the significations evoked. Thus, a "good response of type I" was a choice conforming to the experimenter's prior expectations, that is, one of the three titles judged to conform to the semantic contents of the fragment. However, the questionnaires offered subjects the possibility of making up a title if the ones before them did not seem to be appropriate. Thus occurred "good responses of type II," consisting of verbalizations whose close relationship to the previous type was obvious. Some involved variants of the three acceptable formulas from the list, giving them a more percise turn of phrase; others involved an original insight condensing the essence of the expression or "climate" of the work or arising from selective attention to one element of the fragment.

On reflection, it seems that meaningful responses—those based on actual aspects of the sound patterns—could differ noticeably from those included in the term "good responses of type I." The titles composed by the experimenter and the judges evidenced a certain way of apprehending the fragments—most often synthetic and global—based on the recollection of the title of the work. As other modes of perception were revealed, the problem of signification took on a slightly different form. *Instead of asking to what extent the groups of listeners stayed with the theme of induction that had been proposed to them, we had to uncover the ones that most often appeared in their minds.*

Likewise, reading certain invented responses corresponding to Series I and II revealed a duality between the objective and the subjective not permitted by the use of the slips bearing suggested titles. To test the simple dichotomy between descriptive music and expressive music, I had given all those titles an objective turn, since they were connected with excerpts of descriptive music. But some listeners, on hearing them, thought more of psychological states than of contexts in the external world, and other achieved a synthesis by situating a feeling in an appropriate setting, in a dramatic moment that accompanied or produced it.

All the complexity of the problem of signification was revealed through these several responses, a complexity that the guided method could only mask. It was thus necessary to free the listener from the shackles of the questionnaire procedure in order to penetrate the variety of modes of apprehension of musical form, each of which led to a distinct semantic judgment. The use of the guided method showed only that it is possible in the great majority of cases to polarize significations around verbal elements that are presented. The words play, so to speak, the role of catalysts, putting the listener in a state of receptivity that makes apparent an aspect of the form corresponding to the proposed title. Table 9.7 shows, for the series with which the guided method was systematically applied, percentages of responses of the first and second type, as well as the overall percentages of the two. The latter varied between 64.5% and 97.01% for Series I, and between 69.7% and 94.2% for Series II. These responses were complemented by negative and nonsemantic responses, and responses not related to meaningful titles. The data indicate that the content of the responses was highly consistent across the 12 fragments and consisted of one of the three titles selected by the judeges or a title directly related to those.

However, it is in discussing the results obtained with the semiguided and free methods that we encounter the problem of consistency head on.

TABLE 9.7

Percentage Semantic Responses of the First Type (Chosen From the List) and Second Type (Invented by Subjects), with the Total, for the Guided Inductive Method

Fragment	Type 1	Type 2	Total	Type 1	Type 2	Total
			Series I			
	Group A (n = 48)			Group B (n = 67)		
A	62.5	2.0	64.5	65.7	5.9	71.6
B	62.5	18.7	81.2	58.2	5.9	64.1
C	56.3	18.7	75.0	62.6	22.4	85.0
D	47.9	20.8	68.7	68.6	11.9	80.5
E	77.0	12.5	89.5	79.1	17.9	97.0
F	60.4	12.5	72.9	71.7	4.4	76.1
			Series II			
	Group A (n = 52)			Group B (n = 43)		
A	67.4	7.6	75.0	58.1	20.9	79.0
B	70.8	23.0	94.2	74.4	13.9	88.4
C	53.9	23.0	76.9	51.2	25.5	76.7
D	70.8	6.1	76.9	76.7	2.3	79.0
E	42.3	23.0	65.3	44.2	25.5	69.7
F	69.2	25.0	94.2	72.0	18.6	90.6

Those results helped reveal the deeply psychological nature of the signi-fications in which the semantic kernel belonging to each fragment was no longer the one suggested by the experimenter, but was extracted from the responses spontaneously generated by the subjects. Examination of these responses showed, first of all, their diversity of grammatical structure and their conceptual variety, identical to that found with "good responses of type II" discussed earlier. Concerning their contents, the regular alterna-tion of objective and subjective elements—images of movement, of light-ing, or of feelings—led to the following conclusion: *The responses clustered around certain themes of signification.* It appeared that these themes were few in number (almost always three for a given fragment, occasionally four) and included those which had been designated by the six titles proposed for the same fragments in the questionnaires of the guided method. The application of the semiguided method merely served to limit the number by excluding those which did not conform to the instructions.

Table 9.8 gives the details of these themes for the fragments of Series II and III in which these methods were applied. Table 9.9 gives the overall percentages of responses that pertained to them and from which the themes were drawn. "Unclassifiable responses" in Table 9.9 refers to nonsemantic and negative responses, as well as semantic responses that were not coherent.

Verification of the grouping of the responses. It was useful to verify the objectivity of this classification by submitting it to a group of judges. Given the length of this undertaking, I carried out the verification with six fragments chosen randomly from Series II and III. I gave four adult judges the 706 semantic responses to those six fragments by the 261 subjects who heard them, some with the semiguided method and some with the method of free induction. I included with that list the list of proposed themes of signification for each fragment. The identity of the fragments was unknown to the judges, who did not hear them until the second stage of this operation. In the first stage, the judges were asked only to classify the responses into themes that they seemed clearly to reveal on the basis of their logical content. Ambiguous and allusive cases were to be left undecided because, as noted in the instructions given to the judges:

> These verbal significations often involve allusions to *certain particular aspects* of the objects indicated—aspects that were expressed by the music. When an allusion is too distant or eliptical, please rely on hearing the fragment in order to understand it. We shall do that later in the course of a group discussion of doubtful cases. For example, when a subject provides a sig-nification such as "straight-jacket" to characterize a fragment, that pertains not to the garment but to the state of mind in which one wears it. We need to refer to music to understand the allusion. Likewise, when a subject writes "Versailles" to characterize an Allegro by Mozart, it alludes to a festive atmosphere of dancing—carefree and light—expressed by the music.

TABLE 9.8

Classification of Semantic Responses According to Themes of Signification

Fragment Theme	Series

Series II

A 1— Daybreak. Morning impressions. Brightening.

   2— Gray sky, heavy, lowering. Stormy impressions.

   3— Unrest, anguish. Anguishing situation.

B 1— Awakening of nature. Morning or Spring. Awakening of joy.

   2— A brook or beach in particular, in a laughing tone.

   3— More generally a pleasant and agreeable landscape.

C 1— Heroism, victory.

   2— Solemnity, apotheosis, stroke of illumination, tempest or storm.

   3— Departure for combat, riding, hunting.

D 1— Spiritual renunciation, or, more generally, a religious impression.

   2— Melancholy calm, sadness.

   3— Village or countryside with night falling.

E 1— Pleasant nature, woodlands, a serene solitude in nature.

   2— Nocturnal repose. A languorous shepherd or dancer.

   3— Oriental impression. Enchantment.

F 1— Darkness, shadows, dim places, nocturnal impression.

   2— Funereal impression. Funerary ritual or feelings.

   3— Assemblage or slow procession of old or weary beings.

Series III

A 1— Impression of serenity, at times religious.

   2— Recollection, calm associated with serene, faintly illuminated landscapes (evening or morning).

   3— Light melancholy, nostalgia. Moderate feelings.

B 1— Clearly soaring feeling, happy or tormented exaltation.

   2— Breathtaking or precipitous landscape. An excursion through nature.

   3— Events, actions, situations implying conquest, power, and hope.

C 1— Game or dance of friendly people (elves, counts and countesses).

   2— Mischievous enjoyment, light gaiety, youthful caprices.

   3— Spring or nature festival, or preparation for a celebration in general.

D 1— Monotonous, sad exercise, at times instrumentally awkward.

   2— Sadness associated with remembrance and nostalgia.

   3— A situation involving sadness and lassitude; grief.

E 1— Exhausting activity, mechanized life in a contemporary city.

   2— Dance or battle of primitive people.

   3— Motion of thoughts or things implicating fury, chaos, haste.

F 1— Psychological or exterior solitude, barren countryside.

   2— Reverie with a nuance of melancholy. Sadness.

   3— Calm, serenity, but with a touch of regret.

   4— Waiting, mystery.

TABLE 9.9

Frequency of Objective, Subjective, and Mixed Responses in Relation to Method

Responses: Fragment	Semiguided Objective	Semiguided Subjective & Mixed	Semiguided Unclassified *	Free Objective	Free Subjective & Mixed	Free Unclassified *	chi-Square alpha level
		Method					
Series II (N = 41 & 44)							
A	90.2	9.7	0.0	50.0	43.1	6.8	.01
B	95.1	0.0	4.8	59.0	36.5	6.8	.01
C	85.3	9.7	4.8	60.9	29.5	14.6	.05
D	78.0	14.6	7.3	41.4	58.5	6.8	.01
E	85.3	7.3	7.3	56.8	41.4	4.5	.01
F	76.6	19.6	4.8	58.5	45.4	0.0	.05
Series III (N = 75 & 77)							
A	21.3	66.6	12.0	35.0	54.5	10.3	n.s.
B	33.3	52.0	14.6	45.4	42.8	11.6	n.s.
C	21.3	62.6	16.0	33.7	37.6	28.5	.05
D	12.0	76.0	12.0	24.6	63.6	11.6	.01
E	29.3	56.0	14.6	71.4	23.3	5.1	.01
F	20.0	68.0	12.0	38.9	49.3	11.6	.05

*Negative and nonsemantic responses were included in this category provided that they were not related to the themes of signification listed in Table 9.8.

This aspect of the instructions, in connection with the discussion in chapter 8 concerning the relationship of musical expression to verbal signification, was borne out in the quantitative analysis of the results. For all the judges one portion of responses at first judged unclassifiable under the themes according to their logical content was, following the hearing of the fragment, integrated into those themes. Significations were sharpened by an appeal to expression. For the experimenter, on the other hand, knowledge of the musical material provided for an immediate grasp of those significations and for an immediate specification of the theme.

Table 9.10 shows the number of unclassifiable responses for each of the four judges (labeled W, X, Y, and Z) for their initial judgements, and including the experimenter) for judgments after listening to the fragments. The evaluations by the judges displays a certain amount of disparity, as much from one to the next as vis-à-vis the experimenter. To arrive at a clear conclusion, I compared the judgments of the experimenter with judgments that were shared by at least two judges. Evaluations by one judge (or the experimenter alone) which did not cohere with any other could be considered to be tainted with subjectivity. I then recalculated, from the total number of semantic responses for each fragment, those

TABLE 9.10

Number of Unclassifiable Responses Out of a Total of 706, According to
Four Judges and the Experimenter, Before and After Listening to the
Musical Fragments

	Judge				Experi-menter
	W	X	Y	Z	
Before listening:	224	75	131	214	—
After listening:	103	64	104	89	67

which had been judged unclassifiable in two, three, four, or five judgments.
Table 9.11 shows rather clearly that the results obtained converge with
the judgments of the experimenter. We can thus suppose that the experimenter's classifications involve sufficient safeguards for the six fragments
considered and, by extension, for all 12.

For the rest, an examination of the responses that were rejected by only
one judge shows that in most cases it was a question of nuances very
closely related to the themes or of statements that did not include a specific
reference to them. For example (limiting ourselves to the first fragment
in Table 9.11): "The mist dissipates and lets the sun shine through,"
"Countryside after a rain," "Awakening of a sleeping village at dawn,"
"Getting up after a troubled night," all have a manifest relationship with
the first theme ("Daybreak, Morning Impressions, Brightening") with
which just one judge hesitated to group them. Similarly, "Difficult walk
through a forest," "The resolution of a tense moment," "Anguish, piety,"
"Descent and return from Hell," "The end of the world, chaos, anguish,"
all refer in a relatively close way to the third theme: "Unrest, anguish,
anguishing situation," often rather literally, so that one could consider
them to be classifiable.

Finally, a great many responses were classified by the judges into two
or three themes at once, which substantiates the concept of the coherence
of the themes, as well as the duality of the objective and the subjective in
signification.

Examination of these tables and examples permits us to understand
what is meant by *consistency* of musical signification. One can see that the
responses classified under the same title typically are, from a logical point
of view, only loosely related. Beside the exceptional univocal themes (for
example, Table 9.8, Series III, fragment E, theme 2), we find especially
abstractions of large extension relating to diverse realities. Incidentally, a
number of responses contained several elements, each belonging to a different theme.

The *comprehension* of these abstractions can be effectively discussed only
after we have discussed the objective bases of signification, which we

discuss later. This is not a matter of logical comprehension by which things subsumed under the same concept are associated with one another by underlying objective connections that escape perceptual notice, which can be disclosed only by scientific analysis. What is there in common, to perceptual appearance, between bacteria and an oak? Only that they are both "vegetable." And what is there in common between "Flight of animals from a forest fire," and "A quarrel in family life" (Series III, fragment E, theme 3)? An analogy of motor style, of rhythm, of lively pulsation. What links "Underwater grotto" with "Dream of a night at the chateau of the Ile d'Yeu" (Series II, fragment F, theme 1)? Doubtless nothing, from a logical point of view. However, at the perceptual level, there is a very apparent character: a gloomy and silent atmosphere. Likewise, between the two elements in a response such as, "Daybreak, the awakening of life, intense at the end," there are analogies that belong uniquely to the *progressive* dynamic character of the phenomena described.

These examples could be multiplied indefinitely. I chose them because each seems to represent a typical aspect of what we must understand by

TABLE 9.11

Results Comparing the Classification of Responses for Two Methods by the Judges and the Experimenter

Fragment and Method	n	Semantic Responses	Responses Not Classified by 1 to 5 Judges:					Classified by:	
			1	2	3	4	5	4/5 of Judges	Experimenter
IIA									
Semiguided	41	39	6	1	1	2	2	33	34
Free	68	63	9	5	2	6	3	47	53
II F									
Semiguided	41	39	11	0	0	4	0	35	35
Free	68	64	8	4	1	4	3	52	55
II D									
Semiguided	41	37	8	1	2	1	0	33	34
Free	68	66	6	2	3	3	4	54	58
III B									
Semiguided	75	64	12	4	0	1	2	67	60
Free	77	70	6	6	1	1	1	61	64
III C									
Semiguided	75	60	2	0	2	1	0	57	57
Free	77	66	3	1	2	0	1	62	63
III E									
Semiguided	75	65	7	3	2	5	0	55	59
Free	77	73	13	4	1	1	3	64	67
Totals	261	706	91	31	17	29	19	610	639

"the comprehension of themes of signification." *Signification does not consist in an intelligible, logical, objective identification or analogy, but in an identification or analogy of a phenomenal or perceptual type.* Things subsumed under the same theme have in common one or more apparent traits, which can be described or designated by means of properties of the musical form (rhythm and agogic accents, tone height, dynamic progression, etc.).

Such is the basis for *consistency* of responses within a given theme. It could be indefinitely debatable if we kept to an objective order of classification. But here we are concerned with an order of mental life that in most cases is prior to reflection, namely, that of the abstraction of percepts and feelings. It is true that "outlines of feelings" (in Souriau's, 1925, terms) can be found here. In the complexity of an affective state, we find only certain essential traits. "Of this rich and rapid detail," Souriau says, "we most often take only a cursory and simplified view; and psychological labels, through their generality, lead us to simplify even more" (pp. 88–89).

To my mind, this partial and simplified view consists of schematic images grasped by exteroceptive senses (when the movement is observed in others) or by interoception and proprioception—images of bodily pulsation, of motor activity, and of expressive tone, all of which correspond to the category of feelings.[5] There will thus be a stylized image, characterized by rapid agitation and disorganization of behavior and of cardiac rhythm, under which anger, fear, nervousness, and exasperation will be integrated (for example, Series III, fragment E, theme 3). There is another image, indicated by a certain slow depression of behavior and cardiac rhythm, in which we can group sadness, horror, religious recollection, the impression of death, etc. (for example, Series II, fragment F, theme 2).

In addition to these abstractions of feelings, we can outline the existence of abstractions of "phenomena," of "atmosphere or climate" corresponding to clusters of apparent physical characteristics (shadow, silence, solitude, or their opposites), the different combinations of which provide for the designation of perceptibly different realities. For example, all the responses classified under Series II, fragment F, theme 1, in spite of their differences,

---

[5] A kinetic interpretation of music expression has been provided by Helmholtz (1877/1954) in terms that nevertheless bear the mark of his time. According to him, music, insofar as it can suggest movement, represents the fluctuation of mental activity. "Melodic progression can become the expression of the most diverse conditions of human disposition, [but] not precisely of human *feelings* . . . Words can represent the cause of the frame of mind, . . . the feeling which lies at its root, while music expresses the kind of mental transition which is due to the feeling. [Music] arrogates to itself by right the representation of states of mind, which the other arts can only indirectly touch by showing the situations which caused the emotions, or by giving the resulting words, acts, or outward appearance of the body" (pp. 250–251).

were developments of the same phenomenal form bringing together shadow silence, and (to some extent) solitude. Likewise, in Series III, fragment B, theme 1, we have an example of a form characterized by movement, light, and a degree of rhythmic vehemence projected into nature. Curious in a number of responses was that movement, instead of being imagined as perceived (images of wind or waves), was experienced by the subject in images of flight, of walking, of climbing—whence a certain number of evocations of "rugged landscapes," that is, of landscapes *in motion*. Series II, fragment A, theme 2 depicts a stormy climate (that is, before or after a storm, rather than the storm itself) with a gray and heavy sky and an oppressive atmosphere.

We are now in a position to understand the results of the group of children 4 to 6 years old, comparing them with results of the nonmusician adults who heard the same fragments under the same conditions. The *nonmusician* adults of Group A produced for fragment C of Series III a large proportion (87.1%) of responses around the following three themes:

1. Game or dance of friendly people (elves; counts and countesses).
2. Mischievous enjoyment, light gaiety, youthful caprices.
3. Spring or nature festival, or preparation for celebration in general.

We shall see later that these themes have a basis in elements of the musical structure. For the young subjects, responses clustered around the same themes to a comparable degree (80% of the total of semantic responses). The rest of their responses concerned directly opposite significations, such as sadness, sleep, and grief.

Fragment A of the same series produced for the adults 96.7% responses included in the following themes:

1. Impression of serenity, at times religious.
2. Calm associated with serene, faintly lighted, landscapes (evening or morning).
3. Light melancholy, nostalgia. Moderate feelings.

For the children, this proportion did not exceed 67.9%. The rest clustered around an impression of a clearly different character: "playing," "dancing," "Father Christmas," "being happy."

Finally, with fragment D the adults produced 90.0% of their responses centered around the following related themes:

1. Monotonous, sad task, at times instrumentally awkward.
2. Sadness associated with remembrance and nostalgia.
3. A situation involving sadness and lassitude; grief.

TABLE 9.12

Distribution of Meaningful and Nonmeaningful Semantic Responses, and Negative and Nonsemantic Responses for Two Groups in Experiment 14

Frag-ment	Group A (N = 36)			Children (N = 45)			chi-square alpha level
	Mean-ingful Semantic	Nonmean-ingful Semantic	Negative & Nonsemantic	Mean-ingful Semantic	Nonmean-ingful Semantic	Negative & Nonsemantic	
C	27	4	5	32	8	5	n.s.
A	30	1	5	23	11	11	.01
D	30	3	3	15	18	12	.01

For the children, only 45.4% of semantic responses conformed to these themes ("grief," "sad," "dreaming," "crying," etc.). The rest were diametrically opposed to them: "dancing," "playing," "amusing," "jumping," "someone is happy," "joy."

Table 9.12 summarizes the difference obsserved between the contents of semantic responses for the nonmusician adults of Group A and the children 4 to 6 years old. We had been considering as acceptable responses those which conformed to the themes just defined. Unacceptable responses were those that were incompatible with those themes, of which we have seen some examples. Table 9.12 presents the distribution of acceptable semantic responses, unacceptable semantic responses, and negative or nonsemantic responses for the two groups. That distribution is significantly different in two out of three cases.[6] Examination of Table 9.12 shows a constant tendency of the children toward indeterminate responses. In a sizeable proportion of cases it seems that the subjects did not produce an impression actually based on an appreciation of the properties of the musical form. We have already shown the extent to which the young children were influenced by suggestions from the experimenters. Here we must also reject the hypothesis of a single semantic attitude and understand the significations between the adults of Group A and these children.

What would such an identification mean? It would be the equivalent of the identification, often rejected by psycholgists of childhood, of the comprehension of mimicry and gestural forms between adults and children. As we shall see further on, the fundamental elements of the expressive language of music reside in the close relationship between the rhythmic and melodic scheme and gestural schemes that accompany behavior. The

---

[6]In calculating chi-square, the numbers in the two right-hand columns for each group (those corresponding to absence of meaningful semantic responses) were added (columns 2 and 3, and 5 and 6, respectively).

basic psychological states (calm, agitation, tension, relaxation, joy, depression), apart from the nuances that they can include due to the diversity of motivations, are usually expressed by gestural forms. These forms have given rhythms, spatial tendencies, and directions (raising, lowering, moving sideways), and patterns of organization of partial forms in the midst of global forms (persistent repetition, diversity, periodicity, development, etc.). All these are provided to the exteroceptors through the perception of others' reactions, or to the interoceptors through observing oneself. The transposition of these rhythms, tendencies, and patterns of movement in terms of sound constitutes the basis of the expressive language of music. Music uses two aspects of the same process of "abstraction of feelings," to which is added an infinite wealth of cultural associations. But such abstraction is not accessible to the child. It, in fact, presupposes a certain "putting aside" of the motivational object and a centration of attention on psychological states and bodily manifestations as such; whereas the child, attending to the object and taken by the situation, does not attain the reflective level that would allow him to achieve these emotional abstractions (see especially Zazzo, 1948). It may be that, for the adult, the process of abstraction precedes that of reflection. He experiences a kind of automatic classifying of exteroceptive sensory messages according to their internal relationships. Nothing prevents us from thinking that such a categorization could occur at the proprioceptive and interceptive level of sensibility. But in the adult this implicit experience is fixed by language, through which it becomes schematized. In the notion that we all have of the fundamental categories of affective life, there is a fringe of images of movements or of bodily attitudes, of interoceptive rhythms, of degrees of tension of muscle tonus. It is that experience that comes into play in semantic judgments applied to music, as is shown in chapter 10.

Subjective and Objective Significations. If we read some of the adults' responses from another point of view they tend to cluster in the following manner:

First, there were associations designating perceived events—perceived forms—without an explicit indication of an impression experienced by actors who could be in their midst or who could be the subject who perceived them. Apparently these were pure descriptions from which all affective concomitants were eliminated; for example, "Rumbling of a night time storm," "Factory hard at work," "Storm and torrents."

Second, there were subjective associations; that is, associations designating psychological states without any reference to context or to a situation that might have caused or accompanied them. These were responses such as "nostalgia" or "hesitation," which fit the outlines of feelings described above.

Third, there were mixed responses exhibiting a psychological state embedded in an objective context: "waiting, evening," "religious reflection," "funeral march," "shuddering, intense and intermittent vibration, city life;" or, conversely, a description accompanied by its affective concomitants: "a night on the heights of Hurlevent—desolation and mystery," "winter night (sadness)," "Sunny midday—gaiety." (Furthermore, it is clear that many responses with an objective aspect were in fact charged with feeling and should be considered as concealed mixed responses. For example, "funeral march," "de profundis," and "straight-jacket" involve indisputable references to well-characterized psychological states. On the other hand, such phrases as "sunrise in the fields," "incomplete darkness," and "swelling and menacing clouds" should be considered cautiously, and we should be careful about projecting certain nuances of emotion into them even if they appear to go without saying.)

Table 9.9 shows percentages of objective responses, and of subjective and mixed responses combined, for the 12 fragments of Series II and III to which the semiguided and free induction methods were applied successively. It appears that the inherent opposition that could exist between affective and objective "possibilities of signification" was expressed in the respective proportions of those two type of response.

Let us recall, for the interpretation of these data, that the instructions accompanying the application of the semiguided method consisted, for Series II (devoted to descriptive music), of giving the fragments an objective interpretation *(times of day, seasons, light)*; and, for Series III (composed of dramatic program music), of providing a subjective or mixed interpretation *(psychological or affeactive states, dramatic situations)*. The first two columns of Table 9.9 show percentages of the two types of response being considered; the third column is devoted to negative and nonsemantic responses. We see, once again, the *suggestive effect of the instructions on the orientation of responses* in relation to the dichotomy that we are discussing. Objective responses clearly predominated in the interpretation of the fragments of Series II, whereas in Series III subjective and mixed responses were almost always twice as frequent as objective responses.

A counterbalance for this effect was provided by changing the instructions for the free method with the same fragments but different groups of subjects of the same cultural level. The distribution of the two types of responses was noticeably modified (see the right side of Table 9.9). These frequencies were compared with a chi-square test, which was consistently significant for Series II but not for Series III, where a constant and clear tendency to "desubjectivization" affected each fragment (Table 9.9, column 7).

Here again it appears that "descriptive" music is always more than descriptive; it carries within itself a potential for subjective significations.

The evocations of the external world that it awakens are affectively charged, or at least serve as cues for the recall of concomitant psychological states. In most cases, also, it is those feelings—those psychological states—that appear as such in the subjects' awareness. Conversely, both program music and "pure" music are capable not only of characterizing a feeling, a situation, or a psychological state, but of recalling at the same time their objective concomitants. The subjective tends to situate itself—to contextualize itself—in an "appropriated" context with associations rooted in individual and social experience. Hence the references of these subjects to certain objective social stereotypes charged with affective nuances evoked by the music—"anguish, apprehension"—which may well also reveal individual experiences.

Once again our discussion goes in the direction of remarks made by Souriau (1925):

> Perhaps there is no evocation that does not in its patterning include components (to some extent determined circumstantially) that provide for embedding the pattern in some context. As a consequence, those components must be consistent with certain clusters of facts, which in themselves can be inherently unique. (pp. 32–33)

There is a strong association between "apprehension" and "anguish," as there is between "sowing, spring," and "hope." It is that association which gives the anguish or the hope their special quality and intensity. Nuances among neighboring feelings are established through the bias of situations in which they are accustomed to occur. Music, by evoking the one, contributes to the recall of the other.

Relationships among themes and the coherence of significations. We must consider the relationships among the themes of signification obtained for the same fragments in several different ways. These relationships can consist in *inclusion, relatedness, parallelism* (on a subjective or objective level), or *coexistence.* One of the themes is more general for inclusion than for the others and appears to contain them as particular aspects, examples, or consequences; for example, a theme such as "Unrest, anguish, anguishing situation" vis-à-vis "gray sky, heavy, lowering, stormy impressions,"[7] or "Pleasant and agreeable countryside" vis-à-vis "A brook or beach, in a laughing tone,"[8] or "Heroism, victory" in relationship to "Departure for combat, riding, hunting."[9] Sometimes one of the themes appears to be a

---

[7]Table 9.8, series II, fragment A, themes 3 and 2, respectively.
[8]Table 9.8, series II, fragment B, themes 3 and 2.
[9]Table 9.8, series II, fragment C, themes 1 and 3.

specific aspect of the general signification of the other, for example, "Awakening of nature. Morning or spring" and "Pleasant and agreeable landscape."[10] This type of semantic overlap can be observed as well among themes with subjective content. Thus, "Situation involving sadness and lassitude" could be thought to contain "Sadness associated with remembrance" and even "Monotonous, sad task."[11]

In the last case, there is a close semantic relationship among themes having equivalent extension. This is frequently encountered with subjective significations. "Impression of serenity, at times religious," "Recollection, calm associated with serene landscapes," and "Light melancholy, nostalgia"[12] designate feelings that have their own specificity, especially if we take into account the objective context in which certain listeners are placed. *But they all reveal the same degree of tension, the same scheme of bodily movement and the same family of attitudes.* Likewise, "Joy, gaiety, lightness, insouciance, caprice," and "Dance, race, or game of lively appearance"[13] have a certain bodily pulsation in common—a similar style of behavior, just as do "Exhausting activity, mechanized life in a contemporary city" and "Dance or battle of primitive peoples."[14]

We defined parallelism earlier in regard to subjective and objective responses. Parallelism necessarily obtains in the relationships among the themes, as between "Melancholy calm, sadness" and "Village or countryside with night falling"[15] and between "Soaring feeling," and "Breathtaking or precipitous landscape."[16] Parallelism can be observed even between constituents of the same theme when it arises from mixed responses. There are numerous examples—all the themes defining a situation fall in this category. Corresponding to the many mixed and subjective responses found especially with the semiguided method are objective responses found with the free method. Attentive examination shows, moreover, that all the themes of descriptive content had some aspect of subjectivity, not only through the phenomenal nature of the imagined abstraction that they designated, but also through their more or less implicit integration of an attitude that they disclosed. Thus, a[17] theme like "Village or countryside with night falling," or "Breathtaking or precipitous landscape; a walk through nature"[18] merely *appear* to be absolutely objective. They are images

---

[10] Table 9.8, series II, fragment B, themes 1 and 3.
[11] Table 9.8, series III, fragment D, themes 3, 2, and 1.
[12] Table 9.8, series III, fragment A, themes 1, 2, and 3.
[13] Table 9.8, series III, fragment C, themes 2 and 1.
[14] Table 9.8, series III, fragment E, themes 1 and 2.
[15] Table 9.8, series II, fragment D, themes 2 and 3.
[16] Table 9.8, series III, fragment B, themes 1 and 2.
[17] Table 9.8, series II, fragment D, theme 3.
[18] Table 9.8, series III, fragment B, theme 2.

that condense expressivity, images into which the subject places himself and that he experiences. The parallelism is not always based on the concommitance between the attitude and the setting, but, more deeply, between the tension and the style of movements that imply phenomenal abstraction and the abstraction of feelings. Thus, relaxation and immobility permeate "Village or countryside with night falling," "Melancholy calm, sadness," and "Spiritual renunciation."[19] Similarly, we find high tension and motor agitation in "Exhausting activity, mechanized life in a contemporary city," "Dance or battle of primitive peoples," and "Motion of thoughts or things implicating fury, chaos, haste"[20]; and slowness of progress and gravity of movement in "Funereal impression. Funerary ritual or feelings," and "Assemblage or procession of old or weary beings."[21]

Finally, it sometimes happened that different themes related to the same fragment had no relationship that could be defined. This was the least frequent type of instance but did occur with "Enchantment. Oriental impression" next to "Pleasant nature, woodlands."[22]

---

[19]Table 9.8, series II, fragment D, themes 3, 2, and 1.
[20]Table 9.8, series III, fragment E, themes 1, 2, and 3.
[21]Table 9.8, series II, fragment F, themes 2 and 3.
[22]Table 9.8, series II, fragment E, themes 3 and 1.

Chapter 10

THEMES OF
SIGNIFICATION:
SYMBOLIC ELEMENTS

DIFFICULTIES IN THE ANALYSIS
OF MUSICAL STRUCTURE

When we seek to account for the extensive data provided by semantic judgments, we encounter difficulties that are inherent in the analysis of a complex reality in which the variables are never isolated but coexist in mutual interaction. Even if we limited ourselves to monodic music, we would undoubtedly observe that the examples selected would change character when transposed to a higher or lower register or when played softly or loudly, in one timbre or another. Experiments that involve the simplest stimuli—isolated tones—provide useful and solid data owing to their restriction of the number of variables, and so they can be relied on. But they are of only indirect relevance to music. I have tried, in the selection of certain of the examples, to find relatively simple structures in which one of the variables (melodic gesture, pitch register, intensity) could be set off distinctly, if not perfectly, isolated. In that, and in taking advantage of the infrequent semantic phenomena given acoustically, I felt I had established well-founded relationships between the contents of the sounds and the subjects' responses. In other fragments there was a complex dialectic involving content that was tempting to analyze, with all its multiple aspects—their compatibilities, their mutual reinforcements, their antagonisms.

The classification of facts thus settled midway between the abstract attributes of the sound and the necessarily individual particularities of the fragments analyzed. Musical spatiality, kinetic schemes, the various schemes of tension and release are concepts that are invoked many times and to which I seek to provide a firmer basis and greater precision.

276

MUSICAL SPATIALITY

It is not only objective significations that bring up the question of a musical space, but also significations that are concerned with aspects of emotional life, as we see at the end of this chapter. There is perhaps no signification that does not include a spatial atribute—at least the suggestion of a movement, of a gestural form. Even those which Hanslick (1854/1957) calls "qualities" (sweetness, energy, violence) can be understood only through the mediation processes of imagination that involve figures in space. In phenomenal experience, spatial events and activities come under the form of time when they become indeterminate, general, or abstract. Dimensions, directions, and distance relationships are the spontaneous orientations of imagination when it tries to fill out and actualize these concepts.

The notion of a sound space subsumes processes at different levels. Even in the psychology of spatial *direction* and *volume*, in the acoustic field the observed facts are not identical. The best known mechanism is lateral localization of sound sources with respect to the sagittal plane. This is due to the temporal asymmetry of binaural reception when the sagittal axis does not correspond to the direction of propagation of the sound waves. Asynchrony and differences of phase and intensity make us place a sound source to the right or left. That is given and does not involve association— and, it seems, the only given of this kind.[1] Distance perception presupposes knowledge of sounds that move away, their character changing with the lowering of intensity, the weakening of upper components and the accentuation of the lower, being less absorbed at a distance. The same thing can be said for the reverberation of sound characteristic of the volume of halls.[2]

The spatial signification of a reverberation "halo" is an "interpretation" that is conferred on the spaciousness and the size of the sound source itself (Bernhart, 1949). These two directions (not dimensions) in the acoustic field, together with spaciousness, constitute what we might call the "actual sound space." It corresponds either to features of objective distance of the source with respect to the subject or to features projected on the source

---

[1]See Piéron (1945); Caussé (1944). According to Caussé, differences in phase have a predominant influence compared with other factors.

[2]Reverberation time varies directly with the volume of the room, and the energy in the reverberating sounds inversely with room volume. In a chamber 50 cubic meters in volume and having a reverberation time of the order of 0.7 sec, the reverberating sound energy is 10 times greater than that of the direct sounds. But the ear does not transmit this relationship: "We have the subjective impression of hearing a selection of direct sounds" (Bernhart, 1949, p. 21). Microphones, in contrast, crudely transmit the relationship of the two forms of energy.

by its context. The former will be on a reflexive level; the latter will be "inferences" (Piéron, 1945) (though this last term raises the same problems as Helmholtz's (1877/1954) "unconscious inferences" did in the visual domain. The apparent distancing of a sound, perceived through the signs that have just been described, is not the result of a deduction, any more than the distancing of an object is with the diminution of visual angle. It is rather the product of automatic associative processes.

Another direction that has considerable importance in the spatial symbolism of music, that of "high" and "low," has been verified experimentally in a way that allays all doubts concerning its phenomenal reality, although its psychophysiological mechanism remains unexplained. Here again, there is no question of inference in the strict sense of the term. Pratt (1930) had subjects listen over a loudspeaker to five tones from an audiometer in the frequency range 256 to 4096 Hz, and asked them to place the source on a scale 2.5 m tall, divided into 14 equal parts. The loudspeaker was hidden from the subjects and was moved up or down the ladder after each tone was presented. Each subject made 10 judgments for each sound. Pratt observed that without exception the order of the perceived spatial heights corresponded to the order of the frequencies. Of course, the means were more or less tightly clustered depending on the subject, but the order always conformed to the hierarchy from low to high in pitch, independent of the actual displacement of the source. "Higher pitches were perceptually higher in space than low pitches" (p. 240).[3] Pratt's conclusions suggest that there is an immediate impression of spatial ordering, without association or thought. They agree with those of Stumpf (1890; see also von Hornbostel, n.d.), who proposed that tones have, apart from their three principal attributes, the immanent attribute of pseudospatiality, distinct from the visual or tactile spatiality with which it is intimately linked in experience.

Possible reservations concerning this dimension of sound height may arise from the obvious shortcomings in the explanation of something that is as yet only a phenomenal feature. Clearly, this is not a matter of a primary process, but does that justify our reducing it to a metaphor, to a merely linguistic relationship?[4] It does not seem to, and experiments show that this involves a firmly constructed phenomenal connection acquired through perceptual education. (All music educators know that prior to

---

[3]Along these same lines, Trimble (cited in Piéron, 1945) observed by means of small microphones placed close to the ear that the apparent source of sound moved in an ascending or descending arc depending on the direction of frequency variation.

[4]Révész (1937; 1953) proposes that the only real experience arising from the pitch of sounds is of a kinesthetic order. The hearing of a tone of a particular frequency is localized through a sensation of "resonance" in some region of the body—the chest, the head, the abdomen—independently of vocal exertion.

any musical education, children do not place high and low pitches in space at all.) And it is an historical acquisition as well. This correlation has been found in the language of very many peoples; in some language, it is reversed. We do not know exactly what determines this.

For Spencer (1886) and others who, following him, saw in song the origin of all music (see Combarieu, 1893; Révész, 1953), vocal register was connected with various kinetic sensations, according to which one sings in the high register with a "head" voice and in the lower register with a "chest" voice. But it is necessary to explain why these sensory differentiations have gone in the opposite direction for the Greeks, the Jews, and the Arabs. If this was the origin of the association, we should find notable differences between men and women in the classification of the pitches of sounds, since *the very same vocal pitch* should produce a different localization for the two sexes. That did not happen in our experiment. It is possible that other factors came into play: for example, the relative lengths of lyre strings, the low string being the longest and thus extending "higher" than the shorter one; or because of the social hierarchy of the sexes giving the masculine priority over the feminine, so that the voice of a man would be considered "higher" than that of a woman.[5] Whatever its origin, the psychoacoustic experiments have demonstrated the phenomenological reality (due to acquired associations) of the high or low spatial localization of tones according to their frequency.

These difficulties, along with other biases concerning the presumed "interior" nature of feeling and of sound, have provoked some authors to cast doubt on the other spatial directions delineated by sound patterns and to deny in general any acoustic spatiality. For Révész (1937, 1953), sound space was a mere *flatus vocis*; Brelet (1949)[6] defined it by "interiority" itself—its content obscure and untranslatable except through metaphor. Here we must dispute the opinion that the only form for psychological space must be the one of three Euclidean dimensions provided by one part of our visual experience. Because dimensions are foreign to sounds, acoustic spatiality is relegated to the realm of metaphors without content. We know, however, of other forms of spatiality in which fewer than three dimensions exist: two, in touch (where they are instead directions induced by movement and kinesthesia); none, in olfaction, in which only volume is sensed. In touch, as in the spatiality of the body itself, diverse sensory messages are integrated through experience with visual

---

[5]Sachs (1943) noted that among the Greeks, the hypaté (a low note) was called higher than the nété (a high note), perhaps because of the relative length of the strings of the lyre that produced them; and among the Jews and the Arabs, a man's voice is said to be higher than that of a woman.

[6]This idea can be found in Hegel (1944) and Schopenhauer (1844/1966).

messages, such that we ultimately see the forms that the hand runs over, the movement performed, or the attitude taken by the body—just as when we hear a train disappear over the horizon. These percepts are not in any way "interior," but their exterior spatial forms, different in each case, are unified through the contagion of the visual.

Musical space, however, does not reduce to acoustic space. It is only a symbolic superstructure that uses certain signs, modifying or transposing them to develop spatial *representations*. Thus, retreat or approach suggested through musical means retain from their acoustic homologs only the weakening or strengthening of overall sound intensity, without changing timbre. We ought not say that such signs as the lateralization of the instruments in the orchestra, placed in diverse points in the actual space in which they are heard, play no spatializing role in the representation of a landscape in sound, nor that the hall's reverberation has no influence on it. A restricted orchestra or an overly absorbent studio definitely reduces the effectiveness of the ensemble. But these acoustic signs and this spaciousness are bearers of signification. They lead back to another, imagined space that extends beyond them. Our previous experiments showed that this space is present in a number of semantic responses (see Table 9.8).

The specific quality of musical space does not reside merely in semantic responses, but in the combination of symbolic means, put into the work by the composer to populate a space designed with simultaneous sound sources and movements, (in order to delineate by means of the weight of the melodic line, etc.). Mindful of the reservations concerning the term "inference," we are correct to state that musical space is inferred from exteroceptive or interoproprioceptive movements inherent in melodies and rhythms, from noises or multiple voices that they evoke in stylizing them, and from the objects whose presence is indicated by those movements and those noises (Combarieu, 1893). This symbol formation is clear in the following example, in which it is combined with the effects of timbre and of the progressive elevation of the tonal register and intensity, giving at once an impression of lightening and opening out.

Example 1

Ravel, *Daphnis et Chloé*, Daybreak (Series II, B).[7] The orchestral complexity of this fragment can be seen in the score (Fig. 10.1). Hearing it, one can discern the following structures: a continuous pedal point of superimposed arpeggiated motives (Figure 10.1a). Each motive, consisting of 12 thirty-second notes, is repeated four times in the measure, which gives the pedal

---

[7]The indications that follow these titles refer to the series of experiments with the fragments described in Table 9.1.

Figure 10.1. Examples from Ravel, *Daphnis et Chloé.*

pattern the appearance of a rapid, continual vibration or of a dusting of luminous particles. The dynamic is *pianissimo* at the start and grows only very gradually to the extent of the intervention of additional instruments. In effect, when given only to the flutes and clarinets alternating from measure to measure, the pedal pattern is at first emphasized by a series of glissandos and then leaps of tenths in the harps. The strings and basses sustain this almost imperceptibly at a *pianissimo*. Triplets of held notes by the basses describe a sort of undulation or subterranean writhing that can be discerned under the luminous palpitation. Then, beginning with the third measure of 156, this is doubled in the flute, the oboe, and the English horn, beginning in the fifth measure by the clarinets, in the seventh by the bass clarinet, and finally by the first and second violins. These different entrances and doublings are not distinctly perceived. You hear only a multiplication of the initial vibration, which appears to fill the space, becoming a sort of universal vibration. This whole pedal is situated in the same register. At the start, from one measure to the next, the tessitura of the upper part is elevated by a minor third, then returned to its initial state (Figure 10.1a and b). The harmonic changes that occur from one measure to another introduce variations of *color*. It is only at 157 (measures 1 to 4) that the violins, joining the other instruments, can rise to the initial tessitura of a fifth.

However, beginning at measure 8 of 155, the basses trace a motive doubled at the octave, obstinately repeated in the form of a climb (Figure 10.1c). This climb passes through the levels of *pianissimo, piano, mezzo forte,* and *forte,* emphasizing the dynamic evolution of the pattern. This motive is taken up by the cellos, then the violas, the bass clarinets, and the bassoons. The overall ascension of the basses in this climb is of limited scope, and it draws all its power from the repetition of the ascending motive—from the dynamic evolution of both the basses and the ensemble.

This example shows the difficulty of separating purely spatial impressions from everything that attaches itself to the "content" of that space, and that can be stylized—reduced to "mobiles" uniquely determined by their rhythmic appearance, by their melodic contour, sometimes by the conventional signification of their timbres, by the symbolism of their intensities, or by the "distance" among the different instrumental registers.[8]

Combarieu (1893) has established an inventory of the descriptive resources of the modern orchestra. Music can suggest:

1. The direction of movement, its rapidity, and its form: gyration, undulation, translation; its rhythm, its total duration.

2. An indeterminate number of natural or artificial noises of the external world, with their nuances.

3. The relative position in space of two immobile objects or of two environments and the variable distance that separates them.

4. By way of analogy, the largeness and smallness of objects.

In the same way, Goblot (1901) emphasized the possibilities belonging to musical structures to indicate presences and processes by their motor style: undulation, propagation, and leaping.

Thus, space in music is the exact opposite of the abstract space of geometry, which can be conceptualized in its emptiness as a system of infinite dimensions. Music space consists, instead, of modalities fixed in their fullness and tension. It closely resembles concrete space with its diversity of qualitatively distinct zones, its vectors attached to one particular content or another, according to its structure, its interest, its impact. It would be an error to believe musical space inherent only in descriptive music. Don't works of apparently formal intention (such as a movement from a suite or concerto by Bach) have, when we listen, characteristics uncontestably implying a form of spatiality, not at all metaphorical, but with an analyzable symbolism based on the intrinsic characters of sound structures? "Grandeur," "majesty," "fluidity," or "heaviness" are attributes that we will grant most easily to such patterns, even if we refuse on principle to formulate a more specific signification about them, for each of those can lead back to spatial directions, to distances or movements, to kinetic or gestural forms.

---

[8]See Table 9.8, Series II, A, "Heavy sky, lowering," is associated with the English horn theme; Series II, C, "Departure for battle, riding, hunting," with the theme from the brasses, more than with the former sound; Series II, E, "Pleasant nature, wooded landscape, serene solitude in nature," with successive wind-instrument solos, set off from the orchestral accompaniment; Series II, F, "Gloom, dark places," and "Assemblage or slow procession of the old and weary," with the rhythmic character of the ensembles, and with the preponderance of low senorities; Series III, A, "Serene landscape, faintly lit" were suggested by the character of the theme given to the clarinet, as well as by its timbre and by its distance from the chordal accompaniment; Series III, B, "Jagged or precipitous landscape" was described by fluctuations of dynamics and tonal distances of instrumental motion; Series II, D, did not suggest space explicitly, being a violin solo.

KINETIC SCHEMES

A melody is a type of line that depicts itself, by contour or by gesture in action, for several reasons:

1. Its temporal articulations, its own way of organizing duration through longer or shorter successive sounds or silences, can be interpreted in terms of motor organization.
2. Furthermore, its overall tonal amplitude, or that of its different intervals, suggests spatial amplitude of movement and of successive moments.
3. Finally, its overall tonal direction, or that of its different intervals, are qualified in terms of their upward or downward direction.

Each melody thus encloses a kinetic scheme consisting of certain of the resources of musical rhythm (metrical accent, dynamic accent, accents of pitch and duration), but lacking the resources belonging to polyphony and harmony. It is a unilinear scheme that can be projected in space, represented as a contour drawn in time, or experientially as a modality of movement or bodily rest pertaining to an attitude, a mental state, or a feeling. Depending on the case, we can have objective or subjective significations, and when the movement is seen in both those aspects, we have mixed responses. The following examples demonstrate how powerful melody is. They include extracts of orchestral works in which the melodic part plays a predominant role, or even an exclusive one (see Example 3). The accompanying parts are described and serve as a harmonic background without any particular distinction. The melody is in the foreground with its appearance, its amplitude, its impulses, its pauses, and its ornamentation.

Example 2

Franck, *Psyché*, symphonic poem for chorus and orchestra, first part: The Sleep of Psyché (Series III, A). The fragment begins with an harmonic accompaniment, slowly swaying, in the cellos. The meter is 6/8, but transformed into a triple meter by the division of each measure into three quarter notes, the second and third notes being syncopated. This gives the accompaniment a certain vague and breathlike character, with the second and third notes starting on weak beats.

The melody is a long phrase for solo clarinet, repeated after a break by the flute and the oboe—a slow, syncopated phrase, with close intervals for the most part, at even note values throughout its length, which accentuates the "breathing" quality of the pattern. The melody here is like a single gesture, slow and calm; or like a continuous contour drawing a simple curve, without noticeable roughness, with an intermediate way-station on the fourth note, which is repeated. The ambitus of the phrase is limited to a seventh, and its general direction is slowly descending.

The break serving as a bridge between the two expositions of the phrase is a sort of furtive escape that runs through almost two octaves in two measures, a brief rest interrupting the steady quasi-immobility of the fragment.

The significations evoked are well summarized by themes 1, 2, and 3: "Impression of serenity, at times religious," "Meditation, calm associated with serene, faintly lit, landscapes (morning or evening)," "Slight melancholy, nostalgia. Moderate feelings." As we can see, the psychological states are here linked to slow gestural forms of slight amplitude close to immobility. The landscapes, when they do occur, generally have unbroken contours (hills, fields), and often include a body of water. Without any doubt, the woodwind sounds utilized in the exposition of the melody contribute to the stimulation of rustic or sylvan impressions.

Example 3

Ravel, *Daphnis et Chloé*, Nocturne (Series II, E). Over an almost imperceptible string accompaniment (trills at a *ppp* level), whose harmonic complexity is examined further on, three solos from the flute, horn, and clarinet stand out (Figure 10.2a, b, and c). These solos consist of phrases of almost identical structure through their first three measures (out of five or four), with variations at the end and in the middle. With the slow presentation during the first three measures, these melodies have, until the second beat of the third measure, an ambitus restricted to a major third, within which they proceed by successive degrees. In what follows, the amplitude of the intervals expands, and they all end with a slowly rising phrase, moving by close intervals in the flute and horn and enriched with ornamental features in the clarinet. The tempo is free and the rhythm flexible, with frequent syncopations and a great variety of note values. The pattern constitutes a slow gesture—flexible, not large at the start, of an easy nonchalance enlivened with ornamented measures. The semantic responses arranged here

Figure 10.2. Examples from Ravel, *Daphnis et Chloé*.

under the second theme ("repose, nonchalance," "Goatherd, or langorous dancer") correspond well to this aspect of the melodic motion.

The most abundant source of kinetic forms is rhythm. As we have seen, every melody involves a rhythm. Conversely, every rhythm is conditioned by the melody or melodies in which it is realized, and even by the battery of resources of musical composition that are involved in differentiating it from the background. We can thus correctly define rhythm as "the structure of a system of sounds conceived under the category of becoming" (de Schloezer, 1947). This brings the following into play:

1. Metrical accents, both temporal and intensive, and accents of pitch within the melody.

2. Relationships inherent in heterophony, among rhythmic systems in horizontal relationship (periodicity, relation or opposition of motives that follow each other in different parts); or in vertical relationship (periodicity, relation, or opposition of motifs that weave together in simultaneous parts). We cannot say that the rhythm of a melody persists in its kinetic aspects even when homophony ceases. It is the whole pattern of the system that determines the specifics of movement, so that it is necessary to add (c).

3. Harmonic accentuation, certain chords that are enhancing due to their "thetic" nature, their stable character; metrical accents, whether temporal or not; and in contrast, certain features such as weak chords and transitions that have a tendency to attenuate the accent.

No doubt the hierarchy of tonal functions operates in tonal music to add the effects of the conventional differentiation of harmonic signals to this specifically kinetic differentiation. Furthermore, the *striking* quality of consonant or dissonant chords can be used to emphasize the other forms of accentuation, both in tonal music and even more in music that rejects the functional signals of tonality. The "complex" harmonic structure of certain chords that are recalcitrant to auditory analysis makes them resemble noises and percussion sounds, which are actually more effective elements of excitation than consonances (elements of relaxation) or classifiable harmonies (elements of intelligibility).

When we distinguish rigorously between musical rhythm and natural rhythm, we understand not only that the two are determined by different means, but also that because the internal *raisons d'etre* of the two are different, their similarity is illusory. Natural rhythm is the result of blind physical forces, uncoordinated and produced without regard for the perceptual unity they offer (as when trees and waves contribute their noise to a pattern that is a "polyphony" to our ears). Musical rhythm, on the other hand, results from an impetus of human thought, subsumed under formal cultural norms whose end is the creation of a *work* and not the imitation of nature or of mechanical rhythms (de Schloezer, 1947). Some Bach fugues are graceful—the Fugue in F-sharp Major from Book 1 of the *Well-Tempered Clavier*, for example—whereas others are meditative (the Fugue in F-sharp Minor from the same book). But those are fugues, forms obeying a conventional determinism and bowing to necessities that are not informed with respect to our motor behavior as it affects bodily attitudes. These distinctions are well founded, and we do not dispute them. Besides, our aim is not to analyze the origins of kinetic forms in the composer.[9] What I seek to show by means of this experiment is that despite their particular origins, the forms inherent in musical rhythm can be symbolic analogs of kinetic forms present in behavior, whether the composer intended this analogy explicitly or not. We know that only music gives us fully the contents of a musical expression. If it is the analog of a feeling or of the movement of things, it is so in a specifically musical manner, and we apprehend it only by way of the detour of signification, to the extent that it contains in itself a kinetic form characteristic of that movement or feeling. This is shown in the following examples.

Example 4

Mozart, *Quartet in C-major*, K. 465, Rondo (allegro molto) (Series III, C). The movement is very rapid in its global aspect. The initial theme presented by the first violin contains a succession of eighth-notes, repeated in staccato pairs, supported by chords in the same rhythm as the three other instruments. The pattern at once takes on a light and bouncy appearance (Figure 10.3a).

The second phrase of this theme is preceded and followed by motives in octaves that sound like knocking, forming an harmonic and dynamic contrast (their *forte* level in contrast to the *pianissimo* level in the two phrases). These constitute fierce interruptions or peremptory questions addressed to the first violin, which responds with a slender and supple song (Figure 10.3b).

Following the conclusion of the theme with a motive of the same type is a passage introduced by broken arpeggios ascending in staccato eighth-notes. The first violin alternates held notes and broken arpeggios in

---

[9]Several authors have, on the contrary, thought in terms of an infiltration, whether implicit or not, of natural rhythms into the composer's subconscious. See, for example, d'Udine (1910) and Willems (1954): "Few composers can account for the way in which the subconscious is saturated with elements which, under the influence of certain mental states, rise into the light of consciousness in a form at first unrecognizable. Through minute introspection one can sometimes succeed in recovering the impression that served as the point of departure of a musical work" (p. 103).

Figure 10.3. Examples from Mozart, *Quartet in C Major*, K. 465, Rondo.

two-measure phrases, while the viola and the second violin support them with an accompaniment in which tremolos and syncopated chords succeed each other in two-measure phrases.

One of these alternating figures seems agitated and roiling; the other, jostling and bouncing. This distinguishes them clearly from the playful theme at the start. The whole passage (14 measures) is *forte* until the cadence in D involving tremolos in the second violin and viola. The fragment is a very lively divertissement for a small string ensemble. The extreme lightness of the opening (35 measures) turns into agitation in the following measures (36–54) as a result of changes to agogic accents and syncopation but remains lighthearted. The motives in octaves add an obvious rigid punctuation, of a severity that is immediately belied by the context.

The semantic responses stimulated by the excerpt fell into themes related either to immediate motor evocations corresponding to a rhythmic scheme *seen from outside* (a game or dance, preparations for a ball), to which was added a more precise historical determination (counts and countesses); or to this rhythmic scheme that was felt and experienced as the proprioceptive accompaniment of certain psychological states (joy and gaiety, with a touch of lightness, youth, and carefreeness).

Example 5

Bartok, *Out of Doors* suite for piano solo: The Pursuit (Series III, E). This fragment sets out in a sort of agogic way. The pattern that will constitute a tumultuous ostinato, maintained throughout the length of the fragment, is divided into duplets and progressively accelerated until it reaches steady speed in quintuplets (Figure 10.4a). This ostinato is punctuated throughout the nine measures of the opening with minor seconds Gb-F, which fall at times on weak beats and at times on the principal beats of the measure and constitute a sort of dull and unpredictable hammering in the

Figure 10.4. Examples from Bartok, *Out of Doors* Suite for piano.

lower part that can be discerned under the growing movement of the upper part.

At the tenth measure, the right hand interrupts the strokes of these seconds to attack a theme beginning with the six notes of an ascending whole-tone scale in the middle register, followed and frequently interrupted by repeated notes, by groups of 10, 7, 10, 3, and 4, cut by eighth-rests arbitrarily situated on the first or second beat. These repeated notes constitute a sort of breathless congo drum of unpredictable rhythm, superimposed on the ostinato (Figure 10.4b). It alternates with groups of melodic notes at close intervals, resting on a pedal of repeated notes (15 Fs in a row), grouped into 3,1,2,3,2,2,2, and separated by eighth-rests. The fragment ends with a sort of melodic cadence repeated three times with variations (Figure 10.4c), cut by chords struck in the extreme high register, alternating with chords in the low register above and below the ostinato.

If we set aside the historical character of its melodic and harmoic syntax (which is examined later), this fragment is distinguished by its complex rhythmic anatomy superimposed on the constant tumult of the bass and the irregular percussion of the repeated notes, the chords, and the melodic groupings. It is to this that we should attribute the general character of the three themes that the excerpt evokes. All are related to activities connected with "supercharged" psychological states, strained in their precipitation. Themes 1 and 2 ("Exhausting activity. Mechanized life in a contemporary city. Dance or battle of African peoples.") are formed of exterior images from those precipitating factors. In theme Number 3 we find the experiential and proprioceptive aspect ("Movement of thought involving an outburst. Chaos. Haste."). The impression of disorder and chaos is connected with the rhythmic opposition between the *regular* ostinato that achieves its unchanging movement through the progressive acceleration at the start and the *irregular* drum pattern given to the right hand.

Seeking to define the nature of kinetic schemes more precisely, we might wonder about the degree of precision with which the suggestions of movement are made. Of the three components described earlier—speed, general direction, and form—the the third is unquestionably the one that appears the least directly transposable into a polyrhythmic sound pattern. In the interest of rigor, we can conceive of a simple linear kinetic scheme described by a "melodic line." (Even so, we shall see that this transposition is never univocal nor mechanical.) But what might the kinetic result of a piece of music be when several lines superimpose their accents and their particular durations? Unless the composer has modeled his global rhythms on an extramusical motor pattern, we have to expect that the suggestion comes to the listener, either through segregation of the melodic line or through a compromise between rhythmic components (each of which is too marked to blend in completely) that the listener perceives.

EXPERIMENT 15

The experiments whose results follow demonstrated much of the foregoing in the following way. Seventy subjects (at experience levels A and B—see Experiment 14 in connection with Table 9.2) were presented four samples of music extracted from works whose titles clearly indicated the attempt of the composer in the direction of kinetic description:

1. Pierné, *Giration*, choreographic divertissement (M. Sénart edition, from p. 2, measure 9, to p. 3, last measure);
2. Pierné, *La Toupie* (M. Senart edition, p. 20, last measure, to p. 22, measure 2);
3. Debussy, *Petite Suite*, En Bateau (Durand edition, pp. 1–4, first 30 measures);
4. Debussy, *Images*, Mouvement (first 31 measures).

Method

The conditions were the same as for Experiment 14 (see chapter 9).[10] The subjects were asked whether each fragment (which they heard twice) gave them the idea of movement or of a moving object. If the answer was affirmative, they were asked to define that movement in itself, or so that it could be imagined in the object, and to describe, if possible, its form and *to try to draw it.*

---

[10]These experiments were done in 1953, in the sound-isolated room of the Electro-Acoustic Laboratory of the Center for Scientific Research at Marseilles, with lycée students in their senior year.

Results and Discussion

The numerical results are shown in Table 10.1. Where two numbers are shown, the upper number refers to responses consisting of only one indication of the type shown at the top of the column. The lower number indicates multiple responses consisting, in addition to the upper number of indications of speed or direction or of other forms of movement. The two last columns at the right give the number of indications of speed or direction occurring alone (the upper number) or in multiple responses (the lower number).

Examination of this data discloses the significant frequency of responses containing an idea of movement and numerous indications concerning the form of that movement. As we can see, the latter are not in strict agreement with each other. In some cases, the headings under which they fell were not entirely precise, so that such rubrics as "march or dance" did not provide a determinate sense concerning the form or the appearance of movement except when accompanied with further qualification. A certain number of multiple responses added a precision of speed, appearance, or direction to those terms; or else the moving object itself served to specify the movement in an analogous sense. Everywhere else, there was a certain unity that became evident in listening to the fragments. As with the other significations, the concrete kinetic schemes were fully perceptible only through involvement of the musical pattern. In the first fragment, the saltatory scheme, which underlies many responses, is made up of the alternation of rhythmic figures such as *a* and *b* in Figure 10.5. This latter effect justified an interpretation going in the direction of a march or light dance, or even a simple to-and-fro motion or zig-zag. Significations involving rotation were associated with the way in which the metrical rhythm (of a waltz) was brought out by accents of pitch on the third beat of several measures.

In the second fragment, the whirling and rapid gyrations were associated with repeated figures such as *a* and *b* in Figure 10.6. Example *a* includes at the same time a progression emphasized by the strokes of the violins. This introduces the idea of pursuit or flight by successive brusque movements. The repetitive aspect of the gyration is found in the analogous pattern from the fourth fragment (Figure 10.7a) where it is combined with, then superimposed on, a trotting scheme in which the moment of accentuation on the fourth beat is either an accent of intensity or of pitch (Figure 10.7b). This accentuation intensifies and occurs at intervals that are twice as short in *c*, bringing about an acceleration of movement. Thus, in this fragment there is an alternation of two kinetic schemes that end by mixing in *c*, in which the acceleration is increased even more by the underlying presence of *b* in the left hand.

TABLE 10.1

Distribution of Semantic Responses According to Ideas of Movement

Fragment	Semantic Responses	Responses with Idea of Movement	Forms of Movement					Indication of Speed	Indication of Direction
			1	2	3	4	5		
1	68	64	leaps and bounds	march or dance	to-and-fro	spiral rotation	other movement		
			15	7	5	2		1	1
			16	12	6	3		2	10
2	69	66	whirling gyration, spiral pirouettes	race, flight pursuit	disorganized agitation	leaps	other movement		
			14	10	3	2	3	0	5
			6	10	2	2	2	5	12
3	67	67	sliding gliding horizontal translation	undulation or subtle swaying	dance or quiet walk	other movement			
			24	16	8	4	3	0	6
			5		4	12	2	0	0
4	68	67	gallop, race	gyration, whirling	leaps, leaping dance	jerky, to-and-fro	other movement		
			19	10	5	4	5	0	1
			14	10	5	1	5	12	8

291

Figure 10.5 Two aspects of a saltatory theme, from Pierné, *Giration* (Fragment 1).

Figure 10.6. Themes evoking gyration from Pierné, *Giration*. Example (a) includes simultaneously an ascending progression emphasized by strokes of the violins (Fragment 2).

Figure 10.7. Combination of two types of motion from Debussy, *Mouvement*. (a) Theme with gyrating pattern; (b) theme evoking a trotting rhythm; (c) combination of the two (Fragment 4).

The third fragment offers a slow, supple melodic line with an ambitus restricted for the most part to a third (Figure 10.8), emphasized by held notes in the basses. The slowly undulating swaying is assured by the harp accompaniment consisting of ascending arpeggios that regularly stop at their peak on the second beat of each measure, delineating a slow gesture of mounting from the depths and repeated at regular intervals.

The subjects made relatively few drawings. Perhaps they could have characterized the complex rhythmic form of the musical fragments more easily with words than with lines. Even so, I have chosen several of the drawings as illustrations and have grouped them according to the fragments that inspired them (Figures 10.9, 10.10, 10.11, and 10.12). In Figure 10.9, indications of discontinuous and repeated leaps and bounds

Figure 10.8. Theme recalling undulations or slow swaying, from Debussy, *En bateau* (Fragment 3).

dominate, alternating with moments of preparation consisting of less ample jumping motives, depending on whether the listener wished to represent the most apparent movement or the pattern of the schematic structure. In Fig. 10.10 there are successive swirls linked together with an idea of general progression indicated by arrows. Figure 10.11 is striking in its almost exclusive dominance by horizontals, often slightly wavering, with translation indicated by arrows. Figure 10.12 shows designs that contain only gyratory, spiral, or swirling elements, or some combination of those elements with repeated jumps that are superimposed in the rhythmic form of the musical fragment.

Thus, the idea that emerges from these experiments is that, even if the suggestion of movement is very frequent and even if listening is accompanied with a clear feeling concerning movement, the verbal or graphic translation of that feeling is not easy. Analysis is required to separate the partial schemes that can be characterized by simple terms (gyration, leap, slide). When that separation does not occur, the result is condensed into global concepts evoked by the combination of several movements (walk, dance, race, pursuit, agitation). The nature of moving objects or beings often provides the specification of their appearance, speed, and direction. Walking and dancing are different depending on whether they are done by a human being, and elf, a squirrel, or a bear.

It is thus difficult to obtain an *abstract kinetic scheme* whose verbal or graphic expression would be the faithful equivalent of the concrete scheme present in the fragment. These experiments show that a certain degree of verbal translation, but no more, can be attained. To obtain more would require the presentation of stimuli constructed in the laboratory and not fragments of works.[11] Thus we can understand that some authors have the idea, quite ligitimate in itself, according to which movement in music

---

[11]Concerning the acoustic suggestion of visual forms by noises, Dijkhuis (1953) has shown that the principal difference between noises characterized by flat and by complex temporal envelopes resides in the brief and sonorous aspect of the clear endings of the former and in the continuous aspect of the slower and more mixed intensity transitions of the latter. In this case the problem is different for both the induced term (geometric figures traced by hand with a stylus on a plate), and the inductor (limited acoustic resources and imprecision of the tracing).

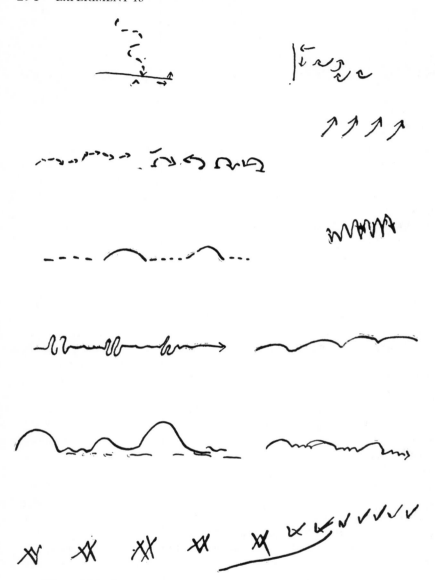

Figure 10.9. Drawings made by subjects hearing Fragment 1 (Pierné, *Giration*). Indications of jumps, repeated or alternating with preparatory movements.

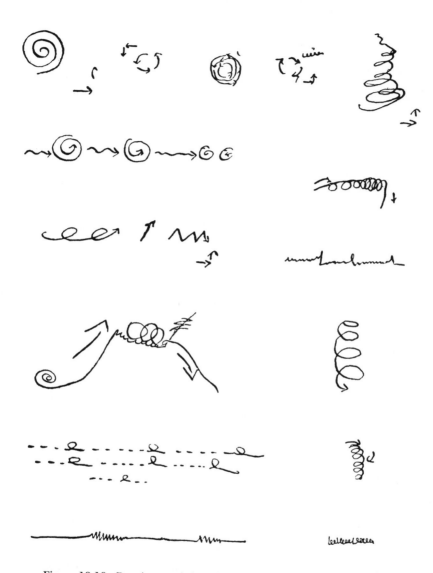

Figure 10.10. Drawings made by subjects hearing Fragment 2 (Pierné, *La Toupie*). Indications of successive or isolated swirls.

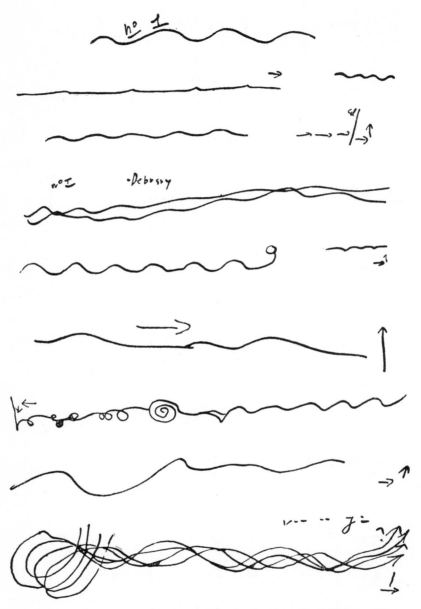

Figure 10.11. Drawings made by subjects hearing Fragment 3 (Debussy, *En bateau*). Horizontal strokes with slight undulations, with translational motion indicated by the arrows.

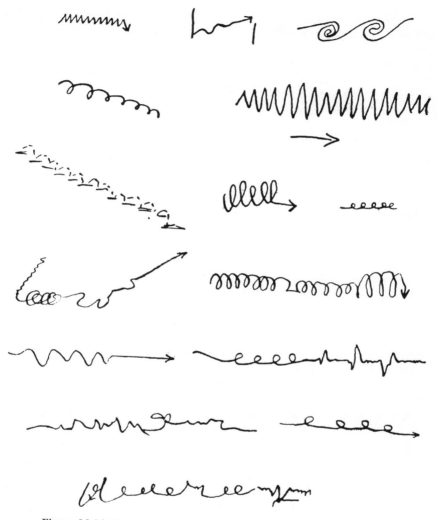

Figure 10.12. Drawings made by subjects hearing Fragment 4 (Debussy, *Mouvement*). Gyrations, spirals, swirls.

is an "automovement," unique in its own space (de Schloezer, 1947), a "pure" movement, "without an object," without relation to other natural or mechanical movements, not even those of the dance (Siohan, 1956). As soon as we seek to analyze works by reading them with the technical precision associated with the multiple means employed in rhythmic writing, we lose sight of what global listening has suggested beyond those means.

Furthermore, it is certain that the analogy between musical movement and physical movement is in many cases excessively mediated, for the necessities of formal construction (always present and operating, whatever the work) impose features on the rythmic figures that might suit only general qualifications, namely those that Hanslick (1854/1957) and many others have adopted: gracefulness, lightness, majesty, calm. Such outlines of movement and appearance are applicable to a number of rhythmic schemes, with specifications appropriate to each work. We know that it is a long way from the outline to the realization and that the outline serves us only in clarifying, through the bias of verbal analysis, an impression that is provided only by the music.

SCHEMES OF TENSION AND RELAXATION

Additional difficulty arises in this analysis because it results in the separation of aspects that are united in the work—that contribute to the building of expression and, in turn, of semantic judgment. We will not attempt to examine all this but rather will take up those aspects that are manifest in the results of these experiments.

The idea of tension and of relaxation can be applied to kinetic schemes. The speed and amplitude of movements inherent in each scheme assume a quantitative variety (whereas the form is only qualitative), expressible in the degress of tension that contribute to determining the differences of accentuation of the heterophonic rhythm. These, then, are schemes of *kinetic tension*.

But the purely quantitative components of tension and relaxation are variations in dynamics and in pitch, and in their combinations.

In itself, the intensity of a sound pattern is a property that can be utilized symbolically to reinforce and differentiate the articulations of musical discourse. Indications of intensity appear to have only a structural function in many classical works. The dynamic contrast established between two themes, between two sections, permits us to distinguish them better. With two repetitions of the same idea, the contrast assures variety to the repetition that sets it off. A progressive change in intensity provides a transition, ending the present development and announcing the following one, whether by priming its dynamic level or by contrasting with it.

However, even in similar cases, dynamics give to the articulations of musical discourse significations related to those of verbal discourse, by analogy with its expressive techniques. A phrase at a *forte* level is positive, affirmative—it says what is important or gives importance to what it says. The *piano* and its different degrees is insidious. It succeeds in capturing attention by a roundabout way. The progressive variations in intensity in the interior of a phrase or a section limit its outlines, make a formal whole. Such significations lead to an aspect of what has been called the "language of intonation" (Dupré & Nathan, 1911, p. 9), vocal mimicry (Dumas, 1933b), and "vocal gesture" (Brelet, 1949, vol. 2), which are based as well on the melodic and rhythmic components I discuss later. But these significations are distinguished from vocal mimicry by their more intellectual aspect. This is less a matter of affective intentions than of logical intentions scattered through the sequence of discourse and connected with the disclosure of its internal hierarchy.

But dynamics also possess a more direct symbolism consisting of transporting into sound the degrees and variations of intensity of external processes, be they visible or audible,[12] or psychological states of tension and release. Even in the first case we do not find, as Hanslick (1854/1957) supposed, a simple copy of schemes of sound or even light intensity but rather an elaborate representation into which the scheme integrates itself and operates to the extent that it is compatible with the others (pitch and kinetic scheme). The following examples from the experiments show this clearly.

Example 6

Ravel, *Daphnis et Chloé*, Daybreak (Series II, B). This fragment starts *pianissimo* with pedal points and broken arpeggios. The climb of the basses begins at measure 8, passing through the levels of *pianissimo, piano, mezzoforte,* and *forte*. The fragment ends in a *fortissimo* which emphasizes at the same time the increased *volume* of the ensemble (through the successive entry of several groups of instruments doubling the pedal point) and the excerpt's tonal elevation (in particular, that of the basses' movement).

Here the dynamic evolution describes a continuous curve, as does the tonal elevation. It contributes to the evocation of progressive lightening of space, gives impressions of wakening, of soaring, of growth—as the semantic responses indicate, clustered around theme number one: "Awakening of nature, morning or spring, awakening of joy."

Example 7

Bartok, *Out of Doors* Suite, The Pursuit (Series III, E). This fragment begins at a *piano* level, which begins to grow in the fourth measure and

---

[12]According to Hanslick (1854/1957), "What part of the feelings then, can music represent, if not the subject involved in them? Only their dynamic properties. It may reproduce the motion accompanying psychical action, according to its momentum: speed, slowness, strength, weakness, increasing and decreasing intensity" (p. 24).

becomes a *mezzo-piano* by the tenth measure: this level is maintained until the final measures *(mezzo-forte)*. However, in the performance selected, the pattern of the fragment gave the impression of scarcely contained dynamic furor. The intensity accents in the upper part and in the accompaniment were perceptible and gave it a very clashing, striking quality.

Themes one and two were related to the dynamic state of the fragment. Both themes concerned boisterous activities: "Mechanized life in the contemporary city" (in particular a factory at work) and "Dance or battle of African peoples." Here again the dynamic tensions and the agogic rhythms are closely united. They start growing rapidly beginning at the level of the opening. A number of responses encoded this evolution: the factory was imagined in the morning, in the initial phase of the rendition; the battle of African peoples became the departure for combat, etc.

Example 8

Respighi, *The Fountains of Rome,* La Fontana di Trevi al Meriggio (Series II, C). Here dynamics played a derivative role. They brought about associations of a general order (compared to the others, which were more particular, resulting from focusing attention on one element or another: the timbre of the brass, the warlike rhythm of the theme, etc.). The level was *hyper-fortissimo* during the first eight measures, the passed to *fortissimo,* then to *forte,* and did not decline perceptibly until the passage to the minor *(mezzo-forte* at measure 17). That is, most of the fragment had a resounding level, accentuated by considerable distances among simultaneous pitch levels in the texture (5 octaves plus a third), the peals of the brass, and the excursions of rhythm and tempo.

The significations of the second theme, "Solemnity, apotheosis, brilliance," seemed to be less subordinated to timbre than the others. By their generality they seemed linked to a global interpretation in which intensity was an integrating element. (It is the equivalent of the force—the attribute of strength.)

This combination of motoric tension and relaxation with intensity appear also, in the following examples, as motives of subjective or mixed significations.

Example 9

Franck, *Psyché,* The Sleep of Psyché (Series III, A). "Religious serenity, meditation, calm, melancholy, nostalgia, muted feelings"—all these nuances would be destroyed by an other dynamic applied to the same pattern of sounds. Almost all the fragment was at the level of *pianissimo.* Only the string interlude that separates the two expositions of the song was stronger at first (a level of *mezzo-forte*), but it did not take long to fade away and end with the initial *pianissimo*.

Example 10

Berlioz, *Roméo et Juliette,* Romeo alone (Series III, F): "Reverie with a hint of melancholy, sadness (theme 2), calming, serenity (theme 3)," and even, to a point, "Waiting, mystery" are also feelings of slight tension, or, in any case, of *a contained tension* that becomes transparent from time to time. The ensemble of violins starts *pianissimo,* with an increase that goes up to *poco forte* on the second phrase, and that accentuates the enlargement of the ambitus. It returns to *pianissimo* at the end of this phrase.

Example 11

Franck, *Psyché et Eros* (Series III, B). Here there are rapid fluctuations of intensity that operate as outbursts of tension, powerful and brusque, giving the impression of vehemence and of taking off into flight. The level at the start is *piano,* but it grows by the seventh measure, passes to *forte,* then to *fortissimo* (measures 12 and 16 of R), then diminishes abruptly (measures 22–23) to a *pianissimo* (measures 1 to 5 of S) from which it returns rapidly to *forte* and *fortissimo* (measures 13 and 23). The corresponding themes evoked were: (a) feeling, in full flight, growing exaltation, but happy; (c) events, action, situation, implying conquest, flight, power.

While the association of "high" with high pitch, and "low" with low pitch could have been experimentally verified with rigor, the association of high and low pitch with such other visual qualities as luminosity and other intensive variables has been made the object of only infrequent and partial control conditions and of few individual studies (e.g., Combarieu, 1893). The observations of Destouches (1899) showed that for 43 of 47 subjects the sensation of brightness was subordinated to the pitch of a heard tone. A small number of subjects (9 of 47) experienced a sensation of *color* more clearly in listening to chords whose components had higher pitches.[13] Later, Révész (1937) showed experimentally that subjects chose consistently, if not unanimously, the same adjectives presented in pairs, for example, *soft-hard, dull-sharp, dim-bright, dark-light.* In comparisons involving pairs of tones of equal intensity, the first term of each pair was

---

[13]Von Hornbostel (n.d.), on the basis of psychological and linguistic observations drawn mostly from germanic languages, supposed that low and high in pitch were primitively associated with dark and light, before becoming associated with "low" and "high."

always applied to low tones, the second to high tones. The four pairs cited were those that elicited unanimity among the subjects. In each pair, the greater degree of muscular or sensory tension is associated with high, and the lesser with low.

This is a resource, in itself polysemic, that combined with such other elements as timbre, rhythm, and dynamics, can become integrated into schemes of tension and relaxation of objective, subjective, or mixed signification. The nature of such schemes would be necessarily different according to the degree of compatibility—of reinforcement or mutual exclusion of elements with respect to one another. In the following example the low register is used, so to speak, in its pure state, and its effect is in harmony with the kinetic relaxation and dynamics belonging to the fragment.

Example 12

Respighi, *The Pines of Rome,* Pini Presso una Catacomba (Series II, F). The orchestra plays an introduction of four measures that at once creates a gloomy impression: the basses, cellos, and muted violas play a series of perfect chords of which the fundamentals descend by half-steps from Eb to C (Figure 10.13a). The first two chords are without thirds, which gives the ensemble a medieval aspect and correspondingly gives rise to an impression of large space and size.[14] The chromatic descent of these chords in the low register signals an increase in darkness. The introduction continues with a lead-in given to the basses and cellos that comes to a brief halt in

Figure 10.13. Examples from Respighi, *The Pines of Rome* (Series II, F).

---

[14]"Doubling at the fifth, and the sound of the fifth in general, gives the impression of limitless space" d'Ollone, 1952, pp. 66–69.

the chromatic descent and descends from the key of C to the key of Cb. The introduction stops on a sixth-chord in that key. On that chord, the horns and bass clarinet attack in unison *(pianissimo)* a slow Gregorian-type theme (Fig. 10.13b). The tessitura of the ensemble has not varied, and the preponderance of low registers remains conspicuous. The clarinets, doubled in the first cellos, start with a fermata on Bb to draw out a slow curve in the Phrygian mode of a generally descending character. Finally we hear a reexposition of the Gregorian theme with the same instruments as before and with slight variations and elaborations, and the fragment ends on an open fifth Eb - Bb held in the basses.

One of the themes of signification corresponding to this fragment is directly related to the association between low and gloomy: "Obscurity, darkness, dim places, night-time impression." Apparently the second, "Funereal impression, funereal ritual or feeling," is based in some of its aspects on that association; in other aspects, on the Gregorian nature of the theme and its slow, unaccented rhythmic character and the low amplitude and falling direction of the melodic gesture.

Example 13

Ravel, *Daphnis et Chloé* Daybreak (Series II, B). In this fragment, analyzed earlier in connection with spatial symbolism, the *progressive lightening* is obtained through the overall ascension in the basses and their dynamic growth, which prime the upper parts, as well as through the multiplication of the pedal-point arpeggios, the entrance of the piccolo, and so forth. The first theme of signification, "Awakening of nature, morning or spring-time," indicates clearly that these aspects were interpreted in terms of a gradual increase in brightness.

Finally, among the themes of tension and relaxation it is necessary to include those (more complex than the preceding) that we can group under the label of "language of intonation," referring to vocal schemes expressing feelings, in which the following are included:

1. The rapidity, slowness, and the marked irregularity of delivery—all of which are transposable into melodic rhythm.[15]

---

[15]Spencer (1886) wrote: "Music takes as raw material the different modifications of the voice and the physiological effects of intense feeling, and combines and complicates them by magnifying resonance and the extremes of pitch, intervals, the rapidity of variations—all of which are, by virtue of organic law, characteristic signs of the language of passion" (p. 402). See also Dumas (1933b): "Sadness elongates vowels and even consonants; depressed emotions slow the delivery, while joy and anger speed it up" (p. 343). Monroe (1929) has shown that muscular effort augments air pressure during expiration while pronouncing vowels.

304 SCHEMES OF TENSION AND RELAXATION

2. The mean pitch height of the register.[16]

3. The size and rapidity of pitch intervals, and accents of pitch.[17]

4. The mean intensity, and variations and accents of intensity.[18]

5. The quality of timbre.[19]

Many authors have proposed the existence of "vocal gestures" analogous to and parallel to muscular gestures, and whose articulations would be mirrored and stylized in melodic phrases. "Every melody," according to Bourguès and Dénéreaz (1921) "is *above all* a series of vocal gestures— an imitative sound image of the dynamogenic rhythm of the composer" (p. 32). Brelet (1949) adds, "As for the quintessential musical gesture— it is the vocal gesture" (p. 41). There we have in effect one of the most perceptible elements of the affective symbolism of music, and it is natural that this should have been observed often. In the sign, as in the signified, we have forms in *sound,* and they do not have to do with the operations of spatial transposition. In the sign and the signified, the sound scheme, even when it involves speech, does not retain its linguistic content, but only its affective intention. (Linguists distinguish between logical, "supra-segmental" intonation cues and affective, "extralinguistic" ones that are superimposed on them. It is the latter that concern us here.)

We are at first struck by how infrequent the mention of vocal symbols is among the semantic judgments of these subjects, even under experimental conditions that should be favorable for their appearance (namely, with the free-induction method and eminently *cantabile* instrumental solos, or recitativelike ones—Series III, A and F). Four such responses occurred for fragment A and six for F, which out of 77 subjects are 5.06% and 6.4% respectively. Table 10.2 lists these responses, all of which were consonant with the attitudes and abstract feelings of the themes of signification with which they were integrated.

Thus vocal symbols were not at all preponderant as motives of signification. On the contrary, they contributed in an entirely ancillary way to

---

[16]According to Dumas (1933b), the melancholy and depressed speak in a low voice, without nuances of pitch.

[17]Dupré and Nathan (1911) reported that the sexual vocalizations of animals, like melodies that express amorous langour, are constructed of close intervals, slowly ascending and descending. Dumas (1933b) and Spencer (1886) both observed that violent states of emotion lead to leaps in pitch of a fifth or an octave or more, while in calm states there is an oscillation of a step or a third around a middle note.

[18]Dumas (1933) noted that muscle tension governing the opening of the glottis, as well as variations in thoracic volume, modified directly by emotional states, produces variations in the stream of air expressed, operating on the intensity of the sound as well as its pitch.

[19]Spencer (1886) and Dumas (1933b) showed that vigorous emotions bring out higher harmonics (metallic timbre), while the depressed emotions suppress them (a flat, white, vocal quality).

TABLE 10.2
Responses of Vocal Character to Series III, Fragments A and F

Response of Vocal Character	Theme of Signification
Fragment A:	
Trusting prayer.	Impression of serenity, at times religious.
Prayer, prayer of thanksgiving.	
Complaint.	Slight melancholy, nostalgia.
Lament.	
Fragment F:	
Lament of an African alone in the desert.	Solitude—either external (barreness of landscape) or psychological.
Song of a solitary shepherd.	
Wanderer's lament.	Reverie with a nuance of melancholy. Sadness.
Lamentation.	
Meditative prayer.	Calm, serenity, but with a nuance of regret. Waiting, mystery.

the kinetic and gestural symbols that make up the schemes of tension and relaxation, by far the most numerous. The vocal schemes that were present in the melodies, whether instrumental or not (but especially when they were), underwent a thoroughgoing cultural elaboration unknown to this degree in primitive art. Of course, it has been shown that certain war cries, musical signals in battle, and certain ritual melodies of the Chilian Indians take up the pattern of the verbal formula rather faithfully (Herzog, 1952). However, even in these extreme cases, the formula has often been included in a musical structure—repeated with variations or combined with other formulae to make a composed song.[20] A fortiori, what still exists of the sound scheme of the cry, the lament, the murmur, in our music, with its multiple resources and its strict structural rules, remains in itself a meager thing. Besides, it interferes with parallel variables involving gesture (amplitude, speed, rhythm), intensity, and pitch, which are difficult to separate in the midst of schemes of tension in which they are combined.

PROBLEM POSED BY SUBJECTIVE SIGNIFICATIONS: ANALYSIS OF SYMBOLIC RELATIONSHIPS IN THE MUSICAL EXPRESSION OF EMOTION

We have analyzed some of the most important symbols inherent in musical signification. Their mechanism in the objective significations poses no

[20]Introductions, strophes, and codas similar to the introduction in conjuring songs (Herzog, 1952). The principal source of the analogy resides, it seems, in the identity of the pitch range for the songs and for speech, codified and limited in accordance with the idea expressed. This has to do not with the borrowing of biological givens, but with social conventions.

problems other than the ones we have just examined. This is not true of subjective and mixed significations, a large number of which occurred among the responses of the subjects. The relationship between among schemes of movement, spatial direction, intensity, and certain objective contexts and "atmospheric" outlines is not in itself a mysterious thing. It is the relationship between these schemes and what are classically referred to as "interior" realities that we need to clarify. In this regard, the experimental observations and their analyses provide an inventory of the means at the disposal of musical symbolism. It remains to be seen whether that catalog of means clarifies the relationship of sign to signified, making it manifest in the experimental observations.

We must take the objections of formalism more seriously than the defenders of musical expressionism have done until now if we are going to elaborate on the elements of an explanation of semantic judgment. When Hanslick (1877/1954) proposed that music could not precisely translate situations or the concrete objects that determine emotions and their concomitant ideas, no one could disagree. But we cannot conclude from that that "no instrumental composition can describe the ideas of love, wrath, or fear, since there is no causal nexus between these ideas and certain combinations of sound" (p. 24). We can no longer suppose, after an examination of the experimental studies, that the only actual processes of translation through sound concern the *qualities* directly represented by the sound (sweetness, violence, energy) or the *spatial movements* and the *variations of spatial processes* (growth, extinction, haste, slowness, intermingling.), through rhythmic and dynamic combinations.

There is in Hanslick, as in many other adversaries of the expression of emotion, a dualist and realist conception of mental life that runs through the philosophy of the period in which they were writing. Emotion is conceived as a mental entity having its own autonomous development absolutely foreign to space—a purely interior event that doubtless has "exterior" manifestations, but that has no intrinsic relations with them. Now, as Wallon (1925) observed, such a representation of feeling or emotion, common to Herbart and James, arises from a hypothetical dichotomy of the organic and the conscious, the "peripheral" theory of emotion being only a reversal and rearrangement of the terms distinguished by intellectualist theories. A faithful description of emotion and feelings captures as many of these states as have a duration and a history and includes a specific mode of consciousness associated with a specific mode of physical disturbance. From the phenomenological point of view, which is the only one that matters here, feelings and emotion, when they occur, are less a cognizance of the situation than they are an obscure cognizance of the diverse degrees of a bodily event produced by the situation and its meaning and projected into it. With children, Wallon explains, situations are known through the agitation they produce, and not in themselves. For adults, too, emotions tend to inundate the notion of objects and of reality with an influx of changes and intimate movements that develop in manifest mimicry that totally monopolizes attention. (p. 26–27)

A more faithful description of consciousness in the affective states makes us understand that it could be musically transmuted. Recall that Helmholtz (1877/1954) had suggested that it is not the emotions themselves that are represented in musical symbolism, but "the way in which the mind vibrates" under the sway of feelings.[21] This duality brings us back to the realist conceptions of Hanslick—on one side, feeling, an occurrence in mental substance; on the other side, the vibration "of the mind," a strangely contradictory expression and one that finds its only justification in a synthetic view of consciousness and of the body proper.

The question that arises is, What, in the experience that persons have of their psychological states—of their emotions and feelings—enters into the schemes of a musical symbolism? Self-evidently it cannot be the innumerable facial expressions that specify the nuances of feelings for others, or even those that accompany shocks of emotion. It is not rhythmic manifestations; and the sensations associated with degree of tonus are in this case much too subtle to be fixed in forms of tension and relaxation.[22] Dumas (1933b), in experiments with persons who were born blind, showed that his subjects were incapable of imitating facial expressions that were suggested to them. Those expressions, however, spontaneously passed across their features when the corresponding situations were created. [This finding indicates that the knowledge that the seeing subject has is not separable from the visual experience acquired by seeing others.] What remains of our emotions in memory thus goes beyond the fine nuances of facial mimicry that determine precisely the forms taken by other resources of motor behavior and expressive tonus. We find in this an explanation, emphasized often in the course of these studies, of the inability of music to express any but the large emotional forms—abstractions of feeling.

What are accessible to musical symbolism are rhythmic *types* of muscular kinesthesia and the *degrees of tension and relaxation* of the tonus of attitude and expression (Dumas, 1933b). There is no difference of nature between the awareness of attitude and the awareness of movement, but only a difference of degree (see André-Thomas & de Ajuriaguerra,

---

[21]See also Riemann (1906): "The motion of sound provides an image of the motions of our minds" (p. 24).

[22]Furthermore, according to Dumas (1933b) and others, facial expressions are only one aspect of the general excitation or depression of the striated muscles that characaterize different affective states.

1948).[23] Of course, the recording of those movements and tensions is very complex and has several levels. Nor does it seem that such recording has been given all possible opportunities since its inception. With adults, Bonnier, Head, and Schilder have demonstrated the importance of tactile, muscular, arthrokinetic sensitivities, which make up the postural senses and whose fusion assures the acquisition of "notions" of effort, relaxation, speed, rhythm, resistance, and restraint—in brief, the temporal, spatial, and intensive dimensions of our bodily reactions (as cited in Lhermitte, 1939; Andre-Thomas & de Ajuriaguerra, 1948).[24]

Furthermore, it seems to have been demonstrated incidentally that these syntheses occur with visual associations serving as the common denominator of each sensory group—a sort of "visual transposition" thanks to which their body-image is constructed (Lhermitte, 1939; Andre-Thomas & de Ajuriaguerra, 1948). In voluntary movement and with phantom limbs (the illusion of amputees) the constant presence of the opticogram beside the somatogram is revealed. The relative importance of these two types of messages (the one more intellectualized than the other insofar as it is linked to a theoretical sense—vision) differs depending on whether it is a matter of passive attitudes, voluntary movements, or of involuntary movements connected with emotions.

We can thus explain the relative facility with which music suggests psychological states in which rhythmic and tonic components are so well differentiated. We can also understand the necessity for music to resort to visual suggestion by the melodic line or by harmonic conventions as soon as it finely graduated feelings and closely related states of thought and reflection are involved (Willems, 1954). Beginning with the sensory messages inherent in the body itself (to which interoceptive sensations should be added), such sensations as heartbeat and feelings of pressure generated by contractions of the smooth muscles,[25] and the awareness of the rhythm and amplitude of respiration, all constitute generic images or somatocognitive types *grouped by families*. Within these images or types, musical

---

[23]Likewise, the distinction between tonus of posture and tonus of attitude has no place here. Whether it is a matter of muscle segments or their antagonists, it is the entire striated musculature that operates in emotional tension and relaxation.

[24]The relative importance of the myoarthrokinetic sensation that we have in conscious awareness of the attitudes of muscle segments has recently been disputed on the basis of experiments and observations that favor the sensation of cutaneous pressure. See Tastevin (1956).

[25]Apart from this, there is a deep sensitivity associated with the very existence of the tissues and with their reactions, which joined with the effects of smooth-muscle contractions, constitute the diffuse and poorly localized protopathic sensibility. See Wallon (1925). For many feelings, pressure in the esophageal and stomach region is an integral part of the experienced impression (Michaud, 1954).

symbolization would not always be able to take accouont of the differences belonging to each nuance of a feeling, to each signification of an attitude.

This fits in with what was observed in the examination of the semantic responses of the subjects. No distinction was made among reverie, meditation, and melancholy, or else it was made through other means than these. It is certain that this categorization is also related to the social norms for the expression of feelings. Only certain affects, certain attitudes close to instinctive life are exempt from the social veneer that imposes rhythm, size, and duration of movements, speed or slowness of gait, or tears or laughter or emotional pain. The language of emotional pain—cries, weeping, silence—is strictly ritualized among many peoples in a manner that astonishes us and makes us understand the ritualization in our own expressions (Mauss, 1921). Movements such as leaps and bounds seem to us strictly tied to the expression of joy. They were, however, associated with funerary rituals in classical China (Granet, 1922). Certain modalities of expressive gesture belonging to antic leaping, itself intertwined with common gestures, are no longear accessible to us (Hacks, 1892). Meyerson (1948) has shown that the analysis of layers of expressive activity uncovers convention in places where we would have believed it to depend on instinct or on pure reflex. Certain groupings such as those of sleep or of physical pain mix indistinctly with others on which ritualization has left its mark. That is why the comprehension of musical expression is in many cases limited to patterns of the former group when the listener is in the presence of works containing other symbols—other images, another agogic pattern and another tempo—symbols other than those he is accustomed to associate with a particular family of emotions and attitudes.

These are, therefore, the heterogeneous realities that are grouped into the somatocognitive types that some authors have attempted to classify. The *experiential* content evoked by these concepts of psychological states is not innate. It is the product of elaborated abstraction, but that abstraction is preconscious, and in it there is a meeting of impressions of the body that in most cases reside on the margins of focal consciousness.[26] These are "affective schemes" analogous to schemes of sensorimotor intelligence, in which, according to Piaget (1945), the part of assimilation is not compensated by an equivalent part of currently operating accommodation. Thus "a sensorimotor transfer, which permits the subject to apply schemes acquired in previous circumstances to a new problem, is entirely unconscious" (p. 223).

---

[26]"In addition to its function as an organ of local attention, the sensory cortex is also the depository of impressions of the past. These can arise into consciousness in the form of images, but most often, if it is a matter of specific impressions, they can remain outside of central consciousness. There they form organized models of ourselves, which can be treated as schemes" (Tchehrazi, 1936, p. 32).

The terms of the language of psychology reflect a double comprehension. On one hand is a clear and reasoned comprehension concerning the goal-directedness or the biological or social causality of the designated state (as when fear is the state released in us *by* danger, desire being the state that orients us *towards* the desired object). On the other hand, they reflect an intuitive comprehension, generated from rhythms and from schemes of tension and relaxation that parallel the reasoned comprehension, and of which it cannot be the precise equivalent. It is this intuitive comprehension that comes into play in the *perception of a feeling in the musical schemes and rhythms* that appear to us to be the stylized analogs of the preceding processes. And, most often, under the influence of that stylization, the analogy cannot be formulated by the subject, who imagines it with a sense of irrefutable evidence. Few subjects among those from whom we collected semantic responses would be able to give us reasons for their choices.

We hold here the key to musical expressivity—so obscure and whose mystery many authors have been all too happy to canonize. For a phenomenology limited by reductionism to that which appears in consciousness while one listens to a musical form, expressivity cannot be reduced to signification because the psychogenetic link between them has not been elaborated.[27] That link is based, in the psychophysiological evolution of the subject, on those somatocognitive types underlying the perception of expressivity, which children before 7th year do not seem to have.[28] We also understand why this perception seldom comes about through of a neuromuscular *resonance,* in which the listener is affected through imitating the perceived schemes (as some authors have thought). As Combarieu (cited in Goblot, 1901) prudently observed, music evokes a movement because it incites us to move ourselves. Others, partisans of musical dynamogenesis, went further, seeking present incipient movements in the listener—kinesthetic messages located in the body (Bourguès & Dénéreaz, 1921), an imitation of movements that would inspire the composer (see d'Udine, 1910), an "emotive pantomime" appearing with hypnotized subjects and operating to a lesser extent with awakened subjects (Despine, 1980; see also de Rochas, Dauriac, & Poiré, 1900).

Now, while it is established that music has dynamogenic effects (Fraisse, Oléron, & Paillard, 1953), those effects have only meager structure compared with the multidimensional richness afforded by musical rhythm. The

---

[27]See Dufrenne (1954), for whom the significations and feelings that become attached to the form were "specific aprioris."

[28]In effect, other reasons could be added to explain the relative failure of 4–6-year-old children to comprehend musical expression: in particular the contents themselves of the child's affective schemes that are homologous to those of the adult. As Pinoteau (1937) concluded, "Each emotion involves reactions characteristic of the age at which it is studied." To this can be added the lack of modes of abstract thought.

better structured and more intense reactions were provoked in cases where musical rhythm coincided with metrical rhythm (marches and dances). It is impossible to suppose that this muscular resonance localized in the extremities of the limbs could be the origin of significations implicating schemes with form, amplitude, and rhythm, as well as schemes of tension and relaxation of great complexity. The entryway to significations does not lie in *imitations,* however rudimentary, of expressive contents that support the significations within the musical form. It consists solely in the implicit or explicit *recognition* of a familiar structure, via an aesthetic construction in which stylization could be more or less prominent, to the point of providing a simple, general appearance that recalls a state of being. In most cases, and especially when the listener does not adopt a semantic attitude, it is this construction that is the focus of consciousness, and the symbolic elements of the signification remain implicitly understood. They do operate, however, in spite of their marginal nature and, functioning as a background for the contemplation of the melodies and harmonies that are *listened to,* revive the echoes and shadows of past bodily experience. It is from this that music derives its ability to accentuate the effects of the image in movies, sharpening and reinforcing the image without being noticed and adding to its expressive power.[29] Hence the importance of the sound track to a scene.

Most classifications of expressions (aside from facial expressions) demonstrate the global, and at times ambivalent, character of movements and rhythms (if they are not determined by sensations of muscle tone). Joy and similar emotions "bring about simple movements that are done without fatigue and, with the greatest of ease, under the influence of excitation, . . . even movements that are coordinated into actions give the impression of being effortless" (Dumas, 1933a). Motoric exuberance also characterizes anger, but there it is accompanied by pushing down on the diaphragm, which can produce dizziness. In intense physical pain, such that recorded by F. Franck, there is at first a slowing of respiration and heart rate, and then an acceleration of both if the pain persists but is reduced (cited in Dumas, 1933a). A generalized contraction goes along with pain, a generalized hypotonus with passive sadness and certain types of fear. Gratiolet (1865) had observed with animals and humans that "motor expressions" of emotion spread through "the entire organism." Some of these observations suggest that closely related states converge in their motoric expression, such as sadness and prayer, hatred and anger.[30] We cannot insist on these classifications, however time-honored.

---

[29]On the effectiveness of music in the interpretation of images in the cinema, see the results described by Francés (1957).

[30]See also Héricourt (1900) "Happy passions are excitatory, and sad passions are inhibitory" (p. 143).

Strehle (1954), relying on cinematographic studies, has provided a classification of external forms and indicators through which the signification of *behavior* and *character* can be revealed. Indications concerning felt tension and relaxation of tonus were necessarily lacking in that classification, in which indicators of movement played a preponderant role. Besides variations and varieties of speed were ranged the rapid onset and slowing of reactions, regularity and irregularity of tempo, the expansiveness or restrictedness of movements, their direction, their linear form, and the smoothness or jumpiness of their articulations. The motoric behavior considered was either restricted to a muscle group (a segment or a limb) or generalized as when it denoted a psychological type. Movement sequences were no less instructive: rhythm could be stereotyped or varied; repetitive stroking, either irregular or calm and easy; the form could be rich or poor; gesticulation, exuberant or limited. Concerning the degrees and forms of externally observable tension, tension could be concentrated or diffuse and proceed by brusque or smooth growth and decline.

All these observed indicators, to which covert events known through proprioception and interoception, and even through protopathic sensibility, should be added, are accessible to musical symbolism. That symbolism, which may or may not be intentional, never merely imitates those indicators[31] but involves a free interpretation that utilizes salient features from kinetic schemes or schemes of tension when those are not incompatible with the aesthetic arrangement of resources in the composition. In this we return to Meyerson's (1948) idea according to which the musical symbol is neither more "natural" nor more "primitive" than the conventional sign. Quite the contrary: the history of music shows that the quest for a concrete symbolism is a preoccupation that retards artistic creativity.[32]

---

[31]Certain of them involved, illusions—in believing, for example, that it suffices to give the impression of "rapid motion" for the unit of measure or a repeated element to surpass the mean cardiac rate (about 72 beats/min). See Yeomans (1955). In fact, more than that is required to obtain passionate movement. The unit of measure is an abstract indication that does not in itself denote the impression of speed.

[32]"We must avoid considering the imaged symbol as being more 'natural' than the conventional sign. On the contrary, it is in some ways a second-order sign. First there was a passage through the abstract and then conventional, the a search for features and properties to give it values along its dimensions, and finally the choice of certain forms, schemas, or models able to portray those properties, making it 'pseudo-concrete' " (Meyerson, 1948, p. 77).

Chapter 11

THEMES OF
SIGNIFICATION:
ASPECTS AND DEGREES
OF CONVENTION

THE SPECIFIC CHARACTER
OF MUSICAL SIGNIFICATION

The often encountered question of extramusical significations applied to music is basically one of their specificity and involves both both aesthetics and the psychology of musical understanding. Of course, it may be said that it is not the search for a representational effect, whatever it might be, that gives a composition its worth. If it were, other arts and other techniques that fulfill that function more easily (and much more faithfully) would render the kind of representation attained by the totality of musical means useless and absurd. What good would there be in the ingenious imitation of procedures that painting, theater, and photography apply incontestably better than music does? And, if the domain of this art is not to express a given feeling, or signify the suggestion of a given atmosphere by symbolism, then true comprehension will not involve seeking them in the works we listen to.

It is easy to respond that no art is a pure copy and that every art is, precisely, expression, utilizing the means that belong uniquely to it. From this viewpoint there is no difference between the nature of music and that of representational painting, except for differences in the manner of expression—forms and colors, on one hand, and sounds and rhythms, on the other.[1] There is complete solidarity between means and content—between sign and signified. A feeling expressed in music does not have the same appearance as one presented in a clear verbal designation, or in a more stylized poetic allusion.[2] It is revealed to us through melodic

---

[1]Hanslick (1854/1957) recognized that the aesthetic character of music does not reside in its power to *awaken* emotions, but rather in the way in which it awakens them.

[2]Cf. Meyerson (1956) on the specificity of art and its objects: "There is no common language for translating all the realities of human experience: painting and music each have their own symbolism, even as physics has its own" (p. 218). See Meyerson (1954).

gesture, rhythm, and harmony, in a temporal development that belongs only to music. Our analysis of musical symbolism makes us grasp the modalities of this relationship in their main aspects. It is therefore correct to say that a feeling "translated" into music is specifically musical. In addition, in each work the *particular* feeling is new and virtually unique. The melodic gestures and rhythmic figures, while at times displaying a certain degree of close relationship from one work to another, have a specific physiognomy in each work and give a concrete and inimitable turn to what verbal language necessarily schematizes. Everything happens as though the expressiveness revealed were that of a being whose message is always unique with respect to voice, accent, gesture, and mimicry.

Symbolism thus involves a specific feature of signification, because what is said in music can be fully expressed nowhere else. It is the same with the nonsymbolic resources whose psychological nature we are seeking to define and that in many cases is still complex and obscure.

In a sense, all the motives of signification, whether symbolic or not, are conventional, if we mean by that that they involve social institutions placed in time, which develop, change, and die. Just as passions are portrayed in the theater or in poetry in particular ways, so do musical means involving sounds and rhythms have a history. Doubtless the ballades of Villon or Marot interpreted by Debussy or Ravel have nothing in common with what Lassus or Palestrina might have done with them. Not only that, but the intention to express by deliberate symbolic procedures at a given level is neither constant nore general, as we have seen. What is specific about symbolic convention is that it involves a *recognition* of the signified through the sign. Between those terms there is not an isomorphism, but an isoschematism, if we may call it that.

In is in this that we find the most accessible side of the musical language. By convention we shall mean in general an *arbitrary* choice at this level (but not one without reason or cause) of a sound vehicle associated with the trait expressed. *The arbitrary thus does not depend on contingency, but rather on the displacement of the necessities of the aesthetic domain into another domain.* Thus, when in the musical systems of the Far East scales or pitches are attributed to planets or seasons or hours of the day, we can say that those are arbitrary relationships in the sense that no commonality between the sign and the signified can be revealed in analysis. The relationship was established in conformity with an external social and religious determinism applied to the art at a moment in its history, and that ultimately became "natural" and evident, like all associations long upheld.

Here we find an especially pure instance of an arbitrary relationship. We encounter such a relationship only rarely in our system, in the basic facts on which other semantic relationships are constructed, conforming to analogies. We could call these relationships semiconventional, in that in them the sign has an intelligible relationship with the signified (although it might be grafted onto an arbitrary relationship). Thus, in the tonal system, the permanence of the initial tonality is perceived as providing unity and stability of discourse insofar as the ear, familiar with the chords and progressions condified in tonal harmony, "understands" their succession as diverse references to the same tonal center. We have there a series of arbitrary relationships, since the feeling of unity has to do principally with harmonic elements whose connection with the tonic chord might have been entirely different. It is different in the innumerable known modes, both practiced and possible. For example, to our ears the chord sequence in Figure 11.1a takes on an indisputable quality of unity because the components of the chords have been integrated into the unity of the major scale through a long and continuous sedimentation. The homologous sequence in another mode shown in Fig. 11.1b does not have the same quality for us, since the fourth and sixth degrees of that mode are "foreign notes" or "alterations" of the "natural" scale.

This illustrates an arbitrary relationship of sign to thing signified.

If we now observe, while in remaining within the rigorous framework of tonality, that a passage in which modulations follow in rapid succession gives us an impression of instability, of restless search, we have put our finger on a second semiconventional relationship grafted onto the first. In effect, such a signification can be constructed psychologically only through the acquisition of the first and through its automatization into "naturalness" at a second level. But it is clear that the relationship of the two—based on the analogy of rapid changes in tonality to rapid changes of state—is not arbitrary. This is not a matter of symbolism in the strict sense, but of a "transfer" of a purely syntactic relationship into the realm of signification.

Note the importance of this distinction between different perceptual processes. On one hand, grasping the unity of the tonal formula comes down to "recognizing" a syntactic order whose basis we have seen in the duration, frequency, and so forth of tonal chords. On the other hand, starting with the sedimentation of the syntactic order, it is a matter of comprehending a more complex musical relationship—that of the succession of different tonalities and their transference by analogy into the realm

Figure 11.1. Chord sequences of different character: (A) Chords based on the diatonic scale; (B) Chords based on a heptatonic mode.

of signification. To be sure, comprehension and transfer operate without reflection, and the modulating passage appears invested with its own semantic power, without the subject's inferring anything. But the process is in itself more complex than conventional association, due to the *plurality* of *mediations* that it involves.

We ought therefore to distinguish a certain number of types of semantic relationships proceeding from simple to complex (without, however, pretending to exhaust the list).

ETHOS

By ηθos the ancient Greeks meant the association of social-psychological qualities to genres, modes, and rhythms (Sachs, 1943). Genres were defined by the interval sizes, ranging from two tones to a quarter-step, that occurred in the types of tetrachords (enharmonic: two tones, quarter-step, quarter-step; chromatic: one and one-half tone, semitone, semitone; diatonic: tone, tone, semitone) and were arranged in different orders in the different modes. According to Ptolemy, the chromatic genre restrained the mind and irritated it, and the diatonic expanded and fortified it. The enharmonic was, before the reign of Alexander, given to the expression of religious veneration and then fell into disuse. According to Plato and Aristotle, the modes differed from one another essentially in the moral and psychological characters that they communicated to those who listened to them. The mixolydian made the mind sad and serious, according to the one; sad and restrained, according to the other. The dorian had, according to Aristotle, a perfect calm; but according to Heraclides (see Bourguès & Dénéreaz, 1921; Reinach, 1892)[3] it was "virile, grandiose, foreign to joy and indolence, serious and energetic (Bourguès & Dénéréaz, 1921, p. 90)." According to certain texts a there was a third ethos in addition to mode and genre—that of final notes. If the melody closed on the tonic, the ethos was active; if it closed on other notes, it was nonactive. Finally, a fourth ethos was associated with pitch region: the high register was depressing and funereal, the middle register had a balanced lyricism, and the low register was exciting.

Here we see a multiplicity of facts ranged under the same label. Only harmony in Greek theory did not admit of ethos. In contrast, our musical

---

[3]According to Plato (1966, *Republic*, III.398f.) the mixolydian and hyperlydian modes ("harmonies") are soft and suitable for drinkers. Only the dorian and the phrygian "fittingly imitate the utterances and accents of a brave man who is engaged in warfare or in any vigorous effort" (399a). In the *Laws* (800c–802b) the power of music over the humors is attributed to rhythm and "harmony" (αρμονια), by which Plato means successions of tones, and not simultaneous combinations.

culture, in which harmonic writing has developed greatly, confers significations on chords whose psychological nature is close to that of the ethos
of the modes and genres (Stumpf, 1896). When we say that our major
and minor modes have affective significations, we mean to confer those
significations on both simultaneous and successive patterns of sound. To
apply the term ethos to those modes hardly makes sense. On one hand,
it would designate acoustic realities that were not part of the ancient
meaning; on the other hand, it would confer on the semantic relationships
that pertain to them an ambiguity that it is impossible to avoid.[4] The
ethos of rhythms and of pitch registers has nothing arbitrary about it,
contrary to the characteristics of major and minor, of tonal unity, or even
of instrumental timbres. I shall therefore discuss these last in terms of
conventional significations.

PURE CONVENTION:
SIGNIFICATIONS OF TIMBRE, MODE,
AND TONALITY

The semantic relationships that are most opaque to reason are those which
compare sound *qualities* to objective or psychological reality, with which
they are connected without any formal reason whatever, inasmuch as they
have no internal structure whatever that could be described. A timbre or
a chord has a perceptual unity close to what language clearly indicates by
comparing them to colors. We say of a chord that it has a certain coloration,
or that a given harmony can be more or less colored by the addition of
supplementary components; in German and Slavic languages timbre is

---

[4]We might wonder how this combination of effects attributable to characteristic rhythmic
modes, to pitch height, and to final notes was accomplished among the Greeks. The same
melody could have an exciting effect in the "higher" (our lower) registers, and a depressant
effect in the "low" (high) registers. In *Problems*, XIX,27–29 Aristotle (1984) threw a strange
light on the nature of the ethos that seems associated essentially with *kinetic forms* as such:
"Why do rhythms and tunes, which after all are only voice, resemble [mental] characters,
whereas savours do not, nor yet colours and odours? Is it because they are movements, as
actions also are? Now activity possesses and instills character, but savours and colours have
no similar effect" (XIX.29). These remarks converge with recent studies of the Greek modes
in which there has been a mistaken tencency to assimilate the tonal conception of the major
and minor modes retrospectively. In fact, it seems clear that the Platonic harmonies were
characterized, not by interval sequences contained in the octave and transposable, but by a
tessitura, a fixed register, a sound, and particular melodic formulas—in brief, *melodic types*
analogous to the Indian raga and the Arabic maqam (Chailley, 1956). The texts from Plato
(1961) cited earlier agree with this interpretation in making the ethos belonging to each a
result involving components of register.

referred to as "tone-color." With regard to timbre—setting aside differ-ences that can remind us of momentary characteristics of the voice[5]—the connection we make with "bucolic" for the flute, "woodland" for the horn, and "religious" or "martial" for the organ or trumpet is purely conven-tional.[6] The origins of these stereotypes lie in usage and very old traditions, though their effects persist in our time in an altered form.[7] It is not the sound of the accordion that is "working class"; it is the instrument itself, the ambiences associated with it. These sorts of significations of *belonging* seem widespread, judging from the examples extracted from these experiments.

Example 1

Respighi, *La Fontana di Trevi al Meriggio* (Series II, C). The warrior theme, presented and repeated several times by the trumpets and trombones, owes all its effectiveness to the timbres of the *brasses* (Fig. 11.2). Whatever the effects of the dynamics might be, we cannot understand otherwise how the fragment evokes so many responses arranged in the following themes: (a) Heroism, victory; (b) Solemnity, apotheosis, brilliance; (c) Departure for battle, riding, hunting. (The brass are associated with activities in which, traditionally, they have a place on the basis of very widespread historical stereotypes.)

Example 2

Respighi, *La Fontana di Villa Medici al Tramonto* (Series II, D). This fragment opens with a series of chords that last a long time (violins in the extreme high register, then two more held by the cellos divisi and the

Figure 11.2. A theme from Respighi, *La Fontana di Trevi al Meriggio*, Series II, C.

---

[5]Under the influence of emotions, these characteristics are reflected in changes in intensity: the metallic voice of anger is inconceivable at a level of *piano*; the white voice of fear cannot be produced *forte*.

[6]See Berlioz (1855), for whom the cornet is endowed with platitudes and an odious vulgarity, for example, and the oboe with a bucolic character full of tenderness and timidity.

[7]Because this happens in many cases, the convention is accepted uncomfortably by certain theoreticians who seek rational explanations there where they are not to be found. Thus the dynamogenic theorists Bourguès and Dénéréaz (1921) see in the power of timbres a phys-iological effect directly linked to the presence or absence of odd harmonics that are more irritating or dynamogenic than others. Stumpf (1883/90) nevertheless admitted analogous "associative" characteristics for timbres, in addition to their acoustic qualities.

basses): a G-minor tonic chord, then the third inversion of the dominant-ninth chord in C. Simultaneously with these chords the sound of the bell is heard—at first twice, separated by a measure of silence, followed by 12 tones struck regularly every two beats. The level is *pianissimo* at the start, with transitory crescendos on the high-register chords and a progressive diminuendo to the final *pianissimo*.

Among the corresponding themes of evocation, two ought to be attributable to the timbre of the bells. Even though that timbre is integrated into the impression of the ensemble, it nevertheless produces a well-determined signification: (1) Religious renunciation, more generally, Religious impression; (3) Village with night falling. The religious impression could have resulted neither from the chords nor the dynamics, but from a direct association with timbre. The image of the village was stimulated by the idea of the bell.

Example 3

Ravel, *Daphnis et Chloé*, Nocturne (Series II, E). Over an indistinct harmonic accompaniment, the flute, then the horn, and finally the clarinet play melodies that have already been described. The flute and clarinet are rustic timbres particularly associated with shepherds, and by extension with nature in general, in a calm and pleasant perspective (here determined by the demeanor of the melody). The horn is a woodland timbre and by extension evokes the solitude of nature. Among the themes of evocation that were brought up, were following significations: (1) Pleasant nature, wooded landscape, serene solitude in nature; (2) Shepherd-boy.

Example 4

The same comparison as in the previous example is applicable to fragment A of Series III (Franck, *Le Sommeil de Psyché*). The slow theme, of serene contour, was presented by the clarinet and then repeated by the flute and oboe. Within the corresponding theme of evocation (2. Meditation, calm, associated with serene landscapes) there ranged several responses based precisely on the stereotype of the shepherd.

The violin solo (as strings in general) is a *subjective* timbre, perhaps because it is not associated with any activity at all not dependent on music. In this regard note:

Example 5

Stravinsky, *Elegie for Violin Solo* (Series III, D). Theme 2: Sadness associated with remembrance, nostalgia; and theme 3: Situation implicating sadness, lassitude, lamentation.

Example 6

Berlioz, *Roméo et Juliette* (Series III, F). The theme is given by the violins in unison: (1) Psychological solitude; (2) Reverie with a nuance of melancholy, sadness; (3) Calming, serenity with a shade of regret; (4) Waiting, mystery.

The arbitrary character of significations of *mode* attributed to major and minor has at times been contested. However, nothing in those explanations offered out of concern for the rationalization of tradition seems decisive. Let us see first what limits might be established for the existence of those significations—what might be their content and by whom perceptible.

Combarieu (1907) and Ogden (1924) in particular have proposed that the major and the minor (both melodically and harmonically) are bearers of an *affective tone* that is well known, though nevertheless conventional. Its conventionality is attested to by numerous 16th- and 17th-century gay dances written in the minor mode, according to Combarieu; and by diminished intervals in Japanese music, analogous to our minor intervals, that are used to express joy, according to Ogden. Experimental work has as yet provided only partial confirmation, not well established because distinctions have not always been made among different categories of subjects. Gilman (1891/92) concluded on the basis of his studies that the major and minor modes "did not decisively determine the affective tone of a piece." Heinlein (1928) and Hevner (1935) working with populations of university students, both musicians and nonmusicians, showed that repeated major and minor chords do not have the attributes ascribed to them by tradition. Changes in intensity and of register could mask those attibutes completely, so that in the low register or at a weak intensity level the major became equivalent to the minor and conversely. This should not surprise us if we consider the purely qualitative nature of chords, whose sound qualities are essentially those of timbre.

Hevner proceeded in the following manner. Ten short pieces for piano were presented, some in a major version and some in a minor version. The subjects heard five pieces belonging to each of the two modes, but never both versions of the same piece. After listening, they were asked either to attribute to each piece one or more adjectives chosen from a list on which they were grouped by similarity of affective tone,[8] or to choose for each piece one adjective from each of 16 pairs of opposites. All the adjectives were closely related to affective states (*tranquil, happy*), personality traits (*sentimental, graceful, fanatic*), or perceptual qualities (*heavy,*

---

[8]This communality is not always easy to perceive, as in groups such as *delicate* grouped with *triumphant, dramatic,* and *gay*; *heavy* with *lyrical, frustrated,* etc.

bright). The results showed that the adjectives that best expressed the properties of the major mode were, in order: *happy, light, sprightly, gay, joyous, bright*; and for the minor; *pathetic, melancholy, plaintive, yearning, gloomy*, etc. But each of the adjectives was linked with both the major and the minor in an appreciable number of cases, so that *happy* was applied to minor 102 times (versus 316 times to the major), *light* 171 (versus 374), and *gay* 127 (versus 297); while *plaintive* was applied to the major 47 times (versus 142 to the minor), *yearning* 39 (versus 113). Hevner then asked whether discrimination of these characteristics was related to musical aptitude or training.[9] She grouped 205 subjects on the basis of their performance on the Seashore (1919) test and on scales for musical talent and training developed by Foster and Tinker (1929). On these scales, the median relationship[10] of the more gifted subjects was 9.36, and that of the less gifted was 7.10; on the Seashore test, the corresponding figures were 6.13 and 6.81. Does this indicate an actual independence of the attribution of affective characteristics of modes with respect ot musical *culture*? No, despite appearances, since nothing in the tests that were used related to the conventional significations of those modes.[11]

The historical arguments furnished by the neutrality of the major and minor modes at the start of the classical period, by the inversion of their semantic attributes in Greek antiquity and in other, present-day musical systems, leaves little room for an explanation of those attributes by anything but convention. Contemporary experimental research confirms this hypothesis by showing that perception requires not a refinement of the ear, but participation in the musical culture and very likely the knowledge of its conventions.

Moreover, what are the attempts at rationalization of which we are aware? And what weight do they have in relation to other facts that have been established?[12] Those of Helmholtz (1877/1954) were applied to major and minor triads and their inversions. They consisted essentially of finding the cause of affective and other historically assigned attributes of the two modes in the combination tones and relationships of harmonics

---

[9]In fact, she also examined the possible relationship with intelligence, a relationship that the application of a scholastic test showed to be nonexistent.

[10]This relationship is a weighted result, obtained via the quotient of the difference over the probable error of the difference: D / PE of D.

[11]Rather, they bring into play sensory discriminations (senses of pitch and of duration) or perceptual capacities (melodic memory) that in no way involve knowledge.

[12]Gilman's (1891/92) explanation of the results of these experiments is purely verbal. It consists of saying that the minor third (6/5) contains "so intimate a connection" with the feeling of sadness that has been attributed to it, that it has become in English synonymous with sadness (as in "a minor strain") (p. 46) See also d'Ollone (1952), according to whom the major and minor have intrinsic colors "to Western ears."

produced by the components of the chords. For the major, whatever the inversion, the combination tones are notes of the chord—at least those formed by the fundamentals and their first harmonics (the only ones audible, according to Helmholtz). For the minor, the combination tones are foreign pitches in (Ab and Bb in the C chord). It is these which make minor chords so appropriate for "the expression of the dismal, the dreary, the enigmatic, the mysterious" (p. 302). Where, however, does the *proprium quid* of these tonal patterns reside? In a certain "roughness" caused by the "dissonance" formed by the fundamentals and these resultants. This dissonance occurs without beats, however, because the components are not very close to each other. Let us suppose for a moment that this dissonance is to some degree perceptible. (Even according to Helmholtz this dissonance "is sensed relatively weakly next to those, much greater, produced by the inexact consonances" [p. 302] in tempered instruments, in particular those of the major triad whose third does not coincide with the fifth harmonic of the tonic.) This brings us to the following conclusion: In the experiments tried by Helmholtz and Hevner, in which only the piano was employed, the major chords were "harsher" than the minors; but to the extent that the subjects were instructed in the traditional system, a difference of another order allowed many of them to conform to that system.

Besides, as in the case of timbres, perceived differences are expressed in terms that have no common measure with *sound quality*. What relationship might be seen between this entirely hypothetical "light roughness" of the minor chord and the adjectives chosen by the subjects in the experiments cited? We know that the chord heard alone is not demonstrably qualifiable but must be joined with melodic intervals and chord progressions. It is to the latter that the dynamogenic explanation of Bourguès and Dénéréaz (1921) is addressed: "Every minor interval is the symbol of a kinesthetic restriction in comparison with the same interval in the major" (p. 90). It thus evokes depression and inhibition, whereas the major makes us experience joy and expansiveness. To reconcile this hypothesis with the inversion of ethos in the Greek modes tending toward the major (the lydian and hypolydian) and minor (dorian and hypodorian), one can say that for the Greeks the kinesthetic restriction and inhibition did not imply sadness at all, but only the domination of desire by the will—the preeminence of reason.

This explanation, however, does not hold. Even though, as has been shown, that a succession of melodic intervals can symbolize kinesthetic restriction or expansion, or the size of a gesture, it does not a distinction between minor melodies in contrast to the major. These preserve their modal character even if interval size militates against it. If the explanation invoked an "unconscious comparison" of the intervals of one mode with the corresponding intervals imagined in the other, as the formulation of Bourguès and Dénéreaz appears to indicate, we would be dealing with an untestable hypothesis that contradicts the conditions under which known psychological experiments are carried out. It is the versions actually heard that have determined the subjects' judgments, and not the comparison of those versions with others the subjects did not hear. It would be more plausible to suppose that hearing two different pieces, one minor and the other major, is accompanied by a global impression (in the first instance) of the *relative lowering of certain scale steps in the abstract*—the mediant and submediant are almost restrained, in most cases, relative to what they are in the major. But this lowering is of a conceptual nature. It can, in the majority of cases, stand in opposition to the melodic line without ceasing to be effective.

Here again we meet the type of explanation that seemed to apply as well to the ethos of tonality. This explanation justifies a convention by a conceptual construct that is ultimately integrated into the feeling. The duality of major and minor succeeded the system of modes and was generalized throughout western Europe following the Renaissance. This duality predates the facts of expression that subsequently were outlined in a definitive manner and that still constitute the perceptual givens of auditory experience for educated musicians in our own time. Underlying those percepts, as an acquired feeling providing for fulfillment of the affective ideas that we grant the modes, is the relative lowering of the second and the sixth scale degrees in the minor—a feeling whose motive is abstract since it does not correspond to an actual experience of lowering of a tone or a series of tones, but to the alteration of a general melodic function. We thus come to understand in the course of our musical education that a certain affective differentiation is admitted between the modes, and we *eventually experience it intimately as a perception that distinguishes the scale degree in concrete sounds*. Facts of this genre are at the origin of the attractions of modal notes by the scale degree below them; we saw this reality in Experiment 2. These alterations can influence the character of even chords in which the characteristic degree is presented simultaneously with others.[13]

An analogous process seems to lie at the origin of what has been called "the ethos of tonality." It is well known that the keys into which our major and minor modes can be transposed are traditionally invested with

---

[13]In *Le Chevalier Gluck*, Hoffmann (1944) imagined that in the course of a dream God taught him the mysteries of music. The Fundamental and the Fifth appeared to him in the guise of two armed giants between whom was placed the third, having the features of a young girl whose song of varied inflection fills his heart with nostalgia.

significations that vary little according to the codifications that we know. We drew a parallel between various significations cited by Charpentier in the 18th century (Borrel, 1934) Helmholtz (1877/1954) in the 19th century,[14] and Alain (1927)[15] in our time, and became convinced that, apart from similar if not analogous characteristics, there are noticeable differences between them. Thus, C-major is, according to each of these authors respectively "gay and warlike," "pure, certain, resolute, expressing innocence, resolution, calm earnestness, profound religious feeling," "balance, strict simplicity, principled acceptance"; F-major is "furious and hotheaded," "peace, joy, light regret, religious feeling," "tenderness"; and B-flat-major is "magnificent and joyous," "sweetness and richness," "gravity."

In the writings of E. T. A. Hoffmann (1949) we find analogous evidence arising from a profoundly musical intelligence. His account takes up traditions to which his time seems to have attached considerable value.[16] We read there, for example, that the tonality of C-sharp has a "disquieting color" (p. 135), that A-flat-major suggests "graceful spirits" that A-flat-minor carries us off to "a country of eternal longing," that the different inversions of the chord of E-major evoke ideas of steadfastness and courage and at the same time of scintillating brilliance, that A-minor introduces an anguished charm, B-flat-major a rustic and vernal image, F-major a passionate dialogue. We know as well that composers never leave the choice of tonality to chance. Between the general spirit of a work and the tonality selected—between the signification of a passage and the modulation established—there are, if not constant correlations, at least tendencies that generally go in the same direction and that can be summarized as follows: The more a key-signature is filled with flats or sharps, the more it develops a feeling of complexity and subtlety of the impressions it suggests.[17] C-major is a white key, flat, and without particular flavor. The more sharps a key contains, the more it engenders ideas of brilliance and tension in the major and tumult and agitation and obscure torment in the minor. The more flats it contains, the more it develops sweetness, attenuates brightness in the major, and engenders ideas of languour, passivity, and sadness in the minor (Révész, 1953). These are general tendencies in

---

[14]These are mentioned only in the English translation of the *Sensations of Tone* (Helmholtz, 1877/1954).

[15]Each of ten chapters is devoted to a key, but each key is often characterized by tis relationships with the others, notably by it distance from C-major.

[16]Brentano, Schubart, and Wackenroder propose, with Hoffmann, the principle according to which each key and each chord are "a humor, or state of mind." cited by Boyer (1938).

[17]Gide (1939) in passing from F-sharp to F "all of nature became humanized, losing with its excessive brilliance that sort of vibrant tartness of green growth that had been captivating us and putting us off at the same time" (Gide, 1939, p. 812). See also Aguettant (1931).

which numerous nuances could be placed. We can see in them pure conventions maintained by the knowledge of works in which they have not only been applied but also have received a surplus of semantic richness depending on the particular genius of each composer. There is no doubt that, from Chopin to Fauré, the keys of *C-sharp-minor* and of *B-flat-minor* have turned in the direction of greater complexity of the mysterious, extending, for example, from the *Fantasie-Impromptu* to the *Theme with Variations*. In this case we have instances of cultural amplification grafted onto initial convention.

Since the advent of temperament, we have known that there are no longer acoustic differences among the transpositions of our major and minor scales. We cannot think of basing "the ethos of tonalities" on the slight pitch differences that once existed between the *chromatic* semitone (*C - C-sharp*) and the "diatonic" semitone (*C - D-flat*). The shifting of a comma up or down in the second key of a modulation in which it occurs is perceived by only few listeners (Montfort, 1945).[18] We know to what a great degree the educated ear substitutes for musically unessential pitch deviations and to what extent, on the other hand, it requires "deviations" that make sense musically (see chapter 2). Furthermore, we cannot seek the origin of the significations of key in the absolute pitches of their fundamentals; we know the extent of fluctuations of tuning that have been observed in Europe for the past century and a half.[19] Besides, the pitch of the fundamental indicates nothing of the register in which the composition will lie.

This question has been often obscured by a confusion. Some, like Helmholtz (1877/1954), have wondered to what degree musicians are capable of *recognizing* the key of transposed sound patterns and by what means they arrive at the answer, when they do not have absolute pitch and when the instruments employed are tuned to tempered tuning. Helmholtz based this discrimination on the perception of slight differences of timbre affecting certain notes of the piano and of string or wind instruments. And experiments carried out by Abraham (1923) showed, along the same lines, that for certain musicians it was the perception of slight differences in intonation or timbre peculiar to their own instrument that guided their discrimination—the task became very difficult with another instrument. And Révész (1953) confirmed these results, showing by experiment that for qualified musicians without absolute pitch, the identification

---

[18]This displacement could not exist, whatever the causal nexus, in tempered instruments with fixed tuning, whose importance in the formation of the ear we have already seen.

[19]Thus, at Berlin A3 changed from 421.8 to 437.3 Hz between 1752 and 1823; at Paris, from 431.3 to 443.3 Hz between 1823 and 1834; at London in 1858, it was 455.2 Hz in some orchestras and 434 Hz in others. These give fluctuations of 15.67, 11.92, and 20.71 savarts, respectively, or in all cases greater than 1/4 tone and close to a tempered semitone.

of the key of a transposed chord could be subject to more than 50% errors. The primary source of confusion was that the differences in timbre produced among the different instruments (assuming that those were clear for everyone) did not affect the same notes in each of them.[20] But we might wonder especially what relationship could exist between those differences and the nuances of ethos attributed to the tonalities. I can see none.

We are, then, still here in the presence of one of the pure conventions to which knowledge gives access and to which practice gives a basis a posteriori, either (as we have seen) by the remembrance of works having a particular character and of which one has read the score or by the development of a feeling of specificity linked to each key signature. On one hand, the multisensory nature of the musical object is involved here and, on the other, the syntactic role of flats and sharps. A chord made of three sharped notes is to both sight and touch (in playing an instrument) a psychological element different from its transposition into C-major, where it loses its accidentals. "When the pianist reads a chord on staff paper, not only does he understand it mentally, but he plays it subconsciously and mentally represents the disposition of the fingers involved" (Maillard, 1952, p. 171). There are already in this fact the rudiments of the concrete individualization of tonalities, but it still does not explain the semantic contents of each tonality. It is in the vocal and kinesthetic sensations attached to the concept of the alterations perhaps that we must look for this individualization. The *sharp* signifies elevation—tension, hardening, growth, warming up, overcharging; the *flat*, lowering—relaxation, softening of light and color, attenuation, weakening. All this is with respect to the tendencies inherent in an abstract vocal gesture or a movement separated from any particular determining factors (since this is not a matter of a specific sound, but of the *degree* to which the key signature alone, in an entirely imagined fashion, inflects the piece one way or another). A tonality is thus made of the pattern of these imagined tendencies; it forms "a veritable *imagined sensory complex* that strongly individualizes it. Each tonality thus becomes (because of as abstract a mental representation as possible) a veritable universe, distinct from other tonal universes" (Maillard, 1952, p. 178). Psychologically it is a process of filling out a convention received through hearsay, having its origin in technical necessity analogous to that of the modes (with the important difference that for the modes we find no acoustical "fundamentals" at all).

---

[20]The notes produced by the open strings on the violin (4 in number), and those produced by the white keys on the piano (50 in number), present only rare instances of timbre contrast with the other notes produced by those instruments. These differences of timbre thus affect the same notes only rarely, given the usual register in which those notes are played.

Thus, into the system of tonalities, swollen with deposits from the historical stream of musical works, fits an experience that could arise only in the developed practitioner, for whom a key signature (whether read or otherwise known) is the signal of the frequent occurrence of flatted or sharped scale degrees and the imagined tendencies that are attached to them.

MEDIATED CONVENTION

As we have seen, the effective practice of tonal music, or even the repeated hearing of harmonic sequences that characterize it, leaves rich and solid cultural sediments, depending on the nature of the education, whether unconscious acculturation or conscious training accompanied or not with theoretical analysis. The auditory experience of harmonic sequences and of the most frequent chords in the tonal syntax can engender a whole network of significations in which the links belonging to the syntax acquire expressivity through *the transfer of syntactic relationships into the psychological domain*. Thus, the consonant chords seem to symbolize *order, balance, rest*; and the dissonant chords *anxiety, desire, torment* (d'Ollone, 1952). For some, the melodic designs resting on a major triad express states of stability, adequacy, and calm; for others, both major and minor triads express those states.[21] It is necessary to specify that melodically or harmonically only the tonic triad gives these sentiments fully; the other chords give them to a lesser degree. There are thus many transfers that occur as the harmonic language becomes rich and complex with resources summoned to provide shades of meaning to the chords traditionally assigned to each function. Appogiaturas have a different appearance depending on whether they are descending or ascending. In the first case, "they glide over the top of the actual note in a movement of matter or mind that lifts them momentarily higher than the point of support—whence the impression of ease, of flexibility, of fullness, generosity, or domination. Ascending appogiaturas, on the other hand, needing to climb for their resolution, to find rest, seem to make a more humble and supplicating effort and gesture" (d'Ollone, 1952, p. 88).

These transfers occur between elements inherent in the tonal system of which we cannot enumerate all. Certain of these, such as chromaticism or the preponderance of foreign notes in a melodic line, belong especially to melody. Those, through their syntactic properties, signify "doubt, fleeting

---

[21]"Whatever their direction or their contour, the figures traced upon the major triad express positive states of mind" (de Schloezer, 1947, p. 235).

and troubled desires, mastered and put in order, but also capable of upsetting order" (d'Ollone, 1952, p. 185).[22] But, as I have noted several times, tonal syntax is not an historically fixed entity; it is, rather, a framework that has been more or less established with the help of essential principles, but that does not cease to admit enrichments—notably in the coloration of harmonies and in the relative importance accorded the secondary scale degress (the second and third) that are rigorously transitory in strict tonality. Thus, we have every reason to suppose that there are in addition to the transfers related to the latter others that draw their power both from the syntactic relationship that they reflect and from the relatively novel and unconventional character that they introduce. Therefore, while the resolution of a dissonance to a consonance is to us a synonym of "calming, reconciliation, solution," its resolution to another dissonance—an uninterrupted chain of dissonances—is equivalent to "incessant movement, agitation, passion, disorder, feelings of development" (d'Ollone, 1952, p. 186; see also Hoffman, 1949). This has to do not with the a priori requirements of the natural ear,[23] but with requirements acquired through contact with the customary sequences of tonal syntax, in which dissonances are resolved to consonances. It is difficult to maintain that the transitory character of the dissonance (when it is observed) results from the unpleasantness that it presents immediately to the ear, in such a way that that purely physiological "unpleasantness" would bring about expectations of consonance.

DISCUSSION OF THE THEORIES
OF HELMHOLTZ AND STUMPF

I shall devote only a little attention to this point. It has been discussed frequently and does not merit much discussion in our time, when dissonant chords have become not the equivalent of consonant chords in terms of sensory qualities (which they are not and never were), but rather a conceptual equivalent in the conscious perception of educated musicians that has lost all its negative attributes. From our psychological perspective it would be arbitrary to refuse to admit that if the ear demands (to a greater or lesser extent) the resolution of dissonances into consonances, it derives this predominant tendency from expectancies produced by the *habitual*

---

[22]According to de Schloezer (1947), who appears to have had a better view of the complexity of these facts, in certain cases chromatic descent in a melody also carries a stylized reference to vocal signs expressing suffering.

[23]Certain songs of primitive peoples contain uninterrupted sequences of dissonances. See chapter 7.

resolution experienced in an incalculable number of occurrences. This process is not different from the one we have proposed concerning the ordering of functions in the genesis of "tonal feeling."

The arguments presented against Helmholtz's (1877/1954) theory are now too numerous for us to see in the frequency of beats generated by two simultaneous tones the origin of this expectancy.[24] There is a considerable difference between *conceptual* dissonance, which is the basis of the progressions the ear uses to educate itself, and dissonance experienced as a physical unpleasantness.[25] The one does not include the other. C1 - C#1 produces 4 beats per second, C6 - C#6 produces 122, but musically the dissonance is "the same"—that is, it must undergo analogous treatment in a chord progression, namely, that treatment which alone is effective in the formation of the musical ear. In contrast C2 - E2 produces 34 beats, and is considered to form a consonance.

It would be unjust, furthermore, not to point out that Helmholtz himself did not see beat frequencies as the unique cause of dissonance: "The roughness arising from sounding two tones together depends, then, in a compound manner on the magnitude of the interval and the number of beats" (p. 172). It is the proximity of fibers in the organ of Corti stimulated in the cochlea by tones "giving way to beats" that would be responsible for that. This is as useless and improbable a hypothesis as that of cochlear projection of phenomena produced only betweenn two sound waves of different periods *in the air*! It is more likely that at the level of the auditory nerve there are produced "pararesonances" that are selective of frequencies less than 3 semitones apart and more than 120 or 121 Hz apart. Hearing two pure tones simultaneously produces a dissonant quality only if it excites the same nerve fiber, which happens only for intervals between 1.6 and about 10 savarts. This quality will be a "weakening of the sensation of tonal pitch due to successive repeated stimulation of the same nerve fiber by the two tones emitted, with more or less rapid alternation" (Husson et al., 1953).[26]

Whatever the nature of the psychological solution envisaged, it is clear that what is called into question here is not musical dissonance, but what the harmonists call "grating," that is, an impression of roughness linked to the perception of a simultaneous interval of one or two semitones. We

---

[24]If we play a series of semitones on the organ, we shall hear 4.125 beats/sec in the low register (B, - C), then 8.25 beats/sec (B - c), then 16.5 (b - c'), on up to 132 beats/sec. However, despite this augmentation, "the character of the sensation remains absolutely invariable."

[25]Helmholtz (1877/1954) considered to start with 30 beats/sec, the disagreeable impression results from the production of a "jarring, hard" tone composed of the beats.

[26]See also Husson (1952): Dissonance results only from a weakening of the sensation of tonal pitch.

can thus explain only a small part of the aggregates classed under the same heading by the theory: the dissonances whose arrangement involves a closeness of two components *smaller than a minor third*. But in perception it is not only these dispositions that require resolution in consonance, but also all the others.[27]

One might think that if it is not physical pleasantness that in characterizing consonances calls for their return, it is perhaps the degree of immediate *simplicity* experienced on hearing them—their unity and fusion, as Stumpf (1883/90) thought. By that we should understand a "possibility of synthesis of sensory impressions" (p. 120) operating to different degrees, depending on the chords, such that some of them form not a summation of auditory sensations but a whole. As a relation immediately given in perception, fusion is neither, according to Stumpf, a psychogenetic process nor an aesthetic impression grafted onto an impression of pleasantness. It is basically identified with a difficulty that certain chords have in submitting to the numerical analysis of their components. The degree of fusion is measured by the number of errors committed by subjects when they are asked to say if the sound impression (always composed of two tones) contains one or two components.

Yet, the cited results, furnished by innumberable experiments, do not permit us to base the sharp distinction between consonance and dissonance (as in classical harmony) upon fusion.

Let us first consider experiments prior to 1888. Carried out with non-musicians, they reveal a hierarchy of degrees of fusion relatively independent of the effects of musical education.[28] Moreover, they bring into play the chord of the second, which Stumpf (1883/90) consequently stopped considering as a dissonance. Table 11.1 shows the results obtained from three experimental series produced in different registers of the organ. Note that between the different consonances the degree of fusion varied much more than between certain consonances and dissonances. Between the fifth and fourth, the difference in percentages was 26; between the major third

---

[27] If we make beats occur that can be produced between the harmonics of two simultaneous fundamentals, we run up against analogous difficulties. First, there will no longer be consonant chords beyond the octave, since even the fifth produces such dissonances in the natural scale as well as in the tempered. Second, in augmenting these intervals by an octave, we "ameliorate" the fifth and the third to some extent, (which become the twelfth and the tenth), while altering the fourth and the sixth (which become the eleventh and thirteenth), so that minor thirds and sixths become minor tenths and thirteenths. Thus, we fall back into a case analogous to the one we have just analyzed: the theory of beats between harmonics involves discriminations among different *states* of the same chord, in the same way that discriminations do among different chords (Helmholtz, 1877/1954).

[28] Note here that Stumpf (1883/90) defining fusion as an immediate sensation, prior to education, observed that the subject completely deprived of musical *experience* did not really exist, at least not in Europe.

TABLE 11.1

Percentage Correct Responses by Nonmusicians in Judging That Two-Tone
Stimuli Contained Two Tones, from Stumpf's Experiments Prior to 1888

		Series			
Interval	Number of Trials	1	2	3	Mean
M 2nd	108	100	83	89	91
Tritone	108	83	86	59	85
m 7th	108	83	78	80	81
M 3rd	210	93	75	50	70
Fourth	210	88	60	51	64
Fifth	210	32	44	37	38
Octave	210	25	28	20	24

TABLE 11.2

Number of Correct Responses by Musicians in Judging That Two-Tone
Stimuli Contained Two Tones, from Stumpf's Experiments of 1888

	Series				
Interval	1 $n = 144$	2 $n = 216$	3 $n = 240$	4 $n = 144$	Total $n = 744$
Tritone	103	178.5	174	111.5	567
M 3rd	99	153	185	108.5	545.5
m 3rd	108	103	169.5	127	507.5
Fourth	64.5	132.5	185.5	106.5	489
Fifth	36	100	156	89.5	381.5

and the fifth, the difference was 32. In contrast, between the minor seventh
and the major third, the difference was only 11; between the tritone and
the major third, it did not exceed 15; between the minor seventh and the
fourth, it was 17.[29]

The experiments of 1888, done in different registers of the organ using
musicians for subjects, produced the analogous results that condensed in
Table 11.2 My statistical analysis by means of chi-square on the overall
results (in the last column) showed that between the tritone and the major
third the difference was not significant (chi-square = 1.72, not significant). It was significant between the tritone and the minor third (chi-
square = 12.02, $p < .01$), but that was equally so between the major

---

[29]The reader will note also the paucity of clear correspondence in the hierarchy of degrees
of fusion from one series to another. In the first series, remarkably, the tritone has more
fusion than the fourth, the minor seventh more than the major third, etc. Between the tritone
and the major third the difference is significant ($p < .05$), but not between the tritone and
minor third, nor between the minor seventh and the major third.

third and the fourth (chi-square = 9.92, $p < .01$) and almost as much between the major and minor thirds (chi-square = 4.682, $p < .05$)—that is, between consonant intervals and between intervals that are both consonant and share the same designation. The only really conclusive observations concerned the fifth and the octave. But do they permit us to determine the differentiation between between the consonant and dissonant harmonies most often used in classical writing? Apparently not, because those harmonies, composed of at least three pitches, contain a fifth and an octave in both cases. In the progression A (Figure 11.3), consisting of a major triad and its dominant-seventh chord, the sum of the degrees of fusion can be considered equivalent, since we have in each of them a fifth, a minor third, and (depending on the case) a major third or a minor seventh, which do not differ in degree of fusion. In contrast, in progressions B and C, composed of four-tone chords, fusion is greater in the consonant chord, either because of the presence of a major second in the dissonant chord (B), or because of the octave G - G in the consonant chord (C). But can we make an harmonic theory depend on the modality of *realization* of the chords—of the particular inversion of each of them? We shall encounter in the subject of fusion the difficulty that was present with the subject of beats: both phenomena permit us to differentiate *certain dissonances with respect to certain consonances*. But the musical ear is formed by hearing a large number of other aggregates that differ among themselves neither by fusion nor by beats, but by pitch relationships that exist between their components and by the syntactic relationships that hold among them. We should ponder the fact that musical perception does not develop on the basis of isolated chords, but from groups of progressions whose ordering is governed by syntactic principles. In the three examples, A, B, and C, the syntactic relationship of the tonic to the dominant seventh is the same, and they sustain the same feeling of suspension and incompleteness, although the relationships between the degrees of fusion are different between A, on one hand, and B and C, on the other. In contrast, in the two progressions of three-tone chords, such as examples D and E, the feeling of repose and relaxation associated with syntactic relationships

Figure 11.3. Syntactic relationships of chords and degrees of fusion: (A) Equivalent fusion of two chords; (B) and (C), Greater fusion in consonant chord; In (D) the third chord is endowed with more fusion than its homolog in (E).

exists only in E and does not appear linked to degrees of fusion. In both, chords are composed of fifths, thirds, fourths, and sevenths. Containing two fourths and a seventh, the final chord in D is endowed with more fusion than in E.

In short, it certainly seems that the transfers of signification related to tonality cannot be explained in all their generality by such attributes as roughness or fusion or their opposites, which indisputably pertain to certain chords to a greater or lesser extent than to others. Besides, it is not impossible that Helmholtz himself was conscious of this relative independence in connection with the augmented-fifth chord, considered by theory as "one of the harshest dissonances" and on that account excluded from classical harmony. Helmholtz (1877/1954) observed that in the tempered scale, this chord is composed of two major thirds—eminently consonant intervals. "This chord," he wrote, "is well adapted for shewing that the original meaning of the intervals asserts itself even with the imperfect tuning of the piano" (p. 213). In effect, it is in spite of temperament that nowadays we consider that a succession of augmented fifths or a whole-tone scale produces "an inhuman impression"—a "wild and primitive" character (d'Ollone, 1952).[30]

HISTORICAL CHARACTER OF TRANSFERS

Helmholtz's example makes us abandon a category of mediated conventions that, in contributing to the tonal system, often developed very fine nuances in the course of its history. I have already sketched the principle steps of that development. Many harmonic acquisitions of the last 150 years have expressed, through the effects of transfers, feelings of anxious waiting, as with the seventh and diminished fifth (in the wait of *Butterfly*, in the anxiety of Juliet at the end of the first act of *Roméo et Juliette*, and in the last movement of Tchaikovsky's *Pathetique* symphony (d'Ollone, 1952). They have also expressed feelings of frenzy, indeterminacy, and confusion, as with the diminished-seventh chord, because of its "inter-tonal" character, which permits it to introduce several tonalities. These are feelings that can resolve into an impression of clarity or triumph when they "are resolved" into a perfect triad (as in Schumann, Chopin, and Liszt); or those feelings can be aggravated when the seventh chord leads to another seventh (as in Meyerbeer and Wagner).

With the augmented fifth in the whole-tone scale, the transfer is effected on the basis of musical forms that are external to the system and make

---

[30]In *Kreisleriana* Hoffmann (1949) tells how Kreisler, having become depressed, decided "to stab himself with an augmented fifth" in the nearby forest.

tonal interpretation impossible. From this arises the impression of strange-ness and of inhumanity that attaches to atonality in general, at least for certain listeners whose musical development has been founded prepon-derantly or exclusively on tonal works. Atonality and its successor systems plunge them into an world of anarchy in which the absence of customary order appears to them as the absence of all order. This impression is experienced in most cases in which conceptual unity does not converge with perceptual unity.[31]

But this involves us in a very general claim that needs to be specified, as much on the objective as on the subjective side. The impression of strangeness may comprise different feelings: either incoherence[32] or else moving into another order. In the latter case, we observe a transfer of cultural relationships into modes of time and space—ideas of exoticism, of distant mysteries, and of anticipation. Mystery of form becomes a form of mystery. In incoherence there are numerous degrees of strangeness, ranging from those attached to unusual or defective modes through the whole-tone scale that can lead to ideas of vague exoticism, to polytonal or dodecaphonic constructions for which there is no possible anchoring in history or geography and that lead to the idea of "alternate worlds" or to ideas of either extreme modernism or extreme primitivism. In short, we have in all these cases transfers in which the impression left by an unusual language is projected onto realities that are beyond the usual spatiotemporal coordinates. Of course, this mechanism interferes with that of symbolization. The kinetic schemes present in the rhythm and in the melody, and the forms of tension and relaxation, determine signification at the same time as the syntactic characteristics with which they are inter-acting. The following examples indicate how this complex dialectic is articulated in concrete cases and how it can invest many other forms in terms of semantic deposits of symbols and transferred elements.

Example 7

Ravel, *Daphnis et Chloé*, Nocturne (Series II, E). The three solos that make up the fragment (see Figure 10.2) rest on an accompaniment of the strings,

---

[31]This even comes through in a letter of Kreisler's: "Unresolved dissonances were crying out in me in a most detestable manner . . . But at a given moment all the sevenths of the tongues of vipers were going to descend and form a luminous world of stalwart thirds" (Hoffman, 1949, pp. 122 & 134).

[32]d'Ollone (1952), v. 1, p. 32: Atonality "is comparable to a social regime that would tend to abolish personality through leveling, and in which human relationships would become false due to the prohibition of any congenial groupings—of any seeking out of natural affinities and particular friendships."

based on a complex chord (Figure 11.4a) held for a long time and then transposed a whole step downward at the entrance of the second solo. The structure of this chord, whose length permits the listener to absorb it fully, is foreign to classical harmony. In analysis one could consider it to be a dominant minor-ninth chord with the addition of an altered tenth and twelfth. But the artificial character of such analyses has often been emphasized—for they attempt to reintegrate novel chords into traditional frameworks by considering the foreign notes to behave like passing tones (appoggiaturas) that are "implicitly" resolved. In fact, to the ear this chord has strange sonority. To this is added a no less important feature of the fragment: the entrance of the solo occurs on a note foreign to the chord (E-sharp), producing a disparity between it and its accompaniment. This becomes accentuated throughout the unfolding of the solo: from an altogether indeterminate tonality during the first two measures (up to the fourth beat), it acquires at the start of its third pitch (the D) a clear tonal character—the tonic is B-flat (even though it is not given) and the scale on which it is constructed is shown in Figure 11.4b. The scale of the second solo (Figure 11.4c) eliminates one of its notes. Thus, the tonality of the solos stands in opposition to the chords in the orchestra.

The significations classified under the third theme of evocation (*Impressions of the Orient, enchantment*) are related to the following characteristics: (a) the mysterious harmonic aspect of the accompaniment; (b) the tonal disparity between that and the melody; and (c) the strangeness of the scale in which it is written. Some examples related to the first two features are: "weighty mystery," "a glade in a virgin forest," "mysterious call," "atmosphere of fairy stories," "enchantment." Other responses contained significations of time or place that gave rather imprecise impressions of "exoticism" created by the whole pattern of the fragment, but perhaps

Figure 11.4. (a) Excerpt from Ravel, *Daphnis et Chloé*, Nocturne (Series II, E); (b) and (c) Scales underlying the accompaniments of the solo passages shown in Figure 10.2.

particularly by the solo: "Morrocan prayers," "oriental evening," "Asiatic mystery," "arrival in the Far East," "Indian chant," "Russian music," "nights in the gardens of Spain."

Example 8

Bartok, *Pursuit* (Series III, E). In all probability the characteristics of the scales employed here are intimately intermingled with those of the rhythm described above. In analysis one can separate them out and establish the role that they play in the determination of semantic responses. The ostinato in the bass is made of a series of intervals that suggests no tonality at all. The lowest note (F) doubled by the seconds struck in the right hand from the beginning can be considered as the tonic of a defective scale (Figure 11.5a). But the entrance of the theme is based on the six notes of a whole-tone scale on F, which differs from the preceding scale (Figure 11.5b) and which introduces two new notes (G and D). The following measures, with the insistent repetition of the same note (D) and the pattern beneath it, which contains a descending scale, suggests a novel mode of G (Figure 11.5c) that is superimposed on the preceding theme, always given to the bass. Finally, from the eighth to the twelfth measure of the theme, two new notes are added to the chromatic total—C4 and D4—bringing their number to eleven. All of these procedures result in the dissolution of tonal character. Tonal unity is broken for several bars, and the diatonic scale gives way to structures that deny it.

The evocations that result from this are transpositions on the socio-historical level of the properly cultural characteristics of syntax: significations of "modernism" applied to life, work, etc., in the first theme: "Life or mechanized and exhausting activity in the contemporary city"; or of primitiveness in the second theme: "Dance or combat of primitive peoples." The coexistence of these two groups of significations might appear contradictory. They are, in fact, explained by the weakness of the means of identification of the syntax at the disposal of certain listeners. The syntax, out of context, is perceived as nonclassical and consequently is either

Figure 11.5. (A) and (B): Scales on which passages in Bartok, *Pursuit*, are based; and (C), a passage containing another scale.

Figure 11.6. Two series of chord progressions from Experiment 16: (A) Series 1 based on classical harmony; (B) The atonal Series 2.

associated with the comtemporary period or perceived as "strange and barbaric" and as a result is associated with a less evolved humanity.

EXPERIMENT 16

In the course of the electropolygraph studies, I had sought to bring to light the nature of the differences among subjects of varied musical culture who heard "usual" and "unusual" chord progressions in classical harmony.[33] The first series of chords consisted of triads and seventh chords (dominant, diminished, and minor), with cadences and resolutions in a fixed tonality (Figure 11.6a). The second series was composed of the same number of progressions having identical rhythm and duration, describing the same melodic line in their upper part, but consisting uniquely of chords foreign to any tonality formed of five chromatic degrees arranged in a spread position (as in the preceding series), and complementary to the chromatic degrees in the chord that followed them (Fig. 11.6b). These patterns suggested no tonality at all, and that was true for each progression taken in isolation.

Method

Each progression lasted 5 sec and was separated from the next progression by an interval of 2.5 sec. The total duration of each series was 1 min, 25 sec. The recording with organ was done at a uniform *mezzo forte* level and was presented each time at a level of constant intensity. The polygraph recording was the same as that described in chapter 5.

---

[33]The technical conditions for this experiment as well as the composition of the groups of subjects was the same as for Experiment 7.

The experiment consisted of presenting the two series to the listeners and asking them which they preferred, as well as their reasons for that preference. They were told to listen attentively first without considering reasons, and to reflect on those later.

The aim of this experiment was essentially to find out:

1. To what extent the listeners of variable musical culture (groups A, B, and C) were able to differentiate the samples of harmonic language, the one based on the tonal system and the other on atonality.

2. What preference the subjects showed for one or the other.

3. How the difference became established—in particular whether it was based on the pleasure or displeasure involved in consonance and dissonance,[34] on aesthetic judgment, on the impression of order and coherence versus disorder and incoherence, etc.

4. Whether this difference was profound enough to produce physiological manifestations recordable by these techniques.

Results and Discussion

The results were as follows:

1. All the listeners, whatever their level of musical culture, established a very clear difference between the two series when they heard them.

2. This differentiation appeared in the very clear preference that most subjects showed for one series or the other. Table 11.3 gives the respective percentages of the opinions expressed. Note that the proportion of subjects without opinion was small in the three groups, especially as concerned the first series. The distribution of choices shows that nonmusicians (group A) preferred the tonal series unequivocally and that none in that group selected the atonal series. The situation was exactly reversed for the musicians in group C, in whose number were included composers, orchestra leaders, and concert virtuosos. Among the mid-level performers (group B), trained in most cases in the study of classical works (but some of whom had had an introduction to nontonal language), the polarization of choice was less pronounced, though those subjects had a clear tendency to favor the tonal series.

3. Analysis of the subjects' reasons showed that rejection of the atonal series was not always based on unpleasantness, but on the impression of

---

[34]In a pilot study I had observed that for many subjects "classic" dissonances such as those of the Series 1 were not very distinguishable from the consonances (for subjects in groups A and B), at least not so they could be contrasted with them with reasonable chances of success. It was thus necessary to find more marked dissonances, which meant going outside the system of tonal chords.

TABLE 11.3
Relative Evaluation of the Series of Chord Progressions by Subjects in
Three Groups

Group	Series 1			Series 2		
	Prefer	Don't Prefer	No Opinion	Prefer	Don't Prefer	No Opinion
A (nonmusicians) n = 16	93.1	0.0	6.2	0.0	87.5	12.5
B (moderate performers) n = 12	75.0	16.6	8.3	16.6	66.6	16.6
C (superior performers & pros) n = 11	0.0	72.7	13.6	72.7	0.0	13.6

incoherence and uneasiness engendered by the contradiction in "what the ear is used to hearing," in the words of a subject in group B. Here are some examples of responses collected from subjects in group A hearing the atonal series: "sad," "not too disagreeable," "crude, grumbling," "annoying, grating," "dissonant, uninteresting," "choppy, discontinuous"; for group B: "not antimusical, but without continuation," "not disagreeable, grating," "inharmonious, contrary to what the ear is used to hearing," "dismal, incoherent, but not too dissonant," "a formless, swarming thing," "profoundly displeasing." Among the subjects of groups B and C the atonal series benefited from a favor that was motivated as follows: "interesting," "these chords hold the attention," "very impressive chords," "dissonant chords, but rich," "mysterious—I like these dissonances very much," "stimulating, interesting, without any unpleasantness," "very original," "agreeable, an exercise in analysis." When this group preferred the first series it was for opposite reasons—the progressions appeared not only agreeable, but "harmonious," "coherent," "connected," "analyzable," "in tune," and "more regular." When they rejected the first series, it was because it appeared, "boring, too predictable, incapable of holding one's attention," "the resolutions are anticipated," "they provide rest, but are boring," and are "indifferent," "banal," "common," "without thought."

4. This clarity of verbal choice contrasted with a general failure to differentiate on the polygraph measures. "Pleasure" and "unpleasantness," and feelings of appropriateness or inappropriateness were not of such a nature to give rise to the autonomic nervous system reactions that had been so readily observed in the same subjects in previous trials (involving hand clapping following a disagreeable word) or in the subsequent listening trials in which they were released by linearly organized musical events. It was the same with the EEG traces, in which we observed hardly any modifications from one series to the other, except at times a relative

increase in eye movements (a sign of distraction) during audition of the series that appeared uninteresting. It would, of course, be risky to conclude from this that the differences in harmonic structure were completely ineffective in producing physiolgical reactions. We might in certain cases observe the opposite if, instead of brief samples, we presented *works* in which the disparity of language would be emphasized through the duration of the piece and that in the end might produce responses. But the interest in our present experiment was in showing that these harmonic oppositions, well differentiated and appreciated in verbal judgments (positively appreciated by some and negatively by others), did not produce the ordinary signs of displeasure or pleasure, of astonishment, of banal expectancy, or the like.

Displeasure is thus rather close of the feeling of inappropriateness, and pleasure close to intellectual interest; and both are relative to the subjects' habits concerning musical language. We have evidence, then, (limited by the sensitivity of the recording techniques) that the transfers of signification based on the fundamental disparities of tonal and atonal harmonic structures are not motivated by primary affects, but by impressions depending on musical education, due to which they appeared either unusual and hence aberrant, or original and worthy of interest, depending on the subjects.[35]

ANTITHESIS OF TRANSFER AND KNOWLEDGE, OF SIGNIFICATION AND REFLECTION

Reflecting on these transfers clarifies an important aspect of the relationship between signifier and signified. For subjects who have undergone tonal acculturation and whose musical education is nonexistent, significations linked to elements of tonal discourse (and those which result from the opposition between tonal and atonal discourse, or merely from partial transgressions of tonal norms) appear magically, so to speak, as the result of the unconscious operation of automatic auditory processing. The transfer occurs unconsciously. What is perceived is "referred" implicitly to what has been laid down in prior experience. Thus, the chord of minor seventh and diminished fifth "recalls" the dominant seventh, a harmony of expectancy and suspension, but by means of something more veiled, more confused, and connected with "alterations." This "recall" is psychologically a fiction—what is definitely given in experience is the expressivity of the

---

[35]For humans, emotional response depends less on stimulation, and more on past experience (See Delay, 1946).

chord consisting of "anxious expectancy." But it can become a reality in a musician listener capable of mentally carrying out the comparison. In that case, we cannot say that the expressivity is destroyed, but that it is taken into the relationship of the signifier to the signified. Its magical character has disappeared. We might even say that the signification gives way to objective judgment.

It is evident that all the expressivities could be dissolved in this manner by the operation of intellectual analysis—those which rely on symbols (being reduced to classified rhythms, interval sequences, etc.) as well as those which involve either pure or mediated convention. This depends both on the listener's conceptual machinery and on his attitudes, which in turn depend on the preponderant aspect of the nature of the signification. Rhythmic-melodic symbols, as well as symbols of spatiality, tension, and relaxation are experienced; they are seldom thought, because they lack clarity concerning such relationships. They impose themselves from the start, and only the global impression bearing expression is felt by the listener. In contrast, conventions and the transfers will sustain analysis more easily, especially in our day, when preoccupations with musical rhetoric and syntax are so frequent.

HISTORICAL–CULTURAL SIGNIFICATIONS

There is, finally, a whole series of significations that are inaccessible to uninitiated subjects.[36] and that, through their clarity, are more closely related to objective judgment than to expressivity. They imply reflective experience of musical works, grasped in their historical progression and confronted with one another. The qualities of banality or originality can come from elements of syntax, from the particulars of form. They evidence an abstraction of harmonic, melodic, and rhythmic relationships and sequential dependencies, constituting conceptual categories to which the music being perceived refers. What makes the personality of a style is the component of invention added to what is typical of cadences, of themes, of genres. De Schloezer (1947) has shown this, apropos of cadences, with a beautiful example borrowed from Bach. We can observe it in Beethoven's last piano sonatas and the *Diabelli Variations*, in which the traditional scheme of the genre is so far surpassed by the richness of invention that the scheme serves, so to speak, as but the pretext for its employment. In

---

[36]By this I do not mean a subject lacking technical instruction in knowledge of musical notation and writing (a musically "illiterate" subject), but rather one who lacks any prolonged perceptual contact with musical works.

such cases the listener recognizes the mark of genius through the conscious experience of this dynamism of an original spirit. There are thus successions of significations that confer on music the power of expressing the highest abstractions—philosophical ideas shorn of any image-like support.

In the same order of ideas, the cultivated listener grasps in the sound form itself the play of influences undergone or exercised by a work. This supposes equally the confrontation (*of an abstract sort*) of an harmonic or symphonic school with the work currently heard. Conceptualizations of this genre are more or less simplistic, depending on the degree of perceptual refinement and the work of reflective analysis associated with it. We could not even observe its existence in group A the subjects, who had categories such as "Mozartian" or "Debussyist" clearly present in memory. It was in the differentiation of details that the difficulties arose, when it was a matter of distinguishing Haydn from Mozart, or Mozart from Cimarosa. Processes of this genre are at the root of the historical significations that Dukas (1948) has analyzed. They rest on the following principle: The worth and meaning of a work are a function of the cultural pattern that extends in time between it and us and even includes what preceded it. Consciousness grasps retrospectively all that there is of anticipations in the harmony and instrumentation of Monteverdi, in confronting what it presently perceives with what it knows of musical movement that has preceded the work and that follows it. The very same opera of Gluck becomes insipid to the extent that the centuries of music that preceded and followed it are revealed (Dukas, 1948). The operas of Mozart, and *The Magic Flute* in particular, impress us with what we hear in them that connects with Wagnerism (Francès, 1951). Likewise, the freshness of certain harmonies, the interest of certain procedures tarnish to the extent that imitators have seized on them and vulgarized them and repeated them endlessly in disguised form (Dukas, 1948).[37] In short, we have here a whole variety of prospective and retrospective views that rely on memory and on the categories that it distinguishes, which are mingled in actual perception. It is impossible to make an abstraction of this. Every hearing of unknown music immediately produces for a cultivated listener an orientation of historical perspective, a play of hypotheses tending to attach it to a particular category, or, better, when the culture is more profound, to distinguish it from them.[38]

I have tried to classify and explain a certain number of nonsymbolic significations that are frequently encountered either in the experimental

---

[37]In Alain (1949) there is a simpler unilinear analysis of this operation of time on the work: "A Beethoven Quartet takes on more meaning year after year. Every masterpiece, apart from the immense thought embodied in it, beyond which we are always projecting, reflects as well all the homage and devotion that it has received, as wreaths on a most venerable altar" (p. 10).

[38]An analogous process has been described concerning the visual arts by Hungerland (1945).

results or in the written testimony of musicians and aestheticians. One can notice that this classification brings out a hierarchy of types examined. Each layer of significations supposes a more or less general type of experience, depending on whether it is a matter of transfers based on the elements of tonal discourse, on the successive enrichments of tonality, on the opposition of the tonal with the atonal—or of significations attached to styles, periods, and to their particularities. But each layer supposes as well a more or less refined form of abstraction depending on whether the signifier is based upon a global impression left by a particular atonal language that refers to tonality, or on the perception of minimal differences in the structure of chords. The play of differentiation and assimilation intervenes in an original way in each case. The process that permit a listener to acquire a "feeling" (for it is one) for the Mozartian style, based on vague assimilations of melodic and rhythmic analogies and on details of construction, is not the same as that which leads one to perceive an expression of anxious expectancy in the chord-of-the-seventh-and-diminished-fifth. In the two cases, moreover, it is a matter of processes that can remain at an unreflective stage of development when the conceptual machinery of the subject does not permit them to be explicit. But they can arise clearly in consciousness, without the corresponding significations being neutralized as a result.

The question of knowing whether all the layers of significations are accessible to a subject deprived of reflective education, by the simple effects of acculturation, is an abstract question that experimentation alone will permit us to resolve. *Theoretically*, except for pure conventions (modes, ethos of tonality) that presuppose knowledge of a code, all the other layers can be perceived by such a subject provided that his ear has been struck a sufficient number of times by the analogies and differences existing among the syntactic elements of tonality. But practically, the experiments on the fugues showed that the analogy and the difference are not isolated by passive sensory experience. As soon as the form of the pattern attains a certain degree of complexity (that is, in effect, as soon as it is musical), active assimilation and differentiation ought to intervene and be equilibrated. If this does not happen, the subject will retain only a confused impression in which, depending on the case, distant analogies will remain without connection, and subtle differences without effect. We have seen this concerning melody, harmony, transposition, and polyphonic forms—distinct perception always presupposes an advanced degree of education. But all perception is distinct to some degree. There is no expressivity that can remain entirely opaque in the wake of sustained efforts. Only experiments can instruct us, in each case, on the nature and extent of the effort required.

Chapter 12
CONCLUSION

PERCEPTION
AND AESTHETIC JUDGMENT

The foregoing analyses can serve as prolegomena to a theory of aesthetic judgment. That judgment itself has doubtless been, in certain legitimate cases, submitted to experimentation. Research on the appreciation of works has led to an empirical classification of taste and to observations concerning its diversity. Investigations of listeners' choices in the programs of radio broadcasts are numerous, and the results they have yielded are useful. They show the listening public distributed according to such variables as social class and age when they are given the option to favor light or serious music, contemporary or classical (Silbermann, 1955).

These investigations are useful not only for the sociology of groups and for programming, but for the knowledge of the mechanisms implicated in the judgment of taste. The studies permit us to locate those mechanisms and to make conjectures concerning their nature. Nevertheless, we do not believe that in determining the terms of the relationship (the public and the chosen work) we have at the same time an understanding of the internal workings of that relationship. When we observe, for example, that a large number of music lovers are hostile to contemporary music, we cannot account for that tendency except in vague terms—we talk of the contradiction of former habits, of an aversion to novelty.

True knowledge of the mechanisms and processes involved in these judgments leads back to a psychological analysis of perception. Lalo (1939) who did so much to illuminate music with the convergent light of all the sciences, concluded by according sociology the ultimate explanation of the aesthetic qualification of the facts of art. Physics, physiology, and psychology, he said, teach us what a chord or a progression is; but sociology teaches us which chords and progressions are preferred to others at some moment in the history of art. Only society confers aesthetic qualification on a fact.

In reality, the two analyses complement one another. Social currents and values impose themselves on individuals by integrating themselves into the personality following a series of adaptations. Thus, for example, the notion of the aesthetic age of a subject refers, on one hand, to a social scale of values—certain forms of art and certain forms of contact with them are considered to be indications of greater maturity in relation to the norms of a group of practicioners or critics. But, on the other hand, what those forms are, and how passage from one to another takes place, only psychological analysis can tell us. It can also, as we have seen, make us understand how transfers of value and eclipses and restorations of merits conferred on a style take place in the course of historical development of a cycle of works and of a school.

In the last analysis, aesthetic judgment is based on the perception of a system of qualities to which more and more complex quantitative relationships correspond. The musical sound itself has for its physical substrate relationships of simultaneous and successive frequencies (for sounds that possess timbre and inasmuch as their objective pitch fluctuates). Then come relatinships that constitute melodies and chords—temporal and dynamic relationships that form, with all the others, simple rhythms. Tonality and modality and the total rhythm are on a higher level. Schemes of composition organize them into forms of simultaneous and successive patterns. Finally, upon the relationships among works that are established in the history of individuals are built significations—secondary qualities whose classification I have sketched. Be they purely conventional or not, they always add to the fullness of the impression that arises from the form. Forms are never perceived without some significations being involved.

We have seen that these qualities and significations sometimes act reciprocally. The feeling of tonality is engendered by prolonged practice of tonal sequences of pitches, principally of harmonies. But isolated tones, in their turn, end up being tonally situated—on some tones we project tonal hypotheses or interpretations. Likewise, tonal feeling confers vectors on single notes; these vectors are born of the attraction of frequent hearing of the usual progressions. These elements are at the base of the system; but the system, once experienced, becomes second nature to the listener and qualifies the elements. We will be able to demonstrate this reciprocal action in examples involving other elements and other patterns if experiments permit us to establish the generality of the reflective observations of musicologists.

The priority of the elements over other patterns in time is meaningless. We do not first hear tones, then chords, then cadences. We do not reflect on the choice of significations that attach to a passage or a work. We do not learn to hear music as we learn the alphabet. In certain cases, the priority of the complex vis-à-vis the simple is evident. What we retain of a work after a first hearing is its overall plan of groupings, if it is apparent enough; if not, we retain a certain relationship of forces developed in time. Details of construction appear only on repetition. As for tones, one never simply hears them, although they condition all the rest.

Such is the perception of music in its complexity. In what sense does its analysis permit us to understand aesthetic judgment? One can say that that judgment presupposes the perception of all these qualities, of all these significations, but that it identifies with none of them insofar as it is the pronouncement of *value*, as opposed to the observation of perceptual givens.

In effect, beauty or ugliness do not seem intrinsically contained in any one of those qualities, nor in the whole group of them. It would be too easy to demonstrate the extent to which their appreciation is relative to a time and place. Concerning harmony, for example, Experiment 16 clearly contrasted listeners attached to customary structures with listeners who consider those structures nonaesthetic because of their usualness. That quality of usualness, relative to a subject's background, is only the threshold beyond which aesthetic judgment becomes possible. It is in no way identified with beauty. Acculturation and, more particularly, artistic education are necessary for sound patterns to organize themselves in perception. That organization is common to many works belonging to the the same system, to modes of writing, and to analogous compositions. How is it that some, but not others, draw the attribution of beauty?

Certain principles governing the constitution of patterns appear to provide the elements of a solution. We can find many examples of works in which "variety in unity," "economy of means," and "balance of parts in the whole" ensure aesthetic effects. But how often do we find examples of works that are admirable—or at least long admired—in which those principles are contradicted! Can we speak of economy of means in the great oratorios of Bach or in *The Ring of the Nibelung*? On the other hand, (and here is an argument based on many examples), the application of these principles appears also to be relative to the style being considered. Compared with contemporary rhythm, the rhythm of many works of Bach is constructed principally in unity, with very little variety. Beethoven's harmony is often restricted for pages to the alternation of two or three tonal chords, and some of those pages are among the most beautiful in the Ninth Symphony. It is more accurate to say that these principles are applied to only one aspect of a work—what rhythm loses in diversity, harmony gains; and what is lacking in balance among sections is compensated by a particular balance of timbre. This sort of tradeoff of resources is noticeable in many masterworks. But we can count some as well in which spareness governs all these aspects at once (as in Schubert's greatest *lieder*), and others where there is exuberance in all of them (as in *The Rite of Spring*).

One should therefore say that these principles are all true and that each provides for the partial and relative justification of the uses of a period and the impression of beauty that emanates from it. But there is another important aspect this is perhaps more directly given in this impression: music is a language, and, as such, it is valued for what it says and for the manner in which it says it. We have seen that even when music is not constructed around a literary argument, it expresses a way of being, a being, a drama, or an experienced impression. Then even when the listener is very far from seeking it, this expressivity takes hold of him unmistakably but without his formulating it verbally. Arnheim (1949) was right to emphasize the temporal procedure of this feeling that accompanies listening—the feeling of a communication, as self-contained as one wishes and as indirect and vague as the style or the author makes it. Most often, the analysis of means and observations on the form and its combinations come only later. Here the impression of beauty is born of the appropriation of means to what is expressed—such is at least the case with masterworks.

We cannot claim that the manner of saying is worth more than what is said. Without doubt, there are numerous examples of works constructed around minor themes (as in portraits of animals or light humorous verse) that are masterpieces by virtue of their expressive invention and choice of means. In the domain of pure music, small genres can be more successful at times than great works. A minuet whose grace is correctly proportioned will touch us more than an oratorio whose heroism and pathos sound false. But the highest aesthetic values can be conferred only on works developing a fundamental human idea, a great theme of the human condition. We cannot put Rameau's *La Poule* and Beethoven's *Ninth Symphony* on the same level, however correct the expression of one or the other might be. This claim ought to be attenuated, considering the historical relativity of taste in this matter. There are periods when great sentiments appear false in themselves, when there is general mistrust of great subjects and grace and elegance alone are *à la mode*. At other times, the reverse is true: grace becomes insipid, an insupportable affectation. All these movements of social sensibility are of a general order and are found in the evolution of the other arts. The fact remains that if we make an abstraction of what has been expressed and if we feel the expression as fitting, regardless of the musical means that vary according to period and style, expression is one of the essential components of the judgment of beauty.

Effective expression depends on formal perfection, for "well said" implies "well made," though the converse is not always true. The absence of expression cannot dissemble behind the artifices and researches of language. The latter, even when pursued in an autonomous manner, end in creating confused facts of expression, badly adapted to the form that bears them. Many contemporary pieces conceived exclusively on an *idea of construction* result in kinetic forms and discontinuous schemes of tension and relaxation whose caprice seems inhuman—a mechanical veneer on life. It is well-made music, in that its form is derived from coherent principles; but it is dependent on no other end than construction itself. That is why its internal movement and its pulses correspond to no known indicator. But these, insofar as they exist and operate on the listener, carry him off into their own world and leave him suspended in the void.

Aesthetic judgment is formed, then, on an expressive communication, which is carried by a formal signifier that the listener places immediately in a sociocultural classification. Even before appreciating it, he knows its type: light or "serious" music, song or melody, or from the folklore of a particular country. Onto this identification is often grafted an especially abstract and superficial type of value judgment, which can be called categorical: certain subjects grant the level of "aesthetic" to one type of work and refuse it to another. One could "love" the contrapuntal style and reject *lieder*, just as one prefers the countryside of Provence to that of Ile-de-France. This choice is not yet a matter of a judgment of beauty—that is always a result of the appreciation of the *individual* qualities in a work. The appreciation of a genre or a style is not necessarily based on non-aesthetic judgments, but it does not do enough to distinguish judgments that apply to works of art from those that pertain to well-adapted, useful, or agreeable objects. There is always something unique in a sonata, a fugue, or a *lied*—we have seen—and it is to that that the listener attaches his judgment.

It is partly for this reason that the most complex significations—those that presuppose the widest artistic experience (sociohistorical significations)—are not the equivalent of judgments of beauty. Several of them were analyzed earlier in outlining the processes of their origin: banality and originality (despite the importance that they have assumed in contemporary aesthetic reflection) are the general qualifications that a subject learns to perceive in the aspects of one work when he has heard many others. But the work is not beautiful because of its originality, for the features of construction that make it so can be found again elsewhere. Furthermore, these significations are empirical and they do not implicate the pronouncement of value. We notice the novelty of a method relative to a period, to a genre, to an accepted tradition, but we need not necessarily adhere to them. Finally, we know well that the knowledge of musical styles increases the number of elements to which we attach the feeling of banality, without necessarily producing a subsequent aesthetic depreciation of the works in which we encounter them. The historical voyage on which the connoisseur and scholar embark modifies the appearance of harmonic elements, cadences, melodic inflections, and generic schemes. In the abridgement of several hours, the listener traverses centuries that have brought about the erosion and decline of ancient elements. He gains access to the elements that have little by little supplanted them. Does that make him stop experiencing the beauty of an ancient work? Yes and no. He feels it, in spite of the erosion engendered by the repetition of the formulas, but he experiences that erosion as a negative quality. The work's other merits must be great for it to win out over adherence to the pattern.

Nor is beauty the *interest* that this operation (so common when one hears a work) sets in motion, (of placing the work in its historical genealogy.) Certain works provide much to think about in this regard. They pose problems and excite curiosity. The connoisseur enjoys this mental exercise that fills out perception. It often takes the place of a more direct access to value. One could even maintain that in certain periods the appreciation of works brings one back to that. The absence of the term "beauty" in the analyses of numerous contemporary musicologists and critics has been remarked many times. They speak more frequently of "importance," of signification, of the historical import of a suite or a symphony. They concentrate on disclosing the particular techniques of the language employed and on explaining them with reference to trends. But aesthetic judgment has been dropped discreetly from their language. It is as if it proceeded from the empirical analyses furnished with abundance and subtlety.

Another category of sociohistorical significations is connected more globally to authors or works because of their fame or because of stories about them. Before any analysis, even before hearing such works, one knows already that they must be admired. This reverential attitude profoundly influences the pleasure we experience and the judgments we make. We must not believe that it affects only conventional pleasures or prescribed judgments, beyond which there is a pure and unmixed sincerity born of immediate contact of the work with the subject. In many cases, the judgment that seem most immediate is based unconsciously on reverence and the knowledge of consecrated value, without which one might suspect the judgment's sincerity. But everyone also knows that impression of beauty given by a work whose author and title are unknown during its entire hearing. Listening to the radio provides such surprises. One places it in the period and in the approximate style of one or two composers. Nevertheless, of the work's aesthetic worth there is no doubt, even when its fame is not established. Along the same lines, all things are not equal and all works are not equally admired in the production of a celebrated artist. Next to his areas of perfection are those which are less attractive and even some that leave us indifferent. This inequality, more or less pronounced depending on authors and on works, could not be accounted for if respect for great names alone formed the basis of the judgment of beauty. Let us go further: beyond a certain point, the fame of a work produces an inability to judge it. Among the misfortunes and risks of history, it is necessary to count not only oblivion and plagiarism, but also excess of celebrity. A Chopin prelude, a Schubert *lied* no longer touch us because they seem caricatures of themselves, reduced to banality in spite of their original brilliance. They have become almost anesthetic. They are institutions, like national anthems that sometimes take their origin from a work destined for concerts.

The multiplicity of components of the judgment of beauty applied to music—their evolving character in the history of art and of the individual— leads to a certain polymorphism of that judgment. The value of a work is derived from different elements that are combined in different proportions according to the period, and even, in certain periods, according to the public. Dukas (1948) said concerning *The Magic Flute* that the admiration by contemporaries of Mozart must have little resembled that which we bring to it now, because the Wagnerian drama has made us see in it the beginnings of a later moment in the history of opera. One could go further and propose that today this admiration varies as much from individual to individual as it does from period to period and from generation to generation.

Historical-cultural significations appeared at first entirely external to actual appreciation. But the formal abundance across which communication is diffused seems to provide a basis for a direct access to beauty. One does not easily consent to liking out of deference; one admits more often to admiration because of sustained interest or historical importance. In reality, no access is immediate, no judgment is possible without a long chain of accommodations, active learning, and knowledge. None of these mediations is explicit in the judgment, but taken all together they serve to ground it. Communication of meaning is poorly established when the form is perceived confusedly. The Western listener, who has for several decades had the opportunity to hear recorded works from the Far East, feels himself so removed from his element by the timbres, the accents of voice, and the strangeness of the "chords" that he does not know how to organize them, place them, and hear them. Musical listening is so far from pure *sensation*, and the musical "sensorium" so little a biological given, that universality of judgment appears to us as an asymptotic limit.

Of course, the judgment of taste can establish itself through misinterpretation. For ancient works it is almost inevitable that this should happen:

onto the form and the meaning imagined by the author and perceived by contemporaries, the listener today grafts an additional value that does not depend on them. The "romanticism" of certain preludes of Bach is an anachronism. But the feeling that that term captures is a real percept experienced by the listener today. It is legitimate to make the effort necessary to have an image of the work as shorn as possible of anachronistic baggage. (The most direct vision is thus also the most informed, the most richly imbued with integrated critical knowledge.) But one is never safe from the interference of perceptual automatisms. They introduce degradations that are also "misinterpretations." One cannot help hearing a perfect cadence, a harmonic progression, as worn-out elements ("tricks easily found out," as Koechlin (1923) says) that the art of today no longer wants. Successions of diminished-seventh chords, such as one finds in certain Preludes of Bach, hardly perturb us anymore, even if we are conscious of the audacity that they presented in their day.

Thoughtless automatism and critical knowledge are thus the two levels on which the contact of form and subject operates, insofar as it is an entity whose sensibility (and even "sensoriality") is historical. Nothing is less immediate than that contact, in spite of appearances. A certain degree of naïveté can be obtained through erudition (for the listener who is not forewarned imagines himself, quite wrongly, to have this naïveté when starting out). In fact, it is laboriously won—as well as contradictory. It is a troublesome situation analogous to that of a subject who wants to reduce the effects of an optical illusion.

With contemporary works also all vision seems indirect and passes through numerous retrospective mediations. Composers have been so conscious of this that, since the start of this century, a large part of their effort has consisted of avoiding reminiscences, especially in their harmonic language. This fear has led some of them to atonalism and to its various successors. Does this not reveal the difficulty that musicians have experienced as emerging from the sedimentary layers left by the works of the past? But what an illusion to believe that a language might be a pure beginning and not be accepted by any previously determined expectancies! I have shown that tonal interpretation can be hung on the slightest elements—whether mistaken or not, it is attempted. The complete break with tonality, when it is consumated, as in serial compositions, is never totally experienced by the public, whatever its good will. The unheard work exists only as the title of a problem—not in reality. By all accounts—even including that of the partisans of dodecaphonism—a language has meaning only within a culture, of which it can be the result. That is, all musical perception is made of a play of references to preexistent formative elements. Atonalism is enhanced by its relationship to tonal music.

Historical-cultural significations, born of simple acculturation or of reflective cognition, thus interpose themselves inevitably in the communication of musical expressivity. This is not a matter of poor judgment—its very nature requires it. The impression of beauty that a completed melodic gesture conveys is always integrated into a culture: the gesture is Mozartean or Ravelian; it is not beautiful in itself. A listener wholly ignorant of Mozart or Ravel could vaguely sense its perfection. He could even be infatuated with it for an instant. His judgment is not the same as that of the connoisseur, but it is rare that he would be deprived of all historical references. We have seen that these exist as more or less imprecise frameworks when more precise knowledge fails. The problem of the survival of a work is thus poorly defined when one postulates a uniform comprehension from century to century. In music, antiquity is not so great as in works of the plastic arts that have been preserved. But changes in language and form have been considerable. Present-day sensibility is the product of this evolution. Appreciation always retains something of the successive steps of this movement.

REFERENCES

Aborn, M., & Rubenstein, H. (1952). Information theory and immediate recall. *Journal of Experimental Psychology, 44,* 260–266.

Abraham, O. (1923). Tonometrische Untersuchungen an einem deutschen Volkslied. [Tomometric studies of a German folksong.] *Psychologische Forschung, 2* 1–22.

Absil, J. (1937). *Postulats de la musique contemporain.* [Postulates of contemporary music.] Préface de D. Milhaud. La Sarthe-Hay: Editions Orientations.

Ades, H. W. (1943). A secondary acoustic area in the cerebral cortex of the cat. *Journal of Neurophysiology, 6,* 59–63.

Aguettant, L. (1931/Dec). Le sens expressif des tonalités dans la musique de Chopin. [The expressive meaning of key in the music of Chopin.] *Revue Musicale, 12,* 81–86.

Alain, E. C. (1927). *La visite au musicien.* [Visit to a musician.] Paris: Gallimard.

Alain, E. C. (1949). *Propos sur l'esthétique.* [Comments on aesthetics.] Paris: Presses Universitaires de France.

André-Thomas, A. H., & Ajuriaguerra, J. de (1948). *L'axe corporel, musculature et innervation.* [Body axis, musculature, and innervation.] Paris: Masson.

Anniballe Braga, L. d' (1956). Testes musicais. [Musical tests.] *Arquivos Brasilieros de Psicotecnica, 8,* 11–47.

Aristotle (1984). *The complete works,* 2 vols. (J. Barnes, Ed.). Princeton, NJ: Princeton University Press.

Arnheim, R. (1949). The priority of expression. *Journal of Aesthetics & Art Criticism, 8,* 106–109.

Bagchi, B. L. (1937). The adaptation and variability of response of the human brain rhythm. *Journal of Psychology, 3,* 463–485.

Basevi, A. (1865). *Introduction à un nouveau système d'harmonie.* [Introduction to a new system of harmony.] (Delâtre, trans.). Florence: G. G. Guidi.

Baudelaire, C. (1961). *Selected verse.* (F. Scarfe, Ed.) Baltimore: Penguin.

Berlioz, H. (1853). *Grand traité d'instrumentation et d'orchestration moderne.* [Grand treatise of instrumentation and orchestration.] Paris: Schonenberger.

Bernhart, J. (1949). *Traité de prise de son.* [Treatise of auditory perception.] Préface d'A. Honegger. Paris: Eyrolles.

Bertrand, I., Delay, J., & Guillain, J. (1939). *L'electroencéphalogramme normal et pathologique.* [Normal and pathological EEG.] Paris: Masson.

Blondel, R. (1934). *Propos variés de musique et de médicine.* [Various comments on music and medicine.] Paris: Editions d'Art et de Médicine.

Borrel, E. (1934). *L'interpretation de la musique française (de Lully à la Révolution).* [The performance of French music (from Lully to the Revolution).] Paris: Alcan.

Bourguès, L., & Dénéreaz, A. (1921). *La musique et la vie intérieure (Essai d'une histoire psychologique de l'art musicale).* [Music and mental life (Essay on the psychological history of the art).] Paris: Alcan; Lausanne: Bridel.

Boyer, J. (1938). *Le romantisme de Beethoven.* [The romanticism of Beethoven.] Paris: Didier.

Boyer, J. (1943). *Petite histoire de la musique allemande.* [Short history of German music.] Paris: Didier.

Braly, K. W. (1933). The influence of past experience on visual perception. *Journal of Experimental Psychology, 16,* 613–643.

Brazier, D. (1892). Du trouble de la faculté musicale dans l'aphasie. [Difficulties with the musical faculty in aphasia.] *Revue Philosophique, 34,* 337–368.

Brehmer, F. (1925). Melodie Auffassung und melodische Begabung des Kinders. [Children's melodic interpretation and aptitude.] *Zeitschrift für angewandte Psychologie, 36,* 18–28.

Brelet, G. (1947). *Esthétique et création musicale.* [Aesthetics and musical creativity.] Paris: Presses Universitaires de France.

Brelet, G. (1949). *Le temps musical,* [Musical time.] 2 vols. Paris: Presses Universitaires de France.

Brelet, G. (1953). *L'interpretation créatrice.* [Creative interpretation.] Paris: Presses Universitaires de France.

Bresson, F. (1953). Langage et communications. [Language and communications.] *Année Psychologique, 53,* 477–502.

Bruner, J. S., & Postman, L. (1949). On the perception of incongruity: A paradigm. *Journal of Personality, 18,* 206–223.

Bruner, J. S., Postman, L., & Rodrigues, J. (1951). Expectations and the perception of color. *American Journal of Psychology, 64,* 216–227.

Campbell, L. (1942). Basal emotional patterns expressible in music. *American Journal of Psychology, 55,* 1–17.

Caussé, R. (1944). *Cours d'acoustique physiologique.* [Course in acoustical physiology.] Paris: Ecole National des Télécommunications.

Chailley, J. (1951). *Traité historique d'analyse musicale.* [Historical treatise of musical analysis.] Paris: A. Leduc.

Chailley, J. (1956). Le mythe des modes grecs. [The myth of the Greek modes.] *Acta Musicologica, 28,* 137–164.

Chailley, J., & Challan, H. (1947). *Théorie de la musique.* [Music theory.] Paris: A. Leduc.

Combarieu, J. (1893). L'expression objective en musique d'après le langage instinctif. [Objective expression in music based on instinctive language.] *Revue Philosophique, 35,* 124–144.

Combarieu, J. (1907). *La musique, ses lois, son évolution.* [Music: Its laws and evolution.] Paris: Flammarion.

Cornu, A., & Mercadier, E. (1869/72). Sur des intervalles musicaux. [On musical intervals.] *Comptes Rendus Hebdomadaire Académie des Sciences, 68,* 301–308; *74,* 321–323.

Cornu, A., & Mercadier, E. (1873). Sur la mesure des intervalles musicaux. [On the measurement of musical intervals.] *Comptes Rendus Hebdomadaire Académie des Sciences, 1,* 431–434.

Cossa, P., & Paillas, J. L. (1944). *Anatomie des centres nerveux.* [Anatomy of the nerve centers.] Paris: Legrand et Bertrand.

Cuvelier, A. (1949). *L'homme et la musique.* [Man and music.] Paris: Presses Universitaires de France.

Dauriac, L. (1893/95) Psychologie du musicien. [Psychology of the musician.] *Revue Philosophique, 35,* 449–470, 595–617, *39,* 31–56.

David, H. T. (1951). The cultural functions of music. *Journal of the History of Ideas, 12,* 423–439.

Davis, H., & Davis, D. A. (1936). Action potentials of the brain in normal persons and in normal states of cerebral activity. *Archives of Neurology & Psychology, 36,* 1214–1224.

Delacroix, H. (1927). *Psychologie de l'art.* [Psychology of art.] Paris: Alcan.

Delay, J. (1946). *Les dérèglements de l'humeur.* [Disorders of temperament.] Paris: Presses Universitaires de France.

Delay, J. (1950). *Les ondes cérébrales et la psychologie,* (second edition). [Brain waves and psychology.] Paris: Presses Universitaires de France.

Despine, P. (1880). *Etude scientifique sur le somnambulism, sur les phénomènes qu'il présente et sur son action thérapeutique dans certaines maladies nerveuses.* [Scientific study of somnambulism and related phenomena, and of its therapeutic effect on certain nervous disorders.] Paris: F. Savy.

Destouches, L. (1899). *La musique et quelques-uns de ses effets sensoriels.* [Music and some if its sensory effects.] Paris: Thèse Lettres.

Dijkhuis, J. (1953). Recherche sur les représentations provoquées par l'audition des bruits. [Research on the representations provoked by listening to noise.] *Journal de Psychologie, 46,* 188–214.

Downey, J. E. (1897). A musical experiment. *American Journal of Psychology, 9,* 63–69.

Dufrenne, M. (1954). Intentionnalité et esthetique. [Intentionality and aesthetics.] *Revue Philosophique 1,* 75–84.

Dukas, P. (1948). *Ecrits sur la musique.* [Writings on music.] Paris: Société Française et Internationale d'Editions.

Dumas, G. (1933a). L'expression des émotions. [The expression of emotion.] *Nouveau Traité de Psychologie,* vol. 3, pp. 39–209.

Dumas, G. (1933b). La mimique vocale. [Vocal mimicry.] *Nouveau Traité de Psychologie,* vol. 3, pp. 339–360.

Duncker, K. (1939). The influence of past experience upon perceptual properties. *American Journal of Psychology, 52,* 255–265.

Dupré, E., & Nathan, M. (1911). *Le langage musicale: Etude médico-psychologique.* [Musical Language: A medico-psychological study.] Paris: Alcan.

Dupré, E., & Nathan, M. (1941). *Propos variés de musique et de médicine.* [Various comments on music and medicine.] Paris: Alcan.

Durup, G., & Fessard, A. (1935). L'electroencéphalogramme de l'homme: Obser-vations psychophysiologiques relatives à l'action des stimuli visuels et auditifs. [Human EEG: Psychophyisiological observations relating to the effects of visual and auditory stimuli] *Année Psychologique, 36,* 1–32.

Durup, G., & Fessard, A. (1936). L'electroencéphalogramme de l'homme: Données quantitives sur l'arrêt provoqué par des stimuli visuels et auditives. [Human EEG: Quantitative results on blockage produced by visual and auditory stimuli.] *Comptes Rendus Société de Biologie, 122,* 756–758.

Ehrenstein, W. (1954). *Probleme der ganzheitpsychologische Wahrnehmungslehre,* [Prob-lems of an entirely psychological perceptual theory.] (3rd ed.). Leipzig: J. A. Barth.

Emmanuel, M. (1951). *Histoire de la langue musicale,* [History of the language of music.] 2 vols. Paris: H. Laurens.

Esbroeck, J. van, & Montfort, F. (1946). *Qu'est-ce que jouer juste?* [What is playing in tune?] Préface de Paul Collaer. Brussels: Edit. Lumière.

Fallot, J. (1951). *La réalité de l'oeuvre d'art.* [The reality of the work of art.] Paris: Julliard.

Faverge, J. M. (1953a). Le langage des communications dans l'analyse du travail. [The language of communication in the analysis of work.] *Bulletin du Centre d'Etudes et de Recherche Psychotechniques, 2,* 2–12.

Faverge, J. M. (1953b). La théorie de l'information en psychologie expérimentale. [Information theory in experimental psychology.] *Année Psychologique, 53,* 463–476.

Foster, W. S., & Tinker, M. A. Notes for instructors: Experiments in psychology.

Fraisse, P. (1949). Influence des attitudes et de la personnalité sur la perception. [Influence of attitudes and personality on perception.] *Année Psychologique, 49,* 237–247.

Fraisse, P. (1956). *Les structures rythmiques: Etude psychologique.* [Rhythmic structures: A psychological study.] Préface de A. Michotte. Louvain: Publications Univer-sitaires; Paris & Brussels: Edit. Erasme.

Fraisse, P., & Fraisse, R. (1937). Etudes sur la mémoire immédiate. [Studies on immediate memory.] *Année Psychologique, 38,* 48–85.

Fraisse, P., Oléron, G., & Paillard, J. (1953). Les effets dynamogéniques de la musique: étude expérimentale. [Dynamogenic effects of music—An experimental study.] *Année Psychologique, 53,* 1–34.

Francastel, P. (1951). *Peinture et société.* [Painting and society.] Lyon: Audin.

Francès, R. (1951). La constitution de l'oeuvre musicale. [The constitution of the musical work.] *Etudes Philosophiques, 6,* 343–353.

Francès, R. (1952). Recherches expérimentales sur la perception des structures mus-icales. [Experimental research on the perception of musical structures.] *Journal de Psychologie, 45,* 78–96.

Francès, R. (1953). Les niveaux de la perception d'après des recherches récentes. [Perceptual thresholds according to recent research.] *Journal de Psychologie, 46,* 87–96.

Francès, R. (1954). Recherches expérimentales sur la perception de la mélodie. [Exper-imental research on the perception of melody. *Journal de Psychologie, 47–51,* 439–457.

Francès, R. (1955). Problèmes et méthodes en psychologie de l'expression musicale.

[Problems and methods in the psychology of musical expression.] *Journal de Psychologie, 52,* 504–519.

Francès, R. (1957). Le problème de l'expression musicale: Quelques données expérimentales. [The problem of musical expression: Some experimental results.] *Psychologie Française, 2,* 168–180.

Fulton, J. F. (1947). *Physiologie du système nerveux.* [Physiology of the nervous system.] (French trans., 2nd ed. C. Chatagnon). Paris: Vigot.

Gantenbein, M. M. (1952). Recherches sur le développement de la perception du mouvement avec l'age (mouvement dit stroboscopique). [Research on the development of the perception of stroboscopic movement with age.] *Archives de Psychologie.* Geneva, no. 131–132.

Gariel, C. (1925). Acoustique musicale. [Musical acoustics.] In *Encyclopédie Lavignac,* part 2. Paris: Delagrave, pp. 403–518.

Gatewood, E. (1927). A study in the use of similes for describing music and its effects. In M. Schoen (Ed.), *The effects of music.* London: Kegan Paul.

Gelb, A. (1933). Remarques générales sur l'utilisation des données pathologiques pour la psychologie et la philosophie du langage. [General remarks on the use of observations of pathology in the psychology and philosophy of language.] *Journal de Psychologie, 33,* 403–429.

Gelb, A., & Goldstein, K. (1925). Über Farbennamenamnesie nebst Bemerkungen über das Wesen der amnetischen Aphasie überhaupt und die Beziehungen zwischen Sprache und dem Verhalten zur Umwelt. [On color-name amnesia, including remarks on the nature of amnesic general aphasia and the relationship between speech and behavior in the environment.] *Psychologische Forschung, 6,* 127–186.

Gide, A. (1939). *Journal (1889–1939), Feuillets.* Paris: La Pléiade & Nouvelle Revue Française.

Gilman, B. I. (1891/92). Report of an experimental test of musical expressiveness. *American Journal of Psychology, 4,* 558–586; *5,* 42–73.

Goblot, E. (1901). La musique descriptive. [Descriptive music.] *Revue Philosophique, 52,* 58–77.

Goldstein, K. (1933). L'analyse de l'aphasie et l'étude de l'essence du langge. [The analysis of aphasia and the study of the essence of language.] *Journal de Psychologie, 30,* 430–496.

Gottschaldt, K. (1926). Über den Einfluss der Erfahrung auf die Wahrnehmung von Figuren. [On the influence of past experience on the perception of figures.] *Psychologische Forschung, 8,* 261–317.

Granet, M. (1922). Le langage de la douleur d'après le rituel funéraire de la Chine classique. [The language of sorrow in the funeral rites of classical China.] *Journal de Psychologie, 19,* 98–117.

Gratiolet, P. (1865). *De la physionomie et des mouvements d'expression.* [Physiognomy and expressive movements.] Paris: J. Hetzel.

Greene, P. C. (1936). Violin performance, with reference to tempered, natural, and Pythagorean intonation. *University of Iowa Studies in the Psychology of Music, 4,* 232–251.

Greene, P. C. (1937) Violin intonation. *Journal of the Acoustical Society of America, 9,* 22–33.

Gribensky, A. (1951). *L'audition.* [Audition.] Paris: Presses Universitaires de France.

Guilford, J. P., & Hilton, R. A. (1933). Some configurational properties of short musical melodies. *Journal of Experimental Psychology, 16,* 32–54.

Hacks, C. (1892). *Le geste.* [Gesture.] Paris: Flammarion.

Hanslick, E. (1957). *The beautiful in music.* (G. Cohen, Trans.). Indianapolis: Bobbs-Merrill. (Originally published 1854)

Hegel, G. W. F. (1944). *Esthétique,* [Aesthetics.] 4 vols. (French trans. V. Jankélévitch). Paris: Aubier.

Heinlein, G. P. (1928). The affective character of the major and minor modes in music. *Journal of Comparative Psychology, 8,* 101–141.

Helmholtz, H. von (1954). *On the sensations of tone.* (A. J. Ellis, Trans.). New York: Dover. (Originally published 1877)

Héricourt, J. (1900). Rapport entre les sensations, la musique, et le geste. [Relationships among sensations, music, and gesture.] *Annales des Sciences Psychologiques, 10,* 143–156.

Herzog, G. (1952). La melodia hablada y la musica primitiva. [Spoken melody and primitive music.] *Revista Musical Chilena* (Santiago de Chili), *43,* 49–67.

Hevner, K. (1935). The affective character of the major and minor modes in music. *American Journal of Psychology, 47,* 103–118.

Hevner, K. (1936). Experimental studies on the elements of expression in music. *American Journal of Psychology, 48,* 246–268.

Hoffman, E. T. A. (1944). *Le chevalier Gluck.* In *Contes.* (French trans. B. Gidon-Netter). Paris: Payot.

Hoffman, E. T. A. (1949). *Kreisleriana.* (French trans. A. Béguin). Paris: Gallimard.

Hornbostel, E. M. von (n.d.). Das räumlische Hören. [Spatial hearing.] *Handbuch des Normal und Pathologische Physiologie,* vol. 11, pp. 701–715.

Hungerland, H. (1945). Problems of descriptive analysis in the visual arts. *Journal of Aesthetics & Art Criticism, 4,* 20–25.

Husson, R. (1952). La beauté musicale et les lois de l'acoustique. [Musical beauty and the laws of acoustics.] *Almanach des Sciences,* pp. 145–151.

Husson, R. *et al.* (1953). Etude expérimentale des conditionnements acoustiques et physiologiques de l'esthétique musicale. [Experimental study of the acoustic and physiological conditions of musical aesthetics.] *Année des Télécommunications: Cahiers d'Acoustique, 3,* 51–72.

Indy, V. d' (1897/98). *Cours de composition musicale.* [Course in musical composition.] Paris: Durand.

Ireland, W. W. (1894). On the affections of the musical faculty in cerebral diseases. *Journal of Mental Science, 40,* 354–367.

Ittelson, W. (1951). The constancies in perceptual theory. *Psychological Review, 58,* 285–294.

Jacobsen, C. F., & Elder, J. H. (1936) The effect of temporal lobe lesions on delayed responses in monkeys. *Comparative Psychology Monographs, 13,* 61–65.

Jasper, H. H., Cruikshank, R. M., & Howard, H. (1935). Action currents from the occipital region of the brain, as affected by variables of attention and external stimulation. *Psychological Bulletin, 8,* 565–571.

Katz, D. (1955). *Introduction à la psychologie de la forme.* [Introduction to the psychology of form.] (French trans. David & Voute). Paris: M. Rivière.

Käufer, H. (1931). *Beitrage zur Frage der sensorischen Amnesie.* [Contribution to the question of sensory amnesia.] Bonn.

Koechlin, C. (1923). L'évolution de l'harmonie, période contemporaine. [The evolution of harmony, contemporary period.] In *Encyclopédie Lavignac,* part 2. Paris: Delagrave, pp. 591–760.

Koffka, K. (1935). *Principles of gestalt psychology.* New York: Harcourt Brace.

Köhler, W. (1929). *Gestalt psychology.* New York: Liveright.

Lairy-Bounes, G. C., & Fishgold, H. (1953). Réactions EEG diffuses aux stimulations psycho-sensorielles: Intérêt clinique. [Diffuse EEG reactions to psycho-sensory stimulation: Clinical implications.] *EEG clin. Neuro-physiol., 5,* 343–362.

Lalo, C. (1939). *Esquisse d'une esthétique musicale scientifique.* [Sketch of a scientific musical aesthetics.] Paris: Alcan. (Originally published 1908)

Lamy, H. (1907). Amnésie musicale chez un aphasique sensoriel. [Musical amnesia in a sensory aphasic.] *Revue de Neurologie, 15,* 688–693.

Lashley, K. S. (1953). Dynamic processes in perception. In *Brain mechanisms and consciousness.* Oxford: Blackwell.

Lazarus, D. (1951). Essais pour une esthétique musicale. [Essays for a musical aesthetics.] *Europe, 29,* 66–70.

Lee, V. (1918). Varieties of musical experience. *North American Review, 252,* 748–757.

Lee, V. (1932). *Music and its lovers.* London: Allen & Unwin.

Legge, W. (1894). Music and musical faculty in insanity. *Journal of Mental Science, 40,* 368–375.

Leibowitz, R. (1949). *Introduction à la musique de douze sons.* [Introduction to twelve-tone music.] Paris: L'Arche.

Lenormand, R. (1912). *Etude sur l'harmonie moderne.* [A study of modern harmony.] Supplement to *Monde Musical,* Paris.

Lhermitte, J. (1939). *L'image de notre corps.* [The image of our body.] Paris: Editions de la Nouvelle Revue Critique.

Lloyd, A. L. (1954). The singing style of the Copper family. *Journal of the English Folk Dance and Song Society, 7,* 145–151.

Lloyd, L. S. (1940). *The musical ear.* Oxford: Oxford University Press.

Loomis, A. L., Harvey, E. N., & Hobart, G. (1936). Electric potentials of the human brain. *Journal of Experimental Psychology, 19,* 249–279.

Lundin, R. W. (1953). *An objective psychology of music.* New York: Ronald Press.

Maillard, P. (1952). Tonalité et transposition. [Tonality and transposition.] *Revue Musicale, 33,* 165–179.

Marie, J.-E. (1953). *Musique vivante.* [Living music.] Paris.

Mauss, M. (1921). L'expression obligatoire des sentiments (rituels oraux funéraires australiens). [The obligatory expression of feelings (oral funeral rites in Australia).] *Journal de Psychologie, 18,* 425–434.

McCleary, R. A., & Lazarus, R. S. (1949). Autonomic discrimination without awareness: An interim report. *Journal of Personality, 18,* 171–179.

McGinnies, E., Comer, P. B., & Lacey, D. L. (1952). Visual recognition threshold as a function of word length and word frequency. *Journal of Experimental Psychology, 44,* 65–68.

Metfessel, M. (1928). *Phonophotography in folk music: American songs in new notation.* Chapel Hill: University of North Carolina Press.

Meyer, L. B. (1957). Meaning in music and information theory. *Journal of Aesthetics & Art Criticism, 15,* 412–424.

Meyer, M. (1903). Experimental studies in the psychology of music. *American Journal of Psychology, 14,* 456–468.

Meyerson, I. (1948). *Les fonctions psychologiques et les oeuvres.* [Psychological functions and works of art.] Paris: Vrin.

Meyerson, I. (1953). Les métamorphoses de l'espace en peinture. [Metamorphoses of space in painting.] *Journal de Psychologie, 46,* 405–428.

Meyerson, I. (1954). Problèmes d'histoire et de psychologie des oeuvres: Spécificité, variation, expérience. [Problems in the history and psychology of works of art-specificity, variation, and experience.] In *Homage à Lucien Febvre.* Paris.

Meyerson, I. (1956). Sur la spécificité de l'art et ses objects. [On the specificity of art and its objects.] In *Mélanges G. Jamati.* Paris: Editions du Centre National de la Recherche Scientifique, pp. 217–223.

Michaud, H. (1954). *La sensibilité.* [Sensitivity.] Lyon: E. Vitte.

Miller, R. S. (1936). The pitch of attack in singing. *University of Iowa Studies in the Psychology of Music, 4,* 158–171.

Minturn, A. L., & Reese, T. W. (1951). The effect of differential reinforcement on the discrimination of visual number. *Journal of Psychology, 31,* 203–231.

Moles, A. (1953). La structure physique du signal musical. [The physical structure of the musical signal.] *Revue Scientifique, 3324,* 277–303.

Monroe, A. H. (1929). The effect of bodily action on voice intensity. *Journal of Applied Psychology, 13,* 516–532.

Montfort, F. (1945). L'ethos des tonalités. [The ethos of tonalities.] In *Hommage à Ch. van den Borren.* Antwerp, p. 245.

Myers, C. S. (1927). Individual differences in listening to music. In M. Schoen (Ed.), *The effects of music.* London: Kegan Paul.

Ogden, R. M. (1924). *Hearing.* London: J. Cape.

Ollone, M. d' (1952). *Le langage musical,* [The language of music.] 2 vols. Paris & Geneva: La Palatine.

Ombredane, A. (1939). Le problème de l'aphasie. [The problem of aphasia.] *Conférence de l'Institut de Linguistique de l'Université de Paris, 7.*

Ombredane, A. (1944). Perception et langage. [Perception and language.] *Etudes de Psychologie Médicale,* vol. 1. Rio-de-Janeiro: Atlantica Editera.

Oppenheim, H. (1888). Über das Verhalten der musikalischen Ausdrucksbewegungen und des musikalischen Verständnisses bei Aphasischen. [On musically expressive movement and the musical understanding of aphasics.] *Charité Année, 13,* 345–361.

Ortmann, O. (1927). Types of listeners: Genetic considerations. In M. Schoen (Ed.), *The effects of music.* London: Kegan Paul.

Peirce, C. S. (1931–35) *Collected papers* (Vols. 1–6). Cambridge, MA: Harvard University Press.

Piaget, J. (1945). *La formation du symbole chez l'enfant.* [The formation of symbols in the child.] Neuchâtel: Delachaux & Niestlé.

Piaget, J., & Lambercier, M. (1943). *La comparaison visuelle des hauteurs à distances variables dans le plan frontoparallèle* [Visual comparison of height at various distances in the frontoparallel plane.] Neuchâtel: Delachaux & Niestlé.

Piéron, H. (1945). *La sensation, guide de vie.* [Sensation, guide for life.] (fourth edition). Paris: Gallimard.

Pinoteau, R. (1937). *Les expressions morbides des émotions dans la neurologie et dans l'art.* [The pathological expression of emotion in neurology and art.] Paris: G. Doin.

Plato (1961). *Collected Dialogues.* E. Hamilton & H. Cairns (Eds.). New York: Pantheon.

Pradines, M. (1947). *Traité de psychologie générale.* [Treatise of general psychology.] Paris: Presses Universitaires de France.

Pradines, M. (1954). *L'aventure de l'esprit dans les espèces.* [The emergence of mind among the species.] Paris: Flammarion.

Pratt, C. C. (1930). The spatial character of high and low tones. *Journal of Experimental Psychology, 13,* 278–285.

Probst, M. (1899). Über die Lokalisation des Tonvermögens. [On the localization of tonal capacities.] *Archiv für Psychiatrie und Nervenkrankheit, 32,* 387–346.

Reimers, D. (1927). Untersuchungen über die Entwickelung des Tonalitätsgefühls im Laufe des Schulzeits. [Studies on the development of sensitivity to tonality during the school years.] *Zeitschrift für Angewandt Psychologie, 28,* 193–234.

Reinach, S. (1892). Notes sur les problèmes musicaux dits d'Aristote. [Notes on the musical Problems attributed to Aristotle.] *Revue des Etudes Grecques, 5,* 22–52.

Révész, G. (1937). Gibt es ein Hörraum? [Is there spatial hearing?] *Acta Psychologica, 3,* 137–192.

Révész, G. (1953). *Introduction to the psychology of music.* (G. I. C. de Courcy, Trans.). London: Longmans, Green.

Riemann, H. (1906). *Les éléments de l'esthétique musicale.* [Elements of musical aesthetics.] (French trans. G. Humbert). Paris: Alcan.

Rochas, A. de, Dauriac, L., & Poiré, E. (1900). *Les sentiments, la musique, et le geste.* [Feelings, music, and gesture.] Grenoble: Falque & Perrin.

Roiha, E. (1956). *On the theory and technique of contemporary music.* Helsinki: Academia Fennica Scientiarum.

Rubin, E. (1915). *Synsoplevede Figurer.* [Perceived figures.] Copenhagen: Gyldendalske.

Ruyer, R. (1955). L'expressivité. [Expressivity.] *Revue de Métaphysique et de Morale, 1–2,* 69–100.

Sachs, C. (1943). *The rise of music in the ancient world, east and west.* New York: W. W. Norton.

Schaeffner, A. (1939). Critique et thématique. [Criticism and thematics.] *Revue Musicale,* 241–254.

Scherchen, H. (1946). *Vom Wesen der Musik.* [The essence of music.] Zurich.

Schloezer, B. de (1947). *Introduction à J. S. Bach.* [Introduction to J. S. Bach.] Paris: Nouvelle Revue Française.

Schloezer, B. de (1951). Quelques considérations sur le langage musical. [Some thoughts on the language of music.] *Journal de Psychologie, 1–2,* 225–236.

Schoen, M. (Ed.) (1927). *The effects of music*. London: Kegan Paul.

Schoen, M. (1928). The aesthetic attitude in music. *Psychological Mongraphs, 39*, 162–183.

Schoenberg, A. (1949). La composition à douze sons. [Composition with twelve tones.] *Polyphonie*, no. 4.

Schopenhauer, A. (1966). *The world as will and representation*, 2 vols. (E. J. F. Payne, trans.). New York: Dover. (Originally published 1844)

Seashore, C. E. (1919). *The psychology of musical talent*. New York: Silver, Burdett.

Seashore, C. E. (1923). Measurements of the expression of emotions in music. *Proceedings of the National Academy of Sciences*, pp. 323–331.

Seashore, C. E. (1938). *The psychology of music*. New York: McGraw-Hill.

Seashore, C. E., & Metfessel, M. (1925) Deviations from the regular as an art principle. *Proceedings of the National Academy of Sciences, 11*, 538–542.

Seashore, H. E. (1936). An objective analysis of artistic singing. *University of Iowa Studies in the Psychology of Music, 4*, 12–157.

Seashore, R. H. (1935). Improvability of pitch discrimination. *Psychological Bulletin, 32*, 546–559.

Servien, P. (1953). *Esthétique*. Paris: Payot.

Silbermann, A. (1955). *La musique, la radio et l'auditeur*. [Music, radio, and the listener.] Paris: Presses Universitaires de France.

Siohan, R. (1956). *Horizons sonores*. Paris: Flammarion.

Small, A. M. (1936). An objective analysis of artistic violin performance. *University of Iowa Studies in the Psychology of Music, 4*, 172–231.

Snyders, G. (1955). L'évolution du goût musical en France aux XVIIe et XVIIIe siècles. [The evolution of musical taste in France in the 17th and 18th centuries.] *Revue des Sciences Humaines*, pp. 325–350.

Sokolov, E. N. (1952). La généralisation de la perception. [The generalization of perception.] *Soviet. Pedagogica*. (French trans.). Paris: Centre Culturel France-U. R. S. S.

Solomon, R. L., & Postman, L. (1952). Frequency of usage as a determinant of recognition for words. *Journal of Experimental Psychology, 43*, 195–201.

Souriau, E. (1925). *L'abstraction sentimentale*. [The abstraction of feelings.] Paris: Presses Universitaires de France.

Souriau, E. (1929). *L'avenir de l'esthétique*. [The emergence of aesthetics.] Paris: Alcan.

Souriau, E. (1947). *La correspondance des arts*. [The correspondence of the arts.] Paris: Flammarion.

Souriau, E. (1952). *Pensée vivante et perfection formelle*. [Living ideas and formal perfection.] (2nd ed.). Paris: Presses Universitaires de France.

Spalding, W. R. (1949). *Manuel d'analyse musicale*. [Manual of musical analysis.] Paris: Payot.

Spencer, H. (1886). Origine et fonction de la musique. [The origin and function of music.] In *Essais de morale, de science, et d'esthétique*. (French trans. Burdeau). Paris: G. Ballière.

Stevens, S. S., & Davis, H. (1948). *Hearing*. New York: Wiley.

Stravinsky, I. (1947). *Poetics of music*. Cambridge, MA: Harvard University Press.

Strehle, H. (1954). *Meinen, Gesten, und Gebärden: Analyse des Gebarens*. [Thoughts, gestures, and signs: Behavioral analysis.] Munich: E. Reinhart.

Stumpf, C. (1883/90). *Tonpsychologie*, [Psychology of sound.] 2 vols. Leipzig: S. Hirzel.

Stumpf, C. (1896). Die pseudo-aristotelische Probleme über Musik. [The pseudo-Aristotelian Problems on music.] In *Abhandlungen der Königlich Akademie der Wissenschaft zu Berlin*. Berlin: G. Reimer.

Tastevin, J. (1956). Des sensations musculaires et articulaires et du sentiment des attitudes. [Muscular and articulatory sensations and those of the feelings associated with attitude.] *Journal de Psychologie, 1*, 10–30.

Tchehrazi, E. (1936). *L'image du soi*. [Self image.] Paris: Le François.

Teplov, B. M. (1947). *Psychologie des aptitudes musicales*. [The psychology of musical aptitudes.] Moscow: Editions de l'Academic des Sciences Pédagogiques. (French trans. J. Deprun). Paris: Presses Universitaires de France, 1966)

Udine, J. d' (1910). *L'art et le geste*. [Art and gesture.] Paris: Alcan.

Vial, J. (1952). *De l'être musical*. [The musical being.] Neuchâtel: La Baconnière.

Wallaschek, R. (1891). Über die Bedeutung der Aphasie für den musikalischen Ausdruck. [On the significance of aphasia for musical expression.] In *Wierteljahrschrift für Musikwissenschaft*. Leipzig, pp. 53–73.

Wallon, H. (1925). *L'enfant turbulent*. [The troubled child.] Paris: Alcan.

Watson, K. B. (1942). The nature and measurement of musical meanings. *Psychological Mongraphs, 54*, 1–43.

Wever, E. G. (1949). *Theory of hearing*. New York: Wiley.

Willems, E. (1954). *Le rythme musical: Etude psychologique*. [Musical rhythm: A psychological study.] Paris: Presses Universitaires de France.

Wolner, M., & Pyle, W. H. (1933). An experiment in individual training in pitch-deficient children. *Journal of Educational Psychology, 24*, 602–608.

Wyatt, R. F. (1936). A new instrument for measuring pitch discrimination. *American Journal of Psychology, 48*, 435–441.

Yeomans, W. (1955). The repetitive factor in music. *Monthly Musical Record, 85*, 63–67.

Zazzo, R. (1948). Images du corps et conscience de soi: Matériaux pour l'étude expérimentale de la conscience. [Body image and self-awareness: Materials for an experimental study of consciousness.] *Enfance, 1*, 29–43.

SUPPLEMENTARY BIBLIOGRAPHY

Deutsch, D. (Ed.) (1982). *The psychology of music*. New York: Academic Press.

Dowling, W. J., & Harwood, D. L. (1986). *Music cognition*. New York: Academic Press.

Francès, R. (1948). La structure en musique. [Structure in music.] *Les Temps Modernes, 37*, 721–734.

Francès, R. (1964). La langue musicale dans la societé contemporaine. [The language of music in contemporary society.] *Sciences de l'Art, 1*, 29–46.

Francès, R. (1968). *Psychologie de l'esthétique*. [The psychology of aesthetics.] Paris: Presses Universitaires de France.

Francès, R. (1972). L'enseignement programmé de la langue musicale. [Programmed instruction in the language of music.] *Cahiers de Doc. Pédagog.*, Institut Pédagog. National.

Francès, R. (1974). L'enseignement programmé de la musique. [Programmed instruction in music.] *Sciences d l'Art, 9*, 121–137.

Francès, R. (1983). *Méthode audio-guidée de solfège: Cours élémentaire et cours moyen* (2nd ed.). [Self-guided solfège method—Elementary course and intermediate course.] Issy-les-Moulineaux: Etablissements d'Applications Psychotechniques.

Francès, R., & Bruchon-Schweitzer, M. (1983). Musical expression and body expression. *Perceptual & Motor Skills, 57*, 587–595.

Francès, R., Imberty, M., & Zenatti, A. (1979). Le domaine Musicale. [The domain of music.] In R. Francès (Ed.) *Psychologie de l'art et de l'esthétique*. Paris: Presses Universitaires de France.

Francès, R., Lhermitte, F., & Verdy, M. F. (1973). Le déficit musical des aphasiques. [The musical deficit in aphasics.] *Revue Internationale de Psychologie Appliquée, 22*, 117–136.

Imberty, M. (1968). Recherches sur la genèse du sentiment du consonance. [Research on the origins of the feeling of consonance.] *Sciences de l'Art, 5*, 29–46.

Imberty, M. (1969). *L'acquisition des structures tonales chez l'enfant*. [The acquisition of tonal structures in children.] Paris: Klincksieck.

Imberty, M. (1978). *Entendre la musique*. [Hearing music.] *Sémantique psychologique de la musique*, vol. 1. Paris: Dunod.

Imberty, M. (1981). *Les écritures du temps*. [The writings of the times.] (*Sémantique psychologique de la musique*, vol. 2). Paris: Dunod.

Including additions by the author

Jacobs, C. (1960). Psychology of music: some European studies. *Acta Psychologica*, *17*.

Levelt, W. J. M., & Plomp, R. (1966). Les dimensions dans la perception des intervalles musicaux. [Dimensions in the perception of musical intervals.] *Sciences d l'Art*, *3*, 172–182.

Levelt, W. J. M., & Plomp, R. (1968). The appreciation of musical intervals. In *Proceedings of the Fifth International Congress of Aesthetics*. Paris: Mouton.

Plomp, R., & Levelt, W. J. M. (1965). Tonal consonance and critical bandwidth. *Journal of the Acoustical Society of America*, *38*, 548–560.

Shuter-Dyson, R., & Gabriel, C. (1981). *The psychology of musical ability* (2nd ed.). London: Methuen.

Valentine, C. W. (1962). *The experimental psychology of beauty*. London: Methuen.

Wellek, A. (1966). Expériences comparées sur la perception de la musique tonale et de la musique dodécaphonique. [Comparative experiments on the perception of tonal and twelve-tone music.] *Sciences de l'Art*, *3*, 156–162.

Wellek, A. (1970). *Typologie der Musikbegabung im deutschen Volke: Grundlegung einer Psychologischen Theorie der Musik und Musikgeschichte*. [Typology of musical aptitude in the German people: Foundations for a psychological theory of music and music history.] Munich: Beck.

Zenatti, A. (1969). Le developpement génétique de la perception musicale. [The genetic development of musical perception.] *Monographies Françaises de Psychologie*, no. 17.

Zenatti, A. (1981). *L'enfant et son environnement musical*. [The child and its musical environment.] Issy-les-Moulineaux: Etablissements d'Applications Psychotechniques.

AUTHOR INDEX

SUBJECT INDEX

371